FUNDAMENTAL
ACCOUNTING
PRINCIPLES

EIGHTH CANADIAN EDITION
VOLUME II

FUNDAMENTAL
ACCOUNTING PRINCIPLES

EIGHTH CANADIAN EDITION
VOLUME II

KERMIT D. LARSON
University of Texas—Austin

MORTON NELSON
Wilfrid Laurier University

MICHAEL ZIN
Professor Emeritus
University of Windsor

RAY F. CARROLL
Dalhousie University

Represented in Canada by:

Times Mirror
Professional Publishing Ltd.

IRWIN

Toronto • Chicago • Bogotá • Boston • Buenos Aires
Caracas • London • Madrid • Mexico City • Sydney

Photo Credits

Chapter 11: *Chris Speedie/Tony Stone Images;* Chapter 12: *Michael Rosenfeld/Tony Stone Images;* Chapter 13: *Sharon Hoogstraten;* Chapter 14: *Sharon Hoogstraten;* Chapter 15: *Courtesy of Corel Corporation;* Chapter 16: *Sharon Hoogstraten;* Chapter 17: *Sharon Hoogstraten;* Chapter 18: *Sharon Hoogstraten;* Chapter 19: *Stewart Cohen/Tony Stone Images.*

Irwin Book Team

Publisher:	*Roderick T. Banister*
Developmental editor:	*Sabira Hussain*
Marketing manager:	*Murray Moman*
Project editor:	*Waivah Clement*
Production supervisor:	*Bob Lange*
Assistant manager, graphics:	*Charlene R. Perez*
Senior designer:	*Heidi J. Baughman*
Coordinator, Graphic and Desktop Services:	*Keri Johnson*
Photo researcher:	*Randall Nicholas/ Nicholas Communications, Inc.*
Compositor:	*York Graphic Services, Inc.*
Typeface:	*10½ /12½ Times Roman*
Printer:	*Von Hoffmann Press, Inc.*

Times Mirror
Higher Education Group

ISBN 0-256-17507-1
Library of Congress Catalog Number 95–80682

Printed in the United States of America
1 2 3 4 5 6 7 8 9 0 VH 3 2 1 0 9 8 7 6

Preface

The tradition of *Fundamental Accounting Principles* includes clear explanations of accounting concepts and practices with closely related assignment material. Recent editions also reflect an educational philosophy we call *action learning.* We are firmly convinced that students learn most effectively when their study activities are designed to emphasize active behaviour. The eighth Canadian edition continues this focus on the effective use of student study time.

By providing a wide variety of action-oriented items in the text and in support of the text, we hope to encourage student involvement within the classroom as well as during study outside of class. Newly developed and thoroughly revised assignment materials provide an extensive basis for varied assignments that stimulate interest, promote a sense of accomplishment, show the real-world relevance of the subject matter, and sharpen the analytical and communications abilities of each student. In addition, the study guide and the computerized tutorial give students a number of action-learning opportunities.

The eighth Canadian edition has changed *Fundamental Accounting Principles* in many important ways. Extensive input obtained through surveys, focus groups, reviewers, and personal correspondence has driven the revision plan. Instructors confirm several trends that are affecting the world of accounting. The trends most prevalent in accounting education today include the visual orientation of students, the need for flexibility and innovation in the classroom, new pedagogy, and the impact of technology. The many changes that have been integrated throughout this revision are in response to these trends.

Chapter Opening Scenarios

NEW FEATURES

A scenario at the beginning of each chapter raises questions related to the material covered in the chapter. Later in the chapter, one or more references show how the ideas being explained at that point apply to the company described in the chapter opening. Even before students read a chapter, they realize from the opening scenarios that what they will be learning is useful in solving real problems.

Use of Colour

Conscious, deliberate thought and effort have gone into the use of colour to add more interest and appeal to the book. More importantly, colour is used as a code to aid in learning. Blue indicates financial statements and reports that provide accounting information to be used in decision making. The primary documents that accountants generate for themselves as they develop informative statements and reports are green. Finally, documents that serve as sources of the data that go into accounting reports are yellow.

Progress Checks with Answers

A new feature in this edition is a series of Progress Checks integrated in each chapter. These review questions follow the discussion related to a learning objective. The goal is to have students stop momentarily and reflect on whether they should spend more time studying a given section of the text before moving on. Answers to the Progress Check questions are provided at the end of each chapter.

Excerpts and Assignments from Annual Reports

The financial statements of Imperial Oil Limited and other companies are used throughout as a basis for discussing the different aspects of the financial statements. In this way, the relevance of the discussion to actual decision situations is emphasized. Most chapters also contain one or more assignments relating to the annual report of Geac Computer Corporation Limited.

Using the Information

A new section at the end of each financial chapter reinforces real-world business applications. Most of these sections use real-world examples and many of them relate directly to the company vignettes that open the chapters. A few examples of Using the Information topics are:

    Debt ratio—Chapter 2

    Business segment information—Chapter 6

    Return on total assets—Chapter 12

    Price-earnings ratio—Chapter 16

    Cash flow analyses—Chapter 18

Enhanced Emphasis on Critical Thinking, Analysis, and Communication Skills

The assignment material in the book has been extensively revised. Many assignments have been reoriented to increase the emphasis on critical thinking and communication skills. For example, the requirements for selected problems in each chapter now include a *preparation component* and a separate *analysis component.*

The analysis component generally requires students to think about the financial statement consequences of alternative situations. Students learn to consider the consequences of alternatives and the resulting effects on their interpretation of the results. This complements the more usual preparation component of the end-of-chapter assignments.

Quick Study (Five-Minute Exercises)

Instructors indicate an increasing reliance on shorter problem material for use as in-class illustrations and as homework assignments. Undoubtedly the prospect of solving problems in a short time and the rapid feedback of having done so successfully are motivating factors that lead students to extend their study efforts. Accordingly, this edition contains a new category of very short exercises that are identified as Quick Study. At least one exercise is provided for each learning objective.

Additional Problems

In response to requests for more and varied problem material, we have replaced the alternate problems which previously mirrored the main problems with new, different problems. The traditional alternate problems are available in a separate booklet.

Concept Testers

To encourage additional study of important glossary terms, all chapters conclude the assignment material with a *concept tester* in the form of a short crossword puzzle.

FEATURES RETAINED

Features about which our adopters have expressed enthusiasm have been retained. These include integrated learning objectives, illustrative diagrams, acetate overlays, "As a Matter of Ethics" cases, "As a Matter of Opinion" interviews, the comprehensive accounting cycle illustration, the summary in terms of learning objectives, chapter glossaries, demonstration problems with solutions and the various forms of problem material including Questions, Exercises, Problems, Provocative Problems, Analytical and Review Problems, the Serial Problem and Comprehensive Review Problems (after Chapters 4, 6, 13, and 22).

CONTENT-SPECIFIC CHANGES

Expanded Prologue

An important change in this edition is an expanded Prologue that describes the accounting function in the context of other organizational functions such as finance, human resources, research and development, production, marketing, and executive management. The Prologue also explains the work accountants do—including their certifications and the fields within which they work—and the pervasive importance of ethics in accounting. As a separate learning unit, the Prologue emphasizes the overall importance of these topics to the understanding of the role accounting plays in providing information to a variety of decision makers.

Financial Statement Orientation of Chapter 1

As a result of the Prologue revision, Chapter 1 is now a much shorter and more manageable learning unit with a clear focus on financial statements. This includes the information contained in the statements, the basic concepts that guide the development and use of accounting information, and the relationship of the statements to the transactions and events in the life of a business. Appendix A following Chapter 1 describes the process by which generally accepted accounting principles are established.

Deletions in Chapters 4 and 5

Reviewers and adopters have overwhelmingly encouraged limiting the early examples in the book to proprietorships. As a result, the discussion of partnerships and corporations has been moved from the body of Chapter 4 to Appendix D following Chapter 4. Corporations are considered in the early chapters only as necessary to support student interaction with the financial statements at the back of the book and to recognize the existence of alternative forms of business organization.

Work sheets are now presented as an *optional* step in the accounting cycle. However, we also describe several reasons why an understanding of work sheets is useful. In addition, a more concise discussion of the adjusting entry method of accounting for inventories has reduced the size of the appendix at the end of Chapter 5.

Discounting Notes Receivable

The revision of Chapter 8 recognizes the fact that an increasing number of companies routinely convert their receivables into cash without waiting to receive customer payments. In dealing with this modern business practice, the discussion of discounting notes receivable has been supplemented with a more general examination of the various ways receivables may be converted into cash.

Topics Related to Inventories

The discussion in Chapter 9 of lower of cost or market has been simplified to avoid the details of considering ceiling and floor limits on market value. The treatment of markups and markdowns has been eliminated from the discussion of the retail inventory method. Reviewers agree that all of these topics are better left to intermediate level courses.

Topics Related to Capital Assets

To help students appreciate the differences between financial accounting and tax accounting, we continue to discuss accelerated amortization. However, the discussion has been condensed to exclude the calculations that underlie the apportioning of accelerated amortization between accounting periods. We also eliminated the discussions of capital asset subsidiary records.

Consolidated Financial Statements

Adopters indicate that the consolidated statements chapter in prior editions was the one they most frequently omitted. Nevertheless, long-term investments are an important financial consideration in evaluating many companies. The answer was to eliminate the consolidated statements chapter and to develop a more balanced set of asset chapters. As a result, Chapter 12 completes the asset coverage by discussing natural resources, intangible assets, and long-term investments. The long-term investments portion naturally concludes with a discussion of investments in international operations. The appendix on investments in equity securities from the seventh Canadian edition has been eliminated.

Leases and Accounting for Corporate Income Taxes

In Chapter 13, the discussion of leases has been significantly shortened. Students learn the differences between capital and operating leases without having to journalize the entries related to capital leases. However, Appendix H, "Accounting for Corporate Income Taxes," has been retained.

Streamlined Coverage of Partnerships and Corporations

Reviewers suggested that we compress the coverage of partnerships and corporations and eliminate seldom used procedures and material that are best left for more advanced textbooks. In response, we streamlined discussion of material in these chapters and eliminated coverage of obsolete or nonessential material such as participating preferred, par value shares and the appendix on treasury stock.

Segmental Reporting

The illustration and discussion of segmental reporting have been eliminated from Chapter 19. However, a short section at the close of Chapter 6 recognizes that operating in several business segments complicates the design of the accounting system. Then, the use of business segment information by decision makers is briefly discussed.

Expanded Coverage of Activity-Based Costing

The practice of managerial accounting in Canadian industry continues to undergo a wide range of significant changes. Among these, the increasing implementation of activity-based costing systems is particularly noticeable. Accordingly, the introductory coverage of activity-based costing in Chapter 23 has been expanded in this new edition.

To provide instructors flexibility in planning course content, the eighth Canadian edition includes several appendixes. Those that clearly relate to a single chapter are placed at the end of that chapter. Appendixes F, G, H, and I appear at the end of the book.

APPENDIXES AND END-OF-TEXT ITEMS

Comprehensive List of Accounts Used in Exercises and Problems

This list provides students with the large variety of accounts that companies use and that are needed to solve the exercises and problems provided in the text. This list is located at the end of this text.

SUPPLEMENTS

For the Instructor

The support package for *Fundamental Accounting Principles* includes many items to assist the instructor. They include the following:

- *Solutions Manuals,* Volumes I, II, and III, which have more extensive supporting calculations in this edition.
- *Solutions Transparencies,* Volumes I, II, and III, which include all exercises, problems, and comprehensive problems. These transparencies are now printed in boldface in a new, exceptionally large typeface so that visibility from a distance is strikingly improved.
- *Teaching Transparencies,* many of which are now in colour.
- *Powerpoint Slides,* developed by Bruce MacLean of Dalhousie University, which are designed to support teaching the course using a computer, data display, and an overhead projector.
- *Video tapes,* available upon adoption, which reinforce important topics and procedures. They may be used in the classroom or media lab.
- *Instructor's Resource Manual,* prepared by Ray Carroll of Dalhousie University, which includes sample course syllabi, suggested homework assignments, a series of lecture outlines, demonstration problems, suggested points for emphasis, and background material for discussing ethics in accounting.
- *Testbank,* which contains a wide variety of test questions, including true-false, multiple-choice, quantitative, matching, and essay questions of varying levels of difficulty.
- *Computest,* a computerized version of the manual testbank for more efficient use, which is available in Macintosh, Windows, or DOS versions. The extensive features of this test-generator program include random question selection based on the user's specification of learning objectives, type of question, and level of difficulty.
- *Teletest.* By calling a toll-free number, users can specify the content of exams and have laser-printed copies of the exams mailed or faxed to them.
- *SPATS (Spreadsheet Applications Template Software),* prepared by Jack Terry and Christopher L. Polselli, C.A., which includes Lotus 1-2-3 (or the equivalent) templates for selected problems and exercises from the text. The templates gradually become more complex, requiring students to build a variety of formulas. What-if questions are added to show the power of spreadsheets and a simple tutorial is included. Instructors may request a free master template for students to use or copy, or students can buy shrinkwrapped versions at a nominal fee. Both DOS and Windows versions are available.
- *Tutorial Software,* prepared by Leland Mansuetti, Keith Weidkamp, and J. Russell Curtis of the British Columbia Institute of Technology. Multiple-choice, true-false, journal entry review and glossary review questions are randomly accessed by students. Explanations of right and wrong answers are provided and scores are tallied. Instructors may request a free master template for students to use or copy, or students can buy shrinkwrapped versions for a nominal fee. Both DOS and Windows versions are available.
- *Solutions Manual to accompany the practice sets* will include detailed solutions to all of the practice sets accompanying the text.

For the Student

In addition to the text, the package of support items for the student includes the following:

- *Working Papers,* Volumes I, II, and III, which include working papers for the exercises, problems, serial problem, and comprehensive problems.
- The *Study Guide,* Volumes I, II, and III, which provides a basis for independent study and review and has been expanded to include multiple-choice and true/false questions as well as several additional problems with solutions for each chapter and appendix.
- *Check Figures* for the problems.
- *Barns Bluff Camping Equipment,* by Barrie Yackness of the British Columbia Institute of Technology and Terrie Kroshus. A manual, single proprietorship practice set with business papers that may be assigned after Chapter 7. This practice set is also available in an Alternate Edition prepared by Tilly Jensen of the Northern Alberta Institute of Technology.
- *Student's Name Book Centre,* by Harvey C. Freedman of Humber College of Applied Arts and Technology. A manual, single proprietorship practice set covering a one-month accounting cycle. The set includes business papers and can be assigned after Chapter 7. This practice set is also available in an Alternate Edition.
- *K.J.C. Manufacturing Company,* by Barrie Yackness and Sylvia Ong. A manual practice set with a narrative of transactions for a manufacturing corporation. This may be assigned after Chapter 20.

ACKNOWLEDGMENTS

We are grateful for the encouragement, suggestions, reviews, and counsel provided by students, colleagues, and instructors from across the country. A tremendous amount of useful information was gathered from over 300 responses to an Introductory Accounting Survey organized by the publisher. Although the identities of the respondents were anonymous to the authors, we learned a great deal from you and appreciate the detail you provided.

Many of the improvements in the Eighth Canadian Edition were based on the input from the reviewers of the seventh edition and the manuscript for the eighth edition. We want to thank this important group of people for their contributions to this edition. They include:

Peter McNeil, C.A.
Camosun College

Donna P. Grace
Sheridan College

Terry Fegarty
Seneca College of Applied
Arts and Technology

Barrie Yackness
British Columbia Institute of
Technology

Paul Molgat
Red Deer College

Tilly Jensen
Northern Alberta Institute of
Technology

Gregg Tranter
Southern Alberta Institute of
Technology

Sheila Simpson
Humber College of Applied Arts
and Technology

We also want to recognize the contribution of Robert Nichols of the British Columbia Institute of Technology who prepared the update of the payroll liabilities chapter and solutions for this edition.

Last but not least, we gratefully acknowledge the contribution from students, faculty members, and secretarial staff at the University of Windsor, Wilfrid Laurier University, and Dalhousie University. Special thanks go to Sharon Roth and Sandra J. Berlasty at the University of Windsor, Allan Russell at Wilfrid Laurier University, and Helen Cruickshanks and Carmen Tam at Dalhousie University.

Kermit D. Larson
Morton Nelson
Michael Zin
Ray F. Carroll

To the Student

Fundamental Accounting Principles is designed to get you actively involved in the learning process so you will learn quickly and more thoroughly. The more time you spend expressing what you are learning, the more effectively you will learn. In accounting, you do this primarily by answering questions and solving problems. But this is not the only way to learn. You also can express your ideas by using the book's wide margins for taking notes, summarizing a phrase, or writing down a question that remains unanswered in your mind. Ideas that pop into your head can lead to fruitful exploration. These notes will assist in your later review of the material, and the simple process of writing them will help you learn.

To guide your study, *learning objectives* are listed near the beginning of each chapter. Read these objectives to form some expectations about what you will learn from studying the chapter. Think of them as your goals while you study. Each learning objective is repeated in the margin at the point the chapter begins to provide material related to that objective. You will find each objective repeated at the end of each chapter in the summary. The exercises and problem assignments following each chapter also are coded to these objectives.

As you progress in your study of each chapter, you will periodically encounter Progress Check questions relating to the material you have just studied. Answer the questions and compare your answers with the correct answers at the end of each chapter. If you are not able to answer the questions correctly, review the preceding section of the chapter before going on.

Several features of the text emphasize the real-world usefulness of the material in the book. For example, the *opening paragraphs* of each chapter raise questions about a real business. As you progress through the chapter, keep a sharp eye out for points in the discussion that apply to the scenario in the opening paragraphs. You will find brief inserts entitled *"As a Matter of Opinion"* in which business and community leaders tell how they use accounting in making decisions.

The use of colour in the book has been carefully planned to facilitate your learning. For example, the financial statements and reports that accounting provides as information to be used in decision making are blue. The primary documents that accountants generate for their own use as they develop informative statements and reports are green. Documents that serve as sources of the data that go into an accounting system are yellow.

As you read the text, you will learn many important new terms. These key terms are printed in black boldface the first time they appear, and they are listed again in a *glossary* after each chapter. In addition, you can find these key terms in the index at the end of the book. As a reinforcement to learning, but also as a light break from regular study, all chapters close with a *crossword puzzle* that involves some of the glossary terms.

Computer technology is changing the way businesses operate and will continue to be a driving force in the twenty-first century. To reflect this change and to give you practice with software, some of the assignments in the book are preloaded on a set of computer templates called *SPATS*. These assignments are identified with the following logo:

Ask your instructor or check your school's bookstore for information about other supplemental items that are available to assist your study. The *tutorial software* contains multiple-choice, true/false, journal entry review, and glossary review questions to help you prepare for exams. The *study guide* reviews learning objectives and provides practice problems for each chapter. *Working papers* provide familiarity with the actual framework used in creating accounting information.

Accounting can be an informative, relevant, and engaging field of inquiry. *Fundamental Accounting Principles* offers many tools to lead you into an understanding of the importance of accounting. Read, discuss, and enjoy! What you learn in this course will be useful in your personal and professional affairs for the rest of your life.

Contents in Brief

Contents

FUNDAMENTAL
ACCOUNTING
PRINCIPLES

EIGHTH CANADIAN EDITION
VOLUME II

Capital Assets: Plant and Equipment

Companies invest large amounts in plant assets, such as trucks and equipment, that are used to produce and distribute goods and provide services to customers. Accounting provides information about the costs of obtaining, maintaining, and using these assets.

s part of their continued study of balance sheet items, Karen White and Mark Smith were given sections of Weston's financial statements. In its December 31, 1994, annual report, George Weston Limited indicated that "Fixed asset investment of $552 million represents another record level and strong commitment to the business. Capital expenditures increased because more opportunities meeting the Company's minimum return levels were identified." George Weston Limited is a broadly based Canadian company founded in 1882 that conducts operations in food processing, food distribution, and resource operations in North America. These diverse businesses operate through Weston Foods, a bakery, dairy, and confectionery food processor; Loblaw Companies, the largest food distributor in Canada; and Weston Resources, a forest products and fish processing company.

GEORGE WESTON LIMITED
NOTES TO CONSOLIDATED FINANCIAL STATEMENTS
(in millions)

	Dec. 31, 1994	Dec. 31, 1993
Fixed Assets	$4,712	$4,327
Less Accumulated Depreciation	2,008	1,865
Net Book Value	$2,704	$2,462

George Weston Limited
Consolidated Cash Flow Statement

Investment:		
Purchase of fixed assets	$ 552	$ 418

LEARNING OBJECTIVES

After studying Chapter 11, you should be able to:

1. **Describe the differences between capital (plant) assets and other kinds of assets, and calculate the cost and record the purchase of plant assets.**

2. **Explain amortization accounting (including the reasons for amortization), calculate amortization by the straight-line and units-of-production methods, and calculate amortization after revising the estimated useful life of an asset.**

3. **Describe the use of accelerated amortization for financial accounting purposes and calculate accelerated amortization under the declining-balance method.**

4. **Describe the difference between revenue and capital expenditures and account properly for costs such as repairs and betterments incurred after the original purchase of capital assets.**

5. **Prepare entries to account for the disposal or exchange of capital assets and explain the use of total asset turnover in evaluating a company's efficiency in using its assets.**

6. **Define or explain the words and phrases listed in the chapter glossary.**

The focus of this chapter is long-term, tangible assets used in the operation of a business. These capital assets represent a major category of investment by businesses. Recent financial press predictions call for an approximate 8% increase in spending related to capital assets. For example, in the **Consumers Packaging Inc.** annual report for the year ended December 31, 1994, management made the following statement: "After spending an average of only $20 million per year on capital expenditures in the years 1991 to 1993, the Company spent $44 million in 1994 and plans to spend $48 million in 1995. In the two years to the end of 1995, the Company will have rebuilt 4 of its 13 furnaces, which normally have a life of 8 to 10 years, and replaced almost half of its glass-forming machines with more modern and productive machines."

Learning fundamental concepts of accounting for plant and equipment will enable you to recognize the direct financial statement impact of business activities like those described above. In studying this chapter, you will learn what distinguishes plant and equipment from other types of assets, how to determine their cost, and how companies allocate their costs to the periods that benefit from their use.

CAPITAL (PLANT) ASSETS COMPARED TO OTHER TYPES OF ASSETS

LO 1

Describe the differences between capital (plant) assets and other kinds of assets, and calculate the cost and record the purchase of plant assets.

Tangible assets that are used in the production or sale of other assets or services and that have a useful life longer than one accounting period are called *capital assets*. In the past, such assets were often described as *plant assets* or *fixed assets*. However, more descriptive terms such as *plant and equipment* or perhaps *property, plant, and equipment* are now used.

The main difference between capital assets and merchandise is that capital assets are held for use while merchandise is held for sale. For example, a business that buys a computer for the purpose of reselling it should report the computer on the balance sheet as merchandise inventory. If the same retailer owns another computer that is used to account for business operations and to prepare reports, it is classified as plant and equipment.

The characteristic that distinguishes capital assets from current assets is the length of their useful lives. For example, supplies are usually consumed within a short time after they are placed in use. Thus, their cost is assigned to the single period in which they are used. By comparison, capital assets have longer useful lives that extend over more than one accounting period. As the usefulness of capital assets expires over these periods, their cost must be allocated among them. This allocation should be accomplished in a rational and systematic manner.[1]

Capital assets are also different than the items that are reported on the balance sheet as long-term investments. Although both are held for more than one accounting period, long-term investments are not used in the primary operations of the business. For example, land that is held for future expansion is classified as a long-term investment. On the other hand, land on which the company's factory is located is a capital asset. In addition, standby equipment held for use in case of a breakdown or during peak periods of production is a capital asset. However, equipment that is removed from service and held for sale is no longer considered a capital asset.

COST OF A CAPITAL ASSET

When a capital asset is purchased, it should be recorded at cost. This cost includes all normal and reasonable expenditures necessary to get the asset in place and ready to use. For example, the cost of a factory machine includes its invoice price, less any cash discount for early payment, plus freight, unpacking, and assembling costs. The cost of an asset also includes the costs of installing a machine before placing it in service. Examples are the costs to build a concrete base or foundation for a machine, to provide electrical connections, and to adjust the machine before using it in operations.

An expenditure cannot be charged to and reported as part of the cost of a capital asset unless the expenditure is reasonable and necessary. For example, if a machine is damaged by being dropped during unpacking, the repairs should not be added to its cost. Instead, they should be charged to an expense account. Also, a fine paid for moving a heavy machine on city streets without proper permits is not part of the cost of the machine. However, if proper permits are obtained, their cost is included in the cost of the asset. Sometimes, costs in addition to the purchase price are incurred to modify or customize a new capital asset. These items should be charged to the asset's cost.

When a capital asset is constructed by a business for its own use, cost includes material and labour costs plus a reasonable amount of indirect overhead costs such as the costs of heat, light, power, and amortization on the machinery used to construct the asset. Cost also includes design fees, building permits, and insurance during construction. However, insurance costs for coverage after the asset has been placed in service are an operating expense.

When land is purchased for a building site, its cost includes the total amount paid for the land, including any real estate commissions. Its cost also includes fees for insuring the title, legal fees, and any accrued property taxes paid by the purchaser. In addition, payments for surveying, clearing, grading, draining, and landscaping are included in the cost of land. Other costs of land include assessments

---

[1] *CICA Handbook,* section 3060, "Capital Assets," par. 31.

by the local government, whether incurred at the time of purchase or later, for such things as installing streets, sewers, and sidewalks. These assessments are included because they add a more or less permanent value to the land.

Land purchased as a building site may have an old building that must be removed. In such cases, the total purchase price should be charged to the Land account. Also, the cost of removing the old building, less any amounts recovered through the sale of salvaged materials, should be charged to the Land account.

Because land has an unlimited life and is not consumed when it is used, it is not subject to amortization. However, **land improvements,** such as parking lot surfaces, fences, and lighting systems, have limited useful lives. Although these costs increase the usefulness of the land, they must be charged to separate Land Improvement accounts so that they can be amortized. Of course, a separate Building account must be charged for the costs of purchasing or constructing a building that will be used as a plant asset.

Land, land improvements, and buildings often are purchased in a single transaction for a lump-sum price. When this occurs, you must allocate the cost of the purchase among the different types of assets, based on their relative market values. These market values may be estimated by appraisal or by using the tax-assessed valuations of the assets.

For example, assume that a company pays $90,000 cash to acquire land appraised at $30,000, land improvements appraised at $10,000, and a building appraised at $60,000. The $90,000 cost is allocated on the basis of appraised values as follows:

	Appraised Value	Percentage of Total	Apportioned Cost
Land	$ 30,000	30%	$27,000
Land improvements	10,000	10	9,000
Building	60,000	60	54,000
Totals	$100,000	100%	$90,000

Progress Check
(Answers to Progress Checks are provided at the end of the chapter.)

11–1 Identify the asset classification for: *(a)* office supplies; *(b)* office equipment; *(c)* merchandise; *(d)* land held for future expansion; *(e)* trucks used in operations.

11–2 Identify the account charged for each of the following expenditures: *(a)* the purchase price of a vacant lot; *(b)* the cost of paving that vacant lot.

11–3 What amount should be recorded as the cost of a new production machine, given the following items related to the machine: gross purchase price, $700,000; duty, $49,000; purchase discount taken, $21,000; freight to move machine to plant, $3,500; assembly costs, $3,000; cost of foundation for machine, $2,500; cost of spare parts to be used in maintaining the machine, $4,200?

Because capital assets are purchased for use, you can think of a capital asset as a quantity of usefulness that contributes to the operations of the business throughout the service life of the asset. And, because the life of any capital asset (other than land) is limited, this quantity of usefulness expires as the asset is used. This expiration of a capital asset's quantity of usefulness is generally described as *amortization*. In accounting, this term describes the process of allocating and charging the cost of the usefulness to the accounting periods that benefit from the asset's use.

The term *amortization* is the general term used for many situations where amounts are allocated to different accounts over varying lengths of time. When the Accounting Standards Board revised and reissued the standard on capital assets (Section 3060), they said that the cost of capital assets should be amortized over their useful lives in a rational and systematic manner. In practice, the term *depreciation* still tends to be used for plant assets such as machinery and buildings, and the term *depletion* still tends to be used for natural resources. Amortization continues to be used for intangible assets and other items such as premium or discount on long-term debt. We will continue to use the terms depreciation and depletion from time to time. Remember that they are terms that are specialized names for amortization.

For example, when a company buys an automobile for use as a plant asset, it acquires a quantity of usefulness in the sense that it obtains a quantity of transportation. The total cost of the transportation is the cost of the car less the expected proceeds to be received when the car is sold or traded in at the end of its service life. This net cost must be allocated to the accounting periods that benefit from the car's use. In other words, the asset's cost must be amortized. Note that the amortization process does not measure the decline in the car's market value each period. Nor does it measure the physical deterioration of the car each period. Under generally accepted accounting principles, amortization is a process of allocating a capital asset's cost to income statements of the years in which it is used.

Because amortization represents the cost of using a capital asset, you should not begin recording amortization charges until the asset is actually put to use providing services or producing products.

NATURE OF AMORTIZATION

LO 2

Explain amortization accounting (including the reasons for amortization), calculate amortization by the straight-line and units-of-production methods, and calculate amortization after revising the estimated useful life of an asset.

SERVICE (USEFUL) LIFE OF A CAPITAL ASSET

The **service life** of a capital asset is the length of time it will be used in the operations of the business. This service life (or useful life) may not be as long as the asset's potential life. For example, although computers have a potential life of six to eight years, a company may plan to trade in its old computers for new ones every three years. In this case, the computers have a three-year service life. Therefore, this company should charge the cost of the computers (less their expected trade-in value) to amortization expense over this three-year period.

Several factors often make the service life of a plant asset hard to predict. Wear and tear from use determine the service life of many assets. However, two additional factors, **inadequacy** and **obsolescence,** often need to be considered.

When a business grows more rapidly than anticipated, the capacity of the assets may become too small for the productive demands of the business. As this happens, the assets become inadequate. Obsolescence, like inadequacy, is hard to anticipate because the timing of new inventions and improvements normally cannot be predicted. Yet, new inventions and improvements may cause a company to discard an obsolete asset long before it wears out.

Many times, a company is able to predict the service life of a new asset based on the company's past experience with similar assets. In other cases, when it has no experience with a particular type of asset, a company must depend on the experience of others or on engineering studies and judgment.

In its 1994 annual report, **Corel Corporation** disclosed the following information regarding its amortization procedures:

(e) Capital Assets

Capital assets are recorded at cost. Amortization of licenses commences with the market release of each new software product and versions. Depreciation and amortization are calculated using the following rates and bases:

Furniture and equipment	20–33% declining balance
Computer equipment and software	33.3% straight-line
Research and development equipment	20% declining balance
Software licenses and purchased software, clipart libraries and Photo CD libraries	Shorter of the life of the license or 20.0–33.3% straight-line
Leasehold improvements	Straight-line over the term of the lease

SALVAGE VALUE

The total amount of amortization that should be taken over an asset's service life is the asset's cost minus its estimated **salvage value.** The salvage value of a plant asset is the amount that you expect to receive from selling the asset at the end of its life. If you expect an asset to be traded in on a new asset, the salvage value is the estimated trade-in value.

Sometimes, a company must incur additional costs to dispose of plant assets. For example, a company may plan to clean and paint an old machine before offering it for sale. In this case, the estimated salvage value is the expected proceeds from the sale of the asset less the cleaning and painting costs.

ALLOCATING AMORTIZATION

Many amortization methods for allocating a capital asset's total cost among the several accounting periods in its service life have been suggested and used in the past. However, at present, most companies use the *straight-line method* of amortization in their financial accounting records for presentation in their financial statements. Some types of assets are amortized according to the *units-of-production method.* We explain these two methods next and then consider some *accelerated amortization* methods.

Straight-Line Method

Straight-line amortization (or **depreciation**) charges each year in the asset's life with the same amount of expense. To determine the annual expense, the total cost to be amortized over the asset's life is calculated by first subtracting the asset's estimated salvage value from its cost. This total amount to be amortized is then divided by the estimated number of accounting periods in the asset's service life.

Illustration 11–1   The Financial Statement of Straight-Line Amortization.

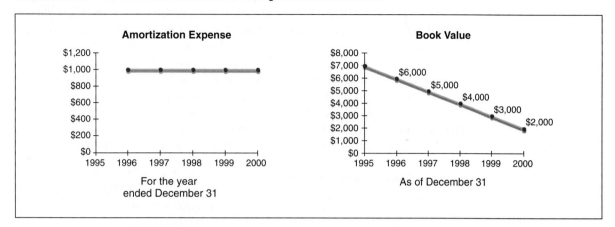

For example, if an asset costs $7,000, has an estimated service life of five years, and has an estimated $2,000 salvage value, its amortization per year by the straight-line method is $1,000. This amount is calculated as follows:

$$\frac{\text{Cost} - \text{Salvage}}{\text{Service life in years}} = \frac{\$7,000 - \$2,000}{5 \text{ years}} = \$1,000 \text{ per year}$$

If this asset is purchased on December 31, 1995, and used throughout its predicted service life of five years, the straight-line method will allocate an equal amount of amortization to each of those years (1996 through 2000). The left graph in Illustration 11–1 shows that this $1,000 per year amount will be reported each year as an expense. The right graph shows the amount that will be reported on each of the six balance sheets that will be produced while the company actually owns the asset. This **book value** of the asset is its original cost less accumulated amortization. The book value goes down by $1,000 each year. Both graphs show why this method is called *straight-line*.

Although most companies use straight-line amortization, other methods are common in certain industries. For example, **Canadian Pacific Limited** uses the units-of-production method in its facilities that produce crude oil and natural gas.

Units-of-Production Method

The purpose of recording amortization, or depreciation, is to provide relevant information about the cost of consuming an asset's usefulness. In general, this means that each accounting period an asset is used should be charged with a fair share of its cost. The straight-line method charges an equal share to each period. If plant assets are used about the same amount in each accounting period, this method produces a reasonable result. However, the use of some plant assets varies greatly from one accounting period to another. For example, a contractor may use a particular piece of construction equipment for a month and then not use it again for a few months.

Because the use of such equipment varies from period to period, **units-of-production amortization** may provide a better matching of expenses with revenues than straight-line amortization. Under the units-of-production method, the cost of an asset minus its estimated salvage value is divided by the total number cost of an asset minus its estimated salvage value is divided by the total number of units that management predicts it will produce during its service life. Units of production may be expressed as units of product or in any other unit of measure such as hours of use or distances driven. In effect, this method computes the amount of amortization per unit of service provided by the asset. Then, the amount of amortization taken in an accounting period is determined by multiplying the units produced in that period by the amortization per unit.

For example, a truck that cost $24,000 has a predicted salvage value of $4,000 and an estimated service life of 200,000 kilometres. The amortization per kilometre, or the amortization per unit of service, is $0.10, which is calculated as follows:

$$\text{Amortization per unit of production} = \frac{\text{Cost} - \text{Salvage value}}{\text{Predicted units of production}}$$

$$= \frac{\$24,000 - \$4,000}{200,000 \text{ kms.}}$$

$$= \$0.10 \text{ per km.}$$

If the truck is driven 32,000 kilometres during its first year, amortization for the first year is $3,200 (32,000 kms. at $.10 per km.). If the truck is driven 24,000 kilometres in the second year, amortization for the second year is 24,000 kilometres times $0.10 per km., or $2,400.

AMORTIZATION FOR PARTIAL YEARS

Of course, capital assets may be purchased or disposed of at any time during the year. When an asset is purchased (or disposed of) at some time other than the beginning or end of an accounting period, amortization must be recorded for part of a year. Otherwise, the year of purchase or the year of disposal is not charged with its share of the asset's amortization.

For example, assume that a machine was purchased and placed in service on October 8, 1996, and that the annual accounting period ends on December 31. The machine cost $4,600; it has an estimated service life of five years and an estimated salvage value of $600. Because the machine was purchased and used nearly three months during 1996, the annual income statement should reflect amortization expense on the machine for that part of the year. The amount of amortization to be reported is often based on the assumption that the machine was purchased on the first of the month nearest the actual date of purchase. Therefore, since the purchase occurred on October 8, three months' amortization is recorded on December 31. If the purchase had been on October 16 or later during October, amortization would be calculated as if the purchase had been on November 1. Using straight-line amortization, the three months' amortization of $200 is calculated as follows:

$$\frac{\$4,600 - \$600}{5} \times \frac{3}{12} = \$200$$

A similar calculation is necessary when the disposal of an asset occurs during a year. For example, suppose that the preceding asset is sold on June 24, 2000. On the date of the disposal, amortization should be recognized. The partial year's amortization, calculated to the nearest whole month, is:

$$\frac{\$4,600 - \$600}{5} \times \frac{6}{12} = \$400$$

In presenting information about the capital assets of a business, both the cost and accumulated amortization of capital assets should be reported. For example, **CGC, Inc.'s** balance sheet at the close of its 1994 fiscal year included the following:

Property, Plant and Equipment

Property, plant and equipment consists of the following:

(in thousands of dollars)		1994		1993
	Cost	Accumulated Depletion, Depreciation & Amortization	Net	Net
Land, land improvements and mineral deposits	$ 2,721	$ 511	$ 2,210	$ 2,223
Buildings	19,431	9,034	10,397	10,857
Furniture, fixtures and equipment	89,288	63,769	25,519	27,596
Vehicles	2,682	2,341	341	394
Leasehold improvements	2,341	1,098	1,243	1,318
Construction in progress	5,720	—	5,720	2,824
Total	$122,183	$76,753	$45,430	$45,212

Notice that CGC reported only the amount of accumulated depletion, depreciation, and amortization for all property, plant, and equipment. This is not necessarily the usual practice in published financial statements. In fact, many companies show property, plant, and equipment on one line with the net amount of cost less accumulated amortization. When this is done, however, the amount of accumulated amortization is disclosed in a note. To satisfy the *full-disclosure principle,* companies also describe the amortization method or methods used.[2] Usually, they do this in a note.

Reporting both the cost and the accumulated amortization of capital assets may help balance sheet readers compare the status of different companies. For example, a company that holds assets having an original cost of $50,000 and accumulated amortization of $40,000 may be in quite a different situation than another company with new assets that cost $10,000. Although the net unamortized cost is the same in both cases, the first company may have more productive capacity available but probably is facing the need to replace its older assets. These differences are not conveyed if the balance sheets report only the $10,000 book values.

From the discussion so far, you should recognize that amortization is a process of cost allocation rather than valuation. Capital assets are reported on balance sheets at their remaining unamortized costs (book value), not at market values.

Some people argue that financial statements should report the market value of plant assets. However, this practice has not gained general acceptance. Instead, most accountants believe that financial statements should be based on the *going-concern principle* described in Chapter 1. This principle states that, unless there is adequate evidence to the contrary, the accountant should assume the company will

---

[2]Ibid., par. 3060.58.

continue in business. This leads to a related assumption that capital assets will be held and used long enough to recover their original cost through the sale of products and services. Therefore, since the capital assets will not be sold, their market values are not reported in the financial statements. Instead, the assets are carried on the balance sheet at cost less accumulated amortization. This is the remaining portion of the original cost that is expected to be recovered in future periods.

Inexperienced financial statement readers may make the mistake of thinking that the accumulated amortization shown on a balance sheet represents funds accumulated to buy new assets when the presently owned assets must be replaced. However, you know that accumulated amortization is a contra account with a credit balance that cannot be used to buy anything. If a business has funds available to buy assets, the funds are shown on the balance sheet as liquid assets such as *Cash,* not as accumulated amortization.

REVISING AMORTIZATION RATES

Because the calculation of amortization or depreciation must be based on an asset's *predicted* useful life, amortization expense is an estimate. Therefore, during the life of an asset, new information may indicate that the original prediction of useful life was inaccurate. If your estimate of an asset's useful life changes, what should be done? The answer is to use the new estimate of the remaining useful life to calculate amortization in the future. In other words, revise the estimate of annual amortization expense in the future by spreading the remaining cost to be amortized over the revised remaining useful life. This approach should be followed whether the amortization method is straight-line, units-of-production, or some other method.

For example, assume that a machine was purchased seven years ago at a cost of $10,500. At that time, the machine was predicted to have a 10-year life with a $500 salvage value. Therefore, it was amortized by the straight-line method at the rate of $1,000 per year [($10,500 − $500)/10 = $1,000]. At the beginning of the asset's eighth year, its book value is $3,500, calculated as follows:

Cost	$10,500
Less seven years' accumulated amortization . . .	7,000
Book value	$ 3,500

At the beginning of its eighth year, the predicted number of years remaining in the useful life is changed from three to five years. The estimated salvage value is also changed to $300. Amortization for each of the machine's five remaining years should be calculated as follows:

$$\frac{\text{Book value} - \text{Revised salvage value}}{\text{Revised remaining useful life}} = \frac{\$3,500 - \$300}{5 \text{ years}} = \$640 \text{ per year}$$

Thus, $640 of amortization should be recorded for the machine at the end of the eighth and each remaining year in its useful life.

Because this asset was amortized at the rate of $1,000 per year for the first seven years, you might contend that amortization expense was overstated during the first seven years. While that view may have merit, accountants have concluded that past years' financial statements generally should not be restated to reflect facts that were not known when the statements were originally prepared.

A revision of the predicted useful life of a plant asset is an example of a **change in an accounting estimate.** Such changes result "from new information or subsequent developments and accordingly from better insight or improved judgment." Generally accepted accounting principles require that changes in accounting estimates, such as a change in estimated useful life or salvage value, be reflected only in future financial statements, not by modifying past statements.[3]

Progress Check

11-4 For accounting purposes, what is the meaning of the term *amortization?*

11-5 Clandestine Gift Shop purchased a new machine for $96,000 on January 1, 1996. Its predicted useful life is five years or 100,000 units of product, and salvage value is $8,000. During 1996, 10,000 units of product were produced. Find the book value of the machine on December 31, 1996, assuming *(a)* straight-line amortization and *(b)* units-of-production amortization.

11-6 In early January of 1996, Betty's Brownies acquired mixing equipment at a cost of $3,800. The company estimated that this equipment would be used for three years and then have a salvage of $200. Early in 1998, they changed the estimate to a four-year life with no residual value. Assuming straight-line amortization, how much will be reported as amortization on this equipment for the year ended 1998?

An annual survey of 300 Canadian companies indicates that straight-line is the most widely used method of amortization. However, note in the following table that **accelerated amortization** methods were used 20% of the time in 1992:

ACCELERATED AMORTIZATION

LO 3
Describe the use of accelerated amortization for financial accounting purposes and calculate accelerated amortization under the declining-balance method.

	Amortization Methods Used	
	1992	1991
Straight-line	62%	61%
An accelerated method	20	21
Units-of-production	16	16
Other	2	2
Total	100%	100%

Source: *Financial Reporting in Canada 1993,* Canadian Institute of Chartered Accountants (Toronto: 1993), p. 154.

Accelerated amortization methods produce larger amortization charges during the early years of an asset's life and smaller charges in the later years. Although more

[3]Ibid., par. 1506.25.

than one accelerated method is used in financial reporting, the most commonly used is the declining-balance method.

Declining-Balance Method

Under **declining-balance amortization,** an amortization rate of up to twice the straight-line rate is applied each year to the book value of the asset at the beginning of the year. Because the book value *declines* each year, the amount of amortization gets smaller each year.

The **Income Tax Act** requires that companies use a declining-balance method for calculating the maximum capital cost allowance (amortization or depreciation for tax purposes) that may be claimed in any period. The Act specifies the rates for various classes of assets. For example, a rate of 20% would be used for general machinery and equipment, and a rate of 4% for most buildings. Further discussion of the details of tax accounting for capital assets is deferred to a more advanced course.

When the amortization rate used is twice the straight-line rate, the method is called the *double-declining-balance method.* To use the double-declining-balance method: (1) calculate the straight-line amortization rate for the asset; (2) double it; and (3) calculate amortization expense for the year by applying this rate to the asset's book value at the beginning of that year. Note that the salvage value is not used in the calculation.

For example, assume that the double-declining-balance method is used to calculate amortization on a new $10,000 asset; it has an estimated life of five years and an estimated salvage value of $1,000. The steps to follow are:

1. Divide 100% by five years to determine the straight-line annual amortization rate of 20% per year.
2. Double this 20% rate to get a declining-balance rate of 40% per year.
3. Calculate the annual amortization charges as shown in the following table:

Year	Beginning Book Value	Annual Amortization (40% of Book Value)	Accumulated Amortization at Year-End	Ending Book Value ($10,000 Cost Less Accumulated Amortization)
First	$10,000	$4,000	$4,000	$6,000
Second	6,000	2,400	6,400	3,600
Third	3,600	1,440	7,840	2,160
Fourth	2,160	864	8,704	1,296
Fifth	1,296	296*	9,000	1,000
Total		$9,000		

*Fifth year amortization is $1,296 − $1,000 = $296.

In the table, notice that the annual amortization of $296 for the fifth year does not equal 40% × $1,296, or $518.40. Instead, the $296 was calculated by subtracting the $1,000 salvage value from the $1,296 book value at the beginning of the fifth year. This was done because, according to generally accepted accounting principles, an asset should not be amortized below its salvage value. If the declining-balance procedure had been applied in the fifth year, the $518.40 of annual amortization would have reduced the ending book value to $777.60, which is less than the $1,000 estimated salvage value.

Earlier in the chapter we discussed the calculation of a partial year's amortization when the straight-line method is used. Recall that when an asset is purchased (or disposed of) at some time other than the end of an accounting period, amortization must be recorded for part of a year. Declining-balance amortization does not complicate this calculation. For example, if amortization must be calculated for three months, the annual amount of amortization is simply multiplied by $^3/_{12}$. So, if an asset that cost $10,000 is purchased three months before the end of the year and the annual declining-balance amortization rate is 20%, amortization for the last three months is $10,000 × 20% × $^3/_{12}$ = $500.

The following year's amortization would be based on the unamortized balance of $9,500 ($10,000 − $500). Thus, the amortization for the next full year would be $1,900 ($9,500 × .2). Another, somewhat more complex calculation may be used to verify the amortization of $1,900, as follows:

Year 1 $10,000 × 20% × ¾₂	$ 500
Year 2 ($10,000 × 20% × ½₂) + ($8,000 × 20% × ¾₂)	1,900

By this time, you have learned that some expenditures are recorded as expenses right away while others are recorded as assets with expenses coming later. After a plant asset is acquired and put into service, additional expenditures may be incurred to operate, maintain, repair, and improve it. In recording these additional expenditures, the accountant must decide whether they should be debited to expense ac-

REVENUE AND CAPITAL EXPENDITURES

LO 4

Describe the difference between revenue and capital expenditures and account properly for costs such as repairs and betterments incurred after the original purchase of capital assets.

counts or asset accounts. The issue is whether more useful information is provided by reporting these expenditures as current expenses or by adding them to the plant asset's cost and amortizing them over its remaining useful life.

Expenditures that are recorded as expenses and deducted from revenues on the current period's income statement are called **revenue expenditures.** They are reported on the income statement because they do not provide material benefits in future periods. Examples of revenue expenditures that relate to plant assets are supplies, fuel, lubricants, and electrical power.

In contrast to revenue expenditures, **capital expenditures** produce economic benefits that do not fully expire before the end of the current period. Because they are debited to asset accounts and reported on the balance sheet, they are also called **balance sheet expenditures.** Capital expenditures increase or improve the kind or amount of service that an asset provides.

Because the information in the financial statements is affected for several years by the choice you make in recording costs as revenue or capital expenditures, managers must be careful in deciding how to classify them. In making these decisions, it is helpful to identify the costs as repairs, betterments, or purchases of assets with low costs.

Repairs

Repairs are made to keep an asset in normal, good operating condition. These expenditures are necessary if an asset is to provide its expected level of service over its estimated useful life. However, repairs do not extend the useful life beyond the original estimate and do not increase the productivity of the asset beyond the levels originally estimated. For example, machines must be cleaned, lubricated, and adjusted, and small parts must be replaced when they wear out. These repairs typically are made every year, and accountants treat them as *revenue expenditures.* Thus, their costs should be reported on the current income statement as expenses.

Consistent with the guidelines given here, **Air Canada** expenses routine maintenance and repairs as incurred. However, the cost of scheduled airframe and engine overhauls is capitalized as a betterment because such expenditures are expected to benefit future periods.

Betterments

A **betterment** (or an improvement) occurs when a plant asset is modified to improve service potential. A betterment might increase the physical output or service capacity, lower operating costs, extend the useful life or improve output quality. A betterment often involves adding a component to an asset or replacing one of its old components with an improved or superior component. While a betterment might make an asset more productive, it may not necessarily increase the asset's useful life. For example, replacing the manual controls on a machine with automatic controls reduces future labour costs. But, the machine still wears out just as fast as it would have with the manual controls.

A betterment benefits future periods and should be debited to the asset account as a capital expenditure. Then, the new book value (less salvage) should be amortized over the remaining service life of the asset. For example, suppose that a company paid $80,000 for a machine with an eight-year service life and no salvage value. On January 2, after three years and $30,000 of amortization, it adds an automatic control system to the machine at a cost of $18,000. As a result, the company's labour cost to operate the machine in future periods will be reduced. The cost of the betterment is added to the Machinery account with this entry:

Jan.	2	Machinery	18,000.00	
		Cash		18,000.00
		To record the installation of the automatic control system.		

At this point, the remaining cost to be amortized is $80,000 + $18,000 − $30,000 = $68,000. Because five years remain in the useful life, the annual amortization expense hereafter will be $13,600 per year ($68,000/5 years).

Capital Assets with Low Costs

Even with the help of computers, keeping individual plant asset records can be expensive. Therefore, many companies do not keep detailed records for assets that cost less than some minimum amount such as $50 or $100. Instead, they treat the acquisition as a revenue expenditure and charge the cost directly to an expense account at the time of purchase. As long as the amounts are small, this practice is acceptable under the *materiality principle*. That is, treating these capital expenditures as revenue expenditures is unlikely to mislead a user of the financial statements.

Progress Check

11-7 **At the beginning of the fifth year of a machine's estimated six-year useful life, the machine was completely overhauled and its estimated useful life was extended to nine years in total. The machine originally cost $108,000, and the overhaul cost was $12,000. Prepare the journal entry to record the cost of the overhaul.**

11-8 **What is the difference between revenue expenditures and capital expenditures and how should they be recorded?**

11-9 **What is a betterment? How should a betterment to a machine be recorded?**

CAPITAL ASSET DISPOSALS

A variety of events might lead to the disposal of capital assets. Some assets wear out or become obsolete. Other assets may be sold because of changing business plans. Sometimes, an asset is discarded or sold because it is damaged by a fire or other accident. Regardless of what leads to a disposal, the journal entry or entries related to the disposal should:

1. Record amortization expense up to the date of the disposal and bring the accumulated amortization account up to date.

LO 5

Prepare entries to account for the disposal or exchange of plant assets and explain the use of total asset turnover in evaluating a company's efficiency in using its assets.

2. Remove the asset and accumulated amortization account balances that relate to the disposal.
3. Record any cash received or paid as a result of the disposal.
4. Record any gain or loss that results from comparing the book value of the asset with the cash received or paid as a result of the disposal.

For example, assume a machine that cost $9,000 was totally destroyed in a fire on June 25. Accumulated amortization at the end of the previous year was $3,000 and unrecorded amortization for the first six months of the current year is $500. The following entry brings the accumulated amortization account up to date:

June	25	Amortization Expense	500.00	
		Accumulated Amortization, Machinery		500.00
		To record amortization up to the date of the fire.		

Assume the owner of the machine carried insurance against fire losses and received a $4,400 cash settlement for the loss. The following entry records the loss of the machine and the cash settlement:

June	25	Cash	4,400.00	
		Loss on Fire[4]	1,100.00	
		Accumulated Amortization, Machinery	3,500.00	
		Machinery		9,000.00
		To record the destruction of machinery, the receipt of		
		insurance settlement, and the net loss resulting from		
		the fire.		

Notice that the two entries accomplish all four of the necessary changes that occurred as a result of the asset disposal. Of course, an asset disposal might involve a gain instead of a loss. Also, a disposal might involve a cash payment instead of a receipt. Regardless of the specific facts, entries similar to these must be made so the income statement shows any gain or loss resulting from the disposal and the balance sheet reflects the necessary changes in the asset and accumulated amortization accounts.

EXCHANGING CAPITAL ASSETS

Many capital assets are sold for cash when they are retired from use. Others, such as machinery, automobiles, and office equipment, are commonly exchanged for new assets. In a typical exchange of assets, a trade-in allowance is received on the old asset, and any balance is paid in cash.

Accounting for the exchange of nonmonetary assets depends on whether the old and the new assets are similar in the functions they perform. For example, trading

---

[4]Note that the recorded loss of $1,100 probably does not equal the economic loss from the fire. The economic loss depends on the difference between the cost of replacing the asset and any insurance settlement. A difference between this economic loss and the reported loss arises from the fact that the accounting records do not attempt to reflect the replacement value of plant assets.

an old truck for a new truck is an exchange of similar assets. An example of exchanging dissimilar assets would be trading a parcel of land for a truck.

Exchanges of Dissimilar Assets

If a company exchanges a plant asset for another asset that is *dissimilar* in use or purpose, any gain or loss on the exchange must be recorded. The gain or loss can be determined by comparing the book value of the assets given up with the fair market value of the assets received. For example, assume that a company exchanges an old machine plus $16,500 cash for some merchandise inventory. The old machine originally cost $18,000 and had accumulated amortization of $15,000 at the time of the exchange. Also assume that the fair market value of the merchandise received in the exchange was $21,000. This entry would record the exchange:

Jan.	5	Merchandise Inventory (or Purchases)	21,000.00	
		Accumulated Amortization, Machinery	15,000.00	
		Machinery		18,000.00
		Cash		16,500.00
		Gain on Exchange of Machinery		1,500.00
		Exchanged old machine and cash for merchandise		
		inventory.		

Note that the book value of the assets given up totaled $19,500, which included $16,500 cash plus $3,000 ($18,000 − $15,000) for the machine. Because the merchandise had a fair market value of $21,000, the entry recorded a gain of $1,500 ($21,000 − $19,500).

Another way to calculate the gain or loss is to compare the machine's book value with the trade-in allowance granted for the machine. Since the fair market value of the merchandise was $21,000 and the cash paid was $16,500, the trade-in allowance granted for the machine was $4,500. The difference between the machine's $3,000 book value and the $4,500 trade-in allowance equals the $1,500 gain on the exchange.

Exchanges of Similar Assets

In general, accounting for exchanges of similar assets depends on whether the amount of cash involved is more or less than 10% of the total consideration given up or received. If the amount of cash is more than 10%, the transaction is a monetary transaction and a gain or loss on the exchange is recorded in the same manner as for exchanges of dissimilar assets.

Nonmonetary Exchanges. Accountants have determined that when an exchange of similar assets occurs and the cash involved is less than 10% of the total consideration, an earnings process has not been completed. The usual rule then is that no gain or loss should be recorded on the exchange. Therefore, the cost of the asset received is recorded as the book value of the asset delivered plus any cash paid or minus any cash received.

To illustrate, assume we decide to trade trucks with another company because they are in more convenient locations. Our truck has an original cost of $90,000 and accumulated amortization of $25,000. We have determined that the market value of the truck we are to receive is approximately $65,000, the book value of the truck we are giving up.

The entry to record the exchange when no cash is involved is

Jan.	5	Automotive equipment (new truck)	65,000	
		Accumulated amortization	25,000	
		Automotive equipment (old truck)		90,000

If we assume that we receive $1,000 as part of the exchange, the entry is

Jan.	5	Cash	1,000	
		Automotive equipment (new truck)	64,000	
		Accumulated amortization	25,000	
		Automotive equipment (old truck)		90,000

Notice that no gain is recorded. Instead the truck's cost is recorded as $64,000. This is still a nonmonetary transaction because the cash involved is less than 10% of the total consideration (10% of $65,000 = $6,500) and similar assets are being exchanged.

Now assume that we pay $3,000 as part of the exchange. The entry to record the transaction is

Jan.	5	Automotive equipment (new truck)	65,000	
		Accumulated amortization	25,000	
		Loss on exchange of trucks	3,000	
		Cash		3,000
		Automotive equipment (old truck)		90,000

Although the general rule is that no gains or losses should be recorded on non-monetary exchanges of similar assets, the maximum amount at which we may record the new asset is its market value. In this example the value of the assets delivered is $68,000 ($3,000 cash plus a truck with a $65,000 book value). However, the market value of the truck received is $65,000. The cost of the truck received must not be recorded at more than $65,000. Therefore, we must record a $3,000 loss.

In nonmonetary exchanges of similar assets, the cost of the asset received is recorded at the book value of the asset given up, minus any cash received or plus any cash paid, as long as this amount is no greater than the market value of the asset being received.[5] A loss might need to be recorded but it is unlikely that a gain would arise.

---

[5] *CICA Handbook,* section 3830, "Non-Monetary Transactions," par. .10.

We have not yet discussed all of the different assets a business might own. Nevertheless, you can see from this and previous chapters that a company's assets are usually very important factors in determining the company's ability to earn profits. Managers spend a great deal of time and energy deciding which assets a company should acquire, how much should be acquired, and how the assets can be used most efficiently. Outside investors and other financial statement readers are also interested in evaluating whether a company uses its assets efficiently.

USING THE INFORMATION— TOTAL ASSET TURNOVER

One way to describe the efficiency of a company's use of its assets is to calculate **total asset turnover.** The formula for this calculation is

$$\text{Total asset turnover} = \frac{\text{Net sales}}{\text{Average total assets}}$$

In this calculation, average total assets is often approximated by averaging the total assets at the beginning of the year with total assets at the end of the year.

For example, suppose that a company with total assets of $9,650,000 at the beginning of the year and $10,850,000 at the end of the year generated sales of $44,000,000 during the year. The company's total asset turnover for the year is calculated as follows:

$$\text{Total asset turnover} = \frac{\$44,000,000}{(\$9,650,000 + \$10,850,000)/2} = 4.3$$

Thus, in describing the efficiency of the company in using its assets to generate sales, we can say that it turned its assets over 4.3 times during the year. Or, we might say that each $1.00 of assets produced $4.30 of sales during the year.

As is true for other financial ratios, a company's total asset turnover is meaningful only when compared to the results in other years and of similar companies. Interpreting the total asset turnover also requires that users understand the company's operations. Some operations are capital intensive, meaning that a relatively large amount must be invested in assets to generate sales. This suggests a relatively low total asset turnover. On the other hand, if operations are labour intensive, sales are generated more by the efforts of people than the use of assets. Thus, we would expect a higher total asset turnover.

Imperial Oil Limited's asset turnover ratio for 1994 is ($ millions):

$$\frac{\$9,011}{(\$11,928 + \$12,861) \div 2} = 0.73$$

Canadian Tire Corporation Limited's asset turnover ratio for 1994 is ($ thousands):

$$\frac{\$3,599,231}{(\$2,668,863 + \$2,400,279) \div 2} = 1.42$$

Progress Check

11-10   **Melanie Co. acquired equipment on January 10, 1996, at a cost of $42,000. The estimated useful life of equipment was five years with an estimated salvage value of $7,000. On June 27, 1997, the company decided to change their manufacturing methods and sold this equipment for $32,000. Prepare the appropriate entry or entries for June 27, 1997.**

11-11   **Standard Company traded an old truck for a new one. The original cost of the old truck was $30,000, and its accumulated amortization at the time of the trade was $23,400. The new truck had a cash price of $45,000. Prepare entries to record the trade assuming Standard received a $3,000 trade-in allowance.**

11-12   **Using the annual report for Geac Computer Corporation in Appendix I, calculate the total asset turnover for the year ended April 30, 1994.**

SUMMARY OF THE CHAPTER IN TERMS OF LEARNING OBJECTIVES

LO 1.   Describe the differences between capital assets and other kinds of assets, and calculate the cost and record the purchase of capital assets. Capital assets are tangible items that have a useful life longer than one accounting period. Capital assets are not held for sale but are used in the production or sale of other assets or services. The cost of capital assets includes all normal and reasonable expenditures necessary to get the assets in place and ready to use. The cost of a lump-sum purchase should be allocated among the individual assets based on their relative market values.

LO 2.   Explain amortization accounting (including the reasons for amortization), calculate amortization by the straight-line and units-of-production methods, and calculate amortization after revising the estimated useful life of an asset. The cost of capital assets that have limited service lives must be allocated to the accounting periods that benefit from their use. The straight-line method of amortization divides the cost minus salvage value by the number of periods in the service life of the asset to determine the amortization expense of each period. The units-of-production method divides the cost minus salvage value by the estimated number of units the asset will produce to determine the amortization per unit. If the estimated useful life of a capital asset is changed, the remaining cost to be amortized is spread over the remaining (revised) useful life of the asset.

LO 3.   Describe the use of accelerated amortization for financial accounting purposes and calculate accelerated amortization under the declining-balance method. Accelerated amortization methods such as the declining-balance method are acceptable for financial accounting purposes if they are based on realistic estimates of useful life.

LO 4.   Describe the difference between revenue and capital expenditures and account properly for costs such as repairs and betterments incurred after the original purchase of capital assets. The benefit of revenue expenditures expires during the current period. Thus, revenue expenditures are debited to expense accounts and matched with current revenues. Capital expenditures are debited to asset accounts because they benefit future periods. Repairs are revenue expenditures. Capital expenditures include betterments. Amounts paid for assets with low costs are technically capital expenditures but can be treated as revenue expenditures if they are not material.

LO 5.   Prepare entries to account for the disposal or exchange of plant assets and explain the use of total asset turnover in evaluating a company's efficiency in using its assets. When a plant asset is discarded or sold, the cost and accumulated amortization are removed from the accounts. Any cash proceeds are recorded and compared to the asset's book value to determine gain or loss. When nonmonetary assets are exchanged and they are dissimilar, either a gain or a loss on disposal is recognized. When similar assets are exchanged in a nonmonetary transaction, gains and losses are seldom recognized. Instead, the new asset account is debited for the book value of the old asset plus any cash paid or minus any cash received. Total asset turnover measures the efficiency of a company's use of its assets to generate sales.

On July 14, 1996, Truro Company paid $600,000 to acquire a fully equipped factory. The purchase included the following:

DEMONSTRATION PROBLEM

Asset	Appraised Value	Estimated Salvage Value	Estimated Service Life	Amortization Method
Land	$160,000			Not amortized
Land improvements . .	80,000	$ –0–	10 years	Straight line
Building	320,000	100,000	10 years	Double declining balance
Machinery	240,000	20,000	10,000 units	Units of production*
Total	$800,000			

*The machinery was used to produce 700 units in 1996 and 1,800 units in 1997.

Required

1. Allocate the total $600,000 cost among the separate assets.
2. Calculate the 1996 (six months) and 1997 amortization expense for each type of asset and calculate the total each year for all assets.

• Complete a three-column worksheet showing these amounts for each asset: appraised value, percent of total value, and allocated cost.

• Using the allocated costs, compute the amount of amortization for 1996 (only one-half year) and 1997 for each asset. Then, summarize those calculations in a table showing the total amortization for each year.

Planning the Solution

1. Allocation of total cost among the assets:

Solution to Demonstration Problem

Asset	Appraised Value	Percent of Total Value	Allocated Cost
Land	$160,000	20%	$120,000
Land improvements	80,000	10	60,000
Building	320,000	40	240,000
Machinery	240,000	30	180,000
Total	$800,000	100%	$600,000

2. Amortization for each asset:

Land Improvements:
Cost	$60,000
Salvage value	–0–
Net cost	$60,000
Service life	10 years
Annual expense ($60,000/10)	$6,000
1996 amortization ($6,000 × 6/12)	$3,000
1997 amortization	$6,000

Building:
  Straight-line rate = 100%/10 = 10%
  Double-declining-balance rate = 10% × 2 = 20%

1996 amortization ($240,000 × 20% × 6/12)	$24,000
1997 amortization [($240,000 − $24,000) × 20%] ..	$43,200

Machinery:

Cost	$180,000
Salvage value	20,000
Net cost	$160,000
Total expected units	10,000
Expected cost per unit ($160,000/10,000)	$ 16

Year	Units × Unit Cost	Amortization
1996	700 × $16	$11,200
1997	1,800 × $16	28,800

Total amortization expense:

	1997	1996
Land improvements	$ 6,000	$ 3,000
Building	43,200	24,000
Machinery	28,800	11,200
Total	$78,000	$38,200

GLOSSARY

Accelerated amortization amortization methods that produce larger amortization charges during the early years of an asset's life and smaller charges in the later years. p. 533

Balance sheet expenditure another name for *capital expenditure.* p. 536

Betterment a modification to an asset to increase its service potential or physical output or to lower its operating costs, extend its useful life, or improve the quality of its output. p. 536

Book value the amount assigned to an item in the accounting records and in the financial statements; for a plant asset, book value is its original cost less accumulated amortization. p. 529

Capital expenditure an expenditure that produces economic benefits that do not fully expire before the end of the current period; because it creates or adds to existing assets, it should appear on the balance sheet as the cost of an asset. Also called a *balance sheet expenditure.* p. 536

Change in an accounting estimate a change in a calculated amount used in the financial statements that results from new information or subsequent developments and from better insight or improved judgment. p. 533

Declining-balance amortization an amortization method in which a plant asset's amortization charge for the period is determined by applying a constant amortization rate each year to the asset's beginning book value. p. 534

Inadequacy a condition in which the capacity of plant assets becomes too small for the productive demands of the business. p. 527

Income Tax Act the codification of the Canadian federal tax laws. p. 534

Land improvements assets that increase the usefulness of land but that have a limited useful life and are subject to amortization. p. 526

Obsolescence a condition in which, because of new inventions and improvements, a capital asset can no longer be used to produce goods or services with a competitive advantage. p. 527

Repairs expenditures made to keep a plant asset in normal, good operating condition; treated as a revenue expenditure. p. 536

Revenue expenditure an expenditure that should appear on the current income statement as an expense and be deducted from the period's revenues because it does not provide a material benefit in future periods. p. 536

Salvage value the amount that management predicts will be recovered at the end of a plant asset's service life through a sale or as a trade-in allowance on the purchase of a new asset. p. 528

Service life the length of time in which a plant asset will be used in the operations of the business. p. 527

Straight-line amortization a method that allocates an equal portion of the total amortization for a plant asset

(cost minus salvage) to each accounting period in its service life. p. 528

Total asset turnover a measure of how efficiently a company uses its assets to generate sales; calculated by dividing net sales by average total assets. p. 541

Units-of-production amortization a method that allocates an equal portion of the total amortization for a plant asset (cost minus salvage) to each unit of product or service that it produces, or on a similar basis, such as hours of use or kilometres driven. p. 529

SYNONYMOUS TERMS

Amortizable cost depreciable cost.

Capital assets plant assets; property, plant, and equipment; fixed assets.

Depletion amortization.

Depreciation amortization.

Service life useful life.

QUESTIONS

1. What characteristics of a capital asset make it different from other assets?

2. What is the balance sheet classification of land held for future expansion? Why is the land not classified as a plant asset?

3. In general, what is included in the cost of a plant asset?

4. What is the difference between land and land improvements?

5. Does the balance of the account, Accumulated Amortization, Machinery, represent funds accumulated to replace the machinery when it wears out? What does the balance of Accumulated Amortization represent?

6. What is the difference between repairs and betterments and how should they be recorded?

7. What accounting principle justifies charging the $75 cost of a plant asset immediately to an expense account?

8. What are some of the events that might lead to the disposal of a plant asset?

9. Should a gain on an exchange of plant assets be recorded?

10. How is total asset turnover calculated? Why would a financial statement user be interested in calculating total asset turnover?

11. Refer to the consolidated balance sheets for Geac Computer Corporation Limited in Appendix I. What phrase does Geac use to describe its capital assets? What is the book value of capital assets as of December 31, 1994, and December 31, 1993?

QUICK STUDY (Five-Minute Exercises)

Explain the difference between *(a)* capital assets and long-term investments; *(b)* capital assets and inventory; and *(c)* capital assets and current assets.

QS 11–1
(LO 1)

Mattituck Lanes installed automatic scorekeeping equipment. The electrical work required to prepare for the installation was $12,000. The invoice price of the equipment was $120,000. Additional costs were $2,000 for delivery and $8,400, sales tax. During the installation, a

QS 11–2
(LO 1)

component of the equipment was damaged because it was carelessly left on a lane and hit by the automatic lane cleaning machine during a daily maintenance run. The cost of repairing the component was $1,500. What is the cost of the automatic scorekeeping equipment?

QS 11–3
(LO 2)

January 5, 1996, Blind Man's Sun acquired sound equipment for concert performances at a cost of $111,800. The rock band estimated that they would use this equipment for four years, during which time they anticipated performing about 12 concerts. They estimated at that point they could sell the equipment for $3,800. During 1996, the band performed four concerts. Calculate the 1996 amortization using (a) straight-line method and (b) the units-of-production method.

QS 11–4
(LO 2)

Refer to the facts in QS 11–3. Assume that Blind Man's Sun chose straight-line amortization but recognized during the second year that due to concert bookings beyond expectations, this equipment would only last a total of three years. The salvage value would remain unchanged. Calculate the revised amortization for the second year and the third year.

QS 11–5
(LO 3)

A fleet of refrigerated delivery trucks acquired on January 4, 1996, at a cost of $620,000 had an estimated useful life of eight years and an estimated salvage value of $100,000. Calculate the 1996 amortization under the double-declining-balance method for financial accounting purposes.

QS 11–6
(LO 4)

a. Classify the following expenditures as revenue or capital expenditures:
   (1) Monthly replacement cost of filters on an air conditioning system, $120.
   (2) Cost of replacing a compressor for a meatpacking firm's refrigeration system that extends the estimated life of the system four years, $40,000.
   (3) The cost of $175,000 for an addition of a new wing on an office building.
   (4) The cost of annual tune-ups for delivery trucks.
b. Prepare the journal entry to record (2) and (3).

QS 11–7
(LO 5)

Dean's Carpet Stores owned an automobile with a $20,000 cost and $18,000 accumulated amortization. In a transaction with a neighbouring computer retailer, Dean exchanged this auto for a computer with a fair market value of $6,000. Dean was required to pay an additional $5,000 cash. Prepare the entry to record this transaction for Dean.

QS 11–8
(LO 5)

Frolic, Inc., owns an industrial machine that cost $19,200 and has been amortized $10,200. Frolic exchanged the machine for a newer model that has a fair value of $24,000. Record the exchange assuming a trade-in allowance of (a) $8,000 and (b) $12,000.

QS 11–9
(LO 5)

Goodyear Tire & Rubber Company reported the following facts in its 1993 annual report: net sales of $11,643.4 million for 1993 and $11,784.9 million for 1992; total end-of-year assets of $8,436.1 million for 1993 and $8,563.7 million for 1992. Calculate the total asset turnover for 1993.

EXERCISES

Exercise 11–1
Cost of a capital asset
(LO 1)

Hot Sox purchased a machine for $23,000, terms 2/10, n/60, FOB shipping point. The seller prepaid the freight charges, $520, adding the amount to the invoice and bringing its total to $23,520. The machine required a special steel mounting and power connections costing

$1,590, and another $750 was paid to assemble the machine and get it into operation. In moving the machine onto its steel mounting, it was dropped and damaged. The repairs cost $380. Later, $60 of raw materials were consumed in adjusting the machine so that it would produce a satisfactory product. The adjustments were normal for this type of machine and were not the result of the damage. However, the items produced while the adjustments were being made were not sellable. Prepare a calculation to show the cost of this machine for accounting purposes. (Assume Hot Sox pays for the purchase within the discount period.)

Piper Plumbing Company paid $184,125 for real estate plus $9,800 in closing costs. The real estate included land appraised at $83,160; land improvements appraised at $27,720; and a building appraised at $87,120. Prepare a calculation showing the allocation of the total cost among the three purchased assets and present the journal entry to record the purchase.

Exercise 11–2
Lump-sum purchase of capital assets
(LO 1)

After planning to build a new manufacturing plant, Jammers Casual Wear purchased a large lot on which a small building was located. The negotiated purchase price for this real estate was $150,000 for the lot plus $80,000 for the building. The company paid $23,000 to have the old building torn down and $34,000 for landscaping the lot. Finally, it paid $960,000 in construction costs, which included the cost of a new building plus $57,000 for lighting and paving a parking lot next to the building. Present a single journal entry to record the costs incurred by Jammers, all of which were paid in cash.

Exercise 11–3
Recording costs of real estate
(LO 1)

Moon Paper Company installed a computerized machine in its factory at a cost of $84,600. The machine's useful life was estimated at 10 years, or 363,000 units of product, with a $12,000 trade-in value. During its second year, the machine produced 35,000 units of product. Determine the machine's second-year amortization under the (a) straight-line, (b) units-of-production, and (c) double-declining-balance methods.

Exercise 11–4
Alternative amortization methods
(LO 2, 3)

On April 1, 1996, Lake Excavating Services purchased a trencher for $500,000. The machine was expected to last five years and have a salvage value of $50,000. Calculate amortization expense for 1997, using (a) the straight-line method and (b) the double-declining-balance method.

Exercise 11–5
Alternative amortization methods; partial year's amortization
(LO 2, 3)

Gemini Fitness Club used straight-line amortization for a machine that cost $43,500, under the assumption it would have a four-year life and a $4,500 trade-in value. After two years, Gemini determined that the machine still had three more years of remaining useful life, after which it would have an estimated $3,600 trade-in value. (a) Calculate the machine's book value at the end of its second year. (b) Calculate the amount of amortization to be charged during each of the remaining years in the machine's revised useful life.

Exercise 11–6
Revising amortization rates
(LO 2)

Starnes Enterprises recently paid $156,800 for equipment that will last five years and have a salvage value of $35,000. By using the machine in its operations for five years, the company expects to earn $57,000 annually, after deducting all expenses except amortization. Present a schedule showing income before amortization, amortization expense, and net income for each year and the total amounts for the five-year period, assuming (a) straight-line amortization and (b) double-declining-balance amortization.

Exercise 11–7
Income statement effects of alternative amortization methods
(LO 2, 3)

In January 1996, Labenski Labs purchased computer equipment for $98,000. The equipment will be used in research and development activities for four years and then sold at an estimated salvage value of $20,000. Prepare schedules showing the amortization assuming (a) straight-line amortization and (b) double-declining-balance amortization.

Exercise 11–8
Alternative amortization methods
(LO 2, 3)

Exercise 11–9
Repairs and betterments
(LO 4)

Eden Extract Company paid $175,000 for equipment that was expected to last four years and have a salvage value of $20,000. Prepare journal entries to record the following costs related to the equipment:

a. During the second year of the equipment's life, $14,000 cash was paid for a new component that was expected to increase the equipment's productivity by 10% each year.

b. During the third year, $3,500 cash was paid for repairs necessary to keep the equipment in good working order.

c. During the fourth year, $9,300 was paid for repairs that were expected to increase the service life of the equipment from four to six years.

Exercise 11–10
Betterments
(LO 4)

Hot Dog Heaven owns a building that appeared on its balance sheet at the end of last year at its original $374,000 cost less $280,500 accumulated amortization. The building has been amortized on a straight-line basis under the assumption that it would have a 20-year life and no salvage value. During the first week in January of the current year, major structural repairs were completed on the building at a cost of $44,800. The repairs did not increase the building's capacity, but they did extend its expected life for 7 years beyond the 20 years originally estimated.

a. Determine the building's age as of the end of last year.

b. Give the entry to record the repairs, which were paid with cash.

c. Determine the book value of the building after the repairs were recorded.

d. Give the entry to record the current year's amortization.

Exercise 11–11
Partial year's
amortization; disposal
of capital asset
(LO 2, 5)

Plum Hill Industries purchased and installed a machine on January 1, 1996, at a total cost of $185,500. Straight-line amortization was taken each year for four years, based on the assumption of a seven-year life and no salvage value. The machine was disposed of on July 1, 2000, during its fifth year of service. Present the entries to record the partial year's amortization on July 1, 2000, and to record the disposal under each of the following unrelated assumptions: *(a)* The machine was sold for $70,000 cash; and *(b)* Plum Hill received an insurance settlement of $60,000 resulting from the total destruction of the machine in a fire.

Exercise 11–12
Exchanging capital assets
(LO 5)

The Rourke Group traded in an old tractor for a new tractor, receiving a $56,000 trade-in allowance and paying the remaining $164,000 in cash. The old tractor cost $190,000, and straight-line amortization of $105,000 had been recorded under the assumption that it would last eight years and have a $22,000 salvage value. Answer the following questions:

a. What was the book value of the old tractor?

b. What is the loss on the exchange?

c. What amount should be debited to the new Tractor account?

Exercise 11–13
Recording capital asset
disposal or exchange
(LO 5)

On January 2, 1996, Kelly Camera Shop disposed of a machine that cost $84,000 and had been amortized $45,250. Present the journal entries to record the disposal under each of the following unrelated assumptions:

a. The machine was sold for $32,500 cash.

b. The machine was traded in on a new machine of like purpose having a $117,000 cash price. A $40,000 trade-in allowance was received, and the balance was paid in cash.

c. The machine was traded for another machine of like purpose, and Kelly paid $3,000 as part of the exchange. The market value of the machine received is approximately $45,000.

d. The machine was traded for vacant land adjacent to the shop to be used as a parking lot. The land had a fair value of $75,000, and Kelly paid $25,000 cash in addition to giving the seller the machine.

Lamb's Antiques reported net sales of $2,431,000 for 1995 and $3,771,000 for 1996. End of year balances for total assets were: 1994, $793,000; 1995, $850,000; and 1996, $941,000. Calculate Lamb's total asset turnover for 1995 and 1996, and comment on the store's efficiency in the use of its assets.

Exercise 11–14
Evaluating efficient use of assets
(LO 5)

PROBLEMS

In 1996, ProSports paid $1,400,000 for a tract of land and two buildings on it. The plan was to demolish Building One and build a new store in its place. Building Two was to be used as a company office and was appraised at a value of $291,500, with a useful life of 20 years and an $80,000 salvage value. A lighted parking lot near Building One had improvements (Land Improvements One) valued at $185,500 that were expected to last another 14 years and have no salvage value. Without considering the buildings or improvements, the tract of land was estimated to have a value of $848,000. ProSports incurred the following additional costs:

Problem 11–1
Real estate costs; partial year's amortization
(LO 1, 2)

Cost to demolish Building One	$ 211,300
Cost of additional landscaping	83,600
Cost to construct new building (Building Three), having a useful life of 25 years and a $195,050 salvage value	1,009,500
Cost of new land improvements near Building Two (Land Improvements Two) which have a 20-year useful life and no salvage value	79,000

Required

1. Prepare a schedule having the following column headings: Land, Building Two, Building Three, Land Improvements One, and Land Improvements Two. Allocate the costs incurred by ProSports to the appropriate columns and total each column.

2. Prepare a single journal entry dated March 31 to record all the incurred costs, assuming they were paid in cash on that date.

3. Using the straight-line method, prepare December 31 adjusting entries to record amortization for the nine months of 1996 during which the assets were in use.

Valley Wide Industries recently negotiated a lump-sum purchase of several assets from a vending machine service company that was going out of business. The purchase was completed on March 1, 1996, at a total cash price of $1,575,000, and included a building, land, certain land improvements, and 12 vehicles. The estimated market value of each asset was: building, $816,000; land, $578,000; land improvements, $85,000; and vehicles, $221,000.

Problem 11–2
Plant asset costs; partial year's amortization; alternative methods
(LO 1, 2, 3)

Required

Preparation component:

1. Prepare a schedule to allocate the lump-sum purchase price to the separate assets that were purchased. Also present the journal entry to record the purchase.

2. Calculate the 1996 amortization expense on the building using the straight-line method, assuming a 15-year life and a $51,300 salvage value.

3. Calculate the 1996 amortization expense on the land improvements assuming an eight-year life and double-declining-balance amortization.

Analysis component:

4. Defend or refute this statement: Accelerated amortization results in lower income over the life of the asset.

Problem 11–3
Alternative amortization methods; partial year's amortization; disposal of plant asset
(LO 2, 3, 5)

Part 1. A machine that cost $105,000, with a four-year life and an estimated $10,000 salvage value, was installed in Patterson Company's factory on January 1. The factory manager estimated that the machine would produce 237,500 units of product during its life. It actually produced the following units: year 1, 60,700; year 2, 61,200; year 3, 59,800; and year 4, 59,100. Note the total number of units produced by the end of year 4 exceeded the original estimate. Nevertheless, the machine should not be amortized below the estimated salvage value.

Required

1. Prepare a calculation showing the amount that should be charged to amortization over the machine's four-year life.

2. Prepare a form with the following column headings:

Year	Straight Line	Units of Production	Double-Declining Balance

Then show the amortization for each year and the total amortization for the machine under each amortization method.

Part 2. Patterson purchased a used machine for $83,500 on January 2. It was repaired the next day at a cost of $1,710 and installed on a new platform that cost $540. The company predicted that the machine would be used for six years and would then have a $7,300 salvage value. Amortization was to be charged on a straight-line basis. A full year's amortization was charged on December 31, the end of the first year of the machine's use. On September 30 of its sixth year in service, it was retired.

Required

1. Prepare journal entries to record the purchase of the machine, the cost of repairing it, and the installation. Assume that cash was paid.

2. Prepare entries to record amortization on the machine on December 31 of its first year and on September 30 in the year of its disposal.

3. Prepare entries to record the retirement of the machine under each of the following unrelated assumptions: (*a*) it was sold for $6,750; (*b*) it was sold for $18,000; and (*c*) it was destroyed in a fire and the insurance company paid $12,000 in full settlement of the loss claim.

Finlay General Contractors completed these transactions involving the purchase and operation of heavy equipment:

1995

June 30   Paid $127,720 cash for a new front-end loader, plus $7,600 in state sales tax and $1,250 for transportation charges. The loader was estimated to have a four-year life and a $17,370 salvage value.

Oct. 4   Paid $1,830 to enclose the cab and install air conditioning in the loader. This increased the estimated salvage value of the loader by $555.

Dec. 31   Recorded straight-line amortization on the loader.

1996

Feb. 16   Paid $460 to repair the loader after the operator backed it into a tree.

July 1   Paid $2,250 to overhaul the loader's engine. As a result, the estimated useful life of the loader was increased by two years.

Dec. 31   Recorded straight-line amortization on the loader.

Required

Prepare journal entries to record the transactions.

Problem 11–4
Partial year's amortization; revising amortization rates; revenue and capital expenditures
(LO 2, 3, 4)

Cyber Systems completed the following transactions involving delivery trucks:

1996

Mar. 29   Paid cash for a new delivery truck, $38,830 plus $2,330 sales tax. The truck was estimated to have a five-year life and a $6,000 trade-in value.

Dec. 31   Recorded straight-line amortization on the truck.

1997

Dec. 31   Recorded straight-line amortization on the truck. However, due to new information obtained earlier in the year, the original estimated service life of the truck was changed from five years to four years, and the original estimated trade-in value was increased to $7,000.

1998

July 5   Traded in the old truck and paid $27,130 in cash for a new truck. The new truck was estimated to have a six-year life and a $6,250 trade-in value. The invoice for the exchange showed these items:

Price of the new truck	$45,100
Trade-in allowance granted on the old truck . .	(19,500)
Balance of purchase price	$25,600
Sales tax	1,530
Total paid in cash	$27,130

Dec. 31   Recorded straight-line amortization on the new truck.

Required

Prepare journal entries to record the transactions.

Problem 11–5
Partial year's amortization; revising amortization rates; exchanging capital assets
(LO 2, 3, 5)

Problem 11–6
Partial year's
amortization; alternative
methods; disposal of
capital assets
(LO 2, 3, 5)

Menck Interiors completed the following transactions involving machinery:

Machine No. 15-50 was purchased for cash on May 1, 1996, at an installed cost of $52,900. Its useful life was estimated to be six years with a $4,300 trade-in value. Straight-line amortization was recorded for the machine at the end of 1996, 1997, and 1998; on April 29, 1999, it was traded for Machine No. 17-95, a similar asset with an installed cash price of $61,900. A trade-in allowance of $30,110 was received for Machine No. 15-50, and the balance was paid in cash.

Machine No. 17-95's life was predicted to be four years with an $8,200 trade-in value. Double-declining-balance amortization was recorded on each December 31 of its life. On November 2, 2000, it was traded for Machine No. BT-311, which was a dissimilar asset with an installed cash price of $179,000. A trade-in allowance of $27,000 was received for Machine No. 17-95, and the balance was paid in cash.

It was estimated that Machine No. BT-311 would produce 200,000 units of product during its five-year useful life, after which it would have a $35,000 trade-in value. Units-of-production amortization was recorded for the machine for 2000, a period in which it produced 31,000 units of product. Between January 1, 2001, and August 21, 2003, the machine produced 108,000 more units. On the latter date, it was sold for $81,200.

Required

Prepare journal entries to record: *(a)* the purchase of each machine, *(b)* the amortization expense recorded on the first December 31 of each machine's life, and *(c)* the disposal of each machine. (Only one entry is needed to record the exchange of one machine for another.)

Problem 11–7
Analytical essay
(LO 4)

It is January 9, 1996, and you have just been hired as an accountant for Brinks Supply Company. The previous accountant brought the accounting records up to date through December 31, 1995, the end of the fiscal year, including the year-end adjusting entries. In reviewing the entries made last year, you discover the following three items:

a.   An expenditure to have a factory machine reconditioned by the manufacturer so it would last three years longer than originally estimated was recorded as a debit to Repairs Expense, Machinery.

b.   The lubrication of factory machinery was recorded as a debit to Machinery.

c.   The installation of a security system for the building was recorded as a debit to Building Improvements. The new system allowed the company to reduce the number of security guards.

Required

For each of the three items, explain why you think a correction is or is not necessary. Also, describe any correcting entry that should be made.

Problem 11–8
Alternative amortization
methods; retirement of
capital assets
(LO 2, 3, 5)

Part 1. FlatIrons Company purchased and installed a new machine that cost $195,000, had a five-year life, and an estimated $27,300 salvage value. Management estimated that the machine would produce 120,000 units of product during its life. Actual production of units of product was as follows: year 1, 16,800; year 2, 26,400; year 3, 24,000; year 4, 22,800; and year 5, 30,000.

Required

1.   Prepare a calculation showing the number of dollars of this machine's cost that should be charged to amortization over its five-year life.

2. Prepare a form with the following column headings:

Year	Straight Line	Units of Production	Double-Declining Balance

Then show the amortization for each year and the total amortization for the machine under each amortization method.

Part 2. On January 9, Gilman Company purchased a used machine for $68,400. The next day it was repaired at a cost of $8,100 and was mounted on a new cradle that cost $6,300. It was estimated the machine would be used for three years and would then have a $10,800 salvage value. Amortization was to be charged on a straight-line basis. A full year's amortization was charged on December 31 of the first and the second years of the machine's use; and on March 29 of its third year of use, the machine was retired from service.

Required

1. Prepare general journal entries to record the purchase of the machine, the cost of repairing it, and its installation. Assume cash was paid in each case.

2. Prepare entries to record amortization on the machine at the end of the first and second years and on March 29 of the third year.

3. Prepare entries to record the retirement of the machine under each of the following unrelated assumptions: (*a*) the machine was sold for $35,250; (*b*) it was sold for $24,150; and (*c*) it was destroyed in a fire, and the insurance company paid $22,050 in full settlement of the loss claim.

Parker Lewis Company completed the following transactions involving plant assets:

Problem 11–9
Plant asset records
(LO 2, 4)

1995

Jan. 2 Purchased on credit from Southwest Equipment an electric packer priced at $19,875. The serial number of the packer was S-67422, its service life was estimated at five years with a trade-in value of $1,875, and it was assigned plant asset No. 420-1.

Apr. 4 Purchased on credit from Southwest Equipment a Donen vibrator priced at $30,705. The serial number of the vibrator was S-33246, its service life was estimated at six years with a trade-in value of $2,625, and it was assigned plant asset No. 430-2.

Dec. 31 Recorded straight-line amortization on the plant equipment for 1995.

1996

Nov. 3 Sold the Donen vibrator to Cement Products for $18,750 cash.

7 Purchased a new Supermix vibrator from Stonework Equipment for $27,000. The serial number of the vibrator was CS-83215, its service life was estimated at eight years with a trade-in value of $3,600, and it was assigned plant asset No. 430-3.

Dec. 31 Recorded straight-line amortization on the plant equipment for 1996.

Required

1. Prepare general journal entries to record the transactions and post to the proper general ledger and subsidiary ledger accounts.

2. Prove the December 31, 1996, balances of the Plant Equipment and Accumulated Amortization, Plant Equipment accounts by preparing a list showing the cost and accumulated amortization on each item of plant equipment owned by Parker Lewis Company on that date.

Problem 11–10
Real estate costs and partial year's amortization
(LO 1, 2)

In early 1996, Nobles Company paid $975,000 for real estate that included a tract of land on which two buildings were located. The plan was to demolish Building A and build a new factory in its place. Building B was to be used as a company office and was appraised at a value of $315,000, with a useful life of 20 years and a $45,000 salvage value. A lighted parking lot near Building B had improvements valued at $105,000 that were expected to last another five years and have no salvage value. In its existing condition, the tract of land was estimated to have a value of $630,000.

Nobles Company incurred the following additional costs:

Cost to demolish Building A	$ 71,250
Cost to landscape new building site	81,000
Cost to build new building (Building C), having a useful life of 25 years and a $75,000 salvage value	1,125,000
Cost of new land improvements near Building C, which have an 8-year useful life and no salvage value	187,500

Required

1. Prepare a form having the following column headings: Land, Building B, Building C, Land Improvements B, and Land Improvements C. Allocate the costs incurred by Nobles Company to the appropriate columns and total each column.

2. Prepare a single journal entry dated June 1 to record all of the costs incurred, assuming they were all paid in cash.

3. Prepare December 31 adjusting entries to record amortization for the seven months of 1996 during which the assets were in use. Use double-declining-balance amortization for the newly constructed Building C and Land Improvements C and straight-line amortization for Building B and Land Improvements B.

Problem 11–11
Capital asset costs and amortization
(LO 1, 2, 3)

Willo Company recently negotiated a lump-sum purchase of several assets from a road equipment dealer who was planning to change locations. The purchase was completed on September 30, 1995, at a total cash price of $870,000 and included a garage with land and certain land improvements and a new heavy, general-purpose truck. The estimated market values of the assets were: sales garage, $552,750; land, $331,650; land improvements, $100,500; and truck, $20,100.

Required

1. Prepare a schedule to allocate the lump-sum purchase price to the separate assets that were purchased. Also present the general journal entry to record the purchase.

2. Calculate the 1996 amortization expense on the garage using the straight-line method and assuming a 15-year life and a $37,500 salvage value.

3. Calculate the 1995 amortization expense on the land improvements assuming an eight-year life and double-declining-balance amortization.

4. The truck is expected to last five years and have a salvage value of $2,250. Prepare a schedule showing each year's amortization on the truck, assuming (a) five-year straight-line amortization and (b) double-declining-balance amortization.

The Whitestone Company completed these transactions involving the purchase and operation of delivery trucks:

Problem 11–12
Purchases, betterments, and sales of capital assets
(LO 4, 5)

1995

June 26 Paid cash for a new truck, $34,200 plus $1,710 provincial sales taxes. The truck was estimated to have a four-year life and a $9,000 salvage value.

July 5 Paid $1,890 for special racks and cleats installed in the truck. The racks and cleats did not increase the truck's estimated trade-in value.

Dec. 31 Recorded straight-line amortization on the truck.

1996

June 25 Paid $2,460 to install an air-conditioning unit in the truck. The unit increased the truck's estimated trade-in value by $300.

Dec. 31 Recorded straight-line amortization on the truck.

1997

Mar. 15 Paid $330 for repairs to the truck's fender damaged when the driver backed into a loading dock.

Dec. 31 Recorded straight-line amortization on the truck.

1998

Aug. 31 Traded the old truck and $29,310 in cash for a new truck. The new truck was estimated to have a three-year life and a $9,600 trade-in value, and the invoice for the exchange showed these items:

Price of the truck	$37,200
Trade-in allowance granted	(9,000)
Balance	$28,200
Provincial sales tax	1,100
Balance paid in cash	$29,310

Sept. 4 Paid $3,690 for special cleats and racks installed in the truck.

Dec. 31 Recorded straight-line amortization on the new truck.

Required

Prepare general journal entries to record the transactions.

A company completed the following transactions involving machinery:

Problem 11–13
Amortizing and exchanging plant assets
(LO 4, 5)

Machine No. 366-90 was purchased on May 1, 1996, at an installed cost of $48,600. Its useful life was estimated at four years with a $5,400 trade-in value. Straight-line amortization was recorded on the machine at the end of 1996 and 1997, and on August 5, 1998, it was traded on Machine No. 366-91. A $27,000 trade-in allowance was received, and the balance was paid in cash.

Machine No. 366-91 was purchased on August 5, 1998, at an installed cash price of $63,000, less the trade-in allowance received on Machine No. 366-90. The new machine's life was estimated at five years with a $6,300 trade-in value. Double-declining-balance amortization was recorded on each December 31 of its life; and on January 5, 2003, it was sold for $9,000.

Machine No. 367-10 was purchased on January 6, 1998, at an installed cost of $45,000. Its useful life was estimated at five years, after which it would have a $4,500 trade-in value. Double-declining-balance amortization was recorded on the machine at the end of 1998,

1999, and 2000; and on January 3, 2001, it was traded on Machine No. 367-11. An $8,100 trade-in allowance was received and the balance was paid in cash.

Machine No. 367-11 was purchased on January 3, 2001, at an installed cash price of $53,100, less the trade-in allowance received on Machine No. 367-10. It was estimated the new machine would produce 75,000 units of product during its useful life, after which it would have a $5,400 trade-in value. Units-of-production depreciation was recorded on the machine for 2001, a period in which it produced 7,500 units of product. Between January 1 and October 3, 2002, the machine produced 11,250 more units, and on the latter date it was sold for $36,000.

Required

Prepare general journal entries to record: (*a*) the purchase of each machine, (*b*) the amortization recorded on the first December 31 of each machine's life, and (*c*) the disposal of each machine. Treat the entries for the first two machines as one series of transactions and those of the next two machines as an unrelated second series. Only one entry is needed to record the exchange of one machine for another.

Problem 11–14
Exchange of assets
(LO 5)

Highway Construction had a piece of road equipment which it purchased in January 1994, at a cost of $180,000. The equipment has been amortized over 8 years, assuming no salvage value, on the straight-line method. At the beginning of May 1996, the company exchanged the equipment for a similar machine. No amortization has been recorded on the old machine for 1996. The market value of the new equipment has been estimated at $132,000.

Required

Prepare a journal entry to record the exchange of the equipment assuming that

a.   No cash is paid or received.

b.   Highway Construction pays $4,000.

c.   Highway Construction receives $2,000.

d.   Highway Construction receives $15,000.

PROVOCATIVE PROBLEMS

**Provocative Problem
11–1**
Business communications case
(LO 1, 5)

While examining the accounting records of Fortunato Company on December 15, 1995, you discover two 1995 entries that appear questionable. The first entry recorded the cash proceeds from an insurance settlement as follows:

Apr.	30	Cash	29,000.00	
		Loss on Fire	8,800.00	
		Accumulated Amortization, Machinery	25,200.00	
		Machinery		63,000.00
		Received payment of fire loss claim.		

Your investigation shows that this entry was made to record the receipt of an insurance company's $29,000 cheque to settle a claim resulting from the destruction of a machine in a small fire on April 2, 1995. The machine originally cost $58,800 and was put into operation on January 3, 1992. It was amortized on a straight-line basis for three years, under the assumptions that it would have a seven-year life and no salvage value. During the first week of January 1995, the machine was overhauled at a cost of $4,200. The overhaul did not increase the machine's capacity or its salvage value. However, it was expected that the overhaul would lengthen the machine's service life two years beyond the seven originally expected.

The second entry that appears questionable was made to record the receipt of a cheque from selling a portion of a tract of land. The land was adjacent to the company's plant and had been purchased the year before. It cost $105,000, and another $18,000 was paid for clearing and grading it. Both amounts had been debited to the Land account. The land was to be used for storing finished products but, sometime after the grading was completed, it became obvious the company did not need the entire tract. Fortunato received an offer from a purchaser to buy the north section for $94,550 or the south section for $60,450. The company decided to sell the north section and recorded the receipt of the purchaser's cheque with the following entry:

Nov.	16	Cash	94,550.00	
		Land		94,550.00
		Sold unneeded land.		

Required

Write a memo to the company's Corrections File describing any errors made in recording these transactions. Since the Corrections File is used in making the year-end adjusting journal entries, show the entry or entries needed to correct each error described in your memo.

Manufax Company temporarily recorded the costs of a new plant in a single account called Land and Buildings. Now, management has asked you to examine this account and prepare any necessary entries to correct the account balances. In doing so, you find the following debits and credits to the account:

Provocative Problem 11–2

Financial reporting problem

(LO 1, 2)

Debits

Jan.	4	Cost of land and building acquired for new plant site	$ 564,000
	9	Attorney's fee for title search	1,500
	18	Cost of demolishing old building on plant site	37,500
	30	Nine months' liability and fire insurance during construction	6,075
Sept.	28	Payment to building contractor on completion	819,000
Oct.	1	Architect's fee for new building	25,200
	10	City assessment for street improvements	42,000
	21	Cost of landscaping new plant site	10,500
			$1,505,775

Credits

Jan.	21	Proceeds from sale of salvaged materials from building	$ 7,900
Oct.	5	Refund of one month's liability and fire insurance premium	675
Dec.	31	Amortization at 2-1/2% per year	28,069
			$ 36,644
		Debit balance	$1,469,131

An account called Amortization Expense, Land and Buildings was debited in recording the $28,069 of amortization. Your investigation suggests that 40 years is a reasonable life expectancy for a building of the type involved and that an assumption of zero salvage value is reasonable.

To summarize your analysis, set up a schedule with columns headed Date, Description, Total Amount, Land, Buildings, and Other Accounts. Next, enter the items found in the

Land and Buildings account on the schedule, distributing the amounts to the proper columns. Show credits on the schedule by enclosing the amounts in parentheses. Also, draft any required correcting entry or entries, under the assumption that the accounts have not been closed.

Provocative Problem 11–3
Financial statement analysis case
(LO 1, 2)

Geac

Refer to the annual report for Geac Computer Corporation Limited in Appendix I. Give particular attention to the balance sheet, income statement, and notes to financial statements before answering the following questions:

1. What percentage of the original cost of Geac's fixed assets remains to be amortized as of April 30, 1994, and April 30, 1993? (Assume the assets have no salvage value.)

2. What method of depreciation does Geac use in amortizing its plant assets?

Provocative Problem 11–4
Ethical issues essay

Review the As a Matter of Ethics case on page 534 and write a short essay discussing the situation faced by Sue Ann Meyer. Include a discussion of the alternative courses of action available to Meyer and indicate how you think she should deal with the situation.

ANALYTICAL AND REVIEW PROBLEMS

A&R Problem 11–1

At the last meeting of the executive committee of Kearins, Ltd., Milton Vacon, controller, was severely criticized by both President Kearins and Kate Ryan, vice president of production. The subject of criticism was in the recognition of periodic amortization. President Kearins was unhappy with the fact that what he referred to as "a fictitious item" was deducted, resulting in depressed net income. In his words, "Depreciation is a fiction when the assets being depreciated are worth far more than we paid for them. What the controller is doing is unduly understanding our net income. This in turn is detrimental to our shareholders because it results in the undervaluation of our shares on the market."

Vice President Ryan was equally adamant about the periodic amortization charges; however, she came on from another side. She said, "Our maintenance people tell me that the level of maintenance is such that our plant and equipment will last virtually forever." She further stated that charging amortization on top of maintenance expenses is double-counting—it seems reasonable to charge either maintenance or amortization but not both.

The time taken by other pressing matters did not permit Vacon to answer; instead, the controller was asked to prepare a report to the executive committee to deal with the issues raised by the president and vice president.

Required

The controller asks you, his assistant, to prepare the required report.

A&R Problem 11–2

The Shape Company purchased a large earth-mover four years ago at a cost of $350,000. At that time it was estimated that the economic life of the equipment would be 12 years and that its ultimate salvage value would be $14,000.

Assuming the company uses straight-line amortization, state whether each of the following events requires a revision of the original amortization rate, with reasons for your answer:

a. Due to the persistent inflation, the present replacement cost of the same type of equipment is $410,000.

b. Because of the higher replacement cost, as described in (*a*) above, the ultimate salvage value is now estimated at $25,000.

c. The company, in connection with having its line of credit increased, was required by the bank to have the assets appraised. The earth-mover was estimated to have a current value of $315,000.

d. At the time the appraisal was made in (*c*) above, it was determined that technological change was progressing more slowly than originally estimated and that the earth-mover would probably remain in service for 15 years with the ultimate salvage value as originally estimated at the end of 12 years.

CONCEPT TESTER

Test your understanding of the concepts introduced in this chapter by completing the following crossword puzzle.

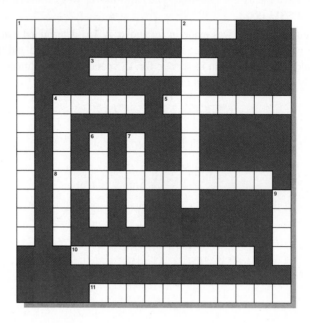

Across Clues

1. Amortization method that allocates an equal amount to each period (2 words).

3. An outlay that produces economic benefits that do not fully expire before the end of the current period (1st of 2 words; also see 11 across).

4. A measure of how efficiently a company uses its assets (1st of 3 words; also see 6 down, 4 down).

5. Expenditures made to keep an asset in normal, good operating condition.

8. A condition in which an asset has lost its usefulness because of new inventions and improvements.

10. A cost incurred to make an asset more efficient.

11. An outlay that produces economic benefits that do not fully expire before the end of the current period (2nd of 2 words; also see 3 across).

Down Clues

1. The expected amount to be recovered at the end of an asset's life (2 words).

2. A condition in which the capacity of an asset becomes too small for the demands of the business.

4. A measure of how efficiently a company uses its assets (3rd of 3 words; also see 4 across, 6 down).

6. A measure of how efficiently a company uses its assets (2nd of 3 words; also see 4 across, 4 down).

7. The original cost of an asset less the accumulated amortization (2nd of 2 words; also see 9 down).

9. The original cost of an asset less the accumulated amortization (1st of 2 words; also see 7 down).

ANSWERS TO PROGRESS CHECKS

11–1 *(a)* office supplies—current assets
    (b) office equipment—plant assets
    (c) merchandise—current assets
    (d) land held for future expansion—long-term investments
    (e) trucks used in operations—plant assets

11–2 *(a)* Land
    (b) Land Improvements

11–3 $700,000 + $49,000 − $21,000 + $3,500 + $3,000 + $2,500 = $737,000$

11–4 Amortization is a process of allocating and charging the cost of plant assets to the accounting periods that benefit from the asset's use.

11–5 *(a)* Book value using straight-line amortization:
    $\$96,000 − [(\$96,000 − \$8,000)/5] = \$78,400$
    (b) Book value using units of production:
    $\$96,000 − [(\$96,000 − \$8,000) \times (10,000/100,000)] = \$87,200$

11–6 $(\$3,800 − \$200)/3 = \$1,200$
    $\$1,200 \times 2 = \$2,400$
    $(\$3,800 − \$2,400)/2 = \$700$

11–7
Machinery	12,000.00	
Cash		12,000.00

11–8 A revenue expenditure benefits only the current period and should be charged to the expense of the current period. A capital expenditure has benefit that extends beyond the end of the current period and should be charged to an asset.

11–9 A betterment involves modifying an existing plant asset to improve its efficiency or lengthen its useful life, usually by replacing part of the asset with an improved or superior part. A betterment should be debited to the improved machine's account.

11–10
Amortization Expense	2,500	
Accumulated Amortization		2,500
Cash	32,000	
Loss on Sales of Equipment	500	
Accumulated Amortization	9,500	
Equipment		42,000

11–11
Truck	45,000	
Loss on Trade-in	3,600	
Accumulated Amortization	23,400	
Truck		30,000
Cash		42,000

11–12 Total asset turnover:

$$\frac{\$152,156}{(\$149,028 + \$117,872) \div 2} = 1.14 \text{ times}$$

Capital Assets: Natural Resources, Intangible Assets, and Long-Term Investments

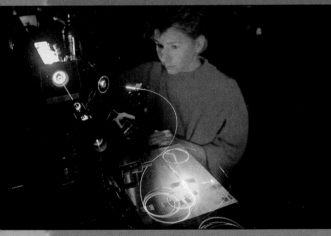

company's assets include many things in addition to tangible equipment and buildings. Patents, ...tural resources, research and development, and outstanding employees all contribute to profits. ...owever, they create unique accounting problems that must be solved.

*K*aren White and Mark Smith are approaching the last chapter dealing with assets. Their instructor has provided some information about Corel Corporation.

In 1993, 1992, and 1991, Corel Corporation, the company that developed and produces CorelDRAW and other related software programs, spent $8.4, $7.2, and $4.4 million on research and development. All of these expenditures were expensed as incurred in accordance with Canadian GAAP. Other assets such as software licences, purchased software, clipart libraries, and photo CD libraries, amounting to $29.0 million, are included in Corel Corporation's Capital Assets.

The above paragraph illustrates an aspect of accounting that is often confusing to the users of financial statements. The amounts incurred to research and develop a valuable asset must be expensed, and the company may not present the asset on the balance sheet. Thus the costs of developing CorelDRAW do not appear on Corel Corporation's statements. However, if a company purchases the rights to produce a product from another party, such as Corel Corporation did with some of its clipart and CD libraries, it may capitalize these costs and show them on the balance sheet.

LEARNING OBJECTIVES

After studying Chapter 12, you should be able to:

1. **Identify assets that should be classified as natural resources or as intangible assets and prepare entries to account for them, including entries to record depletion and amortization.**

2. **State the criteria for classifying assets as long-term investments and describe the categories of securities that are classified as long-term investments.**

3. **Describe the methods used to report long-term securities investments in the financial statements.**

4. **Describe the primary accounting problems of having investments in international operations and prepare entries to account for sales to foreign customers.**

5. **Explain the use of return on total assets in evaluating a company's efficiency in using its assets.**

6. **Define or explain the words and phrases listed in the chapter glossary.**

In Chapters 7 through 9 and 11, you learned about current assets and capital assets. This chapter concludes the focus on assets with a discussion of natural resources, intangible assets, and long-term investments. Natural resources and intangible assets may be particularly important in evaluating the future prospects of some companies. For example, the rights to manufacture computer software products are intangible assets of the companies that developed the products or purchased the rights from the copyright owner.

Many companies make long-term investments in assets such as real estate and debt and equity securities issued by other companies. Also, an increasing number of companies invest in foreign countries or have international operations. The financial statement effects of these investments are often very important. As a result, your study of these topics in this chapter will enrich your ability to understand and interpret financial reports.

NATURAL RESOURCES

LO 1

Identify assets that should be classified as natural resources or as intangible assets and prepare entries to account for them, including entries to record depletion and amortization.

Natural resources include such things as standing timber, mineral deposits, and oil reserves. Because they are physically consumed when they are used, they are known as *wasting assets*. In their natural state, they represent inventories of raw materials that will be converted into a product by cutting, mining, or pumping. However, until the conversion takes place, they are noncurrent assets and appear on a balance sheet under captions such as "Timberlands," "Mineral deposits," or "Oil reserves." Sometimes, this caption appears under the capital asset category of assets and sometimes it is a separate category. **Norcen Energy Resources Limited** combines its natural resources with other fixed assets in one balance sheet item called *Property, plant, and equipment*. However, a note to the financial statements provides more detailed information by separating the total into the following categories: oil and gas, propane marketing, and mineral resources.

Natural resources are initially recorded at cost. Like the cost of capital (or plant) assets, the cost of natural resources is allocated to the periods in which they are consumed. The cost created by consuming the usefulness of natural resources is called **depletion.** On the balance sheet, natural resources are shown at cost less *accumulated depletion*. The amount by which such assets are depleted each year by cutting, mining, or pumping is usually calculated on a units-of-production basis. For example, **Imperial Oil Limited** uses the units-of-production method to amortize the costs of discovering its oil wells.

To illustrate the units-of-production method, assume that a mineral deposit has an estimated 500,000 tonnes of available ore and is purchased for $500,000. The units-of-production depletion charge per tonne of ore mined is $1. Thus, if 85,000 tonnes are mined and sold during the first year, the depletion charge for the year of $85,000 is recorded as follows:

Dec.	31	Depletion Expense, Mineral Deposit	85,000.00	
		Accumulated Depletion, Mineral Deposit		85,000.00
		To record depletion of the mineral deposit.		

On the balance sheet prepared at the end of the first year, the mineral deposit should appear at its $500,000 cost less accumulated depletion of $85,000. Because the 85,000 tonnes of ore were sold during the year, the entire $85,000 depletion charge is reported on the income statement. However, if a portion of the ore had remained unsold at year-end, the depletion cost related to the unsold ore should be carried forward on the balance sheet as part of the cost of the unsold ore inventory, which is a current asset.

The conversion of natural resources through mining, cutting, or pumping often requires the use of machinery and buildings. Because the usefulness of these assets is related to the depletion of the natural resource, their costs should be amortized over the life of the natural resource in proportion to the annual depletion charges. In other words, amortization should be calculated using the units-of-production method. For example, if a machine is installed in a mine and one-eighth of the mine's ore is mined and sold during a year, one-eighth of the machine's cost (less salvage value) should be charged to amortization expense.

INTANGIBLE ASSETS

Some assets represent certain legal rights and economic relationships beneficial to the owner. Because they have no physical existence, they are called **intangible assets.** Patents, copyrights, leaseholds, leasehold improvements, goodwill, and trademarks are intangible assets. We discuss each of these intangible items in more detail in the following sections. Although notes and accounts receivable are also intangible in nature, they are not used to produce products or provide services. Therefore, they are not listed on the balance sheet as intangible assets; instead, they are classified as current assets or investments.

When an intangible asset is purchased, it is recorded at cost. Thereafter, its cost must be systematically written off to expense over its estimated useful life through the process of **amortization.** Generally accepted accounting principles require that the amortization period for an intangible asset be 40 years or less.[1] Companies often disclose the amortization periods they apply to their intangibles. For example, **Onex Corporation's** annual report discloses that it amortizes goodwill principally over 40 years and other intangible assets over their estimated useful lives.

---

[1] *CICA Handbook,* section 3060, "Capital Assets," par. 32.

In many cases, the estimated life of an intangible asset is highly subjective and influenced by a myriad of factors. The selected useful life can have a dramatic impact on reported profits. A few years ago, **Blockbuster Entertainment Corporation** was criticized for changing its amortization period for videotape rights from 9 to 36 months. The change added $3 million, or nearly 20% to Blockbuster's reported income.[2]

Amortization of intangible assets is similar to amortization of plant assets and depletion of natural resources in that all three are processes of cost allocation. However, the straight-line method should be used for amortizing intangibles unless the reporting company can demonstrate that another method is more appropriate. Also, while the effects of depreciation and depletion on the assets are recorded in a contra account (Accumulated Depreciation or Accumulated Depletion), amortization is usually credited directly to the intangible asset account. As a result, the full original cost of intangible assets generally is not reported on the balance sheet. Instead, only the remaining amount of unamortized cost is reported.

Normally, intangible assets are shown in a separate section of the balance sheet that follows immediately after plant and equipment. However, not all companies follow this tradition. The following paragraphs describe several specific intangible assets.

Patents

The federal government grants **patents** to encourage the invention of new machines, mechanical devices, and production processes. A patent gives its owner the exclusive right to manufacture and sell a patented machine or device, or to use a process, for 17 years. When patent rights are purchased, the cost of acquiring the rights is debited to an account called Patents. Also, if the owner engages in lawsuits to defend a patent, the cost of the lawsuits should be debited to the Patents account. However, the costs of research and development leading to a new patent are not debited to an asset account.[3] Instead research costs must be expensed as incurred because of the uncertainty of their future benefits.

Although a patent gives its owner exclusive rights to the patented device or process for 17 years, the cost of the patent should be amortized over its predicted useful life, which might be less than the full 17 years. For example, if a patent that cost $25,000 has an estimated useful life of 10 years, the following adjusting entry is made at the end of each of those years to write off one-tenth of its cost:

Dec.	31	Amortization Expense, Patents	2,500.00	
		Patents		2,500.00
		To write off patent costs over the expected 10-year life.		

The entry's debit causes $2,500 of patent costs to appear on the income statement as one of the costs of the product manufactured and sold under the protection of

[2]*Forbes,* June 12, 1989, p. 150.

[3]*CICA Handbook,* section 3450.

the patent. Note that we have followed the convention of crediting the Patents account rather than a contra account.

Copyrights

A **copyright** is granted by the federal government or by international agreement. In most cases, a copyright gives its owner the exclusive right to publish and sell a musical, literary, or artistic work during the life of the composer, author, or artist and for 50 years thereafter. Most copyrights have value for a much shorter time, and their costs should be amortized over the shorter period. Often, the only identifiable cost of a copyright is the fee paid to the Copyright Office. If this fee is not material, it may be charged directly to an expense account. Otherwise, the copyright costs should be capitalized (recorded as a capital expenditure), and the periodic amortization of a copyright should be debited to an account called *Amortization Expense, Copyrights.*

Leaseholds

Property is rented under a contract called a **lease.** The person or company that owns the property and grants the lease is called the **lessor.** The person or company that secures the right to possess and use the property is called the **lessee.** The rights granted to the lessee by the lessor under the lease are called a **leasehold.** A leasehold is an intangible asset for the lessee.

Some leases require no advance payment from the lessee but do require monthly rent payments. In such cases, a Leasehold account is not needed and the monthly payments are debited to a Rent Expense account. Sometimes, a long-term lease requires the lessee to pay the final year's rent in advance when the lease is signed. If so, the lessee records the advance payment with a debit to its Leasehold asset account. Because the usefulness of the advance payment is not consumed until the final year is reached, the Leasehold account balance remains intact until that year. At that time, the balance is transferred to Rent Expense.[4]

Often, a long-term lease gains value because the current rental rates for similar property increase while the required payments under the lease remain constant. In such cases, the increase in value of the lease is not reported on the lessee's balance sheet since no extra cost was incurred to acquire it. However, if the property is subleased and the new tenant makes a cash payment to the original lessee for the rights under the old lease, the new tenant should debit the payment to a Leasehold account. Then, the balance of the Leasehold account should be amortized to Rent Expense over the remaining life of the lease.

Leasehold Improvements

Long-term leases often require the lessee to pay for any alterations or improvements to the leased property, such as new partitions and store fronts. Normally, the costs of these **leasehold improvements** are debited to an account called Leasehold Improvements. Also, since the improvements become part of the property and revert to the lessor at the end of the lease, the lessee must amortize the cost of the

---

[4]Some long-term leases give the lessee essentially the same rights as a purchaser, and result in tangible assets and liabilities reported by the lessee. Chapter 13 describes these leases.

improvements over the life of the lease or the life of the improvements, whichever is shorter. The amortization entry commonly debits Rent Expense and credits Lease-hold Improvements.

Goodwill

The term **goodwill** has a special meaning in accounting. In theory, a business has an intangible asset called goodwill when its rate of expected future earnings is greater than the rate of earnings normally realized in its industry. Above-average earnings and the existence of theoretical goodwill may be demonstrated with the following information about Companies A and B, both of which are in the same industry:

	Company A	Company B
Net assets (other than goodwill)	$100,000	$100,000
Normal rate of return in this industry	10%	10%
Normal return on net assets	$ 10,000	$ 10,000
Expected net income	10,000	15,000
Expected earnings above average	$ –0–	$ 5,000

Company B is expected to have an above-average earnings rate compared to its industry and, therefore, is said to have goodwill. This goodwill may be the result of excellent customer relations, the location of the business, the quality and unique-ness of its products, monopolistic market advantages, a superior management and work force, or a combination of these and other factors.[5] Consequently, a poten-tial investor would be willing to pay more for Company B than for Company A. Thus, goodwill is theoretically an asset that has value.

Normally, goodwill is purchased only when an entire business operation is ac-quired. In determining the purchase price of a business, the buyer and seller may estimate the amount of goodwill in several different ways. If the business is ex-pected to have $5,000 each year in above-average earnings, its goodwill may be valued at, say, four times its above-average earnings, or $20,000. Or, if the $5,000 is expected to continue indefinitely, they may think of it as a return on an invest-ment at a given rate of return, say, 10%. In this case, the estimated amount of good-will is $5,000/10% = $50,000. However, in the final analysis, the value of good-will is confirmed only by the price the seller is willing to accept and the buyer is willing to pay.

To keep financial statement information from being too subjective, accountants have agreed that goodwill should not be recorded unless it is purchased. The amount of goodwill is measured by subtracting the fair market value of the purchased busi-ness's net assets (excluding goodwill) from the purchase price. In many business acquisitions, goodwill represents a major component of total cost. For example, the **Thompson Corporation's** purchase of **Information Access Company** for

---

[5]Of course, the value of the location may be reflected in a higher cost for the land owned and used by the company.

Intangible Assets

Intangible Assets Disclosed	Number of Companies			
	1992	**1991**	**1990**	**1989**
Goodwill	149	153	149	143
Licences/Broadcast licences	18	20	20	21
Customer lists/circulation	11	10	10	11
Trademarks	11	14	13	12
Patents or patent rights	10	17	15	15
Noncompetition agreements	6	5	4	3
Franchises	4	4	5	5
Publishing rights	4	4	4	4
Technology/Know-how	3	4	5	4

Canadian Institute of Chartered Accountants, *Financial Reporting in Canada, 1993* (Toronto; 1993), p. 120.

$465 million (net of debt acquired) included goodwill of $117 million and other intangibles consisting of publishing rights and circulation of $374 million.

Like other intangible assets, goodwill should be amortized on a straight-line basis over its estimated useful life. However, estimating the useful life of goodwill is very difficult and highly arbitrary in most situations. As a result, you can expect to find companies reporting amortization expense for goodwill based on an estimated useful life of 5 years upward, but not more than 40 years.

Trademarks and Trade Names

Companies often adopt unique symbols or select unique names that they use in marketing their products. Sometimes, the ownership and exclusive right to use such a **trademark** or **trade name** can be established simply by demonstrating that one company has used the trademark or trade name before other businesses. However, ownership generally can be established more definitely by registering the trademark or trade name at the Patent Office. The cost of developing, maintaining, or enhancing the value of a trademark or trade name, perhaps through advertising, should be charged to expense in the period or periods incurred. However, if a trademark or trade name is purchased, the purchase cost should be debited to an asset account and amortized over time.

Amortization of Intangibles

Some intangibles, such as patents, copyrights, and leaseholds, have limited useful lives that are determined by law, contract, or the nature of the asset. Other intangibles, such as goodwill, trademarks, and trade names, have indeterminable lives. In general, the cost of intangible assets should be amortized over the periods expected to be benefited by their use, which in no case is longer than their legal existence. However, as we stated earlier, generally accepted accounting principles require that the amortization period of intangible assets not be longer than 40 years. This limitation applies even if the life of the asset (for example, goodwill) may continue indefinitely into the future.

Progress Check
(Answers to Progress Checks are provided at the end of this chapter.)

12-1   Give an example of an intangible asset and a natural resource.

12-2   Prospect Mining Company paid $650,000 for an ore deposit. The deposit had an estimated 325,000 tonnes of ore that would be fully mined during the next 10 years. During the current year, 91,000 tonnes were mined, processed, and sold. What is the amount of depletion for the year?

12-3   On January 6, 1996, Fun-4-U Toy Company paid $120,000 for a patent with a 17-year legal life to produce a toy that is expected to be marketable for about 3 years. Prepare the entries necessary to record the acquisition and the December 31, 1996, adjustment.

CLASSIFYING INVESTMENTS

LO 2

State the criteria for classifying securities investments as long-term investments and describe the categories of securities that are reported as long-term investments.

In Chapter 8, you learned how to account for temporary investments in debt and equity securities. (We encourage you to review pages 398–402 before you study this section.) Recall that temporary investments are current assets; they are expected to be converted into cash within one year or the current operating cycle of the business, whichever is longer. In general, temporary investments such as T-bills and term deposits are those that are "capable of reasonably prompt liquidation."[6] They either mature within one year or the current operating cycle or are easily sold and therefore qualify as being *marketable.*

Securities investments that do not qualify as current assets are called **long-term investments.** Long-term investments include investments in bonds and shares that are not marketable or that, although marketable, are not intended to serve as a ready source of cash. Long-term investments also include funds earmarked for a special purpose, such as bond sinking funds, and land or other assets owned but not used in the regular operations of the business. In general, these assets are reported on the balance sheet in a separate *Long-term investments* section.

In Illustration 12–1, the boxes on the left side show the different long-term investments in securities. Note that they include (1) debt securities held to maturity, (2) debt and equity securities available for sale, (3) equity securities which give the investor a significant influence over the investee, and (4) equity securities which give the investor control over the investee. We discuss each of these types of investments in the following sections.

Progress Check

12-4   What types of assets are classified as long-term investments?

12-5   Under what conditions should an equity investment be classified on the balance sheet as a long-term investment?

LONG-TERM INVESTMENTS IN SECURITIES

Much of what you learned about temporary investments in Chapter 8 also applies to long-term investments. For example, at the time of purchase, investments are recorded at cost, which includes any commissions or brokerage fees paid to make the purchase. After the purchase, the accounting treatment depends on the type of investment.

---

[6]*CICA Handbook,* par. 3010.02.

Illustration 12-1 Accounting for Long-Term Investments in Securities

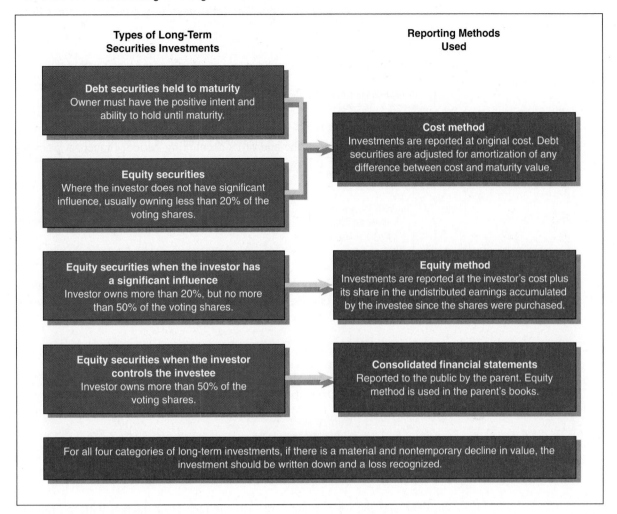

Investments in Debt Securities Held to Maturity

Debt securities held to maturity may be short-term or long-term investments. In either case, the owner should have the intent and the ability to hold the securities until they mature. At the time of purchase, these investments are recorded at cost. Then, interest revenue is recorded as it accrues.

The cost of an investment in debt securities may be more or less than the maturity value of the securities. When the investment is long-term, any difference between cost and maturity value must be amortized over the remaining life of the security. Chapter 13 explains the process of amortizing this difference. In this chapter, however, we assume that the costs of debt investments equal their maturity values.

For example, on August 31, 1996, Francis, Inc., paid $29,500 plus a brokerage fee of $500 to buy $30,000 par value of Candice Corp.'s 7% bonds payable. The bonds pay interest semiannually on August 31 and February 28. The amount of each

LO 3

Describe the methods used to report long-term securities investments in the financial statements.

payment is $30,000 \times 7\% \times 6/12 = \$1,050$. Francis has the intent to hold the bonds until they mature on August 31, 1998. The following entry records the purchase:

1996				
Aug.	31	Investment in Candice Corp. Bonds	30,000.00	
		Cash		30,000.00
		Purchased bonds to be held to maturity.		

On December 31, 1996, at the end of its accounting period, Francis accrues interest receivable with the following entry:

Dec.	31	Interest Receivable	700.00	
		Interest Earned		700.00
		$1,050 \times 4/6 = \$700$.		

In this entry, the $700 represents 4/6 of the semiannual cash receipt for interest. As a result of these entries, Francis's financial statements for 1996 show the following items:

On the income statement for 1996:
    Interest earned .... $ 700

On the December 31, 1996, balance sheet:
Assets:
    Current assets:
        Interest receivable .... $ 700
    Long-term investments:
        Investment in Candice Corp. bonds $30,000

On February 28, 1997, Francis records the receipt of interest with the following entry:

1997				
Feb.	28	Cash	1,050.00	
		Interest Receivable		700.00
		Interest Earned		350.00
		Received 6 months' interest on Candice Corp. bonds.		

When the bonds mature, this entry records the proceeds from the matured bonds:

1998				
Aug.	31	Cash	30,000.00	
		Investment in Candice Corp. Bonds		30,000.00
		Received cash from matured bonds.		

Investments in Equity Securities

The second box on the left side of Illustration 12–1 includes certain equity securities. To be included in this group of long-term investments, the investor in equity securities must not have a significant influence over the investee. Normally, this means that the investor owns less than 20% of the investee corporation's voting shares.[7]

Chapter 8 (pages 398–402) explained the procedures of accounting for temporary investments in equity securities. These same procedures are used for long-term investments accounted for by the cost method. At the time of purchase, the investments are recorded at cost. As dividends are received, they are credited to Dividends Earned and reported in the income statement. When the shares are sold, the proceeds from the sale are compared with the cost of the investment and any gain or loss realized on the sale is reported in the income statement.

Continuing with Francis, Inc., assume that on October 10, 1996, Francis purchased 1,000 common shares of Intex Corp. for $86,000. The following entry records the purchase:

Oct.	10	Investment in Intex Corp. Common Shares	86,000.00	
		Cash		86,000.00
		Purchased 1,000 shares.		

On November 2, Francis received a $1,720 quarterly dividend on the Intex shares. The following entry records the receipt:

Nov.	2	Cash	1,720.00	
		Dividends Earned		1,720.00
		Received dividend of $1.72 per share.		

On December 20, Francis sold 500 of the Intex shares for $45,000, and records the sale with the following entry:

Dec.	20	Cash	45,000.00	
		Investment in Intex Corp. Common Shares		43,000.00
		Gain on Sale of Long-Term Investment		2,000.00
		$86,000/2 = $43,000		

Reporting Long-Term Investments. Long-term investments are shown at cost with market value disclosed even if market value is below cost as long as the decline in value is temporary. However, when there has been a loss in value that

---

[7]The 20% limit is not an absolute rule. Other factors may overrule. See *CICA Handbook,* section 3050, "Long-Term Investments," par. .04.

is other than temporary, the investment is written down to recognize the loss.[8] The writedown (loss) would be included in determining net income. When a long-term investment has been written down to recognize the loss, the new carrying value is deemed to be the new cost basis for subsequent accounting purposes. A subsequent increase in value would be recognized only when realized (i.e., when the shares are sold). For purposes of calculating a gain or loss on sale of the investment, the cost of the investments sold should be calculated on the basis of the average carrying value (total cost of the shares ÷ number of shares held).[9]

Investment in Equity Securities; Investor Has a Significant Influence or Has Control

Sometimes, an investor buys a large block of a corporation's voting shares and is able to exercise a significant influence over the investee corporation. An investor who owns 20% or more of a corporation's voting shares is normally presumed to have a significant influence over the investee. There may be cases, however, where the accountant concludes that the 20% test of significant influence should be over-ruled by other, more persuasive, evidence.

An investor who owns more than 50% of a corporation's voting shares can dom-inate all of the other shareholders in electing the corporation's board of directors. Thus, the investor usually has control which is the power to determine the corpo-ration's strategic, operating, investing, and financing decisions without the coop-eration of others.[10]

As we stated earlier, the method of accounting for an equity investment depends on the relationship between the investor and the investee. In studying Illustration 12–1, note that if the investor has a significant influence, the *equity method* of ac-counting and reporting is used. Finally, if the investor controls the investee, the in-vestor uses the equity method in its records, but reports *consolidated financial state-ments* to the public. We discuss the equity method and consolidated statements in the following sections.

The Equity Method of Accounting for Common Share Investments

If an investor in common shares has significant influence over the investee, the **eq-uity method** of accounting for the investment must be used. When the shares are acquired, the investor records the purchase at cost. For example, on January 1, 1996, Gordon Company purchased 3,000 common shares (30%) of JWM, Inc., for a total cost of $70,650. This entry records the purchase on Gordon's books:

Jan.	1	Investment in JWM Common Shares	70,650.00	
		Cash		70,650.00
		Purchased 3,000 shares.		

---

[8]Ibid., par. 3050.20.

[9]Ibid., par. 3050.27.

[10]Ibid., par. 1590.03.

Under the equity method, the earnings of the investee corporation not only increase the investee's net assets but also increase the investor's equity claims against the investee's assets. Therefore, when the investee closes its books and reports the amount of its earnings, the investor takes up its share of those earnings in its investment account. For example, assume that JWM reported net income of $20,000 for 1996. Gordon's entry to record its 30% share of these earnings is:

Dec.	31	Investment in JWM Common Shares	6,000.00	
		Earnings from Investment in JWM, Inc.		6,000.00
		To record 30% equity in investee's earnings of		
		$20,000		

The debit records the increase in Gordon Company's equity in JWM. The credit causes 30% of JWM's net income to appear on Gordon Company's income statement as earnings from the investment. As with any other revenue, Gordon closes the earnings to Income Summary.

If the investee corporation incurs a net loss instead of a net income, the investor records its share of the loss and reduces (credits) its investment account. Then, the investor closes the loss to Income Summary.

Under the equity method, the receipt of cash dividends is not recorded as revenue because the investor has already recorded its share of the earnings reported by the investee. Instead, dividends received from the investee simply convert the form of the investor's asset from a share investment to cash. Thus, the equity method records dividends as a reduction in the balance of the investment account.

For example, assume that JWM declared and paid $10,000 in cash dividends on its common shares. Gordon's entry to record its 30% share of these dividends, which it received on January 9, 1997, is:

Jan.	9	Cash	3,000.00	
		Investment in JWM Common Shares		3,000.00
		To record receipt of 30% of the $10,000 dividend		
		paid by JWM, Inc.		

Thus, when the equity method is used, the carrying value of a common share investment equals the cost of the investment plus the investor's equity in the *undistributed* earnings of the investee. For example, after the preceding transactions are recorded on the books of Gordon Company, the investment account appears as follows:

Investment in JWM Common Shares

Date		Explanation	Debit	Credit	Balance
1996					
Jan.	1	Investment	70,650		70,650
Dec.	31	Share of earnings	6,000		76,650
1997					
Jan.	9	Share of dividend		3,000	73,650

If Gordon prepared a balance sheet on January 9, the investment in JWM would be reported as $73,650. This is the original cost of the investment, plus Gordon's equity in JWM's earnings since the date of purchase, less Gordon's equity in JWM's dividends since the date of purchase.

When an equity method share investment is sold, the gain or loss on the sale is determined by comparing the proceeds from the sale with the carrying value (book value) of the investment on the date of sale. For example, suppose that Gordon Company sold its JWM stock for $80,000 on January 10, 1997. The entry to record the sale is:

Jan.	10	Cash	80,000.00	
		Investment in JWM Common Shares		73,650.00
		Gain on Sale of Investments		6,350.00
		Sold 3,000 shares of stock for $80,000.		

Investments that Require Consolidated Financial Statements

Corporations often own shares in and may even control other corporations. For example, if Par Company owns more than 50% of the voting shares of Sub Company, Par Company can elect Sub Company's board of directors and thus control its activities and resources. The controlling corporation, Par Company, is known as the **parent company** and Sub Company is called a **subsidiary.**

Many large companies are parents with subsidiaries. For example, **George Weston Limited** is the parent of several subsidiaries, including Loblaw, Neilson/Cadbury, Zehrmart, E.B. Eddy Paper, and National Grocers.

When a corporation owns all the outstanding shares of a subsidiary, it can take over the subsidiary's assets, cancel the subsidiary's shares, and merge the subsidiary into the parent company. However, there often are financial, legal, and tax advantages if a large business is operated as a parent corporation that controls one or more subsidiary corporations. In fact, many large companies are parent corporations that own one or more subsidiaries.

When a business operates as a parent company with subsidiaries, separate accounting records are maintained by each corporation. From a legal viewpoint, the parent and each subsidiary are still separate entities with all the rights, duties, and responsibilities of individual corporations. However, investors in the parent company indirectly are investors in the subsidiaries. To evaluate their investments, parent company investors must consider the financial status and operations of the subsidiaries as well as the parent. This information is provided in **consolidated financial statements.**

Consolidated statements show the financial position, the results of operations, and the cash flows of all corporations under the parent's control, including the subsidiaries. These statements are prepared as if the business is organized as a single company. Although the parent uses the equity method in its accounts, the investment account is not reported on the parent's financial statements. Instead, the individual assets and liabilities of the affiliated companies are combined on a single balance sheet. Also, their revenues and expenses are combined on a single income statement and their cash flows are combined on a single statement of cash flows.

More detailed explanations of consolidated statements are included in advanced accounting courses.

Progress Check

12–6 **What are the similarities and differences in accounting for long-term investments in debt securities that are held to maturity and those that are held as temporary investments?**

12–7 **What are the three categories of long-term equity investments? Describe the criteria for each category and the method used to account for each.**

In today's complex world, many companies conduct business activities in more than one country. In fact, the operations of some large corporations involve so many different countries that they are called **multinational businesses.** The problems of managing and accounting for companies that have international operations can be very complex. Because of this complexity, the following pages present only a brief discussion. A more detailed study of these issues is reserved for advanced business courses.

Two primary problems in accounting for international operations occur because businesses with transactions in more than one country have to deal with more than one currency. These two problems are (1) accounting for sales or purchases denominated in a foreign currency and (2) preparing consolidated financial statements with foreign subsidiaries. To simplify the discussion of these problems, we assume that the companies have a base of operations in Canada and prepare their financial statements in the Canadian dollar. Hence, the **reporting currency** of such firms is the Canadian dollar.

Exchange Rates between Currencies

Active markets for the purchase and sale of foreign currencies exist all over the world. In these markets, Canadian dollars can be exchanged for U.S. dollars, British pounds, French francs, Japanese yen, or other currencies. The price of one currency stated in terms of another currency is called a **foreign exchange rate.** For example, assume that the current exchange rate for British pounds and Canadian dollars was $2.2770 on January 31, 1996. This rate means that one pound could have been acquired for $2.2770. On the same day, assume that the exchange rate between German marks and Canadian dollars was $0.6917. This number means that one mark could be purchased for $0.6917. Foreign exchange rates fluctuate daily (or even hourly) in accordance with the changing supply and demand for each currency and expectations about future events.

Sales or Purchases Denominated in a Foreign Currency

When a Canadian company makes a credit sale to a foreign customer, a special problem can arise in accounting for the sale and the account receivable. If the sales terms require the foreign customer's payment to be in Canadian dollars, no special accounting problem arises. But, if the terms of the sale state that payment is to be made in a foreign currency, the Canadian company must go through special steps to account for the sale and the account receivable.

INVESTMENTS IN INTERNATIONAL OPERATIONS

LO 4

Describe the primary accounting problems of having investments in international operations and prepare entries to account for sales to foreign customers.

For example, suppose that a Canadian company, the Brandon Company, makes a credit sale to London Outfitters, a British company. The sale occurs on December 12, 1996, and the price is £10,000, which is due on February 10, 1997. Naturally, Brandon Company keeps its accounting records in Canadian dollars. Therefore, to record the sale, Brandon Company must translate the sales price from pounds to dollars. This is done using the current exchange rate on the date of the sale. Assuming that the current exchange rate on December 12 is $2.40, Brandon records the sale as follows:

Dec.	12	Accounts Receivable—London Outfitters	24,000.00	
		Sales (10,000 × $2.40)		24,000.00
		To record a sale of £10,000, when the exchange rate equals $2.40.		

Now, assume that Brandon Company prepares annual financial statements on December 31, 1996. On that date, the current exchange rate has increased to $2.45. Therefore, the current dollar value of Brandon Company's receivable is $24,500 (10,000 × $2.45). This amount is now $500 greater than the amount originally recorded on December 12. According to generally accepted accounting principles, the receivable must be reported in the balance sheet at its current dollar value. Hence, Brandon Company must make the following entry to record the increase in the dollar value of the receivable:

Dec.	31	Accounts Receivable—London Outfitters	500.00	
		Foreign Exchange Gain or Loss		500.00
		To record the effects of the increased value of the British pound on our receivable.		

The Foreign Exchange Gain or Loss is closed to the Income Summary account and reported on the income statement.[11]

Assume that Brandon Company receives London Outfitters' payment of £10,000 on February 10, and immediately exchanges the pounds for Canadian dollars. On this date, the exchange rate for pounds has declined to $2.43. Therefore, Brandon Company receives only $24,300 (10,000 × $2.43). The firm records the receipt and the loss associated with the decline in the exchange rate as follows:

Feb.	10	Cash	24,300.00	
		Foreign Exchange Gain or Loss	200.00	
		Accounts Receivable—London Outfitters		24,500.00
		Received foreign currency payment of account and converted it into dollars.		

[11] Ibid., section 1650, "Foreign Currency Translation," par. 20.

Accounting for credit purchases from a foreign supplier is similar to the previous example of a credit sale to a foreign customer. If the Canadian company is required to make a payment in a foreign currency, the account payable must be translated into dollars before it can be recorded by the Canadian company. Then, if the exchange rate changes, an exchange gain or loss must be recognized by the Canadian company at any intervening balance sheet date and at the payment date.

Consolidated Statements with Foreign Subsidiaries

A second problem of accounting for international operations involves the preparation of consolidated financial statements when the parent company has one or more foreign subsidiaries. For example, suppose that a Canadian company owns a controlling interest in a French subsidiary. The reporting currency of the Canadian parent is the dollar. However, the French subsidiary maintains its financial records in francs. Before preparing consolidated statements, the parent must translate financial statements of the French company into Canadian dollars. After the translation is completed, the preparation of consolidated statements is not any different than for any other subsidiary.[12]

The procedures for translating a foreign subsidiary's account balances depend on the nature of the subsidiary's operations. In simple terms, the general process requires the parent company to select appropriate foreign exchange rates and then to apply those rates to the account balances of the foreign subsidiary.

Progress Check

12–8　If a Canadian company makes a credit sale of merchandise to a French customer and the sales terms require payment in francs:
　　a. The Canadian company will incur an exchange loss if the foreign exchange rate between francs and dollars increases from $0.246 at the date of sale to $0.256 at the date the account is settled.
　　b. The French company may eventually have to record an exchange gain or loss.
　　c. The Canadian company may be required to record an exchange gain or loss on the date of the sale.
　　d. None of the above is correct.

After studying this and the previous chapters, you have learned about all of the important classes of assets that businesses own. Recall from Chapter 11 that in evaluating the efficiency of a company in using its assets, a ratio that is often calculated and reviewed is total asset turnover. Another ratio that provides information about a company's efficiency in using its assets is **return on total assets.** You can calculate the return on total assets with this formula:

$$\text{Return on total assets} = \frac{\text{Net income}}{\text{Average total assets}}$$

USING THE INFORMATION— RETURN ON TOTAL ASSETS

LO 5

Explain the use of return on total assets in evaluating a company's efficiency in using its assets.

---

[12]The problem grows much more complicated when the accounts of the French subsidiary are maintained in acccordance with the French version of GAAP. The French statements must be converted to Canadian GAAP before the consolidation can be completed.

For example, **Canstar Sports Inc.,** the manufacturer of Bauer skates and other sports equipment, earned a net income of $15.3 million during 1993. At the beginning of 1993, Canstar had total assets of $137.2 million, and at the end of the year total assets were $159.2 million. If the average total assets owned during the year is approximated by averaging the beginning and ending asset balances, Canstar's return on total assets for 1993 was:

$$\text{Return on total assets} = \frac{\$15.3}{(\$137.2 + \$159.2)/2} = 10.3\%$$

As we have seen for other ratios, a company's return on total assets should be compared with past performance and with the ratios of similar companies. In addition, you must be careful not to place too much importance on the evaluation of any single ratio. For past performance comparisons, Canstar's return on total assets and total asset turnover over a four-year period were as follows:

Year	Return on Total Assets	Total Asset Turnover
1993	10.3%	1.4
1992	11.5	1.4
1991	7.3	1.3
1990	8.6	1.5

Notice that the change in return on total assets suggests that the company's efficiency in using its assets declined from 1992 to 1993. However, the total asset turnover remained relatively constant. A possible explanation for this might be that Canstar decided to increase expenses at a faster rate than sales in an effort to gain an increasing share of the market for its products. Such a strategy would explain a reduced return on total assets and an increased total asset turnover.

Progress Check

12-9 **A company had net income of $140,000 for 1996 and $100,000 for 1997. At December 31, 1996 and 1997, total assets reported were $800,000 and $900,000, respectively. What was the return on total assets for 1997?**

SUMMARY OF THE CHAPTER IN TERMS OF LEARNING OBJECTIVES

LO 1. Identify assets that should be classified as natural resources or as intangible assets and prepare entries to account for them, including entries to record depletion and amortization. The cost of a natural resource is recorded in an asset account. Then, depletion of the natural resource is recorded by allocating the cost to expense according to a units-of-production basis. The depletion is credited to an accumulated depletion account. Intangible assets are recorded at the cost incurred to purchase the assets. The allocation of intangible asset cost to expense is done on a straight-line basis and is called amortization. Normally, amortization is recorded with credits made directly to the asset account instead of a contra account.

LO 2. State the criteria for classifying assets as long-term investments and describe the categories of securities that are classified as long-term

investments. Securities investments are classified as current assets if they are held as a source of cash to be used in current operations and if they mature within one year or the current operating cycle of the business or are marketable. All other investments in securities are long-term investments, which also include assets held for a special purpose and not used in operations.

Long-term investments in securities are classified in four groups: (*a*) debt securities held to maturity, (*b*) equity securities where investor has no significant influence, (*c*) equity securities where the investor has a significant influence over the investee, and (*d*) equity securities when the investor controls the investee.

LO 3. Describe the methods used to report long-term securities investments in the financial statements. Debt held to maturity is reported at its original cost adjusted for amortization of any difference between cost and maturity value. Long-term investments in debt and equity securities are reported at cost unless there is a nontemporary decline in value. Then the investment is written down and a loss is recognized.

The equity method is used if the investor has a significant influence over the investee. This situation usually exists when the investor owns 20% or more of the investee's voting stock. If an investor owns more than 50% of another corporation's voting stock and controls the investee, the investor's financial reports are prepared on a consolidated basis.

Under the equity method, the investor records its share of the investee's earnings with a debit to the investment account and a credit to a revenue account. Dividends received satisfy the investor's equity claims, and reduce the investment account balance.

LO 4. Describe the primary accounting problems of having investments in international operations and prepare entries to account for sales to foreign customers. If a Canadian company makes a credit sale to a foreign customer and the sales terms call for payment with a foreign currency, the company must translate the foreign currency into dollars to record the receivable. If the exchange rate changes before payment is received, foreign exchange gains or losses are recognized in the year in which they occur. The same treatment is used if a Canadian company makes a credit purchase from a foreign supplier and is required to make payment in a foreign currency. Also, if a Canadian company has a foreign subsidiary that maintains its accounts in a foreign currency, the account balances must be translated into dollars before they can be consolidated with the parent's accounts.

LO 5. Explain the use of return on total assets in evaluating a company's efficiency in using its assets. Return on total assets is used along with other ratios such as total asset turnover to evaluate the efficiency of a company in using its assets. Return on total assets is usually calculated as the annual net income divided by the average amount of total assets.

The following transactions relate to Brown Company's long-term investment activities during 1996 and 1997. Brown did not own any long-term investments prior to 1996. Show the appropriate journal entries and the portions of each year's balance sheet and income statement that describe these transactions.

DEMONSTRATION PROBLEM

1996

Sept. 9 Purchased 1,000 common shares of Packard, Inc., for $80,000 cash. These shares represent 30% of Packard's outstanding shares.

Oct.   2   Purchased 2,000 common shares of BCE for $60,000 cash. These shares represent less than a 1% ownership in BCE.

        17   Purchased as a long-term investment 1,000 common shares of Apple Computer for $40,000 cash. These shares are less than 1% of Apple's outstanding shares.

Nov.   1   Received $5,000 cash dividend from Packard.

        30   Received $3,000 cash dividend from BCE.

Dec.   15   Received $1,400 cash dividend from Apple.

        31   Packard's 1996 net income was $70,000.

        31   Market values for the investments in equity securities are Packard, $94,000; BCE, $48,000; and Apple Computer, $45,000.

1997

Jan.   1   Packard, Inc., was taken over by other investors, and Brown sold its shares for $108,000 cash.

May 30   Received $3,100 cash dividend from BCE.

June 15 Received $1,600 cash dividend from Apple.

Aug. 17 Sold the BCE shares for $52,000 cash.

        19   Purchased 2,000 shares of Loblaw common shares for $50,000 as a long-term investment. The stock represents less than a 5% ownership in Loblaw.

Dec. 15 Received $1,800 cash dividend from Apple.

        31   Market values of the investments in equity securities are Apple, $39,000 and Loblaw, $48,000.

Planning the Solution

- Account for the investment in Packard under the equity method.
- Account for the investments in BCE, Apple, and Loblaw as long-term investments using the cost method.
- Prepare the information for the two balance sheets by including the appropriate assets and shareholders' equity accounts.

Solution to Demonstration Problem

Journal entries during 1996:

Sept.	9	Investment in Packard Common Shares	80,000.00	
		Cash		80,000.00
		Acquired 1,000 shares representing a 30% equity in Packard, Inc.		
Oct.	2	Investment in BCE Common Shares	60,000.00	
		Cash		60,000.00
		Acquired 2,000 shares as a long-term investment in securities.		
	17	Investment in Apple Common Shares	40,000.00	
		Cash		40,000.00
		Acquired 1,000 shares as a long-term investment in securities.		

Nov.	1	Cash	5,000.00	
		Investment in Packard Common Shares		5,000.00
		Received dividend from Packard, Inc.		
	30	Cash	3,000.00	
		Dividends Earned		3,000.00
		Received dividend from BCE.		
Dec.	15	Cash	1,400.00	
		Dividends Earned		1,400.00
		Received dividend from Apple.		
	31	Investment in Packard Common Shares	21,000.00	
		Earnings from Investment in Packard		21,000.00
		To record our 30% share of Packard's annual		
		earnings of $70,000.		

	Cost	Market Value
BCE	$ 60,000	$48,000
Apple	40,000	45,000
Total	$100,000	$93,000

Given the usual fluctuations in market prices, it
is reasonable to assume that the reduction is
temporary. Therefore, no adjustment is necessary.

December 31, 1996, balance sheet items:

Assets

Long-term investments:
Equity securities, at cost (market value, $93,000) ... $100,000
Investment in Packard, Inc. (market value, $94,000) . 96,000
    Total $196,000

Income statement items for the year ended December 31, 1996

Dividends earned .... $ 4,400
Earnings from equity method investment 21,000

Journal entries during 1997:

Jan.	1	Cash	108,000.00	
		Investment in Packard Common Shares		96,000.00
		Gain on Sale of Investments		12,000.00
		Sold 1,000 shares for cash.		
May	30	Cash	3,100.00	
		Dividends Earned		3,100.00
		Received dividend from BCE.		

June	15	Cash	1,600.00	
		Dividends Earned		1,600.00
		Received dividend from Apple.		
Aug.	17	Cash	52,000.00	
		Loss on Sale of Investments	8,000.00	
		Investment in BCE Common Shares		60,000.00
		Sold 2,000 shares for cash.		
	19	Investment in Loblaw Common Shares	50,000.00	
		Cash		50,000.00
		Acquired 2,000 shares as a long-term investment in securities available for sale.		
Dec.	15	Cash	1,800.00	
		Dividends Earned		1,800.00
		Received dividend from Apple.		

	Cost	Market Value
Apple	$40,000	$39,000
Loblaw	50,000	48,000
Total	$90,000	$87,000

December 31, 1997, balance sheet items:

Assets

Long-term investments:
  Equity securities, at cost (market value, $87,000) .. $ 90,000

Income statement items for the year ended December 31, 1997:

Dividends earned	$ 6,500
Gain on sale of investments	12,000
Loss on sale of investments	(8,000)

GLOSSARY

Amortization the process of systematically writing off the cost of an intangible asset to expense over its estimated useful life p. 565

Consolidated financial statements financial statements that show the results of all operations under the parent's control, including those of any subsidiaries; assets and liabilities of all affiliated companies are combined on a single balance sheet, revenues and expenses are combined on a single income statement, and cash flows are combined on a single statement of cash flows as though the business were in fact a single company. p. 576

Copyright an exclusive right granted by the federal government or by international agreement to publish and sell a musical, literary, or artistic work for a period of years. p. 567

Depletion the cost created by consuming the usefulness of natural resources. p. 564

Equity method an accounting method used when the investor has influence over the investee; the investment account is initially debited for cost and then is increased to reflect the investor's share of the investee's earnings and decreased to reflect the investor's receipt of dividends paid by the investee. p. 574

Foreign exchange rate the price of one currency stated in terms of another currency. p. 577

Goodwill an intangible asset of a business that represents future earnings greater than the average in its industry; recognized in the financial statements only when a business is acquired at a price in excess of the fair market value of its net assets (excluding goodwill). p. 568

Intangible asset an asset representing certain legal rights and economic relationships; it has no physical existence but is beneficial to the owner. p. 565

Lease a contract under which the owner of property (the lessor) grants to a lessee the right to use the property. p. 567

Leasehold the rights granted to a lessee by the lessor under the terms of a lease contract. p. 567

Leasehold improvements improvements to leased property made and paid for by the lessee. p. 567

Lessee the individual or company that acquires the right to use property under the terms of a lease. p. 567

Lessor the individual or company that owns property to be used by a lessee under the terms of a lease. p. 567

Long-term investments investments in shares and bonds that are not marketable or, if marketable, are not intended to be a ready source of cash in case of need;

also funds earmarked for a special purpose, such as bond sinking funds, and land or other assets not used in regular operations. p. 570

Multinational business a company that operates in a large number of different countries. p. 577

Parent company a corporation that owns a controlling interest in another corporation (more than 50% of the voting stock is required). p. 576

Patent exclusive right granted by the federal government to manufacture and sell a patented machine or device, or to use a process, for 17 years. p. 566

Reporting currency the currency in which a company presents its financial statements. p. 577

Return on total assets a measure of a company's operating efficiency, calculated by expressing net income as a percentage of average total assets. p. 579

Subsidiary a corporation that is controlled by another corporation (the parent) because the parent owns more than 50% of the subsidiary's voting stock. p. 576

Trademark a unique symbol used by a company in marketing its products or services. p. 569

Trade name a unique name used by a company in marketing its products or services. p. 569

SYNONYMOUS TERMS

Amortization depreciation, depletion.
Natural resources wasting assets.

Equity investment share or stock investment.

QUESTIONS

1. What is the name for the process of allocating the cost of natural resources to expense as the natural resources are used?

2. What are the characteristics of an intangible asset?

3. Is the declining-balance method an acceptable means of calculating depletion of natural resources?

4. What general procedures are followed in accounting for intangible assets?

5. When does a business have goodwill? Under what conditions can goodwill appear in a company's balance sheet?

6. X Company bought an established business and paid for goodwill. If X Company plans to incur substantial advertising and promotional costs each year

to maintain the value of the goodwill, must the company also amortize the goodwill?

7. In accounting for common share investments, when should the equity method be used?

8. Under what circumstances would a company prepare consolidated financial statements?

9. Under what circumstances are long-term investments in debt securities reported at their original cost adjusted for amortization of any difference between cost and maturity value?

10. What are two basic problems of accounting for international operations?

11. If a Canadian company makes a credit sale to a foreign customer and the customer is required to make

payment in Canadian dollars, can the Canadian company have an exchange gain or loss as a result of the sale?

12. A Canadian company makes a credit sale to a foreign customer, and the customer is required to make payment in a foreign currency. The foreign exchange rate was $1.40 on the date of the sale and is $1.30 on the date the customer pays the receivable.

Will the Canadian company record an exchange gain or an exchange loss?

13. Refer to Geac Computer Corporation Limited consolidated balance sheets in Appendix I. What percentage of total assets is represented by goodwill at April 30, 1994?

QUICK STUDY (Five-Minute Exercises)

QS 12–1
(LO 1)

Three Z Mining Co. acquired an ore mine at a cost of $615,000. It was necessary to incur a $60,000 cost to access the mine. The mine is estimated to hold 200,000 tonnes of ore and the estimated value of the land after the ore is removed is $80,000.

a. Prepare the entry to record the acquisition.

b. Prepare the year-end adjusting entry assuming that 46,000 tonnes of ore were removed from the mine this year.

QS 12–2
(LO 1)

Which of the following assets should be reported on the balance sheet as an intangible asset? Which should be reported as a natural resource? (a) copper mine, (b) copyright, (c) building, (d) goodwill, (e) timberland.

QS 12–3
(LO 1)

In early January of the current year, Big Mountain Ski Shop incurred a $160,000 cost to modernize the shop. The improvements included new floors, lighting, and fitting platforms for rental equipment. These improvements would last for 10 years of use. Big Mountain leases its retail space and has eight years remaining on the lease. Prepare the entry to record the modernization, and the adjusting entry at the end of the current year.

QS 12–4
(LO 2)

On April 1, 1996, Demi Dean purchased 8% bonds of Multi Media Inc. at a cost of $50,000, which equals their par value. The bonds carry an 8% rate of interest to be paid semiannually on September 30 and March 31. Prepare the entries to record the September 30 receipt of interest and the December 31 accrual.

QS 12–5
(LO 2)

On January 2, 1996, Nassau Co. paid $500,000 to acquire 10,000 (10%) of Suffolk Corp.'s outstanding common shares as a long-term investment. On March 25, 1998, Nassau sold half of the shares for $260,000. What method should be used to account for this investment? Prepare entries to record the acquisition of the shares and the sale.

QS 12–6
(LO 3)

Assume the same facts as in QS 12–5 except assume that the shares acquired represented 30% of the shares outstanding. Suffolk Co. paid a $100,000 dividend on October 12, 1996, and reported a net income of $400,000 for the 1996 year. Prepare the entry to record the receipt of the dividend and the year-end adjustment of the investment account.

QS 12–7
(LO 4)

On November 21, 1996, a Canadian company, NCN, made a sale with credit terms requiring payment in 30 days to a German company, Ehlers Inc. The price of the sale was 50,000 marks. Assuming the exchange rate between German marks and Canadian dollars was

$0.6214 on the date of sale and $0.5942 on December 21, prepare the entries to record the sale and cash receipt on December 21.

How is the return on total assets calculated? What does this ratio evaluate?

QS 12–8
(LO 5)

EXERCISES

On March 30, 1996, Clementine Investments paid $7,275,000 for an ore deposit containing 4,850,000 tonnes. The company also installed machinery in the mine that cost $339,500, had an estimated 10-year life with no salvage value, and was capable of removing all the ore in 8 years. The machine will be abandoned when the ore is completely mined. Clementine began operations on July 1, 1996, and mined and sold 582,000 tonnes of ore during the remaining six months of the year. Give the December 31, 1996, entries to record the depletion of the ore deposit and the amortization of the mining machinery.

Exercise 12–1
Depletion of natural resources
(LO 1)

Majestic Productions purchased the copyright to a painting for $369,000 on January 1, 1996. The copyright legally protects its owner for 24 more years. However, the company plans to market and sell prints of the original for only 15 more years. Prepare journal entries to record the purchase of the copyright and the annual amortization of the copyright on December 31, 1996.

Exercise 12–2
Amortization of intangible assets
(LO 1)

Rocky Lane has devoted years to developing a profitable business that earns an attractive return. Lane is now considering the possibility of selling the business and is attempting to estimate the value of the goodwill in the business. The fair value of the net assets of the business (excluding goodwill) is $625,000, and in a typical year net income is about $90,000. Most businesses of this type are expected to earn a return of about 12% on net assets. Estimate the value of the goodwill assuming (a) the value is equal to eight times the excess earnings above average, and (b) the value can be found by capitalizing the excess earnings above average at a rate of 10%.

Exercise 12–3
Estimating goodwill
(LO 1)

During 1996, Stockton Company's investments in securities included five items. These securities, with their December 31, 1996, market values, are as follows:

Exercise 12–4
Classifying equity investments, recording market values
(LO 2, 3)

a. Antel Corporation bonds payable: $167,400 cost; $182,000 market value. Stockton intends and is able to hold these bonds until they mature in 1999.

b. Foxfire, Inc., common stock: 30,800 shares; $132,980 cost; $143,500 market value. Stockton owns 22% of Foxfire's voting stock and has a significant influence on Foxfire.

c. Techcon Corp. common stock: 10,300 shares; $67,900 cost; $73,240 market value. The goal of this investment is to earn dividends over the next few years.

d. Bali common stock: 4,500 shares; $46,120 cost; $45,770 market value. The goal of this investment is an expected increase in market value of the stock over the next three to five years. Bali has 30,000 common shares outstanding.

e. Joskey common stock: 18,400 shares; $57,100 cost; $55,900 market value. This stock is marketable and is held as an investment of cash available for operations.

State whether each of these investments should be classified as a current asset or as a long-term investment.

Exercise 12–5
Investments in securities
(LO 3)

Pratt Company began operations in 1996 and regularly makes long-term investments in securities. The total cost and market value of these investments at the end of several years were:

	Cost	Market Value
On December 31, 1996	$170,000	$164,800
On December 31, 1997	194,000	206,000
On December 31, 1998	264,000	312,000
On December 31, 1999	398,000	354,000

Required

Prepare journal entries to record the LCM of Pratt's investments at the end of each year. Explain the entries you recorded.

Exercise 12–6
Equity investment transactions; equity method
(LO 3)

Prepare general journal entries to record the following events on the books of MCM Company:

1996

Jan. 14   Purchased 18,000 common shares of Putnam, Inc., for $156,900 plus broker's fee of $1,000. Putnam has 90,000 common shares outstanding and has acknowledged the fact that its policies will be significantly influenced by MCM.

Oct. 1   Putnam declared and paid a cash dividend of $2.60 per share.

Dec. 31   Putnam announced that net income for the year amounted to $650,000.

1997

Apr. 1   Putnam declared and paid a cash dividend of $2.70 per share.

Dec. 31   Putnam announced that net income for the year amounted to $733,100.

    31   MCM sold 6,000 shares of Putnam for $119,370.

Exercise 12–7
Receivables denominated in a foreign currency
(LO 4)

On June 2, 1996, Comco Company made a credit sale to a French company. The terms of the sale required the French company to pay 980,000 francs on January 3, 1997. Comco prepares quarterly financial statements on March 31, June 30, September 30, and December 31. The foreign exchange rates for francs during the time the receivable was outstanding were:

June 2, 1996	$0.16720
June 30, 1996	0.17100
September 30, 1996	0.17225
December 31, 1996	0.16885
January 3, 1997	0.17310

Calculate the foreign exchange gain or loss that Comco should report on each of its quarterly income statements during the last three quarters of 1996 and the first quarter of 1997. Also calculate the amount that should be reported on Comco's balance sheets at the end of the last three quarters of 1996.

Donham Company of Montvale, New Brunswick, sells its products to customers in Canada and in the United States. On December 3, 1996, Donham sold merchandise on credit to Swensons, Ltd., of London, Maine, at a price of U.S. $6,500. The exchange rate on that day was $1U.S. equals $1.4685 Canadian. On December 31, 1996, when Donham prepared its financial statements, the exchange rate was $1 U.S. for $1.4230. Swensons, Ltd., paid its bill in full on January 3, 1997, at which time the exchange rate was $1U.S. for $1.4460. Donham immediately exchanged the U.S. $6,500 for Canadian dollars. Prepare journal entries on December 3, December 31, and January 3, to account for the sale and account receivable on the books of Donham.

Exercise 12–8
Foreign currency transactions
(LO 4)

The following information is available from the financial statements of NRE Company:

	1996	1997	1998
Total assets, December 31	$320,000	$580,000	$1,200,000
Net income	46,000	75,000	106,000

Exercise 12–9
Return on total assets
(LO 5)

Calculate NRE's return on total assets for 1997 and 1998. Comment on the company's efficiency in using its assets in 1997 and 1998.

PROBLEMS

Part 1. Five years ago, Zeno Insurance Company leased space in a building for 15 years. The lease contract calls for annual rental payments of $28,000 to be made on each July 1 throughout the life of the lease and also provides that the lessee must pay for all additions and improvements to the leased property. Because recent nearby construction has made the location more valuable, Zeno decided to sublease the space to Bogart & Company for the remaining 10 years of the lease. On June 25, Bogart paid $75,000 to Zeno for the right to sublease the property and agreed to assume the obligation to pay the $28,000 annual rental charges to the building owner, beginning the next July 1. After taking possession of the leased space, Bogart paid for improving the office portion of the leased space at a cost of $90,950. The improvement was paid for on July 8 and is estimated to have a life equal to the 17 years remaining in the life of the building.

Problem 12–1
Intangible assets and natural resources
(LO 1)

Required

Prepare entries for Bogart & Company to record (*a*) its payment to Zeno for the right to sublease the building space, (*b*) its payment of the next annual rental charge to the building owner, and (*c*) payment for the improvements. Also, prepare the adjusting entries required at the end of the first year of the sublease to amortize (*d*) a proper share of the $75,000 cost of the sublease and (*e*) a proper share of the office improvement.

Part 2. On February 20 of the current year, Amazon Industries paid $8,700,000 for land estimated to contain 11.6 million tonnes of recoverable ore of a valuable mineral. It installed machinery costing $348,000, which had a 12-year life and no salvage value, and was capable of exhausting the ore deposit in 9 years. The machinery was paid for on May 24, six days before mining operations began. The company removed 744,000 tonnes of ore during the first seven months' operations.

Required

Preparation component:

Prepare entries to record (*a*) the purchase of the land, (*b*) the installation of the machinery, (*c*) the first seven months' depletion under the assumption that the land will be valueless after the ore is mined, and (*d*) the first seven months' amortization on the machinery, which will be abandoned after the ore is fully mined.

Analysis component:

Describe the similarities and differences in amortization, depletion, and depreciation.

**Problem 12–2
Goodwill
(LO 1)**

Flowers Unlimited has the following balance sheet on December 31, 1996:

Cash	$ 57,800
Merchandise inventory	43,650
Buildings	320,000
Accumulated amortization	(112,000)
Land	101,750
Total assets	$411,200
Accounts payable	$ 9,400
Long-term note payable	124,925
D. E. Flowers, capital	276,875
Total liabilities and owner's equity . .	$411,200

In this industry, earnings average 32% of owner's equity. Flowers Unlimited, however, is expected to earn $100,000 annually. The owner believes that the balance sheet amounts are reasonable estimates of fair market values for all assets except goodwill, which does not appear on the financial statement. In discussing a plan to sell the company, D. E. Flowers has suggested to the potential buyer that goodwill can be measured by capitalizing the amount of above-average earnings at a rate of 12%. On the other hand, the potential buyer thinks that goodwill should be valued at six times the amount of excess earnings above the average for the industry.

Required

1. Calculate the amount of goodwill claimed by Flowers.

2. Calculate the amount of goodwill according to the potential buyer.

3. Suppose that the buyer finally agrees to pay the full price requested by Flowers. If the amount of expected earnings (before amortization of goodwill) is obtained and the goodwill is amortized over the longest permissible time period, what amount of net income will be reported for the first year after the company is purchased?

4. If the buyer pays the full price requested by Flowers, what rate of return on the purchaser's investment will be earned as net income the first year?

**Problem 12–3
Accounting for equity
investments
(LO 3)**

Austex Company was organized on January 2, 1996. The following transactions and events subsequently occurred:

1996

Jan.   7   Austex purchased 50,000 shares (20%) of Staat, Inc.'s outstanding common shares for $565,500.

Apr. 30   Staat declared and paid a cash dividend of $1.10 per share.

Dec. 31   Staat announced that its net income for 1996 was $480,000. Market value of
          the shares was $11.80 per share.

1997

Nov. 30   Staat declared and paid a cash dividend of $0.70 per share.

Dec. 31   Staat announced that its net income for 1997 was $630,000. Market value of
          the shares was $12.18 per share.

1998

Jan. 5   Austex sold all of its investment in Staat for $682,000 cash.

Part 1. Assume that Austex has a significant influence over Staat because it owns 20% of
the shares.

Required

1. Give the entries on the books of Austex to record the preceding events.
2. Calculate the carrying value per share of Austex's investment as reflected in the investment account on January 4, 1998.
3. Calculate the change in Austex's equity from January 7, 1996, through January 5, 1998, that resulted from its investment in Staat.

Part 2. Assume that even though Austex owns 20% of Staat's outstanding shares, a thorough investigation of the surrounding circumstances indicates that it does not have a significant influence over the investee.

Required

1. Give the entries on the books of Austex to record the preceding events.
2. Calculate the cost per share of Austex's investment as reflected in the investment account on January 4, 1998.
3. Calculate the change in Austex's equity from January 7, 1996, through January 5, 1998, that resulted from its investment in Staat.

Leling Company's long-term investments portfolio at December 31, 1996, consisted of the following:

Problem 12–4
Accounting for long-term investments
(LO 2, 3)

Long-Term Investments	Cost	Market Value
10,000 shares of Company X common shares	$163,500	$145,000
1,500 shares of Company Y common shares	65,000	62,000
120,000 shares of Company Z common shares	40,000	35,600

Leling made the following long-term investments transactions during 1997:

Jan.   17   Sold 750 common shares of Company Y for $36,000 less a brokerage fee
            of $180.

Mar.   3   Purchased 5,000 common shares of Company A for $300,000 plus a brokerage
            fee of $1,500. The shares represent a 30% ownership in Company A.

May   12   Purchased 3,000 common shares of Company B for $96,000 plus a brokerage
            fee of $400. The shares represent a 10% ownership in Company B.

Dec. 11 Purchased 10,000 common shares of Company D for $89,000 plus a brokerage fee of $445. The shares represent a 5% ownership in Company D.

20 Sold 10,000 common shares of Company X for $160,000 less a brokerage fee of $800.

Dec. 31 Company A announced a net profit of $280,000 for the year.

The market values of Leling's investments at December 31, 1997, follow: A, $418,000; B, $92,000; D, $90,800; Y, $38,200; Z, $31,000.

Required

1. Determine what amount should be reported on Leling's December 31, 1997, balance sheet for its investments in equity securities.

2. Prepare a December 31, 1997, adjusting entry, if necessary, to record the LCM adjustment of the long-term investments in securities.

3. What amount of gain or loss on those transactions relating to securities should be reported on Leling's December 31, 1997, income statement?

Problem 12–5
Foreign currency transactions
(LO 4)

Lupold Company is a Canadian company that has customers in several foreign countries. The company had the following transactions in 1996 and 1997:

1996

May 22 Sold merchandise for 15,000 marks to Weishaar Imports of Germany, payment in full to be received in 90 days. On this day, the foreign exchange rate for marks was $0.5654.

Sept. 9 Sold merchandise to Campos Company of Mexico for $24,780 cash. The exchange rate for pesos was $0.322154.

Aug. 25 Received Weishaar Imports' payment for its purchase of May 22, and exchanged the marks for dollars. The current foreign exchange rate for marks was $0.5995.

Nov. 29 Sold merchandise on credit to ONI Company located in Japan. The price of 1.1 million yen was to be paid 60 days from the date of sale. The exchange rate for yen was $0.009195 on November 29.

Dec. 23 Sold merchandise for 158,000 francs to Martinique Company of France, payment in full to be received in 30 days. The exchange rate for francs was $0.16722.

Dec. 31 Prepared adjusting entries to recognize exchange gains or losses on the annual financial statements. Rates for exchanging foreign currencies on this day included the following:

Marks (Germany)	$0.5690
Pesos (Mexico)	0.331256
Yen (Japan)	0.010110
Francs (France)	0.16530

1997

Jan. 24 Received full payment from Martinique for the sale of December 23 and immediately exchanged the francs for dollars. The exchange rate for francs was $0.16342.

30 Received ONI's full payment for the sale of November 29 and immediately exchanged the yen for dollars. The exchange rate for yen was $0.010290.

Required

Preparation component:

1. Prepare general journal entries to account for these transactions of Lupold.

2. Calculate the foreign exchange gain or loss to be reported on Lupold's 1996 income statement.

Analysis component:

3. What actions might Lupold consider to reduce its risk of foreign exchange gains or losses?

On January 3, Tragor Company purchased 20,000 common shares of Entech Company for $10 per share, or $200,000. Tragor's purchase represents a 30% ownership in Entech. Tragor did not own any investments prior to the Entech stock purchase. Entech did not declare any dividends on its common shares during the year, and on December 31 reported a net loss of $80,000. The market value of the Entech shares on December 31 was $11.00 per share. The accountant for Tragor made the following adjusting entry to update the account balances for the investment in Entech:

Problem 12–6
Analytical essay
(LO 3)

Dec.	31	Long-Term Investments	20,000.00	
		Gain on Investments		20,000.00
		(20,000 × $11) − $200,000 = $20,000		

Explain why this entry is incorrect. Without providing specific amounts, determine what impact the accountant's error had on the financial statements.

Part 1. Five years ago, D. C. Corporation leased space in a building for a period of 20 years. The lease contract calls for $81,000 in annual rental payments on each January 1 throughout the life of the lease and also provides that the lessee must pay for all additions and improvements to the leased property. Recent construction nearby has made the location more valuable; and on December 30, D. C. Corporation subleased the space to T. P., Inc., for the remaining 15 years of the lease, beginning on the next January 1. T. P., Inc., paid $360,000 for the privilege of subleasing the property and in addition agreed to assume and pay the building owner the $81,000 annual rental charges. After taking possession of the leased space T. P., Inc., paid for remodeling the office portion of the leased space at a cost of $270,000. The remodeled office portion is estimated to have a life equal to the remaining life of the building, 25 years, and was paid for on January 10.

Problem 12–7
Intangible assets and natural resources
(LO 5)

Required

Prepare entries for T. P., Inc., to record: (*a*) T. P., Inc.'s payment to sublease the building space, (*b*) its payment of the annual rental charge to the building owner, and (*c*) payment for the new office portion. Also, prepare the adjusting entries required at the end of the first year of the sublease to amortize (*d*) a proper share of the $360,000 cost of the sublease and (*e*) a proper share of the office remodeling cost.

Part 2. On May 8 of the current year, Huber Company paid $1,080,000 for mineral land estimated to contain 9,000,000 tonnes of recoverable ore. It installed machinery costing $187,500, having an eight-year life and no salvage value, and capable of exhausting the mine in five years. The machinery was paid for on June 28, four days before mining operations began. During the first six months' operations the company mined 720,000 tonnes of ore.

Required

Prepare entries to record (*a*) the purchase of the mineral land, (*b*) the installation of the machinery, (*c*) the first six months' depletion under the assumption that the land will be valueless after the ore is mined, and (*d*) the first six months' amortization on the machinery, which will be abandoned after the ore is fully mined.

Problem 12–8
Goodwill
(LO 5)

Batts Company's balance sheet on December 31, 1996, is as follows:

Cash	$ 170,100
Merchandise inventory	245,700
Buildings	756,000
Accumulated amortization	(198,450)
Land	425,250
Total assets	$1,398,600
Accounts payable	$113,400
Long-term note payable	295,200
Common shares	706,500
Retained earnings	283,500
Total liabilities and owners' equity ..	$1,398,600

In Batts Company's industry, earnings average 11% of common shareholders' equity. Batts Company, however, is expected to earn $198,900 annually. The owners of Batts Company believe that the balance sheet amounts are reasonable estimates of fair market values except for goodwill. In discussing a plan to sell the company, they argue that goodwill should be recognized by capitalizing the amount of earnings above average at a rate of 20%. On the other hand, the prospective purchaser argues that goodwill should be valued at four times the earnings above average.

Required

1. Calculate the amount of goodwill claimed by Batts Company's owners.
2. Calculate the amount of goodwill according to the purchaser.
3. Suppose the purchaser finally agrees to pay the full price requested by Batts Company's owners. If the expected earnings level is obtained and the goodwill is amortized over the longest permissible time period, what will be the net income for the first year after the company is purchased?
4. If the purchaser pays the full price requested by Batts Company's owners, what percentage of the purchaser's investment will be earned as net income the first year?

Problem 12–9
Equity investments—cost and equity methods
(LO 2, 3)

Ranger Company was organized on January 2, 1996, for the purpose of investing in the shares of other companies. Ranger Company immediately issued 50,000 common shares for which it received $250,000 cash. On January 9, 1996, Ranger Company purchased 10,000 shares (20%) of Trumpe Company's outstanding shares at a cost of $250,000. The following transactions and events subsequently occurred:

1996

Apr. 30 Trumpe Company declared and paid a cash dividend of $1 per share.

Dec. 31 Trumpe Company announced that its net income for the year was $125,000.

1997

Aug. 10 Trumpe Company declared and paid a cash dividend of $0.80 per share.

Dec. 31 Trumpe Company announced that its net income for the year was $95,000.

1998

Jan.   4 Ranger Company sold all of its investment in Trumpe Company for $275,000
          cash.

Part 1. Because Ranger Company owns 20% of Trumpe Company's outstanding shares.
Ranger Company is presumed to have a significant influence over Trumpe Company.

Required

1. Give the entries on the books of Ranger Company to record the above events regarding its investment in Trumpe Company.
2. Calculate the cost per share of Ranger Company's investment as reflected in the investment account on January 1, 1998.
3. Calculate Ranger Company's retained earnings balance on January 5, 1998, after
   closing of the books.

Part 2. Although Ranger Company owns 20% of Trumpe Company's outstanding shares,
a thorough investigation of the surrounding circumstances indicates that Ranger Company
does not have a significant influence over Trumpe Company, and the cost method is the appropriate method of accounting for the investment.

Required

1. Give the entries on the books of Ranger Company to record the above events regarding its investment in Trumpe Company.
2. Calculate the cost per share of Ranger Company's investment as reflected in the investment account on January 1, 1998.
3. Calculate Ranger Company's retained earnings balance on January 5, 1998, after a
   closing of the books.

Paramount Sales Corporation, a Canadian company that has customers in several foreign
countries, had the following transactions in 1996 and 1997:

Problem 12–10
Foreign currency
transactions
(LO 5)

1996

June   6 Sold merchandise for 125,000 francs to Poirot Co. of Brussels, payment in
          full to be received in 60 days. On this day, the foreign exchange rate for
          francs into dollars was $0.02822.

July 17 Sold merchandise to Nordhoff Distributors of West Germany for $8,880 cash.
          The exchange rate for marks into dollars was $0.5920.

Aug.   1 Received Poirot Company's payment for its purchase of June 6 and exchanged
          the francs for dollars. The current foreign exchange rate for francs into dollars
          was $0.02840.

Oct. 25 Sold merchandise on credit to British Imports, Ltd., a company located in
          London, England. The price of 3,000 pounds was to be paid 90 days from the
          date of sale. On October 25, the exchange rate for pounds into dollars was
          $1.7730.

Nov. 30 Sold merchandise for 350,000 yen to Yamoto Company of Japan; payment in
          full to be in 60 days. The exchange rate for yen into dollars was $0.007710.

Dec. 31 Prepared adjusting entries to recognize exchange gains or losses on the annual financial statements. Rates for exchanging foreign currencies into dollars on this day included the following:

Francs (Belgium)	$ 0.02833
Marks (W. German)	0.5944
Pounds (England)	1.7125
Yen (Japan)	0.007897

1997

Jan. 23 Received British Imports, Ltd.'s full payment for the sale of October 25 and immediately exchanged the pounds for dollars. The exchange rate for pounds into dollars was $1.7628.

29 Received full payment from Yamoto Company for the sale of November 30 and immediately exchanged the yen for dollars. The exchange rate for yen into dollars was $0.007779.

Required

1. Prepare general journal entries to account for these transactions of Paramount Sales Corporation.

2. Calculate the exchange gain or loss to be reported on Paramount Sales Corporation's 1996 income statement.

PROVOCATIVE PROBLEMS

Provocative Problem 12–1

Business communications case

(LO 2, 3)

You are the accountant for PCI Company. The owner of PCI, Lester Murphy, has finished reviewing the financial statements you prepared for 1997 and questions the $40,000 loss reported on PCI's sale of its investment in the shares of Runyan Company.

PCI acquired 100,000 shares of Runyan's outstanding common shares on December 31, 1996, at a cost of $500,000. This shares purchase represented a 30% interest in Runyan. The 1997 income statement showed that the investments made by PCI proved to be very profitable and that the earnings from all investments were $340,000. On January 5, 1998, PCI sold the Runyan shares for $580,000. Runyan did not pay any dividends during 1997 and reported $400,000 net income for the year.

Murphy believes that because the purchase price of the Runyan shares was $500,000 and it was sold for $580,000, the 1998 income statement should report an $80,000 gain on the sale.

Draft a memo to Murphy explaining why the $40,000 loss on the sale of the Runyan shares is correctly reported.

Provocative Problem 12–2

Managerial analysis problem

(A review problem)

UNI Company is considering buying either Riteway Company or Best Company, similar businesses that acquired their equipment and began operating four years ago. In evaluating the two companies, UNI has determined that they have not used the same accounting procedures so their financial statements are not comparable. Over the past four years, Riteway has reported an average annual net income of $197,840 and Best has reported $254,190. The current balance sheets of the two companies show the following:

	Riteway	**Best**
Cash	$ 131,500	$ 144,400
Accounts receivable	972,400	1,077,000
Allowance for doubtful accounts	(57,000)	–0–
Merchandise inventory	1,268,200	1,666,000
Office equipment	496,800	420,800
Accumulated amortization, office equipment ..	(293,310)	(168,320)
Total assets	$2,518,590	$3,139,880
Total liabilities	$1,176,800	$1,408,600

Riteway has used the allowance method of accounting for bad debts and Best has used the direct write-off method. An examination of each company's accounts revealed that only $30,000 of Riteway's accounts are probably uncollectible and that Best's estimated uncollectible accounts total $54,000.

Because Best uses FIFO, its ending inventory amounts approximate replacement cost. However, Riteway uses LIFO. As a result, Riteway's current inventory is reported $176,000 below replacement cost.

In taking amortization for the past four years, both companies have assumed 10-year lives and no salvage value for their equipment. However, Riteway has used double-declining-balance amortization, while Best has used straight-line. UNI believes that straight-line amortization results in reporting equipment on the balance sheet at its approximate market value.

UNI is willing to pay fair market value for the net assets (including goodwill) of either business. UNI estimates goodwill to be four times the average annual earnings in excess of 14% of the fair market value of the net tangible assets (assets, other than goodwill, minus liabilities).

Required

Prepare the following schedules: (*a*) the net tangible assets of each company at fair market values assessed by UNI, (*b*) the revised net incomes of the companies based on adjusted amounts of bad debts expense, FIFO inventories, and straight-line amortization, (*c*) the calculation of each company's goodwill, and (*d*) the maximum purchase price UNI would pay for each business, if it assumed the liabilities of the purchased business. (Note: Round all calculations to the nearest dollar.)

Examine Geac Computer Corporation Limited's financial statements and supplemental information in Appendix I and answer the following questions:

1. Are Geac's financial statements consolidated? How can you tell?

2. Does Geac have more than one subsidiary? How can you tell?

3. Does Geac have any foreign operations? How can you tell?

4. Is there a foreign exchange gain or loss on the income statement? Provide an explanation for what you find or do not find.

5. What intangible assets does Geac own? Assuming it will not take advantage of any renewal options, what is the maximum time period that Geac can use to amortize these intangibles?

6. Calculate Geac's return on total assets for 1994.

Provocative Problem 12–3

Financial statement analysis case

(LO 1, 4, 5)

Geac

ANALYTICAL AND REVIEW PROBLEMS

A & R Problem 12–1

On January 1, 1996, Tony Company purchases 40% of Danny Company's outstanding voting shares. On December 31, 1997, Tony Company's account Investment in Danny Company showed a balance of $400,000. Danny Company reported the following information for the years of 1996 and 1997:

	Net Income	Dividends Paid
1996	$150,000	$50,000
1997	200,000	50,000

Required

Calculate the purchase price paid by Tony Company for the Danny Company shares.

A & R Problem 12–2

The following is an excerpt from the notes to the financial statements of ABC Sciences Ltd.:

> ABC Sciences holds a 35.4% interest in Halifax-based Eastern Laboratories which develops, manufactures, and distributes chemicals solely in the Canadian market. ABC Sciences accounts for its investment in Eastern Chemicals by the equity method. During 1996, Eastern had a strong year, with revenues increasing 79.6% while net income more than doubled to $7.6 million. ABC Science's share of this net income was . . .

Required

1. Is ABC Sciences using the cost or equity method to account for its investment in Eastern Chemicals? Support your answer.
2. Prepare the journal entry to record ABC Sciences's share of Eastern's net income.
3. If Eastern paid out 50% of its 1996 net income as cash dividends, what entry would ABC Sciences make to record the receipt of cash?

CONCEPT TESTER

Check your understanding of the concepts introduced in this chapter by completing the following crossword puzzle.

Across Clues

1. The process of systematically writing off the cost of an intangible asset.

4. A cost created by consuming the usefulness of a natural resource.

7. A contract under which the owner of the property grants another the right to the property's use.

9. An exclusive right to publish and sell artistic works.

11. An exclusive right to manufacture and sell a product or process.

12. A corporation that holds a controlling interest in another corporation (2 words).

Down Clues

2. A unique symbol used by a company in marketing its product or services.

3. Changes to a leased property made by the lessee (1st of 2 words; also see 6 down).

5. An accounting method used when the investor has influence over the investee (2 words).

6. Changes to a leased property made by the lessee (2nd of 2 words; also see 3 down).

8. An intangible asset of a business represented by future earnings of a business above the norm.

10. A corporation that is controlled by another corporation.

ANSWERS TO PROGRESS CHECKS

12–1 Some possible answers:

   Intangible Assets:

   Patents

   Copyrights

   Leaseholds

   Leasehold Improvements

   Goodwill

   Trademarks

   Exclusive Licenses

   Natural Resources:

   Timberlands

   Mineral Deposits

   Oil Reserves

12–2 $650,000 \times (91,000/325,000) = \$182,000$

12–3

Jan.	6	Patents	120,000	
		Cash		120,000
Dec.	31	Amortization Expense	40,000	
		Patents		40,000

12–4 Long-term investments include funds earmarked for a special purpose, bonds and shares that do not meet the test of a current asset, and other assets that are not used in the regular operations of the business.

12–5 An equity investment is classified as a long-term investment if it is not marketable or, if marketable, it is not held as an available source of cash to meet the needs of current operations.

12–6 Long-term investments in debt securities and temporary investments in debt securities are recorded at cost and interest on both is accrued as earned. However, long-term debt securities require amortization of the difference between cost and maturity value.

12–7 Long-term equity investments are placed in the following three categories and accounted for using the method indicated:

   a. Noninfluential holding (less than 20% of outstanding shares) − Cost Method.

   b. Significantly influential holding (20% to 50% of outstanding shares) − Equity Method.

   c. Controlling holding (more than 50%) − Consolidated Statements.

12–8 d

12–9 ($800,000 + $900,000)/2 = $850,000
$100,000/$850,000 = 11.8%

Despite the risks of being in debt, companies with liabilities enjoy many advantages. For example, sales can be increased if a company agrees to repair or replace defective products under a warranty obligation. Careful borrowing also allows companies to increase their income and assets.

Current and Long-Term Liabilities

Karen White and Mark Smith have been given an assignment to evaluate Safeway's financial condition. They are confused about the nature of the company's liabilities. The balance sheet reports four different categories of liabilities, and the differences between these categories are not clear to Karen and Mark.

Safeway, Inc., is one of the world's largest food retailers. At the end of its 1993 year, Safeway operated approximately 1,080 stores in Canada and the United States. The company's 1993 annual report appears to indicate that Safeway has been successfully emerging from a very difficult period of losses. At the end of its 1989 year, total shareholders' equity was a negative $388.9 million (a deficit). In other words, total liabilities exceeded total assets by $388.9 million. This situation improved each year until, at the end of 1993, total shareholders' equity was a positive $382.9 million.

Safeway Inc. and Subsidiaries
(In millions)

	Year-end 1993	Year-end 1992
Current liabilities:		
Current maturities of notes and debentures	$ 188.6	$ 92.0
Current obligations under capital leases	19.3	20.4
Accounts payable	880.5	811.0
Accrued salaries and wages	216.3	192.5
Other accrued liabilities	406.7	385.9
Total current liabilities	$1,711.4	$1,501.8
Long-term debt:		
Notes and debentures	$2,287.7	$2,736.6
Obligations under capital leases	193.6	199.6
Total long-term debt	$2,481.3	$2,936.2
Deferred income taxes	145.5	176.0
Accrued claims and other liabilities	353.6	368.7
Total liabilities	$4,691.8	$4,982.7

LEARNING OBJECTIVES

After studying Chapter 13, you should be able to:

1. **Define liabilities, explain the difference between current and long-term liabilities, and describe the uncertainties related to some liabilities.**

2. **Describe how accountants record and report estimated liabilities such as warranties and income taxes and how they report contingent liabilities.**

3. **Describe how accountants record and report short-term notes payable.**

4. **Explain and calculate the present value of an amount to be paid at a future date and the present value of a series of equal amounts to be paid at future dates.**

5. **Describe how accountants use present value concepts in accounting for long-term notes, and how liabilities may result from leasing assets.**

6. **Calculate the number of times a company earns its fixed interest charges and describe what it reveals about a company's situation.**

7. **Define or explain the words and phrases listed in the chapter glossary.**

Previous chapters have described liabilities for accounts payable, notes payable, wages payable, and unearned revenues. In this chapter, you will learn about liabilities arising from warranties, income taxes, borrowing, asset purchases and leases. We also describe contingent liabilities and the important concept of present value. As you study this chapter, you will learn how accountants define, classify, and measure liabilities for the purpose of reporting useful information about them.

DEFINING AND CLASSIFYING LIABILITIES

LO 1

Define liabilities, explain the difference between current and long-term liabilities, and describe the uncertainties related to some liabilities.

In general, a liability means that because of a past event, a business has a present obligation to make a future payment. More precisely, liabilities are probable future payments of assets or services that an entity is presently obligated to make as a result of past transactions or events.[1] As shown in the diagram, this definition involves three dimensions in time:

• The company is obligated in the present

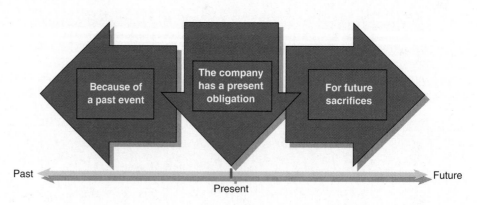

[1]*CICA Handbook*, section 1000, "Financial Statement Concepts," par. 32.

- To pay out assets or deliver services in the future
- Because of an event in the past

This definition also tells us that liabilities do not include all expected future payments. For example, suppose that a company expects to pay wages to its employees in the coming months. These future payments are not liabilities because the company is not presently obligated to pay them. The company is not presently obligated because the employees have not yet earned the future wages. In other words, no past transaction has resulted in a present obligation. The liabilities will be created in the future only when the employees actually perform the work.

Current and Long-Term Liabilities

Information about liabilities is more useful when the balance sheet identifies the liabilities as current and long-term. *Current liabilities* are due within one year or the company's operating cycle, whichever is longer.[2] Typical current liabilities include accounts payable, short-term notes payable, wages payable, warranty liabilities, lease liabilities, payroll and other taxes payable, and unearned revenues.

Obligations that are not expected to be paid within one year (or a longer operating cycle) should be classified as *long-term liabilities.* Typical long-term liabilities include long-term notes payable, warranty liabilities, lease liabilities, and bonds payable. On the balance sheet, these may be presented in a single long-term liabilities section. However, many companies show them as two or more items such as *long-term debt* and *other liabilities.* For example, the liabilities of Safeway Inc., on page 601 include long-term debt, deferred income taxes, and accrued claims and other liabilities. All of these are reported below current liabilities and are understood to be non-current (long-term) liabilities.

Some kinds of liabilities may be either current or long term. A specific debt is assigned to a category on the basis of how soon it will be paid. In fact, a single liability is divided between the two categories if the company expects to make payments in both the near and more distant future. For example, recall the liabilities of **Safeway Inc.** Notice that the first two current liabilities represent the current portions of the two items listed as long-term debt.

A few liabilities do not have a fixed due date because they are payable on the creditor's demand. They are reported as current liabilities because they may have to be paid within the year or a longer operating cycle.

Three important questions concerning liabilities are: Who must be paid? When is payment due? How much is to be paid? In many situations, the answers to these three questions are determined at the time the liability is incurred. For example, assume that Coleman Company has an account payable for precisely $100, payable on August 15, 1996, to R. L. Tucker. There is no uncertainty about any of the questions. The company knows whom to pay, when to pay, and how much to pay. Other types of liabilities may be uncertain with respect to one or more of the three questions.

UNCERTAIN ASPECTS OF SOME LIABILITIES

---

[2]Ibid., section 1510, "Current Assets and Current Liabilities," par. .03.

When the Identity of the Creditor Is Uncertain. Some liabilities have uncertainty about who will be paid. For example, a corporation's board of directors creates a liability with a known amount when it declares a dividend payable to the shareholders. Because the dividend will be paid to the investors who actually own shares on a specified future date, the recipients are not known with certainty until that date. Despite this uncertainty, the corporation has a liability that is reported on the balance sheet.

When the Due Date Is Uncertain. In other situations, a company may have an obligation of a known amount to a known creditor, but not know exactly when the debt must be settled. For example, a copy services company may accept fees in advance from a customer who expects to need copies later. Thus, the copy service company has a liability that will be settled by providing services at an unknown future date. Even though this uncertainty exists, the company's balance sheet is complete only if it includes this liability to its customer. (These obligations are reported as current liabilities because they may have to be settled in the short term.)

When the Amount Is Uncertain. In addition, a company may know that an obligation exists but may not know exactly how much will be required to settle it. For example, a company uses electrical power every day but is billed only after the meter has been read. The cost has been incurred and the liability has been created, even though the bill has not been received. As a result, a liability to the utility company is reported with an estimated amount if the balance sheet is prepared before the bill arrives.

Progress Check

(Answers to Progress Checks are provided at the end of the chapter.)

13-1   What is a liability?

13-2   Is every expected future payment a liability?

13-3   If a liability is payable in 15 months, should it be classified as current or long-term?

ESTIMATED LIABILITIES

LO 2

Describe how accountants record and report estimated liabilities such as warranties and income taxes, and how they report contingent liabilities.

Obligations of uncertain amounts that can be reasonably estimated are called **estimated liabilities.** A common example of an estimated liability involves warranties offered by a seller. Other estimated liabilities are created for contracts to provide future services, income taxes, property taxes, and employee benefits such as pensions and health care.

Warranty Liabilities

An estimated liability is created when a company sells products covered by a warranty. In effect, a **warranty** obligates the seller or manufacturer to pay for replacing or repairing the product when it breaks or otherwise fails to perform within a specified period. For example, a used car might be sold with a warranty that covers parts and labour.

To comply with the *full disclosure* and the *matching principles,* the seller must report the expense of providing a warranty during the same period as the revenue from the sales of the product. The seller must also report the obligation under the warranty as a liability, even though it is uncertain about the existence, amount, payee, and date of its future sacrifices. The seller's warranty obligation does not require payments unless the products break and are returned for repairs. Nonetheless, future payments are probable, and the amount of the liability can be estimated using the company's past experience with warranties.

For example, suppose that a dealer sells a used car for $8,000 on December 1, 1996, with a one-year or 15,000-km. warranty that covers repair parts and labour charges. Experience shows that the warranty expense averages about 4% of a car's selling price. In this case, the expense is expected to be $320 ($8,000 × 4%). The dealer records the expense and liability with this entry:

1996				
Dec.	1	Warranty Expense	320.00	
		Estimated Warranty Liability		320.00
		To record the warranty expense and liability at 4%		
		of the selling price.		

This entry causes the expense to be reported on the 1996 income statement. It also causes the warranty liability to appear on the balance sheet for December 31, 1996.

Now, suppose that the customer returns the car for warranty repairs on January 9, 1997. The dealer performs the work by replacing parts that cost $90 and using labour at a cost of $110. This entry records the partial settlement of the estimated warranty liability:

1997				
Jan.	9	Estimated Warranty Liability	200.00	
		Auto Parts Inventory		90.00
		Cash		110.00
		To record the cost of warranty repairs.		

Notice that this entry does not record any additional expense in 1997. Instead, the entry reduces the balance of the estimated warranty liability. The warranty expense was already recorded in 1996, the year the car was sold under the warranty.

What happens if the total warranty costs actually turn out to be more or less than the predicted $320? In fact, some difference is highly likely for any particular car. Over the long term, management should monitor the actual warranty costs to see whether the 4% rate provides useful information. If actual experience reveals a large difference, the rate should be modified for future sales.

Income Tax Liabilities for Corporations

A proprietorship's financial statements do not include income taxes because they do not pay income taxes; instead, they are assessed directly against the owner. However, corporations are subject to income taxes and must estimate the amount of their income tax liability when they prepare interim financial statements. We explain this process in the following paragraphs. Then, in the next section, we discuss deferred income tax liabilities that arise from temporary differences between GAAP and income tax rules.

Income tax expense for a corporation creates a liability that exists until payments are made to the government. Because the taxes are created by the process of earning income, a liability is incurred as soon as the income is earned. However, the taxes must be paid monthly under federal regulations.

For example, suppose that a corporation, Foster, Inc., prepares monthly financial statements. Based on the income earned in January, the company estimates that it owes income taxes of $12,100. The following adjusting entry records the estimate:

Jan.	31	Income Tax Expense	12,100.00	
		Income Taxes Payable		12,100.00
		Accrued income tax expense and liability based on the estimated income for the month of January.		

The estimated tax liability is paid each month. Assuming the tax installment is paid the next month, the following entry records the payment:

Feb.	10	Income Taxes Payable	12,100.00	
		Cash		12,100.00
		Paid the monthly income taxes based on the estimated income for January.		

The process of accruing and then paying the taxes continues throughout the year. However, by the time the annual financial statements are prepared at the end of the year, the company's accountant knows the amount of income that has been earned and the actual amount of income taxes that must be paid. This information allows the accountant to update the expense and liability accounts.

For example, suppose that Foster, Inc.'s accounts include a $22,000 credit balance in the Income Taxes Liability account at December 31, 1996. Information about the company's income for the year shows that the actual liability should be $33,500. This entry records the additional expense and liability:

Dec.	31	Income Tax Expense	11,500.00	
		Income Taxes Payable		11,500.00
		To record additional tax expense and liability.		

The liability will be settled when the company makes its final payment in 1997.

Deferred Income Tax Liabilities

Another special type of income tax liability may be incurred when the amount of income before taxes reported on a corporation's income statement is not the same as the amount of income reported on its income tax return. These differences arise because income tax laws define income differently from GAAP.[3]

---

[3]The differences between the tax laws and GAAP arise because Parliament uses the tax law to generate revenues, stimulate the economy, and otherwise influence behaviour. GAAP, on the other hand, are intended to provide financial information that is useful for decision making.

Some of the differences between the tax law and GAAP are temporary. These *temporary differences* arise when the tax return and the income statement report a revenue or expense in different years. As an example, for tax purposes, companies are often able to deduct higher amounts of amortization in the early years of an asset's life and smaller amounts in the later years. On their income statements, they often report an equal amount of amortization expense in each year. Thus, in the early years, amortization for tax purposes is more than amortization expense on the income statement. Then, in the later years, amortization for tax purposes is less than amortization expense on the income statement.

When there are temporary differences between taxable income on the tax return and income before taxes on the income statement, GAAP requires corporations to calculate income tax expense based on the income reported on the income statement. In the previous example involving amortization, the result is that the income tax expense reported in the early years is more than the amount of income tax payable. This difference is called **deferred income tax.**

For example, assume that after making and recording its income tax payments, a company determines at the end of the year that an additional $25,000 of income tax expense should be recorded. It also determines that only $21,000 is currently due and $4,000 is deferred to future years. The following entry records the end-of-year adjustment:

Dec.	31	Income Tax Expense	25,000.00	
		Income Taxes Payable		21,000.00
		Deferred Income Tax		4,000.00
		To record tax expense and deferred tax.		

In this entry, the credit to Income Taxes Payable represents the amount that is currently due to be paid. The credit to Deferred Income Tax represents the tax payments that are deferred until future years when the temporary difference reverses.

Many companies report deferred income tax liabilities. For example, **Alcan Aluminium Limited's** December 31, 1994, balance sheet shows that Alcan had a deferred income tax liability of $441 million.

In some circumstances, temporary differences may cause a company to pay income taxes before they are reported on the income statement as an expense. If so, the company usually reports a *deferred income tax debit* on its balance sheet that is similar to a prepaid expense. For example, **Dofasco Inc.'s** December 31, 1994, balance sheet reported deferred income taxes of $14.1 million as a current asset.

Goods and Services Tax and Sales Taxes Payable

Sales tax liabilities arise because the federal government and most provincial governments require businesses to act as collection agencies for the Goods and Services Tax (GST) and provincial sales taxes (PSTs). When a business makes a sale, the customer is charged for the sales tax on top of the selling price, in most cases, and the tax is later paid to the government(s).

Chapter 6 illustrated how the sales taxes would be accumulated in the sales journal. Assume that Superior Clothing Store collected $8,750 of GST and $7,500 of PST during September. At the end of September these amounts would appear on the balance sheet as current liabilities. The entry to pay these taxes during October would be as follows:

Oct.	25	GST Payable	8,750	
		Cash		8,750
		To pay GST for September.		
		PST Payable	7,500	
		Cash		7,500
		To pay PST for September.		

Note that the sales taxes are neither a revenue nor an expense for the enterprise. However, when a business purchases goods and services for its own use, the sales taxes paid become part of the cost of these items. In the case of goods purchased for resale, either the business would be exempt from paying the sales taxes on the purchase or the sales taxes paid could be deducted from the sales taxes collected when determining the amount to be remitted to the government(s).

Progress Check

13-4   Estimated liabilities would include an obligation to pay
  a. An uncertain but reasonably estimated amount to a specific person on a specific date.
  b. A known amount to a specific person on an uncertain due date.
  c. A known amount to an uncertain person on a known due date.
  d. All of the above.

13-5   An automobile was sold for $15,000 on June 1, 1996, with a one-year warranty that covers parts and labour. Based on past experience, warranty expense is estimated at 1.5% of the selling price. On March 1, 1997, the customer returned the car for warranty repairs that used replacement parts at a cost of $75 and labour at a cost of $60. The amount that should be recorded as warranty expense at the time of the March 1 repairs is *(a)* $0, *(b)* $60, *(c)* $75, *(d)* $135, *(e)* $225.

13-6   Why would a corporation accrue an income tax liability for interim reports?

CONTINGENT LIABILITIES

Sometimes, past transactions have the effect of requiring a future payment only if some uncertain future event takes place. If the likelihood that the uncertain future event will occur is remote, the company is not required to report a liability in the statements or the notes. However, if the uncertain future event is likely and the amount of the payment can be reasonably estimated, the company is required to report the anticipated payment as a liability.[4]

Contingent liabilities involve situations that fall between these two extremes. One situation is that the uncertain future event is likely but the amount of the payment cannot be reasonably estimated. For example, the company is being sued by a customer but is defending itself and cannot determine what the final outcome will be.

---

[4]Ibid, section 3290, "Contingencies," par. .06.

The other is that the uncertain future event is not likely but has a reasonable possibility of occurring. The company has guaranteed a loan for an affiliated company and it is unlikely that the loan will go into default. These contingent liabilities are not recorded in the books as liabilities. However, the *full-disclosure principle* requires disclosure of contingent liabilities in the financial statements or in the notes.

Distinguishing between Liabilities and Contingent Liabilities

Contingent liabilities become definite obligations only if some previously uncertain event actually takes place. For example, a typical contingent liability is a discounted note receivable that becomes a definite obligation only if the original signer of the note fails to pay it at maturity. We discussed this example in Chapter 8.

Does a product warranty create a liability or a contingent liability? A product warranty requires service or payment only if the product fails and the customer returns it for service. These conditions make it appear to be like a contingent liability. However, the contingent obligation should be recorded in the books as a liability if the occurrence of the future contingency is likely and if the amount of the liability can be reasonably estimated. Therefore, product warranties are usually recorded as liabilities because: (1) the failure of some percentage of the sold products is likely, and (2) past experience allows the seller to develop a reasonable estimate of the amount to be paid.

Other Examples of Contingent Liabilities

Potential Legal Claims. In today's legal environment, many companies find themselves being sued for damages for a variety of reasons. The accounting question is this: Should the defendant recognize a liability on the balance sheet or disclose a contingent liability in the notes while a lawsuit is outstanding and not yet settled? The answer is that the potential claim should be recorded as a liability only if a payment for damages is likely and the amount can be reasonably estimated. If the potential claim cannot be reasonably estimated or its occurrence is not determinable, it should be described as a contingent liability.

Debt Guarantees. Sometimes a company will guarantee the payment of a debt owed by a supplier, customer, or other company. Usually, the guarantor describes the guarantee in the notes to the financial statements as a contingent liability. However, if it is likely that the original debtor will default, the guarantor needs to record and report the guarantee as a liability.

Other Uncertainties

All companies and other organizations face major uncertainties from future economic events, including natural disasters and the development of new competing products. If these events do occur, they may destroy the company's assets or drive it out of business. However, these uncertainties are not liabilities because they are future events that are not a result of past transactions. Financial statements are not useful if they include speculation about possible effects of events that have not yet occurred.

Be sure to read the comment by Susan Selfe in As a Matter of Opinion. She discusses additional liabilities that companies may need to describe in the future if accounting principles are changed.

As a Matter of Opinion

Susan Selfe (Suominen) is a 1990 graduate of Wilfrid Laurier University's Business Administration CO-OP program. She joined Shell Canada in Toronto as a business analyst and later Household Financial as an internal auditor. In 1993 she was hired by Fidelity Investments Canada as a financial analyst. Fidelity Investments is the 6th largest mutual fund company in Canada and is the Canadian subsidiary of Boston based Fidelity Investments Limited, the world's largest mutual fund company. Since joining Fidelity, Susan obtained her CMA designation and successfully passed the Canadian Securities Course (CSC). In 1995 she was promoted to Senior Financial Analyst where she leads a team that is responsible for reporting the monthly financial and business results to Fidelity's senior management in Canada and the United States. In addition to being involved in project analysis, she also coordinates the quarterly forecast for over 30 cost centres.

Over the past several years, accountants have begun to pay much more attention to the potential future payments that businesses may be obligated to make as a result of current operations. A good example involves the promises of employers to pay health care benefits for their retired employees. The CICA's Accounting Standards Board expects to issue an Exposure Draft in 1996. Companies presently do not report this obligation except by reporting an expense for actual payments they had already made. The Exposure Draft may require them to provide information about their obligations and to recognize the expenses for probable future payments.

Are there other obligations that we presently ignore but someday may have to recognize as liabilities? I would not be surprised. One that comes to mind is potential claims from injuries to product users. Some juries have given large awards many years after a product was sold. Another possible liability is the cost of cleaning up toxic wastes discarded before anyone was aware of the danger.

Nobody can say whether these particular examples will eventually result in new liabilities or disclosures. But, I have no doubt that accounting will continue to evolve in response to an increasing emphasis on the obligations of doing business responsibly.

Susan Selfe, BBA, CMA

Progress Check

13-7 A future payment should be reported as a liability on a company's balance sheet if the payment is contingent on a future event that:
a. Is not likely but is reasonably possible and the amount of the payment cannot be reasonably estimated.
b. Is likely and the amount of the payment can be reasonably estimated.
c. Is not likely but the amount of the payment is known.

13-8 Under what circumstances should a future payment be reported in the financial statements as a contingent liability?

ACCOUNTING FOR KNOWN LIABILITIES

Most liabilities arise in situations with little uncertainty. The procedures used to account for these debts are described in the following sections of the chapter. The topics include:

• Short-term notes payable.
• Long-term notes payable.
• Lease liabilities.

In addition, we introduce you to present value calculations that accountants use when accounting for long-term liabilities and interest expense. Payroll liabilities were discussed in Chapter 10.

A short-term note payable may be created when a company purchases merchandise on credit and then extends the credit period by signing a note that replaces the account. Short-term notes payable also arise when money is borrowed from a financial institution.

SHORT-TERM NOTES PAYABLE

LO 3
Describe how accountants record and report short-term notes payable.

Note Given to Extend a Credit Period

In some cases, a company may create a note payable to replace an account payable. For example, a creditor may ask that an interest-bearing note be substituted for an account that does not bear interest. In other situations, the borrower's weak financial condition may encourage the creditor to obtain a note and close the account to ensure that additional credit sales are not made to this customer.

For example, assume that on August 23, Broke Company asks to extend its past-due $600 account payable to Smart Company. After some negotiations, Smart agrees to accept $100 cash and a 60-day, 12%, $500 note payable to replace the account payable. The accountant for Broke records the substitution with this entry:

Aug.	23	Accounts Payable—Smart Company	600.00	
		Cash		100.00
		Notes Payable		500.00
		Paid $100 cash and gave a 60-day, 12% note to extend the due date on the account.		

Notice that signing the note does not pay off the debt. Instead, the debt's form is merely changed from an account to a note payable. Smart Company may prefer to have the note because it earns interest and because it provides reliable documentation of the debt's existence, term, and amount.

When the note becomes due, Broke will pay the note and interest by giving Smart a cheque for $509.86 and then record the payment with this entry:

Oct.	22	Notes Payable	500.00	
		Interest Expense	9.86	
		Cash		509.86
		Paid note with interest ($500 × 12% × 60/365).		

Note that the interest expense is calculated by multiplying the principal of the note by the original rate for the fraction of the year the note was outstanding.

Borrowing from a Bank

When making a loan, a bank typically requires the borrower to sign a promissory note. When the note matures, the borrower pays back a larger amount. The difference between the two amounts is *interest*. In many situations, the note states that the signer of the note promises to pay the *principal* (the amount borrowed) plus the interest. If so, the *face value* of the note equals the principal.

In other situations, the bank may have the borrower sign a note with a face value that includes both the principal and the interest. In these cases, the signer of the note borrows less than the note's face value. The difference between the borrowed amount and the note's face value is interest. Because the borrowed amount is less than the face value, the difference is sometimes called the **discount on note payable.** To illustrate these two kinds of loans, assume that Robin Goode borrows $2,000 from a bank on behalf of the Goode Company. The loan is made on September 30 and will be repaid in 60 days. It has a 12% annual interest rate.

Face Value Equals the Amount Borrowed. Suppose that the bank requires Goode to sign a loan with a face value equal to the borrowed $2,000. If so, the note will include the following phrase: "I promise to pay $2,000 plus interest at 12% sixty days after September 30." The Goode Company records the increase in cash and the new liability with this entry:

Sept.	30	Cash	2,000.00	
		Notes Payable		2,000.00
		Borrowed cash with a 60-day, 12% note.		

When the note and interest are paid 60 days later, Goode records the event with this entry:

Nov.	29	Notes Payable	2,000.00	
		Interest Expense	39.45	
		Cash		2,039.45
		Paid note with interest ($2,000 × 12% × 60/365).		

Face Value Equals the Amount Borrowed and the Interest. If Goode's bank wishes, it may draw up a note that includes the 12% interest in its face value. If so, the note contains the following promise: "I promise to pay $2,039.45 sixty days after September 30." Notice that the note does not refer to the rate that was used to compute the $39.45 of interest included in the $2,039.45 face value. In all other respects, the note is exactly the same. However, the lack of a stated rate of interest sometimes causes an agreement like this one to be called a **noninterest-bearing note.** In fact, this widely used term is not precise because the note does bear interest, which is included in the face value.

When the face value of the note includes principal and interest, Goode could record the debt with an entry exactly like the previous September 30 entry. However, the more typical practice is to credit Notes Payable for the face value of the note and record the discount in a contra account. The following entry takes this approach:

Sept.	30	Cash	2,000.00	
		Discount on Notes Payable	39.45	
		Notes Payable		2,039.45
		Borrowed cash with a 60-day, 12% note (Discount		
		= $2,000 × 12% × 60/365).		

The Discount on Notes Payable account is contra to the Notes Payable account. If a balance sheet is prepared on September 30, the $39.45 discount is subtracted from the $2,039.45 balance in the Notes Payable account to reflect the $2,000 net amount borrowed.

When the note matures 60 days later on November 29, the entry to record Goode's $2,039.45 payment to the bank is:

Nov.	29	Notes Payable	2,039.45	
		Interest Expense	39.45	
		Cash		2,039.45
		Discount on Notes Payable		39.45
		Paid note with interest.		

If the end of an accounting period falls between the signing of a note payable and its maturity date, the *matching principle* requires the accountant to record the accrued but unpaid interest on the note. For example, suppose that Robin Goode borrowed $2,000 on December 16, 1996, instead of September 30. The 60-day note matures on February 14, 1997. Because the company's fiscal year ends on December 31, the accountant records interest expense for the 15 days in December. The entries depend on the form of the note.

Face Value Equals the Amount Borrowed. If the note's face value equals the amount borrowed, the accrued interest is charged to expense and credited to an Interest Payable account. To illustrate, assume that the $2,000 note signed by Goode on December 16 bears 12% interest. Because 15 out of the 60 days covered by the note have elapsed by December 31, one-fourth (15 days/60 days) of the $39.45 total interest is an expense of 1996. Goode records this expense with the following adjusting entry at the end of 1996:

1996 Dec.	31	Interest Expense	9.86	
		Interest Payable		9.86
		To record accrued interest on note payable		
		($2,000 × 12% × 15/365).		

When the note matures on February 14, Goode records this entry:

ADJUSTMENTS AT THE END OF THE REPORTING PERIOD

1997				
Feb.	14	Interest Expense ($2,000 × 12% × 45/365)	29.59	
		Interest Payable	9.86	
		Notes Payable	2,000.00	
		Cash		2,039.45
		Paid note with interest.		

The entry recognizes the 45 days of interest expense for 1997 and removes the balances of the two liability accounts.

Face Value Equals the Amount Borrowed and the Interest. Now assume that the face value of the note includes the interest. For example, assume that Goode signed a $2,039.45 noninterest-bearing note on December 15. In recording the note, Goode credited the $2,039.45 face value of the note to Notes Payable and debited the $39.45 discount to a contra account. This adjusting entry is needed to record the accrual of 15 days of interest at the end of 1996:

Dec.	31	Interest Expense	9.86	
		Discount on Notes Payable		9.86
		To record accrued interest on note payable		
		($2,000 × 12% × 15/365).		

Observe that the accrued interest is not credited to Interest Payable. Instead, the entry reduces the balance of the contra account from $39.45 to $29.59. As a result, it increases the net liability to $2,009.46 ($2,039.45 − $29.59).

When the note matures, the following entry accrues the interest expense for the last 45 days of the note and records its payment:

1997				
Feb.	14	Interest Expense	29.59	
		Notes Payable	2,039.45	
		Discount on Notes Payable		29.59
		Cash		2,039.45
		Paid note with interest ($2,000 × 12% × 45/365).		

Progress Check

13-9   **Why would a creditor want a past-due account to be replaced by a note?**

13-10   **A company borrows money for six months by signing a $1,050 note payable. In recording the transaction, the company's bookkeeper correctly debited $50 to Discount on Notes Payable. How much was borrowed? What annual rate of interest was charged?**

LONG-TERM LIABILITIES

In addition to current liabilities, companies often have liabilities that are repaid after one year (or a longer operating cycle). These *long-term liabilities* can arise when money is borrowed from a bank or when a note is issued to buy an asset. A long-term liability also may be created when a company enters into a multiyear lease agreement that is similar to buying the asset. Each of these liability arrangements is described in this chapter. In addition, large companies often borrow money by issuing *bonds* to a number of creditors. These securities are usually long-term liabilities that exist as long as 30 years or more. Accounting for bonds is described in Chapter 17.

Because of the extended lives of long-term liabilities, accounting for them is often more complicated than accounting for short-term liabilities. In particular, the accountant may need to apply present value techniques to measure a long-term liability when it is created and to assign interest expense to each of the years in the liability's life.

Information based on the concept of **present value** enters into many financing and investing decisions. It also enters into accounting for liabilities resulting from those decisions. Therefore, an understanding of present value is important for all business students.

Because this chapter focuses on liabilities, we explain present value concepts by referring to future cash outflows, payables, and interest expense. However, the same concepts also apply to future cash inflows, receivables, and interest income. The most fundamental present value concept is based on the idea that an amount of cash to be paid (or received) in the future has less value now than the same amount of cash to be paid (or received) today.

For example, $1 to be paid one year from now has a present value that is less than $1. To see why this is true, assume that $0.9259 is borrowed for one year at 8% interest. The amount of interest that will be incurred is $0.9259 × 8% = $0.0741. When the $0.0741 interest is added to the $0.9259, the sum equals the $1 payment that is necessary to repay the debt with interest, as shown here:

Amount borrowed	$0.9259
Interest for one year at 8%	0.0741
Total debt after one year	$1.0000

In this example, the $0.9259 borrowed amount is the present value of the $1 future payment. To state the concept more generally, a borrowed amount is the present value of a future payment if the borrowed amount generates interest at a given rate and the future payment will repay the debt with interest.[5]

To carry this example of present value further, assume that the $1 payment is to be made after two years and the 8% interest is to be compounded annually. Compounding means that interest during the second period is based on the sum of the amount borrowed plus the interest accrued during the first period. In other words,

PRESENT
VALUE
CONCEPTS

LO 4
Explain and calculate the present value of an amount to be paid at a future date and the present value of a series of equal amounts to be paid at future dates.

---

[5]Exactly the same analysis applies to an investment. If $0.9259 is invested at 8%, it will generate $0.0741 interest revenue in one year, thereby amounting to a $1 receipt of principal and interest.

the second period's interest is 8% multiplied by the sum of the original amount borrowed plus the interest earned during the first period.

In this example, where $1 is to be paid back after two years, the amount that can be borrowed (the present value) is $0.8573. The following calculation shows why $0.8573 is the present value:

Amount borrowed during first year	$0.8573
Interest during first year ($0.8573 × 8%)	0.0686
Amount borrowed during second year	$0.9259
Interest during second year ($0.9259 × 8%)	0.0741
Total debt after two years	$1.0000

Notice that the first year's interest is added to the principal amount borrowed so that the second year's interest is based on $0.9259.[6]

Unless otherwise noted, the interest rates used in this text are annual rates and interest is compounded annually.

Present Value Tables

The present value of $1 to be paid after a number of periods in the future can be calculated by using this formula: $1/(1 + i)^n$. The symbol i in the equation is the interest rate per period and n is the number of periods until the future payment must be made. For example, the present value of $1 to be paid after two periods at 8% is $1/(1.08)^2$, which equals $0.8573.

Although you can use this formula to find present values, other techniques are available. For example, many electronic calculators are preprogrammed to find present values. You can also use a **present value table** that shows present values computed with the formula at various interest rates for different time periods. In fact, many students find it helpful to learn how to make the calculations with the tables and then move on to use a calculator when they become comfortable with present value concepts.

Table 13–1 shows present values of a future payment of $1 for up to 10 periods at five different interest rates. The present values in the table have been rounded to four decimal places.[7] (This table is taken from a larger and more complete table in Appendix F at the end of the book.)

To use this table, notice that the first value in the 8% column in Table 13–1 is 0.9259. We used this value in the previous section as the present value of $1 at 8%. Go down one row in the same 8% column to find the present value of $1 discounted at 8% for two years. You should find the value of 0.8573 that we used in the second example. This value means that $0.8573 is the present value of the obligation to pay $1 after two periods, discounted at 8% per period.

---

[6]Benjamin Franklin is said to have described compounding with this expression: "The money money makes makes more money."

[7]Four decimal places are sufficient for the applications described in this book. Other situations may require more precision.

Table 13-1
Present Value of $1

	Rate				
Periods	**2%**	**4%**	**6%**	**8%**	**10%**
1	0.9804	0.9615	0.9434	0.9259	0.9091
2	0.9612	0.9246	0.8900	0.8573	0.8264
3	0.9423	0.8890	0.8396	0.7938	0.7513
4	0.9238	0.8548	0.7921	0.7350	0.6830
5	0.9057	0.8219	0.7473	0.6806	0.6209
6	0.8880	0.7903	0.7050	0.6302	0.5645
7	0.8706	0.7599	0.6651	0.5835	0.5132
8	0.8535	0.7307	0.6274	0.5403	0.4665
9	0.8368	0.7026	0.5919	0.5002	0.4241
10	0.8203	0.6756	0.5584	0.4632	0.3855

Using a Present Value Table

To demonstrate how an accountant can measure a liability by using a present value table like Table 13–1, assume that a company plans to borrow cash and then repay it as follows:

To be paid back after one year	$ 2,000
To be paid back after two years	3,000
To be paid back after three years	5,000
Total to be paid back	$10,000

If the company will have to pay 10% interest on this loan, how much will it be able to borrow? The answer is that it can borrow the present value of the three future payments, discounted at 10%. This is calculated in Illustration 13–1 with values from Table 13–1. The illustration shows that the company can borrow $8,054 at 10% in exchange for its promise to make the three payments at the scheduled dates.

Present Values of Annuities

The $8,054 present value of the loan in Illustration 13–1 is the sum of the present values of the three different payments. If the expected cash flows for a liability are not equal, their combined present value must be found by calculating each of their individual present values. In other cases, a loan may create an **annuity,** this is a series of equal payments occurring at equal time intervals. The present value of an annuity can be found with fewer calculations.

For example, suppose that a company can repay a 6% loan by making a $5,000 payment at the end of each year for the next four years. The amount to be borrowed under this loan equals the present value of the four payments discounted at 6%. The present value is calculated in Illustration 13–2 by multiplying each payment by the appropriate value from Table 13–1. The illustration shows that the company can borrow $17,326 under these terms.

Illustration 13–1
Finding the Present
Value of a Series of
Unequal Payments

Years from Now	Expected Payments	Present Value of $1 at 10%	Present Value of Expected Payments
1	$2,000	0.9091	$1,818
2	3,000	0.8264	2,479
3	5,000	0.7513	3,757
Total present value of the payments . .			$8,054

Illustration 13–2
Finding the Present
Value of a Series of
Equal Payments (an
Annuity) by Discounting
Each Payment

Years from Now	Expected Payments	Present Value of $1 at 6%	Present Value of Expected Payments
1	$5,000	0.9434	$ 4,717
2	5,000	0.8900	4,450
3	5,000	0.8396	4,198
4	5,000	0.7921	3,961
Total		3.4651	$17,326

Because the series of $5,000 payments is an annuity, the accountant can determine the present value with either of two shortcuts. As shown in the third column of Illustration 13–2, the total of the present values of $1 at 6% for 1 through 4 periods equals 3.4651. One shortcut multiplies this total of 3.4651 by the $5,000 annual payment to get the combined present value of $17,326. This shortcut requires only one multiplication instead of four.

The second shortcut uses an *annuity table* such as Table 13–2.[8] (Table 13–2 is taken from a more complete table in Appendix F at the end of the book.) Instead of having to take the sum of the individual present values from Table 13–1, you can go directly to the annuity table to find the present (table) value that relates to a specific number of payments and a specific interest rate. Then, you multiply this table value by the amount of the payment to find the present value of all the payments in the annuity.

To continue the example, the second shortcut proceeds as follows: Enter Table 13–2 on the row for four payments and go across until you reach the column for 6%; you will find the value 3.4651. This amount equals the present value of an annuity with four payments of $1, discounted at 6%. Then, multiply 3.4651 times $5,000 to get the $17,326 present value of the annuity.

---

[8]The formula for finding the Table values is: $\dfrac{1 - \dfrac{1}{(1 + i)^n}}{i}$

However, the present values in Table 13–2 can be found by adding the values of the individual payments in Table 13–1. (Because the tables show only four decimal places, there are some ± 0.0001 rounding differences between them.)

Table 13-2
Present Value of an
Annuity of $1

Payments	2%	4%	6%	8%	10%
1	0.9804	0.9615	0.9434	0.9259	0.9091
2	1.9416	1.8861	1.8334	1.7833	1.7355
3	2.8839	2.7751	2.6730	2.5771	2.4869
4	3.8077	3.6299	3.4651	3.3121	3.1699
5	4.7135	4.4518	4.2124	3.9927	3.7908
6	5.6014	5.2421	4.9173	4.6229	4.3553
7	6.4720	6.0021	5.5824	5.2064	4.8684
8	7.3255	6.7327	6.2098	5.7466	5.3349
9	8.1622	7.4353	6.8017	6.2469	5.7590
10	8.9826	8.1109	7.3601	6.7101	6.1446

Table header: **Rate**

COMPOUNDING PERIODS SHORTER THAN A YEAR

In the previous examples, the interest rates were applied to periods of one year. However, in many situations, interest is compounded over shorter periods. For example, the interest rate on bonds is usually described as an annual rate but the interest is actually paid every six months. As a result, the present value of the interest payments to be received from these bonds must be based on interest periods that are six months long.

To illustrate a calculation based on six-month interest periods, suppose that a borrower wants to know the present value of a series of ten $4,000 semiannual payments to be made over five years. These payments are to be discounted with an *annual* interest rate of 8%. Although the interest rate is described as an annual rate of 8%, it is actually a rate of 4% per six-month interest period. To find the present value of the series of $4,000 payments, enter Table 13–2 on row 10 and go across to the 4% column. The table value is 8.1109, and the present value of the annuity is $32,444 (8.1109 × $4,000).

Study Appendix F at the end of the book to learn more about present value concepts. The appendix includes more complete present value tables and provides future value tables. It also includes exercises that will help you understand discounting.

Progress Check

13–11 A company enters into an agreement to make four annual payments of $1,000 each, starting one year from now. The annual interest rate is 8%. The present value of these four payments is: *(a)* $2,923; *(b)* $2,940; *(c)* $3,312; *(d)* $4,000; *(e)* $6,733.

13–12 Suppose that a company has an option to pay either $10,000 after one year or $5,000 after six months and another $5,000 after one year. Which choice always has the smaller present value?

APPLYING PRESENT VALUE CONCEPTS TO LONG-TERM NOTES

Earlier in the chapter, we stated that accountants use present value concepts to measure liabilities and to assign or allocate interest expense to each reporting period in a liability's life. In doing this, the liability is initially measured as the present value of the future payments. Over the life of the note, the amount of interest allocated to each period equals the product of multiplying the original interest rate by the balance of the liability at the beginning of the period. The balance at any

LO 5

Describe how accountants use present value concepts in accounting for long-term notes and how liabilities may result from leasing assets.

point in time equals the original balance plus any allocated interest less any payments.[9]

Interest-Bearing Notes that Require a Single Payment

Suppose that a company buys equipment on January 2 with a fair market value of $45,000 by issuing an 8%, three-year note, with all of the interest paid at maturity. If the 8% interest is at the prevailing market rate, the face value of the note should be $45,000. The buyer records the purchase with this entry:

Jan.	2	Store Equipment	45,000.00	
		Notes Payable		45,000.00
		Issued a $45,000, three-year, 8% note payable for		
		store equipment.		

Over the life of the note, the issuer reports annual interest expense equal to the original interest rate times each year's beginning balance for the liability. Illustration 13–3 shows the interest allocation. Note that the interest is allocated by multiplying each year's beginning balance by the original 8% interest rate. Then, the interest is added to the beginning balance to find the ending balance, which then becomes the next year's beginning balance. Because the balance grows through compounding, the amount of interest allocated to each year increases over the life of the note. The final ending balance of $56,687 equals the original $45,000 borrowed plus the total interest of $11,687.

Noninterest-Bearing Notes

Earlier in the chapter, we described so-called noninterest-bearing notes, which include the interest in their initial face values. When a noninterest-bearing note is used to purchase an asset, the note's face value is greater than the asset's fair value. As a result, the asset and the note should be recorded at the asset's fair value or at the note's fair value, whichever is more clearly determinable. The note's fair value can be estimated by finding the present value of its payments discounted at the market interest rate when it was issued.

For example, suppose that Harborg Company buys machinery on January 2, 1996, by issuing a noninterest-bearing, five-year, $10,000 note payable. The company's managers conclude that their estimate of the asset's fair value is less reliable than is the current 10% interest rate available to the company.

When the note is issued, its fair value equals the present value of the $10,000 payment due after five years discounted at 10%. Table 13–1 shows us that the present value of 1 discounted at 10% for five years is 0.6209. Thus, the present (fair) value of the note is calculated as $10,000 × 0.6209 = $6,209. This is also the implied fair value of the asset. The following entry records the purchase:

---

[9]The liability's balance at any date equals the present value of all remaining future payments, discounted at the original interest rate.

Illustration 13–3   Allocation of Interest on a Note with All Interest Paid at Maturity

Beginning balance	$45,000	$48,600	$52,488
Interest rate	x 8%	x 8%	x 8%
Interest expense	$ 3,600	$ 3,888	$ 4,199
Ending balance	$48,600	$52,488	$56,687

```
1996
Jan.   2 | Machinery ...............................   6,209.00
           Discount on Notes Payable ...............   3,791.00
             Long-Term Notes Payable ..............
             Cash ..................................              10,000.00
           Exchanged a five-year noninterest-bearing note
           for a machine.
```

By recording the maturity value in one account and the discount in a contra account, the entry follows the typical approach of recording a noninterest-bearing note. In the entry, the $3,791 debit to Discount on Notes Payable equals the total amount of interest that must be allocated to the five years in the note's life.

In Illustration 13–4, we calculate each year's interest and show the effect of the allocation on the discount and the net liability. The net liability balance grows over the five years until it reaches the maturity amount of $10,000. Note also that the discount balance decreases to $0 after five years. Because the discount is gradually reduced to zero, this process is often referred to as *amortizing the discount.*

Notice that the process of calculating each year's interest is the same as it was in the previous discussion of interest-bearing notes that require a single payment. The net liability balance at the beginning of each year is multiplied by the 10% interest rate to determine the interest for the year.

The first year's interest and reduction of the discount are recorded when the accountant makes this year-end adjusting entry:

Illustration 13-4   Allocating Interest Expense over the Life of a Noninterest-Bearing Note

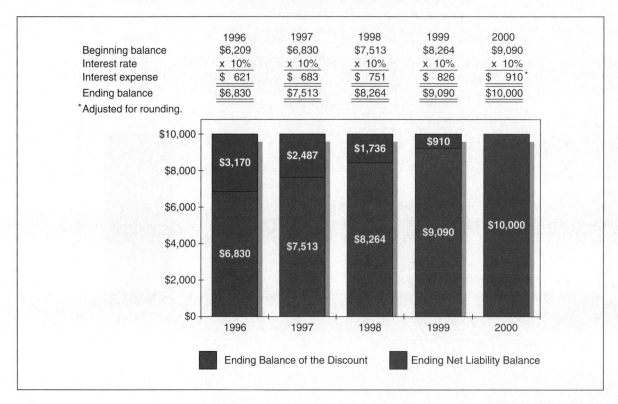

	1996	1997	1998	1999	2000
Beginning balance	$6,209	$6,830	$7,513	$8,264	$9,090
Interest rate	x 10%	x 10%	x 10%	x 10%	x 10%
Interest expense	$ 621	$ 683	$ 751	$ 826	$ 910*
Ending balance	$6,830	$7,513	$8,264	$9,090	$10,000

*Adjusted for rounding.

1996				
Dec.	31	Interest Expense	621.00	
		Discount on Notes Payable		621.00
		To record interest expense accrued on a		
		noninterest-bearing note.		

Similar entries are recorded at the end of each year until the balance of the discount account equals $0, and the net liability balance equals $10,000.

When the note matures on January 2, 2001, the issuer records the payment with this entry:

2001				
Jan.	2	Long-Term Notes Payable	10,000.00	
		Cash		10,000.00
		Paid noninterest-bearing note.		

LIABILITIES FROM LEASING

As an alternative to purchasing property, companies can lease it by agreeing to make a series of rental payments to the property owner, who is called the *lessor*. Because a lease gives the property's user (called the *lessee*) exclusive control over the property's usefulness, the lessee can use it to earn revenues. In addition, a lease creates a liability if it has essentially the same effect as purchasing the asset on credit.

According to the generally accepted accounting principles described in *CICA Handbook,* section 3065, "Leases," the lessee's financial statements must report a leased asset and a lease liability if the lease qualifies as a **capital lease.** The essence of a capital lease is that the lease agreement gives the lessee the risks and benefits normally associated with ownership. In general, a capital lease covers a number of years and creates a long-term liability that is paid off with a series of equal payments. For example, **Loblaw Companies Limited** reported that its capital leases for equipment and facilities covered assets with a cost of $88.1 million and a book value of $39.8 million as of December 31, 1994. The leases also involved liabilities of $65.6 million.

When a capital lease is created, the lessee recognizes a leased asset and amortizes it over its useful life. The lessee also recognizes a lease liability and allocates interest expense to the years in the lease. The interest allocation process is the same as we have seen for notes payable.

Leases that are not capital leases are called **operating leases.** With an operating lease, the lessee does not report the lease as an asset. The lessee's income statement reports rent expense and does not report either interest or depreciation expense.

Intermediate accounting textbooks describe more details about the characteristics of leases that cause them to be accounted for as capital or operating. They also describe the financial accounting practices used by the lessor and lessee for capital leases.

Progress Check

13-13   On January 1, 1996, Fairview Co. signed a $6,000 three-year note payable bearing 6% annual interest. The original principal and all interest is to be paid on December 31, 1998. The interest will compound every year. How much interest should be allocated to 1997? *(a)* $0; *(b)* $360; *(c)* $381.60; *(d)* $404.50.

13-14   Suppose that a company promises to pay a lender $4,000 at the end of four years. If the annual interest rate is 8% and the interest is included in the $4,000, what is the amount that the company originally borrowed?

13-15   Which one of the following requires the lessee to record a liability? *(a)* Operating lease; *(b)* Lessor; *(c)* Contingent liability; *(d)* Capital lease.

USING THE INFORMATION— TIMES FIXED INTEREST CHARGES EARNED

A company incurs interest expense when it issues notes or bonds and when it enters into capital leases. Many of these liabilities are long-term obligations that are likely to remain outstanding for a substantial period of time even if the company experiences a decline in sales. As a result, interest expense is often viewed as a fixed cost. That is, the amount of interest is not likely to fluctuate much as a result of changes in sales volume.

Although fixed costs can be advantageous when a company is growing, they create the risk that the company might not be able to pay them if sales decline. The following example shows a company's results for the current year and two possible outcomes for the next year:

LO 6

Calculate the number of times a company earns its fixed interest charges and describe what it reveals about a company's situation.

	Current Year	Next Year	
		If Sales Increase	If Sales Decrease
Sales	$600,000	$900,000	$300,000
Expenses (75% of sales)	450,000	675,000	225,000
Income before interest	$150,000	$225,000	$ 75,000
Interest expense (fixed)	60,000	60,000	60,000
Net income	$ 90,000	$165,000	$ 15,000

As we show in the table, expenses other than interest are projected to stay at 75% of sales. In contrast, the interest is expected to remain at $60,000 per year. Note in the second column that the company's income would nearly double if its sales increased by 50%. However, the company's profits would fall drastically if the sales decreased by 50%. These numbers show that a company's risk is affected by the amount of fixed interest charges that it incurs each year.

The risk created by these fixed expenses can be described numerically with the **times fixed interest charges earned** ratio. You can use the following formula to find the ratio:

$$\text{Times fixed interest charges earned} = \frac{\text{Income before interest}}{\text{Interest expense}}$$

For this company's current year, the income before interest is $150,000. Therefore, the ratio is $150,000/$60,000, which equals 2.5 times. This result suggests that the company faces a relatively low degree of risk. Its sales would have to go down by a large amount before the company would not be able to cover its interest expenses. This condition should provide comfort to the company's creditors and its owners.

Care must be taken in calculating the times fixed interest charges earned ratio for a corporation. Because interest is deducted in determining taxable income, the numerator for a corporation can be expressed as follows:

Income before interest = Net income + Interest expense + Income taxes expense

The times fixed interest charges earned ratio is best interpreted in light of information about the variability of the company's net income before interest. If this amount is stable from year to year, or is growing, the company can afford to take on some of the risk created by borrowing. However, if the company's income before interest varies greatly from year to year, fixed interest charges can increase the risk that the owner will not earn a return or that the company will be unable to pay the interest.

Progress Check

13-16 **The times fixed interest charges earned ratio**
   a. Equals interest expense divided by net income.
   b. Takes on a larger value as the amount of fixed interest charges gets larger.
   c. Is best interpreted in light of information about the variability of the company's net income before interest.

13-17 Two companies each have net income after interest of $100,000. First Company has fixed interest charges of $200,000 and Second Company has fixed interest charges of $40,000. Which one is in a more risky situation in terms of being affected by a drop in sales?

LO 1. Define liabilities, explain the difference between current and long-term liabilities, and describe the uncertainties related to some liabilities. Liabilities are probable future payments of assets or services that an entity is presently obligated to make as a result of past events. Current liabilities are due within one year or one operating cycle, whichever is longer. All other liabilities are long-term liabilities. Potential uncertainties about a liability include the identity of the creditor, the due date, and the amount to be paid.

LO 2. Describe how accountants record and report estimated liabilities such as warranties and income taxes, and how they report contingent liabilities. If an uncertain future payment depends on a likely future event and the amount can be reasonably estimated, the payment should be reported as a liability. The future payment must be described as a contingent liability if (*a*) the occurrence of the future event is not determinable, or (*b*) the event is likely but the amount of the payment cannot be reasonably estimated.

Liabilities for warranties and income taxes are recorded with estimated amounts to be paid. This practice recognizes the expenses in the time period that they are incurred. Deferred income taxes are recognized if temporary differences between GAAP and tax rules result in recording more or less income tax expense than the amount to be currently paid.

LO 3. Describe how accountants record and report short-term notes payable. Short-term notes payable may be interest-bearing, in which case the face value of the note equals the amount borrowed and the note specifies a rate of interest to be paid until maturity. Noninterest-bearing notes include interest in their face value; thus, the face value equals the amount to be paid when the note matures.

LO 4. Explain and calculate the present value of an amount to be paid at a future date and the present value of a series of equal amounts to be paid at future dates. The primary present value concept is that today's value of an amount of cash to be paid or received in the future is less than today's value of the same amount of cash to be paid or received today. Another present value concept is that interest is compounded, which means that the interest is added to the balance and used to determine interest for succeeding periods. An annuity is a series of equal payments occurring at equal time intervals.

LO 5. Describe how accountants use present value concepts in accounting for long-term notes, and how liabilities may result from leasing assets. Accountants may use present value concepts to determine the fair value of assets purchased in return for issuing debt. They also use present value concepts to allocate interest expense among the periods in a note's life by multiplying the note's beginning-of-period balance by the original interest rate. Noninterest-bearing notes are normally recorded with a discount account that is contra to the liability account. The balance of the discount account is amortized in the process of recognizing interest expense over the note's life.

Leases are an alternative to purchases as a means of gaining the use of assets. Capital leases give the lessee essentially the same risks and potential rewards as ownership. As a result, the leases and related lease obligations are recorded as assets and liabilities. Other leases, which are called operating leases, involve recording rent expense as the asset is used.

LO 6. Calculate the number of times a company earns its fixed interest charges and describe what it reveals about a company's situation. Times fixed interest charges earned is calculated by dividing a company's net income before interest by the amount of fixed interest charges incurred. This ratio describes the cushion that exists to protect the company's ability to pay interest and earn a profit for its owners against declines in its sales.

DEMONSTRATION PROBLEM

The following series of transactions and other events took place at the Kern Company during its calendar reporting year. Describe their effects on the financial statements by presenting the journal entries described in each situation.

a. Throughout September 1996, Kern sold $140,000 of merchandise that was covered by a 180-day warranty. Prior experience shows that the costs of fulfilling the warranty will equal 5% of the sales revenue. Calculate September's warranty expense and the increase in the warranty liability and show how it would be recorded with a September 30 adjusting entry. Also show the journal entry that would be made on October 8 to record an expenditure of $300 cash to provide warranty service on an item sold in September.

b. On October 12, Kern arranged with a supplier to replace an overdue $10,000 account payable by paying $2,500 cash and signing a note for the remainder. The note matured in 90 days and had a 12% interest rate. Show the entries that would be recorded on October 12, December 31, and January 10, 1997 (when the note matures).

c. Kern acquired a machine on December 1 by giving a $60,000 noninterest-bearing note due in one year. The market rate of interest for this type of debt was 10%. Show the entries that would be made when the note is created; as of December 31, 1996, and at maturity on December 1, 1997.

Planning the Solution

*   For *(a),* compute the warranty expense for September and record it with an estimated liability. Record the October expenditure as a decrease in the liability.

*   For *(b),* eliminate the liability for the account payable and create the liability for the note payable. Calculate the interest expense for the 80 days that the note is outstanding in 1996 and record it as an additional liability. Record the payment of the note, being sure to include the interest for the 10 days in 1997.

*   For *(c),* measure the cost of the machinery by finding the present value of the $60,000 cash expected to be paid when the note matures. Record the note at its face value, and use a contra-liability account to record the discount. Accrue 30 days' interest at December 31 by reducing the discount account. At maturity, the journal entry should record additional interest expense for 1997, eliminate the note payable account balance, and eliminate the discount account balance.

Solution to Demonstration Problem

a. Warranty expense = 5% × $140,000 = $7,000

Sept.	30	Warranty Expense	7,000.00	
		Estimated Warranty Liability		7,000.00
		To record warranty expense and liability at 5% of sales for the month.		
Oct.	8	Estimated Warranty Liability	300.00	
		Cash		300.00
		To record the cost of the warranty service.		

b. Interest expense for 1996 = 12% × $7,500 × 80/365 = $197.26
Interest expense for 1997 = 12% × $7,500 × 10/365 = $24.66

Oct.	12	Accounts Payable	10,000.00	
		Notes Payable		7,500.00
		Cash		2,500.00
		Paid $2,500 cash and gave a 90-day, 12% note to extend the due date on the account.		
Dec.	31	Interest Expense	197.26	
		Interest Payable		197.26
		To accrue interest on note payable.		
Jan.	10	Interest Expense	24.66	
		Interest Payable	197.26	
		Notes Payable	7,500.00	
		Cash		7,721.92
		Paid note with interest, including accrued interest payable.		

c. Cost of the asset = Present value of the note
Present value of the note = $60,000 × Table 13–1 value for
n = 1 and i = 10%
Present value of the note = $60,000 × 0.9091 = $54,546
Discount on the note = $60,000 − $54,546 = $5,454

Dec.	1	Machinery	54,546.00	
		Discount on Notes Payable	5,454.00	
		Notes Payable		60,000.00
		Exchanged a one-year, noninterest-bearing note for a machine.		

Interest expense for 1996 = 10% × $54,546 × 1/12 = $455
Interest expense for 1997 = $5,454 − $455 = $4,999

Dec.	31	Interest Expense	455.00	
		Discount on Notes Payable		455.00
		To accrue interest on noninterest-bearing note payable.		
1997 Dec.	1	Interest Expense	4,999.00	
		Notes Payable	60,000.00	
		Cash		60,000.00
		Discount on Notes Payable		4,999.00
		Paid noninterest-bearing note payable.		

GLOSSARY

Annuity a series of equal payments occurring at equal time intervals. p. 617

Capital lease a lease that gives the lessee the risks and benefits normally associated with ownership. p. 623

Deferred income tax payments of income taxes that are deferred until future years because of temporary differences between GAAP and tax rules. p. 607

Discount on note payable the difference between the face value of a noninterest-bearing note payable and the amount borrowed; represents interest that will be paid on the note over its life. p. 612

Estimated liability an obligation that is reported as a liability even though the amount to be paid is uncertain. p. 604

Noninterest-bearing note a note that does not have a stated rate of interest; the interest is included in the face value of the note. p. 612

Operating lease a lease that is not a capital lease. p. 623

Present value the amount that can be invested (borrowed) at a given interest rate to generate a total future investment (debt) that will equal the amount of a specified future receipt (payment). p. 615

Present value table a table that shows the present values of an amount to be received when discounted at various interest rates for various periods of time, or the present values of a series of equal payments to be received for a varying number of periods when discounted at various interest rates. p. 616

Times fixed interest charges earned the ratio of a company's income before interest and income taxes divided by the amount of interest charges; used to evaluate the risk of being committed to make interest payments when income varies. p. 624

Warranty an agreement that obligates the seller or manufacturer to repair or replace a product that fails to perform properly within a specified period. p. 604

SYNONYMOUS TERMS

Capital lease financing lease
Carrying value of a note book value of a note

Warranty guarantee

QUESTIONS

1. What is the difference between a current and a long-term liability?

2. What is an estimated liability?

3. What are the three important questions concerning the certainty of liabilities?

4. Suppose that a company has a facility located in an area where disastrous weather conditions often occur. Should it report a probable loss from a future disaster as a liability on its balance sheet? Why?

5. Why are warranty liabilities usually recognized on the balance sheet as liabilities even when they are uncertain?

6. What factors affect the present value of a future $2,000 payment?

7. How would a lease create an asset and a liability for the lessee?

8. What proportion of Geac Computer Corporation Limited's liabilities are long-term?

QUICK STUDY (Five-Minute Exercises)

Which of the following items would normally be classified as a current liability for a company that has a 14-month operating cycle?

a.   A note payable due in 18 months.

b.   Salaries payable.

c.   Bonds payable that mature in two years.

d.   A note payable due in 10 months.

e.   The portion of a long-term note that is due to be paid in 14 months.

On December 20, Compu sold a computer for $3,500 with a one-year warranty that covers parts and labour. Warranty expense was estimated at 2% of sales. On March 2, the computer was turned in for repairs covered under the warranty requiring $50 in parts and $30 of labour. Prepare the March 2 journal entry to record the warranty repairs.

On December 11, 1996, the Snyder Company borrowed $42,000 and signed a 60-day, 9% note payable with a face value of $42,000. *(a)* Calculate the accrued interest payable on December 31, and *(b)* present the journal entry to record the paying of the note at maturity.

Determine the amount that can be borrowed under each of the following circumstances:

a.   A promise to pay $50,000 in six years at an interest rate of 10%.

b.   An agreement made on January 2, 1996, to make four payments of $4,200 on January 2 of 1997 through 2000. The annual interest rate was 8%.

On January 1, 1996, a company borrowed $40,000 in exchange for an interest-bearing note. The note plus compounded interest at an annual rate of 12% is due on January 1, 1999. Determine the amount that the company will pay on the due date.

Calculate the times fixed interest charges earned for a company that has income before interest of $462,000 and interest expense of $98,000.

EXERCISES

The following list of items might appear as liabilities on the balance sheet of a company that has a two-month operating cycle. Identify the proper classification of each item. In the space beside each item write *C* if it is a current liability, an *L* if it is a long-term liability, or an *N* if it is not a liability.

___ *a.*   Wages payable.

___ *b.*   Notes payable in 60 days.

___ *c.*   Mortgage payable (payments due after next 12 months).

___ *d.*   Notes receivable in 90 days.

___ *e.*   Bonds payable (mature in 10 years).

___ *f.*   Mortgage payable (payments due in next 12 months).

___ *g.*   Notes payable in 6–12 months.

___ *h.*   Income taxes payable.

___ *i.*   Accounts receivable.

___ *j.*   Notes payable in 13–24 months.

Exercise 13–2
Warranty expense and liability
(LO 2)

Sassower Co. sold a computer to a customer on December 4, 1996, for $8,000 cash. Based on prior experience, the company expects to eventually incur warranty costs equal to 5% of this selling price. On January 18, 1997, the customer returned the computer for repairs that were completed on the same day. The cost of the repairs consisted of $198 for the materials taken from the parts inventory and $40 of labour that was fully paid with cash.

a.   How much warranty expense should the company report for December for this computer?

b.   How large is the warranty liability for this computer as of December 31, 1996?

c.   How much warranty expense should the company report for January for this computer?

d.   How large is the warranty liability for this computer as of January 31, 1997?

e.   Show the journal entries that would be made to record (1) the sale; (2) the adjustment as of December 31, 1996, to record the warranty expense; and (3) the repairs that occurred in January.

Exercise 13–3
Accounting for income taxes
(LO 2)

McKeag Corp. prepares interim financial statements each month. As part of the process, estimated income taxes are accrued each month as 30% of the company's income for that month. The estimated income taxes are paid in the next month for the amount accrued in the prior month. These facts are known about the last quarter of 1996:

a.   The company determined that the following amounts of net income occurred for these months:

        October 1996 . . . . . . $ 8,500
        November 1996   6,000
        December 1996   10,000

b.   After the tax return was completed in early January, the accountant determined that the Income Taxes Payable account balance should be $7,480 on December 31.

Required

1.   Determine the amount of the adjustment needed to produce the proper ending balance in the Income Taxes Payable account.

2.   Present the journal entries to record the adjustment to the Income Taxes Payable account upon completion of the return and to record the January 15 payment of the fourth-quarter taxes.

Exercise 13–4
Interest-bearing and noninterest-bearing notes payable
(LO 3)

The Knightwood Co. borrowed $50,000 on September 1, 1996, for 90 days at 8% interest by signing a note.

a.   On what date will this note mature?

b.   How much interest expense is created by this note?

c.   Suppose that the face value of the note equals the principal of the loan. Show the general journal entries to record issuing the note and paying it at maturity.

d.   Suppose that the face value of the note includes the principal of the loan and the interest to be paid at maturity. Show the general journal entries to record issuing the note and paying it at maturity.

The Shelby Co. borrowed $30,000 on December 1, 1996, for 90 days at 10% interest by signing a note.

a. On what date will this note mature?

b. How much interest expense is created by this note in 1995?

c. How much interest expense is created by this note in 1996?

d. Suppose that the face value of the note equals the principal of the loan. Show the general journal entries to record issuing the note, to accrue interest at the end of 1996, and to record paying the note at maturity.

e. Suppose that the face value of the note includes the principal of the loan and the interest to be paid at maturity. Show the general journal entries to record issuing the note, to accrue interest at the end of 1996, and to record paying the note at maturity.

Exercise 13–5
Interest-bearing and noninterest-bearing short-term notes payable with year-end adjustments
(LO 4)

On January 1, 1996, a company has agreed to pay $15,000 after three years. If the annual interest rate is 6%, determine how much cash the company can borrow with this promise. Present a three-column table that shows the beginning balance, interest, and ending balance for 1996, 1997, and 1998.

Exercise 13–6
Present value of a future payment and accumulating interest
(LO 4)

Find the amount of money that can be borrowed with each of the following promises:

Exercise 13–7
Present value of liabilities
(LO 4)

	Future Payment	Number of Years	Interest Rate
a.	$80,000	1	6%
b.	80,000	5	6
c.	80,000	5	8
d.	60,000	7	10
e.	10,000	1	2
f.	25,000	9	4

A company recently borrowed money and agreed to pay it back with a series of three annual payments of $10,000 each. The firm also borrowed cash and agreed to pay it back with a series of seven annual payments of $4,000 each. The annual interest rate for the loans was 10%.

Exercise 13–8
Present value of annuities
(LO 4)

a. Use Table 13–1 to find the present value of these two annuities.

b. Use Table 13–2 to find the present value of these two annuities.

A company borrowed cash on January 2, 1996, by promising to make four payments of $3,000 each at June 30, 1996; December 31, 1996; June 30, 1997; and December 31, 1997.

Exercise 13–9
Semiannual compounding
(LO 4)

a. How much cash was the company able to borrow if the interest rate was 12%, compounded semiannually?

b. How much cash was the company able to borrow if the interest rate was 16%, compounded semiannually?

c. How much cash was the company able to borrow if the interest rate was 20%, compounded semiannually?

The Carson Company purchased some machinery on March 10 that had a cost of $56,000. Show the journal entry that would record this purchase under these four separate situations:

Exercise 13–10
Recording an asset purchase in exchange for a note
(LO 5)

a. The company paid cash for the full purchase price.

b. The company gave an interest-bearing note for the full purchase price.

c. The company gave a noninterest-bearing one-year note for $61,600.

Exercise 13–11
Calculations concerning a noninterest-bearing note
(LO 5)

On January 2, 1996, the Brewster Co. acquired land by issuing a noninterest-bearing note for $20,000. The fair market value of the land was not reliably known, but the company knew that the market interest rate for the note was 6%. The note matures in three years on January 1, 1999.

a. What is the present value of the note at the time of the purchase?

b. What is the initial balance of the discount on the note payable?

c. Prepare a table that shows the amount of interest that will be allocated to each of the three years in the note's life and the ending balance of the net liability for each year.

d. Prepare a table that determines the ending balance of the discount on the note for each of the three years.

Exercise 13–12
Journal entries for a noninterest-bearing note
(LO 5)

Use the data in Exercise 13–11 to prepare journal entries for these dates:

a. January 2, 1996 (land purchase).

b. December 31, 1996 (accrual entry).

c. December 31, 1997 (accrual entry).

d. December 31, 1998 (accrual entry).

e. January 1, 1999 (the payment of the note).

Exercise 13–13
Times fixed interest charges earned
(LO 6)

Use the following information for a proprietorship to compute times fixed interest charges earned:

	Net Income or (Loss)	Interest Expense
a.	$ 85,000	$ 16,000
b.	85,000	40,000
c.	85,000	90,000
d.	240,000	120,000
e.	(25,000)	60,000
f.	96,000	6,000

PROBLEMS

Problem 13–1
Estimated product warranty liabilities
(LO 2)

On November 10, 1996, Bright Beam Co. began to buy and resell high-powered flashlights for $40 each. The flashlights are covered under a warranty that requires the company to replace any nonworking flashlight within 90 days. When a flashlight is returned, the company simply throws it away and mails a new one from inventory to the customer. The company's cost for a new flashlight is only $7. The manufacturer has advised the company to expect warranty costs to equal 8% of the total sales. These events occurred in 1996 and 1997:

1996

Nov. 15 Sold flashlights for $8,000 cash.

30 Recognized warranty expense for November with an adjusting entry.

Dec. 8 Replaced 15 flashlights that were returned under the warranty.

15 Sold flashlights for $22,000 cash.

29 Replaced 40 flashlights that were returned under the warranty.

31 Recognized warranty expense for December with an adjusting entry.

1997

Jan. 14   Sold flashlights for $11,000 cash.

    20   Replaced 63 flashlights that were returned under the warranty.

    31   Recognized warranty expense for January with an adjusting entry.

Required

1. How much warranty expense should be reported for November and December of 1996?

2. How much warranty expense should be reported for January 1997?

3. What is the balance of the estimated warranty liability as of December 31, 1996?

4. What is the balance of the estimated warranty liability as of January 31, 1997?

5   Prepare journal entries to record the transactions and adjustments.

The Northside Co. entered into the following transactions involving short-term liabilities during 1996 and 1997:

1996

Mar. 14   Purchased merchandise on credit from Pete Winston Co. for $12,500. The terms were 1/10, n/30.

Apr. 14   Replaced the account payable to Pete Winston Co. with a 60-day note bearing 10% annual interest. Northside paid $3,500 cash, with the result that the balance of the note was $9,000.

May 21   Borrowed $20,000 from Central Bank by signing an interest-bearing note for $20,000. The annual interest rate was 12%, and the note has a 90-day term.

?   Paid the note to Pete Winston Co. at maturity.

?   Paid the note to Central Bank at maturity.

Dec. 15   Borrowed $35,000 from Eastern Bank by signing a noninterest-bearing note for $36,035.62 that matures in 120 days. (This amount is based on a 9% interest rate.)

    31   Recorded an accrual adjusting entry for the interest on the note to Eastern Bank.

1997

?   Paid the note to Eastern Bank at maturity.

Problem 13–2
Transactions with short-term notes payable
(LO 4)

Required

1. Determine the maturity dates of the three notes just described.

2. Determine the interest due at maturity for the three notes.

3. Determine the interest to be recorded in the adjusting entry at the end of 1996.

4. Determine the interest to be recorded in 1997.

5. Present journal entries for all the preceding events and adjustments.

Sherlock Enterprises is negotiating the purchase of a new building. The seller has offered Sherlock the following three payment plans:

> Plan A: $100,000 cash would be paid at once.
> Plan B: $114,000 cash would be paid after two years.
> Plan C: $58,000 cash would be paid at the end of each of the next two years.

Problem 13–3
Present values of possible liabilities
(LO 4, 5)

The company's owner knows that the market interest rate is 8%.

Required

1. Use the market interest rate to determine present value of each of the three possible payment plans.
2. Show the journal entry that would be made to record the acquisition under each of the three plans. (Assume that the note's face value would include all interest to be paid.)
3. Identify the plan that creates the lowest cost for the company.
4. Assume that Plan B is adopted and the present value of the cash flows is used as the building's cost. Determine the amount of interest expense that will be reported in each of the two years in the note's life.

Problem 13–4
Exchanging a noninterest-bearing note for a plant asset
(LO 5)

On January 2, 1996, Watts Company acquired an item of equipment by issuing a $55,000 noninterest-bearing five-year note payable on December 31, 2000. A reliable cash price for the equipment was not readily available. The market annual rate of interest for similar notes was 4% on the day of the exchange.

Required

(Round all amounts in your answers to the nearest whole dollar.)

1. Determine the initial net liability created by issuing this note.
2. Present a table showing the calculation of the amount of interest expense allocated to each year the note is outstanding and the carrying amount of the net liability at the end of each of those years.
3. Present a table that shows the balance of the discount at the end of each year the note is outstanding.
4. Prepare general journal entries to record the purchase of the equipment, the accrual of interest expense at the end of 1996 and 1997, and the accrual of interest expense and the payment of the note on December 31, 2000.
5. Show how the note should be presented on the balance sheet as of December 31, 1998.

Problem 13–5
Understanding times fixed interest charges earned
(LO 7)

These condensed income statements are for two companies:

Adams Co.		Beene Co.	
Sales	$100,000	Sales	$100,000
Variable expenses (65%) . . .	65,000	Variable expenses (85%) . . .	85,000
Net income before interest . .	$ 35,000	Net income before interest . .	$ 15,000
Interest (fixed)	25,000	Interest (fixed)	5,000
Net income	$ 10,000	Net income	$ 10,000

Required

Preparation component:

1. What is the times fixed interest charges earned for Adams Co.?
2. What is the times fixed interest charges earned for Beene Co.?
3. What happens to each company's net income if sales increase by 20%?
4. What happens to each company's net income if sales increase by 40%?

5. What happens to each company's net income if sales increase by 80%?

6. What happens to each company's net income if sales decrease by 10%?

7. What happens to each company's net income if sales decrease by 20%?

8. What happens to each company's net income if sales decrease by 50%?

Analysis component:

9. Comment on what you observe and relate it to the ratio values that you found in questions 1 and 2.

Collie Company sells a single product subject to a six-month warranty that covers replacement parts but not labour. The company uses a periodic inventory system to account for merchandise. Prepare journal entries to record the following transactions completed by the company during the month of April:

Problem 13–6
Product warranty expense
(LO 2)

Apr. 2 Purchased 1,200 units of merchandise for $30 per unit, paying cash.

   3 Purchased $3,900 of spare parts for making repairs to merchandise that is expected to be returned for warranty work.

   8 Sold 500 units of merchandise for $60 per unit, receiving cash.

   11 Repaired 30 units of merchandise that customers returned under the warranty. Replacement parts cost $750, and the customers paid $570 for labour.

   18 Sold 600 units of merchandise for $65 per unit.

   21 Repaired 22 units of merchandise under the product warranty. Replacement parts cost $506, and the customers paid $396 for labour.

   29 Recorded warranty expense for April. Past experience shows that 4% of the units sold require warranty work, and the average cost of replacement parts is $24 per unit returned. Average labour charges are $18.50.

Prepare general journal entries to record these transactions of Davies Company:

Problem 13–7
Journalizing notes
payable transactions
(LO 3)

1996

Jan. 8 Purchased merchandise on credit from Grant Company, invoice dated January 7, terms 2/10, n/60, $15,600.

Feb. 5 Borrowed money at First Provincial Bank by discounting our own $25,000 note payable for 60 days at 12%. Since the note matures before the end of the year, the discount should be charged to Interest Expense.

Mar. 10 Gave Grant Company $2,100 cash and a $13,500, 60-day, 12% note to secure an extension on our account that was due.

Apr. 5 Paid the note discounted at First Provincial Bank on February 5.

May 10 Paid the note given Grant Company on March 10.

Nov. 1 Borrowed money at First Provincial Bank by discounting our own $30,000 note payable for 90 days at 14%.

Dec. 16 Borrowed money at InterCity Bank by giving a $25,000, 60-day, 15% note payable.

Dec. 31 Made an adjusting entry to record interest on the November 1 note to First Provincial Bank.

   31 Made an adjusting entry to record the accrued interest on the December 16 note to InterCity Bank.

1997

Jan. 30   Paid the November 1 note to First Provincial Bank. Also recorded interest expense related to the note.

Feb. 14   Paid the note given InterCity Bank on December 16.

Problem 13–8
Present values of
alternative payment
patterns
(LO 4)

Tropical Adventures is negotiating with a naval architect and shipyard in planning the construction of a 90-foot trimaran that Tropical Adventures expects to acquire and place in charter service. The yacht will be completed and ready for service four years hence. If Tropical Adventures pays for the yacht on completion (Payment Plan A), it will cost $500,500. However, two alternative payment plans are available. Plan B would require an immediate payment of $365,650. Plan C would require four annual payments of $105,850, the first of which would be made one year hence. In evaluating the three alternatives, the management of Tropical Adventures has decided to assume an interest rate of 10%.

Required

Calculate the present value of each payment and indicate which plan Tropical Adventures should follow.

Problem 13–9
Exchanging a noninterest-
bearing note for a capital
asset
(LO 5)

On January 2, 1996, a company gave its own $150,000 noninterest-bearing, five-year note payable in exchange for a machine the cash price of which was not readily determinable. The market rate for interest on such notes on the day of the exchange was 8% annually.

Required

(*Round all amounts in your answers to the nearest whole dollar.*)

1. Prepare a form with the following column headings and calculate and fill in the required amounts for the five years the note is outstanding.

Year	Face Amount of Note	Unamortized Discount at Beginning of Year	Beginning-of-Year Carrying Amount	Discount to Be Amortized Each Year	Unamortized Discount at the End of Year	End-of-Year Carrying Amount

2. Prepare general journal entries to record (*a*) the acquisition of the machine, (*b*) the discount amortized at the end of each year, and (*c*) the payment of the note on January 2, 2001.

3. Show how the note should appear on the December 31, 1998, balance sheet.

Problem 13–10
Installment notes
(LO 5)

On June 30, 1996, Potter Company borrowed $450,000 at the bank by signing a five-year, 12% installment note. The terms of the note require equal semiannual payments beginning December 31, 1996.

Required

(*Round all amounts in your answers to the nearest whole dollar.*)

1. Calculate the amount of the installment payments. (Use Table 13–2 on page 619.)

2. Prepare a table with column headings like the table below. Complete the table for the Potter Company note.

Period Ending	Beginning of Period Principal Balance	Periodic Payment	Interest Expense for Period	Principal Portion of Payment	End of Period Balance

3. Prepare general journal entries to record the first and the last payments on the note.

4. Assume that the note does not require equal payments. Instead, assume the note requires payments of accrued interest plus equal amounts of principal. Prepare general journal entries to record the first and the last payments on the note.

This problem requires you to demonstrate your understanding of noninterest-bearing notes, interest allocation, and present values by explaining how it would be possible to use incomplete information to discover other facts about a loan. Suppose that a company borrowed some cash on January 1, 1996, with a four-year noninterest-bearing note payable. A year later, on December 31, 1996, you know only these two items of information:

Problem 13–11
Analytical essays
(LO 5)

a.   The net liability (net of the remaining discount) as of December 31, 1996.

b.   The interest expense reported for the year ended December 31, 1996.

Write brief explanations of the calculations you would make to identify the following additional facts about the loan:

1. The amount borrowed on January 1, 1996.

2. The market interest rate on January 1, 1996.

3. The amount of interest that will be reported for 1997.

After a long analysis, the manager of the Greenfield Company has decided to acquire a truck through a long-term noncancellable lease instead of buying it outright. Under the terms of the lease, Greenfield must make regular monthly payments throughout the four-year term of the lease and provide for all the operating costs, including gas, insurance, and repairs. At the end of the lease, the lessor will simply give Greenfield the legal title to the truck. Describe why Greenfield should account for the lease as if it is essentially a purchase.

Problem 13–12
Analytical essay
(LO 5)

PROVOCATIVE PROBLEMS

Sam Ishikawa is the new manager of accounting and finance for a medium-sized manufacturing company. Now that the end of the year is approaching, his problem is determining whether and how to describe some of the company's contingencies in the financial statements. The general manager, Sue Peebles, raised objections to two specific contingencies in his preliminary proposal.

Provocative Problem 13–1
Business communications case
(LO 2)

First, Peebles objected to the proposal to report nothing about a patent infringement suit that the company has filed against a competitor. The manager's written comment on his proposal was, "We KNOW that we have them cold on this one! There is no way that we're not going to win a very large settlement!"

Second, she objected to his proposal to recognize an expense and a liability for warranty service on units of a new product that was just introduced in the company's fourth quarter. Her scribbled comment on this point was "There is no way that we can estimate this warranty cost. Besides, we don't owe anybody anything until the products break down and are returned for service. Let's just report an expense if and when we do the repairs."

Develop a short written response for Ishikawa to the objections raised by the general manager in a one-page memorandum dated December 15.

Provocative Problem 13–2

Financial statement analysis case

(LO 1, 2, 5, 6)

Geac

Answer the following questions by using the information in the financial statements and notes for Geac Computer Corporation Limited that appear in Appendix I at the end of the book:

1. Examine the company's balance sheet to find the amount of long-term debt that it had on April 30, 1994. Also, what is the amount of the company's current notes payable?

2. Examine the statement of operations to find the amount of interest expense during fiscal years 1994 and 1993. Assume that the interest expense represents interest paid. Calculate times fixed interest charges earned for both years and comment on any significant change in the ratio.

3. Does the note on "Commitments and Contingencies" provide information that allows the reader to determine whether the company has entered into any operating or capital leases?

4. What evidence would you look for as an indication that the company has any temporary differences between the income reported on the income statement and the income reported on its tax return? Can you find any evidence of these differences for Geac?

ANALYTICAL AND REVIEW PROBLEMS

A&R Problem 13–1

El Flighter, ace lefthander with the York Bluebirds, is negotiating for renewal of his contract. Prior to making an offer to Flighter, George Megabucks—owner of the team—asks you to check out three alternatives he intends to present to the pitcher. George is only willing to offer a three-year contract but is offering three different payment schemes as follows:

a. $300,000 payable at the end of each year for 10 years.

b. $750,000 payable at the end of each year for 3 years.

c. $1,800,000 payable on signing the three-year contract.

Required

Prepare journal entries for each of the alternatives as of the date of signing the contract and at the end of the first year. Also indicate balance sheet presentation as of the end of the first year. Assume:

1. The going rate of interest is 12%.

2. The company amortizes assets on a straight-line basis.

On September 1, 1996, Chang Company acquired a machine by paying $15,000 cash and signing a two-year note that carried a face amount of $90,000 due at the end of the two-year period; the note did not specify interest. Assume the going rate of interest for this company for this type of loan is 12%. The accounting period ends December 31.

A & R Problem 13–2

Required

Give the entry to record the purchase of the machine and complete a tabulation as follows (round amounts to nearest dollar):

	Straight-Line Method	Interest Method
1. Cash to be paid at maturity	$_____	$_____
2. Total interest expense	$_____	$_____
3. Interest expense on income statement for 1996	$_____	$_____
4. Amount of the liability reported on balance sheet at end of 1996	$_____	$_____
5. Amortization expense for 1996 (assume straight-line, partial year, no residual value, and useful life of five years)	$_____	$_____

CONCEPT TESTER

Test your understanding of the concepts introduced in this chapter by completing the following crossword puzzle.

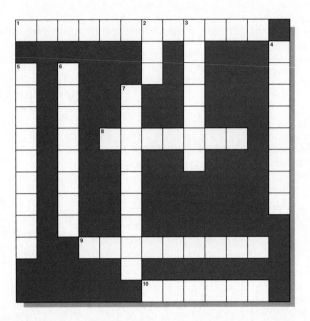

Across Clues

1. The amount, at a given interest rate, that will equate to an amount in the future (2 words).

8. A type of lease that gives the lessee the risks and benefits of ownership.

9. An obligation that is reported even though the amount to be paid is uncertain (1st of 2 words; also see 7 down).

10. Payments of income taxes that arise in future periods due to timing differences (2nd of 3 words; also see 6 down, 2 down).

Down Clues

2. Payments of income taxes that arise in future periods (3rd of 3 words; also see 6 down, 10 across).

3. A series of equal payments occurring at equal time intervals.

4. An agreement that obligates a manufacturer to repair or replace a product that fails to perform.

5. The type of lease that is not a capital lease.

6. Payments of income taxes that arise in future periods due to timing differences (1st of 3 words; also see 10 across, 2 down).

7. An obligation that is reported even though the amount to be paid is uncertain (2nd of 2 words; also see 9 across).

COMPREHENSIVE PROBLEM

The Schwartz Exterminator Company provides pest control services and sells extermination products manufactured by other companies. The following six-column table contains
the company's unadjusted trial balance as of December 31, 1996.

**Schwartz Exterminator
Company
(Review of Chapters
1–13)**

SCHWARTZ EXTERMINATOR COMPANY
Six-column Table
December 31, 1996

	Unadjusted Trial Balance		Adjustments		Adjusted Trial Balance	
Cash	$ 15,000					
Accounts receivable	24,000					
Allowance for doubtful accounts		$ 3,064				
Merchandise inventory	18,000					
Trucks	22,000					
Accum. amortization, trucks		0				
Equipment	75,000					
Accum. amortization, equipment		21,500				
Accounts payable		6,000				
Estimated warranty liability		1,200				
Unearned extermination services revenue		0				
Long-term notes payable		60,000				
Discount on notes payable	15,898					
Arnold Schwartz, capital		58,800				
Arnold Schwartz, withdrawals	21,000					
Extermination services revenue		70,000				
Interest earned		436				
Sales		135,000				
Purchases	81,000					
Amortization expense, trucks	0					
Amortization expense, equip.	0					
Wages expense	45,000					
Interest expense	0					
Rent expense	16,000					
Bad debts expense	0					
Miscellaneous expenses	6,202					
Repairs expense	11,000					
Utilities expense	5,900					
Warranty expense	0					
Totals	$356,000	$356,000				

The following information applies to the company and its situation at the end of the year:

a.   The bank reconciliation as of December 31, 1996, includes these facts:

Balance per bank	$13,200
Balance per books	15,000
Outstanding cheques	2,600
Deposit in transit	3,500
Interest earned	44
Service charges (miscellaneous expense) ..	17

Included with the bank statement was a canceled cheque that the company had failed to record. (This information allows you to determine the amount of the cheque, which was a payment of an account payable.)

b.   An examination of customers' accounts shows that accounts totaling $2,500 should be written off as uncollectible. In addition, the owner has determined that the ending balance of the Allowance for Doubtful Accounts account should be $4,300.

c.   A truck was purchased and placed in service on July 1, 1996. Its cost is being amortized with the straight-line method using these facts and predictions:

Original cost	$22,000
Expected salvage value	6,000
Useful life (years)	4

d.   Two items of equipment (a sprayer and an injector) were purchased and put into service early in January 1994. Their costs are being amortized with the straight-line method using these facts and predictions:

	Sprayer	Injector
Original cost	$45,000	$30,000
Expected salvage value	3,000	2,500
Useful life (years)	8	5

e.   On October 1, 1996, the company was paid $2,640 in advance to provide monthly service on an apartment complex for one year. The company began providing the services in October. When the cash was received, the full amount was credited to the Extermination Services Revenue account.

f.   The company offers a warranty for all of the products it sells. The expected cost of providing warranty service is 2% of sales. No warranty expense has been recorded for 1996. All costs of servicing products under the warranties in 1996 were properly debited to the liability account.

g.   The $60,000 long-term note is a five-year, noninterest-bearing note that was given to Second National Bank on December 31, 1994. The market interest rate on the date of the loan was 8%.

h.   The ending inventory of merchandise was counted and determined to have a cost of $16,300.

Required

1.   Use the provided information to determine the amounts of the following items:

   a.   The correct ending balance of Cash and the amount of the omitted cheque.

   b.   The correct ending balance of the Allowance for Doubtful Accounts.

   c.   The annual amortization expense for the truck that was acquired during the year (calculated to the nearest month).

d. The annual amortization expense for the two items of equipment that were used during the year.

e. The correct ending balances of the Extermination Services Revenue and Unearned Extermination Services Revenue accounts.

f. The correct ending balances of the accounts for Warranty Expense and the Estimated Warranty Liability.

g. The correct ending balances of the accounts for Interest Expense and the Discount on Notes Payable.

h. The cost of goods sold for the year.

2. Use the results of requirement 1 to complete the six-column table by first entering the appropriate adjustments for items *a* through *g* and then completing the adjusted trial balance columns. (Hint: item *b* requires two entries.)

3. Present general journal entries to record the adjustments entered on the six-column table.

4. Present a single-step income statement, a statement of changes in owner's equity, and a classified balance sheet.

ANSWERS TO PROGRESS CHECKS

13–1 Liabilities are probable future payments of assets or services that an entity is presently obligated to make as a result of past transactions or events.

13–2 No; an expected future payment is not a liability unless an obligation was created by a past event or transaction.

13–3 In most cases, a liability due in 15 months should be classified as long-term. However, it should be classified as a current liability if the company's operating cycle is at least 15 months long.

13–4 *a*

13–5 *a*

13–6 A corporation would accrue an income tax liability for its interim financial statements because income tax expense is incurred when income is earned, not just at the end of the year.

13–7 *b*

13–8 A future payment should be reported as a contingent liability if the uncertain future event is likely and the amount of the payment can be reasonably estimated.

13–9 A creditor might want to have a note payable instead of an account payable in order to (*a*) start charging interest and/or (*b*) have positive evidence of the debt and its terms.

13–10 The amount borrowed was $1,000 ($1,050 − $50). The rate of interest was 5% ($50/$1,000) for six months, which is an annual rate of 10%.

13–11 *c*
3.3121 × $1,000 = $3,312

13–12 The option of paying $10,000 after a year always has a lower present value. In effect, it postpones paying the first $5,000 by six months. As a result, the present value of the delayed payment is always less.

13–13 *c*
[$6,000 + ($6,000 × .06)] × .06 = $381.60

13–14 $4,000 × 0.7350 = $2,940

13–15 *d*

13–16 *c*

13–17 The risk can be described by the ratio that shows the number of times the fixed interest charges are covered by the net income *before* interest. The ratio for the first company is only 1.5 [($100,000 + $200,000)/$200,000], while the ratio for the second company is 3.5 [($100,000 + $40,000)/$40,000]. This analysis shows that First Company is more susceptible to the risk of incurring a loss if its sales decline.

Partnership Accounting

As a business enterprise becomes more complex, it needs more human and financial resources. A partnership allows the owners to pool their talents and funds to achieve more than they could individually. A partnership also creates needs for special accounting information.

*F*ive weeks had passed since the instructor asked Karen White and Mark Smith to prepare for a discussion on partnerships. They read the partnership chapter and other related material that came to their attention. They concluded that for their presentation White would take a pro and Smith a con position on the partnership form of business organization.

In summation of positions, White and Smith agreed that:

The partnership form of business organization has many pitfalls and should be entered into only as a last resort. Entry should be made with extreme caution and with as many protective features as can be negotiated.

LEARNING OBJECTIVES

After studying Chapter 14, you should be able to:

1. **List the characteristics of a partnership and explain the concepts of mutual agency and unlimited liability in a partnership.**
2. **Allocate partnership earnings to partners *(a)* on a stated fractional basis, *(b)* in the partners' capital ratio, and *(c)* through the use of salary and interest allowances.**
3. **Prepare entries for *(a)* the sale of a partnership interest, *(b)* the admission of a new partner by investment, and *(c)* the retirement of a partner by the withdrawal of partnership assets.**
4. **Prepare entries required in the liquidation of a partnership.**
5. **Define or explain the words and phrases listed in the chapter glossary.**

The early chapters of this book were devoted, for the most part, to the single proprietorship with only passing references to partnerships and corporations. In this chapter, we examine the partnership form of business in greater detail. The partnership form is widely used, especially in businesses where the owners know each other well. Many professional businesses, including public accounting firms, are organized as partnerships.

CHARACTERISTICS OF PARTNERSHIPS

LO 1

List the characteristics of a partnership and explain the concepts of mutual agency and unlimited liability in a partnership.

Many businesses, such as small retail and service businesses, are organized as partnerships. Also, many professional practitioners—physicians, lawyers, and public accountants—have traditionally organized their practices as partnerships. The provincial Partnership Acts and the Civil Code, with minor variations, define a **partnership** as "the relation which subsists between persons carrying on a business in common with a view of profit." Another definition of a partnership is "an association of two or more competent persons under a contract to combine some or all of their property, labour, and skills in the operation of a business." Both of these definitions say something about the legal nature of a partnership. However, the nature of the partnership form of business becomes clearer when you understand some of the specific features that characterize partnerships.

A Voluntary Association

A partnership is a voluntary association between the partners. All that is required to form a partnership is that two or more legally competent people (that is, people who are of age and of sound mental capacity) must agree to be partners. Their agreement becomes a **partnership contract.** Although it should be in writing, the contract is binding even if it is only expressed orally.

Limited Life

The life of a partnership is always limited. Death, bankruptcy, or anything that takes away the ability of one of the partners to enter into or fulfill a contract automatically ends a partnership. In addition, a partnership may be terminated at will by any one of the partners. Before agreeing to join a partnership, you should understand clearly two important characteristics of a partnership: mutual agency and unlimited liability.

Mutual Agency

Generally, the relationship between the partners in a partnership involves **mutual agency**. Under normal circumstances, every partner is a fully authorized agent of the partnership. As its agent, a partner can commit or bind the partnership to any contract that is within the apparent scope of the partnership's business. For example, a partner in a merchandising business can sign contracts that bind the partnership to buy merchandise, lease a store building, borrow money, or hire employees. These activities are all within the scope of the business of a merchandising firm. On the other hand, a partner in a law firm, acting alone, cannot bind his or her partners to a contract to buy merchandise for resale or rent a retail store building. These actions are not within the normal scope of a law firm's business.

Partners may agree to limit the power of any one or more of the partners to negotiate certain contracts for the partnership. Such an agreement is binding on the partners and on outsiders who know that it exists. However, it is not binding on outsiders who do not know that it exists. Outsiders who are not aware of the agreement have the right to assume that each partner has normal agency powers for the partnership.

Because mutual agency exposes all partners to the risk of unwise actions by any one partner, people should carefully evaluate potential partners before agreeing to join a partnership. The importance of this advice is underscored by the fact that most partnerships are also characterized by unlimited liability.

Unlimited Liability of Partners

When a partnership cannot pay its debts, the creditors normally can satisfy their claims from the *personal* assets of the partners. Also, if some partners do not have enough assets to meet their share of the partnership's debts, the creditors can turn to the assets of the remaining partners who are able to pay. Because partners may be called on to pay all the debts of the partnership, each partner is said to have **unlimited liability** for the partnership's debts. Mutual agency and unlimited liability are the main reasons why most partnerships have only a few members.

Limited Partnerships and Limited Liability Partnerships

Partnerships in which all of the partners have unlimited liability are called **general partnerships**. Sometimes, however, individuals who want to invest in a partnership are not willing to accept the risk of unlimited liability. Their needs may be met by using a **limited partnership**. A limited partnership has two classes of partners, general and limited. At least one partner has to be a **general partner** who must assume unlimited liability for the debts of the partnership. The remaining **limited partners** have no personal liability beyond the amounts that they invest in the business. Usually, a limited partnership is managed by the general partner or partners. The limited partners have no active role except for major decisions specified in the partnership agreement.

A similar form of partnership in some jurisdictions allowing professionals such as lawyers to use is the **limited liability partnership**. This type of partnership is designed to protect innocent partners from malpractice or negligence claims that result from the acts of another partner. When a partner provides service that results in a malpractice claim, that partner has personal liability for the claim. The remaining partners who were not responsible for the actions that resulted in the claim are not personally liable for the claim. However, all partners have personal liability for other partnership debts.

ADVANTAGES AND DISADVANTAGES OF A PARTNERSHIP

Limited life, mutual agency, and unlimited liability are disadvantages of a partnership. Yet, there are other reasons why a partnership may be a preferred form of business organization. A partnership has the advantage of being able to bring together more money and skills than a single proprietorship. A partnership is easier to organize than a corporation. Also, a partnership may escape some of the federal and provincial regulations and taxes that are imposed on corporations. Finally, partners may act without having to hold shareholders' or directors' meetings, which are required of a corporation.

PARTNERSHIP ACCOUNTING

Accounting for a partnership does not differ from accounting for a proprietorship except for transactions that directly affect the partners' equity. Because ownership rights in a partnership are divided among the partners, partnership accounting:

- Uses a capital account for each partner.
- Uses a withdrawals account for each partner.
- Allocates net incomes or losses to the partners according to the provisions of the partnership agreement.

When partners invest in a partnership, their capital accounts are credited for the invested amounts. Partners' withdrawals of assets are debited to their withdrawals accounts. In closing the accounts at the end of the year, the partners' capital accounts are credited or debited for their shares of the net income or loss. Finally, the withdrawals account of each partner is closed to that partner's capital account. These closing procedures are like those used for a single proprietorship. The only difference is that separate capital and withdrawals accounts are maintained for each partner.

NATURE OF PARTNERSHIP EARNINGS

Because they are its owners, partners are not employees of the partnership. If partners devote their time and services to the affairs of their partnership, they are understood to do so for profit, not for salary. Therefore, when the partners calculate the net income of a partnership, salaries to the partners are not deducted as expenses on the income statement. However, when the net income or loss of the partnership is allocated among the partners, the partners may agree to base part of the allocation on salary allowances that reflect the relative values of service provided by the partners.

Partners are also understood to have invested in a partnership for profit, not for interest. Nevertheless, partners may agree that the division of partnership earnings should include a return based on their invested capital. For example, if one

partner contributes five times as much capital as another, it is only fair that this fact be considered when earnings are allocated among the partners. Thus, a partnership agreement may provide for interest allowances based on the partners' capital balances. Like salary allowances, interest allowances are not expenses to be reported on the income statement.

DIVISION OF EARNINGS

LO 2

Allocate partnership earnings to earnings to partners *(a)* on a stated fractional basis, *(b)* in the partners' capital ratio, and *(c)* through the use of salary and interest allowances.

In the absence of a contrary agreement, the law states that the income or loss of a partnership should be shared equally by the partners. However, partners may agree to any method of sharing. If they agree on how they will share income but say nothing about losses, then losses are shared in the same way as income.

Several methods of sharing partnership earnings can be used. Three frequently used methods divide earnings: (1) on a stated fractional basis, (2) in the ratio of capital investments, or (3) using salary and interest allowances and any remainder in a fixed ratio.

Earnings Allocated on a Stated Fractional Basis

An easy way to divide partnership earnings is to give each partner a fraction of the total. All that is necessary is for the partners to agree on the fractional share that each will receive. For example, assume that the partnership agreement of B. A. Jones and S. A. Meyers states that Jones will receive two-thirds and Meyers will receive one-third of the partnership earnings. If the partnership's net income is $30,000, the earnings are allocated to the partners and the Income Summary account is closed with the following entry:

Dec.	31	Income Summary	30,000.00	
		B. A. Jones, Capital		20,000.00
		S. A. Meyers, Capital		10,000.00
		To close the Income Summary account and allocate the earnings.		

When earnings are shared on a fractional basis, the fractions may reflect the relative capital investments of the partners. For example, suppose that B. Donner and H. Flack formed a partnership and agreed to share earnings in the ratio of their investments. Because Donner invested $50,000 and Flack invested $30,000, Donner will receive five-eighths of the earnings ($50,000/$80,000) while Flack will receive three-eighths of the earnings ($30,000/$80,000).

Salaries and Interest as Aids in Sharing

As we have mentioned, the service contributions and capital contributions of the partners often are not equal. If the service contributions are not equal, salary allowances can compensate for the differences. Or, when capital contributions are not equal, interest allowances can compensate for the unequal investments. When both investment and service contributions are unequal, the allocation of net incomes and losses may include both interest and salary allowances.

For example, in Kathy Stanley and David Breck's new partnership, Stanley is to provide services that they agree are worth an annual salary of $36,000. Breck

Illustration 14-1
Sharing Income When
Income Exceeds
Salary and Interest
Allowances

	Share to Stanley	Share to Breck	Income to Be Allocated
Total net income			$70,000
Allocated as salary allowances:			
Stanley	$36,000		
Breck		$24,000	
Total allocated as salary allowances			60,000
Balance of income after salary allowances ..			$10,000
Allocated as interest:			
Stanley (10% on $30,000)	3,000		
Breck (10% on $10,000)		1,000	
Total allocated as interest			4,000
Balance of income after salary and			
interest allowances			$ 6,000
Balance allocated equally:			
Stanley	3,000		
Breck		3,000	
Total allocated equally			6,000
Balance of income			$ 0
Shares of the partners	$42,000	$28,000	
Percentages of total net income	60%	40%	

is less experienced in the business, so his service contribution is worth only $24,000. Also, Stanley will invest $30,000 in the business and Breck will invest $10,000. To compensate Stanley and Breck fairly in light of the differences in their service and capital contributions, they agree to share incomes or losses as follows:

1. Annual salary allowances of $36,000 to Stanley and $24,000 to Breck.
2. Interest allowances equal to 10% of each partner's beginning-of-year capital balance.
3. The remaining balance of income or loss is to be shared equally.

Note that the provisions for salaries and interest in this partnership agreement are called *allowances*. These allowances are not reported on the income statement as salaries and interest expense. They are only a means of splitting up the net income or net loss of the partnership.

Under the Stanley and Breck partnership agreement, a first year's net income of $70,000 is shared as shown in Illustration 14–1. Notice that Stanley gets $42,000, or 60% of the income, while Breck gets $28,000, or 40%.

In Illustration 14–1, notice that the $70,000 net income exceeds the salary and interest allowances of the partners. However, the method of sharing agreed to by Stanley and Breck must be followed even if the net income is smaller than the salary and interest allowances. For example, if the first year's net income was $50,000, it would be allocated to the partners as shown in Illustration 14–2. Notice that this circumstance provides Stanley with 64% of the total income, while Breck gets only 36%.

	Share to Stanley	Share to Breck	Income to Be Allocated
Total net income			$ 50,000
Allocated as salary allowances:			
Stanley	$36,000		
Breck		$24,000	
Total allocated as salary allowances			60,000
Balance of income after salary allowances ..			$(10,000)
Allocated as interest:			
Stanley (10% on $30,000)	3,000		
Breck (10% on $10,000)		1,000	
Total allocated as interest			4,000
Balance of income after salary and interest allowances			$(14,000)
Balance allocated equally:			
Stanley	(7,000)		
Breck		(7,000)	
Total allocated equally			(14,000)
Balance of income			$ 0
Shares of the partners	$32,000	$18,000	
Percentages of total net income	64%	36%	

Illustration 14–2
Sharing Income When
Interest and Salary
Allowances Exceed
Income

A net loss would be shared by Stanley and Breck in the same manner as the $50,000 net income. The only difference is that the income-and-loss-sharing procedure would begin with a negative amount of income because of the net loss. After the salary and interest allowances, the remaining balance to be allocated equally would then be a larger negative amount.

Progress Check

14–1 A partnership is automatically terminated in the event *(a)* the partnership agreement is not in writing; *(b)* a partner dies; or *(c)* a partner exercises mutual agency.

14–2 Mixon and Reed form a partnership by contributing $70,000 and $35,000 respectively. They agree to an interest allowance equal to 10% of each partner's capital balance at the beginning of the year with the remaining income to be shared equally.

14–3 What does the term *unlimited liability* mean when it is applied to a partnership?

PARTNERSHIP FINANCIAL STATEMENTS

In most respects, partnership financial statements are like those of a single proprietorship. On the balance sheet of a partnership, the owner's equity section often shows the separate capital account balance of each partner. The **statement of changes in partners' equity** shows the total capital balances at the beginning of the period, any additional investments made by the partners, the net income or loss of the partnership, withdrawals by the partners, and the ending capital balances. Usually, this statement shows these changes for each partner's capital account and includes the allocation of income among the partners.

Illustration 14–3
A Statement of
Changes in Partners'
Equity

STANLEY AND BRECK
Statement of Changes in Partners' Equity
For Year Ended December 31, 19—

		Stanley		Breck	Total
Beginning capital balances			$ –0–	$ –0–	$ –0–
Plus:					
Investments by owners			30,000	10,000	40,000
Net income:					
Salary allowances	$36,000			$24,000	
Interest allowances	3,000			1,000	
Balance	(7,000)			(7,000)	
Total net income			32,000	18,000	50,000
Total			$62,000	$28,000	$90,000
Less partners' withdrawals			(20,000)	(12,000)	(32,000)
Ending capital balances			$42,000	$16,000	$58,000

For example, recall that Stanley and Breck began their partnership by making investments of $30,000 and $10,000, respectively. During the first year of operations, in which the partnership earned $50,000, assume that Stanley withdrew $20,000 and Breck withdrew $12,000. The statement of changes in partners' equity appears in Illustration 14–3. The inclusion of salary and interest allowances and the allocation of the balances are generally not reported in such a statement. However, the detail in Illustration 14–3 is shown to demonstrate how the division of net income is attained.

WITHDRAWAL OR ADDITION OF A PARTNER

Prepare entries for *(a)* the sale of a partnership interest, *(b)* the admission of a new partner by investment, and *(c)* the retirement of a partner by the withdrawal of partnership assets.

A partnership is based on a contract between specific individuals. Therefore, when a partner withdraws from a partnership, the old partnership ceases to exist. Nevertheless, the business may continue to operate as a new partnership among the remaining partners.

The withdrawal of a partner from a partnership may take place in two ways. First, the withdrawing partner may sell his or her interest to another person who pays for the interest by transferring cash or other assets to the withdrawing partner. Second, cash or other assets of the partnership may be distributed to the withdrawing partner in settlement of his or her interest in the partnership.

When a new partner is admitted to a partnership, the old partnership technically ends and is replaced by a new partnership. Similar to the withdrawal of a partner, there are two ways a new partner may be admitted to an existing partnership: First, the new partner may purchase an interest directly from one or more of its partners. In other words, the new partner may pay cash to one or more of the existing partners in exchange for an interest in the partnership. Second, a new partner may join an existing partnership by investing cash or other assets in the business.

Sale of a Partnership Interest

Assume that the Abbott, Burns, and Camp partnership owes no liabilities and has the following assets and owners' equity:

Assets		Owners' Equity	
Cash	$ 3,000	Abbott, capital	$ 5,000
Other assets	12,000	Burns, capital	5,000
		Camp, capital	5,000
Total assets	$15,000	Total owners' equity	$15,000

Camp's equity in this partnership is $5,000. If Camp sells this equity to Davis for $7,000, Camp is selling a $5,000 recorded interest in the partnership assets. The entry on the partnership books to transfer the equity is

Feb.	4	Camp, Capital	5,000.00	
		Davis, Capital		5,000.00
		To transfer Camp's equity in the partnership to Davis.		

After this entry is posted, the assets and owners' equity of the new partnership are

Assets		Owners' Equity	
Cash	$ 3,000	Abbott, capital	$ 5,000
Other assets	12,000	Burns, capital	5,000
....		Davis, capital	5,000
Total assets	$15,000	Total owners' equity	$15,000

Two aspects of this transaction are especially important. First, the $7,000 Davis paid to Camp is not recorded in the partnership books. Camp sold and transferred a $5,000 recorded equity in the partnership assets to Davis. The entry that records the transfer is a debit to Camp, Capital, and a credit to Davis, Capital, for $5,000. Furthermore, the entry is the same whether Davis pays Camp $7,000, or $70,000. The amount is paid directly to Camp. Because the partnership is not a party to the transaction, its assets and total equity are not affected by the transaction.

The second important aspect of this transaction is the question of whether Davis's purchase of Camp's interest qualifies Davis as a new partner. In fact, Abbott and Burns must agree if Davis is to become a partner. Abbott and Burns cannot prevent Camp from selling the interest to Davis. But Abbott and Burns do not have to accept Davis as a partner. If Abbott and Burns agree to accept Davis, a new partnership is formed and a new contract with a new income-and-loss-sharing ratio must be drawn.

What if either Abbott or Burns refuses to accept Davis as a partner? Under the partnership acts, Davis gets Camp's share of partnership income and losses. And if the partnership is liquidated, Davis gets Camp's share of partnership assets. However, Davis gets no voice in the management of the firm until being admitted as a partner.

14–4 **PQR are partners. Q sells his interest to his son. Are P and R obliged to take the son into the partnership?**

14–5 **KRJ are partners. With the agreement of K and R, J sells his interest to Z. However, J does not disclose to K and R the amount he received. Is he within his right to withhold such information?**

14–6 **MNO are partners. With the agreement of N and O, M sells her interest to P. P assumes that her sharing of income will be the same as M enjoyed. Do you agree with her assumption?**

Investing Assets in an Existing Partnership

Instead of purchasing the equity of an existing partner, an individual may gain an equity by investing assets in the business. The invested assets then become the property of the partnership. For example, assume that the partnership of Evans and Gage has assets and owners' equity as follows:

Assets		Owners' Equity	
Cash	$ 3,000	Evans, capital.	$20,000
Other assets	37,000	Gage, capital	20,000
Total assets	$40,000	Total owners' equity	$40,000

Also, assume that Evans and Gage have agreed to accept Hart as a partner with a one-half interest in the business on his investment of $40,000. This entry records Hart's investment:

Mar.	2	Cash	40,000.00	
		Hart, Capital		40,000.00
		To record the investment of Hart.		

After the entry is posted, the assets and owners' equity of the new partnership appear as follows:

Assets		Owners' Equity	
Cash	$43,000	Evans, capital.	$20,000
Other assets	37,000	Gage, capital	20,000
		Hart, capital.	40,000
Total assets	$80,000	Total owners' equity	$80,000

In this case, Hart has a 50% equity in the assets of the business. However, he does not necessarily have a right to one-half of its net income. The sharing of incomes and losses is a separate matter on which the partners must agree. As you learned earlier in the chapter, the sharing of profits and losses may be in the ratio of the partners' relative capital contributions. However, the method of sharing also may depend on other factors.

A Bonus to the Old Partners

Sometimes, when the current value of a partnership is greater than the recorded amounts of equity, the partners may require an incoming partner to give a bonus for the privilege of joining the firm. For example, Judd and Kirk operate a partnership business, sharing its earnings equally. The partnership's accounting records show that Judd's recorded equity in the business is $38,000 and Kirk's recorded equity is $32,000. Judd and Kirk agree to accept Lee's $50,000 investment in the business in return for a one-third share of the partnership's earnings and a one-third equity in net assets. Lee's equity is determined with a calculation as follows:

Equities of the existing partners ($38,000 + $32,000) ..	$ 70,000
Investment of the new partner	50,000
Total partnership equity	$120,000
Equity of Lee (⅓ of total)	$ 40,000

Notice that although Lee invested $50,000 in the partnership, his equity in the recorded net assets of the partnership is only $40,000. The $10,000 difference usually is described as a bonus allocated to the existing partners (Judd and Kirk). Therefore, this entry records Lee's investment:

May	15	Cash	50,000.00	
		Lee, Capital		40,000.00
		Judd, Capital		5,000.00
		Kirk, Capital		5,000.00
		To record the investment of Lee.		

Notice that the $10,000 difference between the $50,000 invested by Lee and the $40,000 credited to his capital account is shared by Judd and Kirk according to their income-and-loss-sharing ratio. Such a bonus is always shared by the old partners in their income-and-loss-sharing ratio. This ratio is used because the bonus compensates the old partners for increases in the worth of the partnership that have not yet been recorded as income.

Recording Goodwill

As discussed previously, when a new partner's investment exceeds his or her equity in the partnership's net assets, the entry to record the new partner's admission normally allocates a bonus to the existing partners. Occasionally, however, firms use an alternative method to record the admission of a new partner. The alternative method involves recording goodwill on the books of the partnership. The debit to Goodwill is matched with credits that increase the equities of the existing partners.

The goodwill method of recording a new partner's admission would be used only if the evidence indicates that future earnings of the partnership are large enough to justify the increased partnership equity. Evidence of such future earnings might be provided by a historical record of earnings that are consistently in excess of the average for the industry.

In practice, goodwill is seldom recognized upon the admission of a new partner. Instead, the bonus method usually is used.

Bonus to the New Partner

Sometimes, the members of an existing partnership may be very eager to bring a new partner into their firm. The business may need additional cash or the new partner may have exceptional abilities or business contacts that will increase profits. Thus, the old partners may be willing to give the new partner a larger equity in the business than the amount of his or her investment. In this case, the old partners give a bonus to the new partner.

For example, Jay Moss and Mike Owen are partners with capital account balances of $30,000 and $18,000, respectively. They share incomes and losses in a 2:1 ratio. Anxious to have Kay Pitt join their partnership, the partners will grant her a one-fourth equity in the firm if she invests $12,000. If Pitt accepts, her equity in the new firm is calculated as follows:

Equity of the existing partners ($30,000 + $18,000) ..	$48,000
Investment of the new partner	12,000
Total equity in the new partnership	$60,000
Equity of Pitt (¼ of total)	$15,000

This entry records Pitt's investment:

June	1	Cash	12,000.00	
		Moss, Capital ($3,000 × ⅔)	2,000.00	
		Owen, Capital ($3,000 × ⅓)	1,000.00	
		Pitt, Capital		15,000.00
		To record the investment of Pitt.		

Note that Pitt's bonus is contributed by the old partners in their income-and-loss-sharing ratio. Also remember that Pitt's one-fourth equity does not necessarily entitle her to one-fourth of the earnings of the business. The sharing of income and losses is a separate matter for agreement by the partners.

Withdrawal of a Partner

When a new partnership is formed, the contract should include the procedures to follow when a partner retires from the partnership. These procedures often state that a withdrawing partner shall withdraw assets equal to the current value of the

partner's equity. To accomplish this, the procedures may require an audit of the accounting records and a revaluation of the partnership assets. The revaluation places the assets on the books at current values. It also causes the partners' capital accounts to reflect the current value of their equity.

For example, assume that Blue is retiring from the partnership of Smith, Blue, and Short. The partners have always shared incomes and losses in the ratio of one-half to Smith, one-fourth to Blue, and one-fourth to Short. Their partnership agreement provides for an audit and asset revaluation on the retirement of a partner. Just prior to the audit and revaluation, their balance sheet shows the following assets and owners' equity:

Assets			Owners' Equity	
Cash		$11,000	Smith, capital	$22,000
Merchandise inventory		16,000	Blue, capital	10,000
Equipment	$20,000		Short, capital	10,000
Less accum. amort.	5,000	15,000		
Total assets		$42,000	Total owners' equity	$42,000

The audit and appraisal indicate that the merchandise inventory is overvalued by $4,000. Also, due to market changes, the partnership's equipment should be valued at $25,000, less accumulated amortization of $8,000. The entries to record these revaluations are

Oct.	31	Smith, Capital	2,000.00	
		Blue, Capital	1,000.00	
		Short, Capital	1,000.00	
		Merchandise Inventory		4,000.00
		To revalue the inventory.		
	31	Equipment	5,000.00	
		Accumulated Amortization, Equipment		3,000.00
		Smith, Capital		1,000.00
		Blue, Capital		500.00
		Short, Capital		500.00
		To revalue the equipment.		

Note in these entries that the partners share the amount of the revaluations in their income-and-loss-sharing ratio. This is fair because revaluations of assets are actually gains and losses. If the partnership were not terminated, these gains and losses would sooner or later show up on the income statement as increases and decreases in net income. The revaluation simply records the effect of the gains and losses earlier than would have occurred.

After the entries revaluing the partnership assets are recorded, the balance sheet for the Smith, Blue, and Short partnership is as follows:

Assets			Owners' Equity	
Cash		$11,000	Smith, capital.	$21,000
Merchandise inventory . .		12,000	Blue, capital	9,500
Equipment	$25,000		Short, capital	9,500
Less accum. amort. . .	8,000	17,000		
Total assets		$40,000	Total owners' equity	$40,000

After the revaluation, if Blue retires and takes cash equal to his revalued equity, this entry records the withdrawal:

Oct.	31	Blue, Capital	9,500.00	
		Cash		9,500.00
		To record the withdrawal of Blue.		

In withdrawing, Blue does not have to take cash in settlement of his equity. He may take any combination of assets to which the partners agree, or he may take the new partnership's promissory note. Also, the withdrawal of Blue generally creates a new partnership between the remaining partners. Therefore, a new partnership contract and a new income-and-loss-sharing agreement may be required.

Withdrawing Partner Takes Fewer Assets than Recorded Equity

Sometimes, when a partner retires, the remaining partners may not wish to revalue the assets on the books of the partnership. Nevertheless, they must determine the current values of the partnership assets to establish the amount of assets to be taken by the retiring partner. For example, the partners may agree that the assets are overvalued. As a result, the retiring partner should receive assets of less value than the book value of his or her equity. Also, even if the assets are not overvalued, a retiring partner may be willing to take less than the current value of his or her equity just to get out of the partnership.

When a partner retires and takes assets of less value than his or her recorded equity, the partner in effect leaves a portion of the equity in the business. The remaining partners share the unwithdrawn equity portion in accordance with their income-and-loss-sharing ratio. For example, assume that partners Black, Brown, and Green share incomes and losses in a 2:2:1 ratio. Their assets and equities are as follows:

Assets		Owners' Equity	
Cash	$ 5,000	Black, capital.	$ 6,000
Merchandise inventory	9,000	Brown, capital	6,000
Store equipment	4,000	Green, capital	6,000
Total assets	$18,000	Total owners' equity	$18,000

Brown is anxious to withdraw from the partnership and offers to take $4,500 in cash in settlement for his equity. Black and Green agree to the $4,500 withdrawal, and Brown retires. This entry records the retirement:

Mar.	4	Brown, Capital	6,000.00	
		Cash		4,500.00
		Black, Capital		1,000.00
		Green, Capital		500.00
		To record the withdrawal of Brown.		

In retiring, Brown withdrew $1,500 less than his recorded equity. This is divided between Black and Green in their income-and-loss-sharing ratio. The income-and-loss-sharing ratio of the original partnership was Black, 2; Brown, 2; and Green, 1. Therefore, the ratio for sharing between Black and Green was 2:1, and the unwithdrawn book equity of Brown is shared by Black and Green in this ratio.

Withdrawing Partner Takes More Assets than Recorded Equity

There are two common reasons why a retiring partner might withdraw more assets than his or her recorded equity: First, the partnership assets may be undervalued on the books. Second, the continuing partners may want to encourage the retiring partner to withdraw by giving up assets of greater value than the retiring partner's recorded equity.

When assets are undervalued, the partners may not wish to change the recorded values. A retiring partner allowed to withdraw assets of greater value than that partner's recorded equity is, in effect, withdrawing his or her own equity plus a portion of the continuing partners' equities.

For example, assume that partners Jones, Thomas, and Finch share incomes and losses in a 3:2:1 ratio. The assets and owners' equity of the partnership are as follows:

Assets		Owners' Equity	
Cash	$ 5,000	Jones, capital	$ 9,000
Merchandise inventory	10,000	Thomas, capital	6,000
Equipment	3,000	Finch, capital	3,000
Total assets	$18,000	Total owners' equity	$18,000

Finch wishes to withdraw from the partnership. Jones and Thomas plan to continue the business. The partners agree that some of the partnership's assets are undervalued, but they do not wish to increase the recorded values. They further agree that if current values were recorded, the asset total would be increased by $6,000 and the equity of Finch would be increased by $1,000. Therefore, the partners agree that $4,000 is the proper value for Finch's equity and that amount of cash may be withdrawn. This entry records the withdrawal:

May	7	Finch, Capital	3,000.00	
		Jones, Capital	600.00	
		Thomas, Capital	400.00	
		Cash		4,000.00
		To record the withdrawal of Finch.		

DEATH OF A PARTNER

A partner's death automatically dissolves a partnership. As a result, the deceased partner's estate is entitled to receive the amount of his or her equity. The partnership contract should contain provisions for settlement in case a partner dies. Included should be provisions for *(a)* an immediate closing of the books to determine earnings since the end of the previous accounting period and *(b)* a method for determining and recording current values for the assets and liabilities. After these steps are taken, the remaining partners and the deceased partner's estate must agree to a disposition of the deceased partner's equity. This may involve selling the equity to the remaining partners or to an outsider, or it may involve the withdrawal of assets in settlement. We explained the appropriate entries for both cases in the previous paragraphs.

LIQUIDATIONS

LO 4

Prepare entries required in the liquidation of a partnership.

When a partnership is liquidated, its business is ended. The assets are converted into cash, and the creditors are paid. The remaining cash is then distributed to the partners, and the partnership is dissolved. **Partnership liquidations** may follow a variety of different steps. However, we limit the following discussion to three typical situations.

All Assets Are Sold at a Net Gain

One typical partnership liquidation is the situation in which all of the partnership assets are converted into cash at a net gain. Then the cash is distributed and the partnership is dissolved. The following example shows the necessary accounting entries to be made under these conditions.

Ottis, Skinner, and Parr have operated a partnership for a number of years, sharing incomes and losses in a 3:2:1 ratio. Due to several unsatisfactory conditions, the partners decide to liquidate as of December 31. On that date, the books are closed, the income from operations is transferred to the partners' capital accounts, and the partnership's balance sheet appears as follows:

Assets		Liabilities and Owners' Equity	
Cash	$10,000	Accounts payable	$ 5,000
Merchandise inventory	15,000	Ottis, capital	15,000
Other assets	25,000	Skinner, capital	15,000
		Parr, capital	15,000
		Total liabilities and	
Total assets	$50,000	owners' equity	$50,000

In a liquidation, some gains of losses normally result from the sale of noncash assets. These losses and gains are called *losses and gains from liquidation.* Just like any other net incomes or losses, the partners share the losses and gains from liquidation in their income-and-loss-sharing ratio. Assume, for example, Ottis, Skinner, and Parr sell their inventory for $12,000 and their other assets for $34,000. This entry records the sales and the net gain allocation:

Jan.	12	Cash	12,000.00	
		Loss or Gain from Liquidation	3,000.00	
		Merchandise Inventory		15,000.00
		Sold the inventory at a loss.		
	15	Cash	34,000.00	
		Other Assets		25,000.00
		Loss or Gain from Liquidation		9,000.00
		Sold the other assets at a profit.		
	15	Loss or Gain from Liquidation	6,000.00	
		Ottis, Capital		3,000.00
		Skinner, Capital		2,000.00
		Parr, Capital		1,000.00
		To allocate the net gain from sale of assets to the partners in their 3:2:1 income-and-loss-sharing ratio.		

Notice in the last entry that the losses and gains from liquidation were shared in the partners' income-and-loss-sharing ratio. In solving liquidation problems, do not make the mistake of allocating the losses and gains in the ratio of the partners' capital balances.

After the merchandise inventory and other assets of Ottis, Skinner, and Parr are sold and the net gain is allocated, a new balance sheet shows the following:

Assets		Liabilities and Owners' Equity	
Cash	$56,000	Accounts payable	$ 5,000
		Ottis, capital	18,000
		Skinner, capital	17,000
		Parr, capital.	16,000
		Total liabilities and	
Total assets	$56,000	owners' equity	$56,000

Observe that the one asset, cash of $56,000, exactly equals the sum of the liabilities and the equities of the partners.

After partnership assets are sold and the gain or loss shared, the realized cash is distributed to the proper parties. Because creditors have first claim, they are paid first. After the creditors are paid, the remaining cash is divided among the partners. Each partner has the right to cash equal to his or her equity or, in other words, cash equal to the balance of his or her capital account. These entries record the final cash payments and distribution to Ottis, Skinner, and Parr:

Jan.	15	Accounts Payable	5,000.00	
		Cash		5,000.00
		To pay the claims of the creditors.		
	15	Ottis, Capital	18,000.00	
		Skinner, Capital	17,000.00	
		Parr, Capital	16,000.00	
		Cash		51,000.00
		To distribute the remaining cash to the partners according to their capital account balances.		

Notice that after gains and losses are shared and the creditors are paid, each partner receives cash equal to the balance remaining in his or her capital account. The partners receive these amounts because cash is the only remaining partnership asset and a partner's capital account balance represents the partner's equity in that asset. In making the entry to distribute cash to the partners, be sure that you do not make the mistake of distributing it in the partners' income-and-loss-sharing ratio. Gains and losses from liquidations are allocated according to the income-and-loss-sharing ratio; but cash must be distributed to the partners in relation to their capital account balances.

All Assets Are Sold at a Net Loss: Each Partner's Capital Account Is Sufficient to Absorb His or Her Share of the Loss

In a liquidation, the partnership sometimes sells its assets at a net loss. For example, assume that the Ottis, Skinner, and Parr partnership does not sell its assets at a profit. Instead, assume that they sell the inventory for $10,000 and the other assets for $12,000. These entries record the sales and loss allocation:

Jan.	12	Cash	10,000.00	
		Loss or Gain on Liquidation	5,000.00	
		Merchandise Inventory		15,000.00
		Sold the inventory at a loss.		
	15	Cash	12,000.00	
		Loss or Gain on Liquidation	13,000.00	
		Other Assets		25,000.00
		Sold the other assets at a loss.		
	15	Ottis, Capital	9,000.00	
		Skinner, Capital	6,000.00	
		Parr, Capital	3,000.00	
		Loss or Gain on Liquidation		18,000.00
		To allocate the loss from sale of assets to the partners in their income-and-loss-sharing ratio.		

After the entries are posted, a balance sheet shows that the partnership cash exactly equals the liabilities and the equities of the partners:

Assets		Liabilities and Owners' Equity	
Cash	$32,000	Accounts payable	$ 5,000
		Ottis, capital	6,000
		Skinner, capital	9,000
		Parr, capital	12,000
Total assets	$32,000	Total liabilities and owners' equity	$32,000

The following entries record the distribution of the cash to the proper parties:

Jan.	15	Accounts Payable	5,000.00	
		Cash		5,000.00
		To pay the partnership creditors.		
	15	Ottis, Capital	6,000.00	
		Skinner, Capital	9,000.00	
		Parr, Capital	12,000.00	
		Cash		27,000.00
		To distribute the remaining cash to the partners according to the balances of their capital accounts.		

Notice again that after losses are shared and creditors are paid, the partners receive the remaining cash in the ratio of their capital account balances.

All Assets Are Sold at a Net Loss: A Partner's Capital Account Is Not Sufficient to Cover His or Her Share of the Loss

Sometimes the liquidation losses allocated to a partner exceed that partner's capital account balance. In such cases, the partner must, if possible, cover the deficit by paying cash into the partnership. For example, contrary to the situations described in the previous illustrations, assume that the Ottis, Skinner, and Parr partnership sells its merchandise for $3,000 and sells its other assets for $4,000. These entries record the sales and the loss allocation:

Jan.	12	Cash	3,000.00	
		Loss or Gain on Liquidation	12,000.00	
		Merchandise Inventory		15,000.00
		Sold the inventory at a loss.		
	15	Cash	4,000.00	
		Loss or Gain on Liquidation	21,000.00	
		Other Assets		25,000.00
		Sold the other assets at a loss.		
	15	Ottis, Capital	16,500.00	
		Skinner, Capital	11,000.00	
		Parr, Capital	5,500.00	
		Loss or Gain on Liquidation		33,000.00
		To allocate the loss from sale of assets to the partners in their income-and-loss-sharing ratio.		

After posting the entry to allocate the loss, the capital account of Ottis has a $1,500 debit balance and appears as follows:

Otis, Capital

Date		Explanation	Debit	Credit	Balance
Dec.	31	Balance			15,000.00
Jan.	15	Share of loss on sale	16,500.00		1,500.00 dr.

The partnership agreement states that one-half of all losses or gains should be allocated to Ottis. Therefore, since Ottis's capital account balance is not large enough to absorb his share of the loss, he is obligated to pay $1,500 into the partnership to cover the deficit, or debit balance. If Ottis is able to pay, this entry records the receipt:

Dec.	31	Cash	1,500.00	
		Ottis, Capital		1,500.00
		To record the additional investment of Ottis to cover his share of loss.		

After the $1,500 is received, the partnership has $18,500 in cash. The following entries record the cash distributions to the proper parties:

Jan.	15	Accounts Payable	5,000.00	
		Cash		5,000.00
		To pay the partnership creditors.		
	15	Skinner, Capital	4,000.00	
		Parr, Capital	9,500.00	
		Cash		13,500.00
		To distribute the remaining cash to the partners according to the balances of their capital accounts.		

When a partnership's liquidation loss creates a debit balance in one partner's capital account balance, that partner may be unable to make up the deficit. In such cases, since each partner has unlimited liability, the deficit must be borne by the remaining partner or partners. For example, assume that Ottis is unable to pay the $1,500 necessary to cover the deficit in his capital account. If Ottis is unable to pay, his deficit must be shared by Skinner and Parr in their income-and-loss-sharing ratio. The partners share incomes and losses in the ratio of Ottis, 3; Skinner, 2; and Parr, 1. Therefore, Skinner and Parr share in a 2:1 ratio. This means that Skinner and Parr must share the $1,500 by which Ottis's share of the loss exceeded his capital account balance in a 2:1 ratio. Normally, the defaulting partner's deficit is transferred to the capital accounts of the remaining partners. This is accomplished for Ottis, Skinner, and Parr with the following entry:

Jan.	15	Skinner, Capital	1,000.00	
		Parr, Capital	500.00	
		Ottis, Capital		1,500.00
		To transfer the deficit of Ottis to the capital accounts of Skinner and Parr.		

After the deficit is transferred, the capital accounts of the partners appear as in Illustration 14–4. These entries record the final payments to creditors and distribution to the partners:

Jan.	15	Accounts Payable	5,000.00	
		Cash		5,000.00
		To pay the partnership creditors.		
	15	Skinner, Capital	3,000.00	
		Parr, Capital	9,000.00	
		Cash		12,000.00
		To distribute the remaining cash to the partners according to their capital account balances.		

Illustration 14–4 Allocating Liquidation Loss and Partner's Deficit to Capital Accounts

Otis, Capital

Date		Explanation	Debit	Credit	Balance
Dec.	31	Balance			15,000.00
Jan.	15	Share of loss on sale	16,500.00		1,500.00 dr.
	15	Deficit to Skinner and Parr		1,500.00	–0–

Skinner, Capital

Date		Explanation	Debit	Credit	Balance
Dec.	31	Balance			15,000.00
Jan.	15	Share of loss on sale	11,000.00		4,000.00
	15	Deficit to Skinner and Parr	1,000.00		3,000.00

Parr, Capital

Date		Explanation	Debit	Credit	Balance
Dec.	31	Balance			15,000.00
Jan.	15	Share of loss on sale	5,500.00		9,500.00
	15	Deficit to Skinner and Parr	500.00		9,000.00

Note that Ottis's inability to meet his loss share now does not relieve him of liability. If he becomes able to pay at some future time. Skinner and Parr may collect the full $1,500 from him. Skinner may collect $1,000, and Parr, $500.

The sharing of an insolvent partner's deficit by the remaining partners in their original income-and-loss-sharing ratio is generally regarded as equitable. In England, however, in 1904 in the case of *Garner* v. *Murray,* Judge Joyce ruled that the debit balance of the insolvent partner's capital account is a personal debt due to the other partners and to be borne by them in the ratio of their capital account balances immediately prior to liquidation.

While *Garner* v. *Murray* still appears to be good law, it is considered by most to be inequitable. The decision applies only when the partnership agreement does not cover this situation. It is therefore important to provide in the partnership agreement for the sharing of a partner's debit balance by the remaining partners in their income-and-loss-sharing ratio.

THE PARTNERSHIP AGREEMENT

After studying this chapter, you should appreciate White's and Smith's concluding statement on page 645. The partnership form of business organization is indeed replete with pitfalls. It is, therefore, extremely important that the partnership agreement or contract address possible eventualities, however remote they may seem at the time. The enthusiasm generated by embarking on a new venture should not cause the partners to overlook the importance of the content of the partnership agreement.

Progress Check

14–7   Under what conditions would the existing partners offer a new partner a bonus?

14–8   Why would a new partner's investment exceed his/her equity in a partnership?

14–9   On liquidation of ABC, C's capital balance ends up with a $1,000 debit balance. How is this amount closed out?

LO 1. List the characteristics of a partnership and explain the concepts of mutual agency and unlimited liability in a partnership. A partnership is a voluntary association between the partners that is based on a contract. The life of a partnership is limited by agreement or by the death or incapacity of a partner. Normally, each partner can act as an agent of the other partners and commit the partnership to any contract within the apparent scope of its business. All partners in a general partnership are personally liable for all the debts of the partnership. Limited partnerships include one or more general partners plus one or more (limited) partners whose liabilities are limited to the amount of their investments in the partnership. The risk of becoming a partner results in part from the fact that partnership characteristics include mutual agency and unlimited liability.

LO 2. Allocate partnership earnings to partners (a) on a stated fractional basis, (b) in the partners' capital ratio, and (c) through the use of salary and interest allowances. A partnership's net incomes or losses are allocated to the partners according to the terms of the partnership agreement. The agreement may specify that each partner will receive a given fraction, or that the allocation of incomes and losses will reflect salary allowances and/or interest allowances. When salary and/or interest allowances are granted, the residual net income or loss usually is allocated equally or on a stated fractional basis.

LO 3. Prepare entries for (a) the sale of a partnership interest, (b) the admission of a new partner by investment, and (c) the retirement of a partner by the withdrawal of partnership assets. When a new partner buys a partnership interest directly from one or more of the existing partners, the amount of cash paid from one partner to another does not affect the total recorded equity of the partnership. The recorded equity of the selling partner(s) is simply transferred to the capital account of the new partner. Alternatively, a new partner may purchase an equity by investing additional assets in the partnership. When this occurs, part of the new partner's investment may be credited as a bonus to the capital accounts of the existing partners. Also, to gain the participation of the new partner, the existing partners may give the new partner a bonus whereby portions of the existing partners' capital balances are transferred to the new partner's capital account. Occasionally, goodwill is recorded when a new partner invests in a partnership.

LO 4. Prepare entries required in the liquidation of a partnership. When a partnership is liquidated, losses and gains from selling the partnership assets are allocated to the partners according to their income-and-loss-sharing ratio. If a partner's capital account has a deficit balance that the partner cannot pay, the other partners must share the deficit in their relative income-and-loss-sharing ratio.

SUMMARY OF THE CHAPTER IN TERMS OF LEARNING OBJECTIVES

DEMONSTRATION PROBLEM

The following events affect the partner's capital accounts in several successive partnerships. On a work sheet with six money columns, one for each of five partners and a totals column, show the effects of the following events on the partners' capital accounts:

13/4/92   Kelly and Emerson create K&E Co. Each invests $10,000, and they agree to share profits equally.

31/12/92 K&E Co. earns $15,000 in the year. Kelly withdraws $4,000 from the partnership, and Emerson withdraws $7,000.

1/1/93   Reed is made a partner in KE&R Co. after contributing $12,000 cash. The partners agree that each will get a 10% interest allowance on their beginning capital balances. In addition, Emerson and Reed are to receive $5,000 salary allowances. The remainder of the income is to be divided evenly.

31/12/93 The partnership's income for the year is $40,000, and these withdrawals occur: Kelly, $5,000; Emerson, $12,500; and Reed, $11,000.

1/1/94   For $20,000, Kelly sells her interest to Merritt, who is accepted by Emerson and Reed as a partner in the new ER&M Co. The profits are to be shared equally after Emerson and Reed each receive $25,000 salaries.

31/12/94 The partnership's income for the year is $35,000, and these withdrawals occur: Emerson, $2,500, and Reed, $2,000.

1/1/95   Davis is admitted as a partner after investing $60,000 cash in the new Davis & Associates partnership. Davis is given a 50% interest in capital after the other partners transfer $3,000 to his account from each of theirs. A 20% interest allowance (on the beginning-of-year capital balances) will be used in sharing profits, but there will be no salaries. Davis will get 40% of the remainder, and the other three partners will each get 20%.

31/12/95 Davis & Associates earns $127,600 for the year, and these withdrawals occur: Emerson, $25,000; Reed, $27,000; Merritt, $15,000; and Davis, $40,000.

1/1/96   Davis buys out Emerson and Reed for the balances of their capital accounts, after a revaluation of the partnership assets. The revaluation gain is $50,000, which is divided in the previous 1:1:1:2 ratio. Davis pays the others from personal funds. Merritt and Davis will share profits on a 1:9 ratio.

28/2/96   The partnership had $10,000 of income since the beginning of the year. Merritt retires and receives partnership cash equal to her capital balance. Davis takes possession of the partnership assets in his own name, and the company is dissolved.

Planning the Solution

- Evaluate each transaction's effects on the capital accounts of the partners.
- Each time a new partner is admitted or a partner withdraws, allocate any bonus based on the income-or-loss-sharing agreement.
- Each time a new partner is admitted or a partner withdraws, allocate subsequent net incomes or losses in accordance with the new partnership agreement.

Solution to the Demonstration Problem

Event	Kelly	Emerson	Reed	Merritt	Davis	Total	Share of Income
13/4/92							
Initial investment	$10,000	$10,000				$ 20,000	
31/12/92							
Income (equal)	7,500	7,500				15,000	$ 15,000
Withdrawals	(4,000)	(7,000)				(11,000)	
Ending balance	$13,500	$10,500				$ 24,000	
1/1/93							
New investment			$12,000			12,000	
31/12/93							
10% interest	1,350	1,050	1,200			3,600	
Salaries		5,000	5,000			10,000	} 40,000
Remainder (equal)	8,800	8,800	8,800			26,400	
Withdrawals	(5,000)	(12,500)	(11,000)			(28,500)	
Ending balance	$18,650	$12,850	$16,000			$ 47,500	
1/1/94							
Transfer interest	(18,650)			$18,650		–0–	
31/12/94							
Salaries		25,000	25,000			50,000	35,000
Remainder (equal)		(5,000)	(5,000)	(5,000)		(15,000)	
Withdrawals		(2,500)	(2,000)			(4,500)	
Ending balance	$ –0–	$30,350	$34,000	$13,650		$ 78,000	
1/1/95							
New investment					$ 60,000	60,000	
Bonuses to Davis		(3,000)	(3,000)	(3,000)	9,000	–0–	
Adjusted balance		$27,350	$31,000	$10,650	$ 69,000	$138,000	
31/12/95							
20% interest		5,470	6,200	2,130	13,800	27,600	127,600
Remain. (1:1:1:2)		20,000	20,000	20,000	40,000	100,000	
Withdrawals		(25,000)	(27,000)	(15,000)	(40,000)	(107,000)	
Ending balance		$27,820	$30,200	$17,780	$82,800	$158,600	
1/1/96							
Gain (1:1:1:2)		10,000	10,000	10,000	20,000	50,000	
Adjusted balance		$37,820	$40,200	$27,780	$102,800	$208,600	
Transfer interests		(37,820)	(40,200)		78,020	–0–	
Adjusted balance		$ –0–	$ –0–	$27,780	$180,820	$208,600	
28/2/96							
Income (1:9)				1,000	9,000	10,000	10,000
Adjusted balance				$28,780	$189,820	$218,600	$227,600*
Settlements				(28,780)	(189,820)	(218,600)	(227,600)**
Final balance				$ –0–	$ –0–	$ –0–	$ –0–

*Total of reported net incomes.
**Total of allocated net incomes.

GLOSSARY

General partner a partner who assumes unlimited liability for the debts of the partnership; the general partner in a limited partnership is usually responsible for its management. p. 647

General partnership a partnership in which all partners have unlimited liability for partnership debts. p. 647

Limited partners partners who have no personal liability for debts of the limited partnership beyond the amounts they have invested in the partnership. p. 647

Limited partnership a partnership that has two classes of partners, limited partners and one or more general partners. p. 647

Mutual agency the legal relationship among the partners whereby each partner is an agent of the partnership and is able to bind the partnership to contracts within the apparent scope of the partnership's business. p. 647

Partnership an unincorporated association of two or more persons to carry on a business for profit as co-owners. p. 646

Partnership contract the agreement between partners that sets forth the terms under which the affairs of the partnership will be conducted. p. 646

Partnership liquidations the winding up of a partnership business by converting its assets to cash and distributing the cash to the proper parties. p. 660

Statement of changes in partners' equity a financial statement that shows the total capital balances at the beginning of the period, any additional investments by the partners, the net income or loss of the period, the partners' withdrawals during the period, and the ending capital balances. p. 651

Unlimited liability of partners the legal relationship among general partners of a partnership that makes each general partner responsible for paying all the debts of the partnership if the other partners are unable to pay their shares. p. 647

QUESTIONS

1. Amey and Lacey are partners. Lacey dies, and her son claims the right to take his mother's place in the partnership. Does he have this right? Why?

2. If Roscoe cannot legally enter into a contract, can he become a partner?

3. If a partnership contract does not state the period of time the partnership is to exist, when does the partnership end?

4. As applied to a partnership, what does the term *mutual agency* mean?

5. Kurt and Ellen are partners in operating a store. Without consulting Kurt, Ellen enters into a contract for the purchase of merchandise for the store. Kurt contends that he did not authorize the order and refuses to take delivery. The vendor sues the partners for the contract price of the merchandise. Will the partnership have to pay? Why?

6. Would your answer to Question 5 differ if Kurt and Ellen were partners in a public accounting firm?

7. Can partners limit the right of a partner to commit their partnership to contracts? Would the agreement be binding *(a)* on the partners and *(b)* on outsiders?

8. What does the term *unlimited liability* mean when it is applied to members of a partnership?

9. The partnership agreement of Barnes and Ardmore provides for a two-thirds, one-third sharing of income but says nothing about losses. The first year of partnership operations resulted in a loss and Barnes argues that the loss should be shared equally because the partnership agreement said nothing about sharing losses. What do you think?

10. Ace and Bud are partners who agree that Ace will receive a $50,000 salary allowance after which remaining incomes or losses will be shared equally. If Bud's capital account is credited $1,000 as his share of the net income in a given period, how much net income did the partnership earn?

11. Van, Wink, and York are partners with capital account balances of $7,000 each. Zack pays Van $8,000 for his one-third interest and is admitted to the partnership. The bookkeeper debits Van, Capital, and credits Zack, Capital, for $7,000. Zack objects; he wants his capital account to show an $8,000 balance, the amount he paid for his interest. Explain why Zack's capital account is credited for $7,000.

12. If the partners in Blume Partnership want the financial statements to show the procedures used to allocate the partnership income among the partners, on what financial statement should the allocation appear?

13. After all partnership assets are converted to cash and all liabilities have been paid, the remaining cash should equal the sum of the balances of the partners' capital accounts. Why?

14. Kay, Kat, and Kim are partners. In a liquidation, Kay's share of partnership losses exceeds her capital account balance. She is unable to meet the deficit from her personal assets, and the excess losses are shared by her partners. Does this relieve Kay of liability?

15. A partner withdraws from a partnership and receives assets of greater value than the book value of his or her equity. Should the remaining partners share the resulting reduction in their equities in the ratio of their relative capital balances or in their income-and-loss-sharing ratio?

QUICK STUDY (Five-Minute Exercises)

Fred and Jim entered into a partnership and the first year's operation resulted in the following:

QS 14–1
(LO 1)

Sales	$510,000
Cost of goods sold	305,000
Operating expenses excluding salaries and wages	45,000
Salaries and wages:	
Two employees	42,000
Fred	30,000
Jim	25,000

Determine the partnership net income.

Fred Earnest and Jackie Magness are partners in a business they started two years ago. The partnership agreement states that Earnest should receive a salary allowance of $15,000 and Magness should receive $20,000. Any remaining income or loss is to be shared equally. Determine each partner's share of the current year's net income of $52,000.

QS 14–2
(LO 2)

Assume that in QS 14–2 above, the net income was $21,000 instead of $52,000.

QS 14–3
(LO 2)

Anthony, Bonnie, and Carrie are partners in ABC with respective capital balances on February 1, 1997, of $6,000, $9,000, and $11,000. On that date, Bonnie sold her share to Darwin for $10,000. Anthony and Carrie agreed to accept Darwin as a partner. Prepare the journal entry on the partnership's books to record the transfer of equity from Bonnie to Darwin.

QS 14–4
(LO 3)

Ken, Lam, and Mat are partners in KLM, sharing net income and loss in 5:3:2 ratio respectively. Lam decides to retire and agreed with Ken and Mat to withdraw from the partnership for a $50,000 cash consideration for his interest. Just prior to withdrawal, the respective capital balances of the partners were $88,000, $56,000 and $44,000. An audit and appraisal indicated that the $50,000 agreed to by Lam represented fair market value of his stake in the partnership. Consequently, decision was to write down the assets to reflect current valuation. Determine capital balances of Ken and Mat in the new partnership.

QS 14–5
(LO 2, 3)

QS 14–6
(LO 2, 3)

Omni, Paranka, and Quadra are partners in OPQ with respective capital balances of $30,000, $22,000, and $15,000 and income-and-loss-sharing ratio of 3:2:1. Omni and Quadra encouraged Paranka to retire by offering her $30,000 for her stake in the partnership. Paranka accepted the offer. Omni and Quadra agreed that aside from the decrease in the partnership's cash, no other assets would change. Determine the capital balances of Omni and Quadra after the withdrawal of Paranka.

QS 14–7
(LO 2, 3, 4)

Samuel, Amy, and Mary were partners in SAM, sharing income and loss in the 4:3:2 ratio respectively. Their respective capital balances on March 1, 1997, were $65,000, $48,000, and $34,000. On that day they agreed to sell the partnership for an amount sufficient to pay the partnership liabilities and leave $165,000 to be divided by the partners. Determine the amount each partner received.

QS 14–8
(LO 2, 3, 4)

Assume that in 14–7 above, the partnership was sold for an amount that left $120,000 to be divided by the partners. Determine the amount each partner received.

EXERCISES

Exercise 14–1
Journalizing partnership entries
(LO 2)

On February 1, 1996, Young and Olde formed a partnership in which Young contributed $70,000 and Olde contributed land valued at $80,000 and a building valued at $90,000. The partnership also is to assume responsibility for Olde's $30,000 long-term note payable. The partners agreed to share profits as follows: Young is to receive an annual salary allowance of $35,000, each partner is to receive 10% of his or her original capital investment, and any remaining profit or loss is to be shared equally. On November 20, 1996, Young withdrew cash of $40,000 and Olde withdrew $30,000. Present general journal entries to record the initial capital investments of the partners, the cash withdrawals of the partners, and the December 31 closing of the withdrawals accounts and the Income Summary account, which had a credit balance of $68,000.

Exercise 14–2
Income allocation in a partnership
(LO 2)

Newberg and Scampi began a partnership by investing $52,000 and $78,000, respectively. During its first year, the partnership earned $180,000. Prepare calculations that show how the income should be allocated to the partners under each of the following plans for sharing net incomes and losses:

a. The partners failed to agree on a method of sharing income.

b. The partners agreed to share incomes and losses in their investment ratio.

c. The partners agreed to share income by allowing an $85,000 per year salary allowance to Newberg, a $65,000 per year salary allowance to Scampi, 10% interest on beginning capital balances, and the remainder equally.

Exercise 14–3
Income allocation in a partnership
(LO 2)

Assume the partners in Exercise 14–2 agreed to share net incomes and losses by allowing yearly salary allowances of $85,000 to Newberg and $65,000 to Scampi, 10% interest allowances on their investments, and the balance equally. Determine *(a)* the shares of Newberg and Scampi in a first-year net income of $145,300 and *(b)* the partners' shares in a first-year net loss of $30,200.

The partners in the Duprix Partnership have agreed that partner Dupont may sell his $70,000 equity in the partnership to Queen, for which Queen will pay Dupont $55,000. Present the partnership's journal entry to record the sale on April 30.

Exercise 14–4
Sale of a partnership interest
(LO 3)

The Hagen-Baden Partnership has total partners' equity of $380,000, which is made up of Hagen, Capital, $300,000, and Baden, Capital, $80,000. The partners share net incomes and losses in a ratio of 75% to Hagen and 25% to Baden. On July 1, Megan is admitted to the partnership and given a 20% interest in equity and in gains and losses. Prepare the journal entry to record the entry of Megan under each of the following unrelated assumptions: Megan invests cash of (a) $95,000; (b) $115,000; and (c) $55,000.

Exercise 14–5
Admission of a new partner
(LO 3)

Hollis, Evans, and Bowen have been partners sharing net incomes and losses in a 3:5:2 ratio. On October 31, the date Bowen retires from the partnership, the equities of the partners are Hollis, $130,000; Evans, $200,000; and Bowen, $50,000. Present general journal entries to record Bowen's retirement under each of the following unrelated assumptions.

Exercise 14–6
Retirement of a partner
(LO 3)

a.   Bowen is paid $50,000 in partnership cash for his equity.

b.   Bowen is paid $60,000 in partnership cash for his equity.

c.   Bowen is paid $45,000 in partnership cash for his equity.

The Whiz-Bam-Boom partnership was begun with investments by the partners as follows: Whiz, $115,600; Bam, $88,600; and Boom, $95,800. The first year of operations did not go well, and the partners finally decided to liquidate the partnership, sharing all losses equally. On December 13, after all assets were converted to cash and all creditors were paid, only $30,000 in partnership cash remained.

Exercise 14–7
Liquidation of a partnership
(LO 4)

Required

1.   Calculate the capital account balances of the partners after the liquidation of assets and payment of creditors.

2.   Assume that any partner with a deficit pays cash to the partnership to cover the deficit. Then, present the general journal entries on December 31 to record the cash receipt from the deficit partner(s) and the final disbursement of cash to the partners.

3.   Now make the contrary assumption that any partner with a deficit is not able to reimburse the partnership. Present journal entries (a) to transfer the deficit of any deficient partners to the other partners and (b) to record the final disbursement of cash to the partners.

Prince, Count, and Earl are partners who share incomes and losses in a 1:3:4 ratio. After lengthy disagreements among the partners and several unprofitable periods, the partners decided to liquidate the partnership. Before the liquidation, the partnership balance sheet showed total assets, $238,000; liabilities, $200,000; Prince, Capital, $8,000; Count, Capital, $10,000; and Earl, Capital, $20,000. The cash proceeds from selling the assets were sufficient to repay all but $45,000 to the creditors. Calculate the loss from selling the assets, allocate the loss to the partners, and determine how much of the remaining liability should be paid by each partner.

Exercise 14–8
Liquidation of a partnership
(LO 4)

Assume that the Prince, Count, and Earl partnership of Exercise 14–8 is a limited partnership. Prince and Count are general partners, and Earl is a limited partner. How much of the remaining $45,000 liability should be paid by each partner?

Exercise 14–9
Liquidation of a limited partnership
(LO 4)

PROBLEMS

Problem 14–1
Methods of allocating
partnership income
(LO 2)

Del Willis, Lara Hart, and Susan Butler invested $66,400, $58,100, and $41,500, respectively, in a partnership. During its first year, the firm earned $175,500.

Required

Prepare entries to close the firm's Income Summary account as of December 31 and to allocate the net income to the partners under each of the assumptions below. (Round your answers to the nearest whole dollar.)

a. The partners could not agree as to the method of sharing incomes.

b. The partners agreed to share net incomes and losses in the ratio of their beginning investments.

c. The partners agreed to share income by allowing annual salary allowances of $52,000 to Willis, $58,000 to Hart, and $45,000 to Butler; allowing 10% interest on the partners' investments; and sharing the remainder equally.

Problem 14–2
Allocating partnership
incomes and losses;
sequential years
(LO 2)

Linda Meade and Richard Munez are in the process of forming a partnership to which Meade will devote one-third time and Munez will devote full time. They have discussed the following plans for sharing net incomes and losses:

a. In the ratio of their investments which they have agreed to maintain at $33,000 for Meade and $49,500 for Munez.

b. In proportion to the time devoted to the business.

c. A salary allowance of $3,500 per month to Munez and the balance in their investment ratio.

d. A $3,500 per month salary allowance to Munez, 10% interest on their investments, and the balance equally.

The partners expect the business to generate income as follows: year 1, $20,000 net loss; year 2, $60,000 net income; and year 3, $95,000 net income.

Required

1. Prepare three schedules with the following columnar headings:

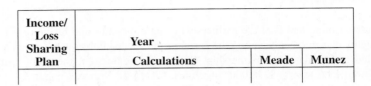

Income/ Loss Sharing Plan	Year _____		
	Calculations	Meade	Munez

2. Complete a schedule for each of the first three years by showing how the partnership net income or loss for each year should be allocated to the partners under each of the four plans being considered. Round your answers to the nearest whole dollar.

Problem 14–3
Allocating partnership
incomes and losses;
sequential years
(LO 2)

Harriet Monroe and Ozzie Young are in the process of forming a partnership to which Monroe will devote one-fourth time and Young will devote full time. They have discussed the following plans for sharing net incomes and losses:

a.   In the ratio of their investments which they have agreed to maintain at $49,800 for Monroe and $74,700 for Young.

b.   In proportion to the time devoted to the business.

c.   A salary allowance of $5,250 per month to Young and the balance in their investment ratio.

d.   A $5,250 per month salary allowance to Young, 10% interest on their investments, and the balance equally.

The partners expect the business to generate income as follows: year 1, $30,500 net income; year 2, $82,500 net loss; and year 3, $215,000 net income.

Required

1.   Prepare three schedules with the following columnar headings:

Income/ Loss Sharing Plan	Year ____		
	Calculations	Monroe	Young

2.   Complete a schedule for each of the first three years by showing how the partnership income for each year would be allocated to the partners under each of the four plans being considered. Round your answers to the nearest whole dollar.

Betty Iris, Jim Dolan, and Bob Carrow formed the IDC Partnership by making capital contributions of $245,000, $280,000, and $175,000, respectively. They anticipate annual net incomes of $390,000 and are considering the following alternative plans of sharing net incomes and losses: (*a*) equally; (*b*) in the ratio of their initial investments; or (*c*) interest allowances of 12% on initial investments, salary allowances of $95,000 to Iris, $46,000 to Dolan, and $60,000 to Carrow, with any remaining balance shared equally.

Problem 14–4
Partnership income allocation, statement of changes in partners' equity, and closing entries
(LO 2)

Required

1.   Prepare a schedule with the following column headings:

Income/Loss Sharing Plan	Calculations	Share to Iris	Share to Dolan	Share to Carrow	Totals

Use the schedule to show how a net income of $390,000 would be distributed under each of the alternative plans being considered. Round your answers to the nearest whole dollar.

2.   Prepare a statement of changes in partners' equity showing the allocation of income to the partners, assuming they agree to use alternative (*c*) and the net income actually earned is $135,000. During the year, Iris, Dolan, and Carrow withdrew $40,000, $30,000, and $20,000, respectively.

3.   Prepare the December 31 journal entry to close Income Summary assuming they agree to use alternative (*c*) and the net income is $135,000. Also close the withdrawals accounts.

Problem 14–5
Partnership income
allocation, statement
of changes in partners'
equity, and closing
entries
(LO 2)

Lou Cass, Red Sanders, and Barbara Archer formed the CSA Partnership by making capital contributions of $116,640, $129,600, and $142,560, respectively. They anticipate annual net incomes of $195,000 and are considering the following alternative plans of sharing net incomes and losses: (*a*) equally; (*b*) in the ratio of their initial investments; or (*c*) salary allowances of $35,000 to Cass, $20,000 to Sanders, and $45,000 to Archer and interest allowances of 10% on initial investments, with any remaining balance shared equally.

Required

1. Prepare a schedule with the following column headings:

Income/Loss Sharing Plan	Calculations	Share to Cass	Share to Sanders	Share to Archer	Totals

Use the schedule to show how a net income of $195,000 would be distributed under each of the alternative plans being considered. Round your answers to the nearest whole dollar.

2. Prepare a statement of changes in partners' equity showing the allocation of income to the partners, assuming they agree to use alternative (*c*) and the net income earned is $85,000. During the year, Cass, Sanders, and Archer withdrew $15,000, $20,000, and $23,000, respectively.

3. Prepare the December 31 journal entry to close Income Summary assuming they agree to use alternative (*c*) and the net income is $85,000. Also close the withdrawals accounts.

Problem 14–6
Withdrawal of a partner
(LO 3)

Part 1. Pushkin, Tolstoy, and Chekhov are partners with capital balances as follows: Pushkin, $183,750; Tolstoy, $131,250; and Chekhov, $315,000. The partners share incomes and losses in a 1:2:3 ratio. Prepare general journal entries to record the August 1 withdrawal of Tolstoy from the partnership under each of the following unrelated assumptions.

a. Tolstoy sells his interest to Gogol for $168,000 after Pushkin and Chekhov approve the entry of Gogol as a partner.

b. Tolstoy gives his interest to a son-in-law, Lermontov. Pushkin and Chekhov accept Lermontov as a partner.

c. Tolstoy is paid $131,250 in partnership cash for his equity.

d. Tolstoy is paid $194,250 in partnership cash for his equity.

e. Tolstoy is paid $27,250 in partnership cash plus delivery equipment recorded on the partnership books at $115,000 less accumulated amortization of $63,000.

Part 2. Assume that Tolstoy does not retire from the partnership described in Part 1. Instead, Nabokov is admitted to the partnership on August 1 with a 25% equity. Prepare general journal entries to record the entry of Nabokov into the partnership under each of the following unrelated assumptions:

a. Nabokov invests $210,000.

b. Nabokov invests $157,500.

c. Nabokov invests $262,500.

Maxwell, Adams, and Nelson plan to liquidate their partnership. They have always shared losses and gains in a 1:4:5 ratio, and on the day of the liquidation their balance sheet appeared as follows:

Problem 14–7
Liquidation of a
partnership
(LO 4)

MAXWELL, ADAMS AND NELSON
Balance Sheet
June 30, 19—

Assets		Liabilities and Owners' Equity	
Cash	$ 27,500	Accounts payable.	$ 52,150
Other assets	180,500	Pam Maxwell, capital.	30,500
		Greg Adams, capital.	80,350
		Linda Nelson, capital	45,000
		Total liabilities and	
Total assets	$208,000	owners' equity	$208,000

Required

Prepare general journal entries to record the sale of the other assets and the distribution of the cash to the proper parties under each of the following unrelated assumptions:

a. The other assets are sold for $195,250.

b. The other assets are sold for $150,000.

c. The other assets are sold for $85,000, and any partners with resulting deficits can and do pay in the amount of their deficits.

d. The other assets are sold for $75,000, and the partners have no assets other than those invested in the business.

Until May 28, 1996, Block, Sun, and Steen were partners that shared incomes and losses in the ratio of their beginning-of-year capital account balances. On May 28, Sun suffered a heart attack and died. Block and Steen immediately ended the business operations and prepared the following adjusted trial balance:

Problem 14–8
Death of a partner
(LO 3)

BLOCK, SUN AND STEEN
Adjusted Trial Balance
May 28, 1996

Cash	$ 23,625	
Accounts receivable	55,125	
Allowance for doubtful accounts		$ 2,625
Supplies inventory	111,750	
Equipment	70,875	
Accumulated amortization, equipment		18,375
Land	23,625	
Building	262,500	
Accumulated amortization, building		49,875
Accounts payable		15,750
Note payable (secured by mortgage)		52,500
Bob Block, capital		157,500
Joan Sun, capital		157,500
Tim Steen, capital		78,750
Bob Block, withdrawals	8,250	
Joan Sun, withdrawals	8,250	
Tim Steen, withdrawals	8,250	
Revenues		204,750
Expenses	165,375	
Totals	$737,625	$737,625

Required

1. Prepare May 28 entries to close the revenue, expense, income summary, and withdrawals accounts of the partnership.

2. Assume the estate of Sun agreed to accept the land and building and to assume the mortgage note thereon in settlement of its claim against the partnership assets, and that Block and Steen planned to continue the business and rent the building from the estate. Give the partnership's June 15 entry to transfer the land, building, and mortgage note in settlement with the estate.

3. Assume that in place of the foregoing, the estate of Sun demanded a cash settlement, and the business had to be sold to a competitor who gave $355,000 for the noncash assets and assumed the mortgage note but not the accounts payable. Give the June 15 entry to transfer the noncash assets and mortgage note to the competitor, and give the entries to allocate the loss to the partners and to distribute the partnership cash to the proper parties.

Required

1. Prepare general journal entries to record the asset sales, the allocation of the realization loss, and the payment of the creditors.

2. Under the assumption that any partners with capital deficits can and do pay the amount of their deficits on July 17, give the entry to record the receipt of the cash and the distribution of partnership cash to the remaining partners.

3. Under the assumption that any partners with capital deficits cannot pay, give the entry to allocate the deficits to the remaining partners. Then give the entry to distribute the partnership cash to the remaining partners.

Problem 14–9
Analytical essay
(LO 2)

Janet Koppen and Beverly Spikes want to form a partnership and are considering two methods of sharing incomes and losses. Method *a* splits all profits and losses in a 2:3 ratio, or 40% to Koppen and 60% to Spikes. Method *b* depends on the income or loss of the partnership. If the partnership incurs a loss, the partners share it equally. If the income is in the range of $0 to $36,000, it is allocated based on an annual salary allowance of $12,000 to Koppen and $24,000 to Spikes. If the net income exceeds $36,000 the residual after the salary allowances is shared equally.

Spikes has retained you to write an evaluation of the two methods indicating which is most favourable to her. Your discussion should include a comparison of the two methods at each of the three possible net income levels. Also, discuss the importance of asking Spikes to estimate the partnership's future earnings.

Problem 14–10
Analytical essay
(LO 3)

Kay Doobie, Ed Foley, and Brian McKenzie have been operating a partnership for several years. Business has not been good recently, and Doobie is withdrawing from the partnership. The partners agree that the market values of the assets are less than their recorded book values. However, they do not want to change the recorded values at his time. As a result, the partners have agreed that Doobie should withdraw cash in an amount that is less than her capital account balance.

Foley and McKenzie are not sure how to calculate the adjustments to their capital accounts (brought about by the difference between Doobie's equity and the cash she is withdrawing). Foley thinks they should split the difference in the ratio of their capital account balances. McKenzie thinks the adjustments should be calculated using their income-and-loss-sharing ratio. Which partner do you think is correct? Explain why.

PROVOCATIVE PROBLEMS

Lisa White and Joe Black agreed to share the annual net incomes or losses of their partnership as follows. If the partnership earns a net income, the first $50,000 is allocated 25% to White and 75% to Black so as to reflect the time devoted to the business by each partner. Income in excess of $50,000 is shared equally. However, if business operations result in a loss for the year, the partners have agreed to share the loss equally.

Provocative Problem 14–1
White and Black Partnership
(LO 2)

Required

1. Prepare a schedule showing how the 1996 net income of $59,000 should be allocated to the partners.

2. Immediately after the closing entries for 1996 were posted on December 31, 1996, the partners discover $70,000 of unrecorded accounts payable. These accounts payable relate to expenses incurred by the business. Black suggests that the $70,000 should be allocated equally between the partners as a loss. White disagrees and argues that an entry should be made to record the accounts payable and correct the capital accounts to reflect an $11,000 net loss for 1996. (*a*) Present the January 1, 1997, journal entry to record the accounts payable and allocate the loss to the partners according to Black's suggestion. (*b*) Now give the January 1, 1997, journal entry to record the accounts payable and correct the capital accounts according to White's argument. Show how you calculated the amounts in the entry.

3. Which partner do you think is right? Why?

Maddie Hall and Amanda Miller are partners that own and operate The Fitness Place, an exercise and casual wear shop. Hall has a $75,000 equity in the business, and Miller has a $60,000 equity. They share incomes and losses by allowing annual salary allowances of $33,750 to Hall and $27,000 to Miller, with any remaining balance being shared 60% to Hall and 40% to Miller.

Provocative Problem 14–2
The Fitness Place
(LO 3)

Susie Hall, Maddie Hall's daughter, has been working in the store on a salary basis. In addition to working in the store, Susie is a popular aerobics teacher and is well known among other aerobics teachers and a number of students. As a result, Susie attracts a great deal of business to the store. The partners believe that a least one-third of the past three years' sales can be traced directly to Susie's association with the store, and it is reasonable to assume she was instrumental in attracting even more.

Susie is paid $1,800 per month but feels this is not sufficient to induce her to remain with the firm as an employee. However, she likes her work and would like to remain in the fitness-wear business. What she really wants is to become a partner in the business.

Her mother is anxious for her to remain in the business and proposes the following:

a. That Susie be admitted to the partnership with a 20% equity in the partnership assets.

b. That she, Maddie Hall, transfer from her capital account to that of Susie's one half the 20% interest; that Susie contribute to the firm's assets a noninterest-bearing note for the other half; and that she, Maddie Hall, will guarantee payment of the note.

c. That incomes and losses be shared by continuing the $33,750 and $27,000 salary allowances of the original partners and that Susie be given a $21,600 annual salary allowance, after which any remaining income or loss would be shared 40% to Maddie Hall, 40% to Amanda Miller, and 20% to Susie Hall.

Prepare a report to Ms. Miller on the advisability of accepting Maddie Hall's proposal. Under the assumption that net incomes for the past three years have been $65,400, $68,500, and $70,500, respectively, prepare schedules showing (a) how net income was allocated during the past three years and (b) how it would have been allocated had the proposed new agreement been in effect. Also, (c) prepare a schedule showing the partners' capital interests as they would be immediately after the admission of Susie.

**Provocative Problem
14–3
Venerable Partnership
(LO 3)**

The following is the balance sheet of the Venerable Partnership on December 31, 1996:

Assets		Liabilities and Owners' Equity	
Cash	$ 45,250	Hamilton, capital	$22,750
Other assets	56,250	Adams, capital	33,700
Land	33,750	Hay, capital	78,750
		Total liabilities and	
Total assets	$135,250	owners' equity	$135,250

The income-and-loss-sharing percentages are: Hamilton, 20%; Adams, 30%; and Hay, 50%. Hamilton wishes to withdraw from the partnership, and the partners finally agree that the land owned by the partnership should be transferred to Hamilton in full payment for his equity. In reaching this decision they recognize that the land has appreciated since it was purchased and is now worth $60,000. If Hamilton retires on January 1, 1997, what journal entries should be made on that date?

**Provocative Problem
14–4
Ethical issues essay**

Review the "As a Matter of Ethics" case on page 661. Then write a brief essay describing Janis Carpenter's engagement and suggestions you would offer the partners. Your essay should include the reasons why your settlement is fair.

ANALYTICAL AND REVIEW PROBLEMS

A & R Problem 14–1

Jay and Mar entered into a partnership to carry on a business under the firm name of Jay-Mar Sportsland. Prior to the final signing of the agreement Jay asks you to evaluate the "income/loss distribution clause" contained in the agreement.

Your examination revealed that the agreement called for the following: Equal sharing of net income and losses after an initial allocation of $40,000 to Jay and $10,000 to Mar in order to reflect the difference in time and expertise devoted to the business by each partner. The initial allocation would be made regardless of the level of net income/loss.

Required

Prepare a report to Jay on the particular clause of the agreement. Your report should show the consequence on each partner of operating results as follows: (a) net income of $80,000; (b) net income of $20,000; (c) operation at break-even, that is, no net income or loss; (d) loss of $20,000; (e) loss of $80,000.

A & R Problem 14–2

The summarized balance sheet of Bell, Trunk, and Field showed:

Assets		Equities	
Cash	$ 20,000	Liabilities	$ 60,000
Other assets	280,000	Bell, capital	80,000
		Trunk, capital	120,000
		Field, capital	$ 40,000
Total assets	$300,000	Total equities	$300,00

The partnership has operated successfully for nearly 25 years, and Field, because of his age and health, is pushing for sale of the business. In fact, he has found Arn, a buyer who is willing to pay $320,000 cash and take over the liabilities. Both Bell and Trunk are not anxious to sell what they refer to as "our little gold mine."

Field is adamant about getting out and has proposed the following:

1. Either sell to Arn, or Bell and Trunk (a new partnership) Should buy out Field at an amount Field would receive if the business was sold to Arn.

2. Admit Arn to partnership upon the purchase of Field's share for an amount Field and Arn will negotiate.

The present partnership agreement calls for a distribution of net income/loss on a 3:5:2 basis. If Arn is admitted to partnership the ratio would not change; he would be entitled to Field's 20% share of net income/loss. If Bell and Trunk buy out for an amount based on the Arn offer, Bell and Trunk would continue to share net income/loss on the same relative basis. They would (the new partnership of Bell and Trunk) have to borrow sufficient funds from the bank to retain a minimum cash balance of $10,000.

Required

1. Prepare the general journal entry for admission of Arn to the partnership upon his purchase of Field's interest for an undisclosed amount.

2. Prepare the necessary entries to record Field's withdrawal from the partnership. The amount paid to Field is equal to the amount he would have received if the partnership was sold to Arn.

CONCEPT TESTER

Test your understanding of the concepts introduced in this chapter by completing the following crossword puzzle:

Across Clues

2. Purpose or motive of partnership.
3. A basis for allocation.
7. Characteristic that each partner is able to bind the partnership (2 words).
9. Cause for dissolution of a partnership.
14. Type of association.
15. Reward to new partner.
17. Particulars of partnership.
18. Judge in *Garner* vs *Murray* case.
19. Gain or loss on disposal of partnership assets.

Down Clues

1. Degree of exposure of general partners.
2. Co-owners of an unincorporated business.
4. Liability protection enjoyed by certain partners.
5. Negative balance in a partner's account.
6. Retirement of partner from the partnership.
8. Winding up of a partnership.
9. Final entry on liquidation for disposal of cash.
10. Division of net income/loss.
11. Excess of new partner's investment over her/his equity.
12. Another cause for dissolution of a partnership.
13. Partner(s) with unlimited liability.
16. If not specified, sharing of income/loss.

ANSWERS TO PROGRESS CHECKS

14–1 *b.*

14–2

	Mixon	**Reed**
10% interest	$ 7,000	$ 3,500
Balance	14,750	14,750
Total allocation	$21,750	$18,250

14–3 The creditors may satisfy their claims from personal assets of the partners if partnership assets are not sufficient.

14–4 No. A partnership is a voluntary association requiring an agreement of all potential partners to associate.

14–5 Yes. The transaction is between J and Z and is outside the scope of the other partners.

14–6 No. A new partnership comes into existence with a negotiated sharing ratio that may be different from the ratio used in the replaced partnership.

14–7 The existing partners would offer a bonus if there is a need for additional cash and/or the particular skills that the new partner would bring to the partnership.

14–8 There is evidence of potential superior profitability of the partnership.

14–9 C should contribute $1,000 to the partnership. If C is unable to meet the $1,000 requirement, the deficit would be allocated to A and B before distribution of cash.

Organization and Operation of Corporations

Business corporations that operate as corporations enjoy many advantages, including the ability to grow larger by selling shares to the public. The annual report presents accounting information that helps bridge the gap between a corporation's owners and its professional managers.

Karen White and Mark Smith looked forward to the study of the next two chapters on corporations. They had already acquired a degree of knowledge through examination of the Annual Report of Imperial Oil Limited and the various handouts by the instructor.

When they had finished reading Chapter 15, White and Smith fantasized as to what they would do if they came into money. They wondered what kind of a return they could expect on investments. Snapping out of their daydream, they realized that the questions they contemplated were real and important. Consequently, they decided that the next day they would be back in the library examining not only Imperial's dividend record, but also those of other companies whose names were familiar to them. Karen and Mark decided that they would take with them to the library the stock quotation page from the local newspaper. The next day they compiled the following information:

Company	Common Dividend 1994	Share Prices Feb. 15, 1995
Imperial Oil Limited	$1.80*	$46 ¼
BCE Inc.	2.72	43 ⅜
Anchor Lamina Inc.	0.12	6
Imasco Inc.	1.92	41 ⅜
Hemlo Gold Ltd.	0.20	11 ⅞

*Excludes special dividend of $3.00.

LEARNING OBJECTIVES

After studying Chapter 15, you should be able to:

1. **Explain the advantages, disadvantages, and organization of corporations and the differences in accounting for partnerships and corporations.**
2. **Record the issuance of no-par value shares.**
3. **Record transactions involving share subscriptions and explain the effects of subscribed shares on a corporation's assets and shareholders' equity.**
4. **State the differences between common and preferred shares, and allocate dividends between the common and preferred shares.**
5. **Describe convertible preferred shares and explain the meaning of redemption, book, and market values of shares.**
6. **Calculate dividend yield and explain its meaning.**
7. **Define or explain the words and phrases listed in the chapter glossary.**

Of the three common types of business organizations (proprietorships, partnerships, and corporations), corporations are fewest in number. However, they transact more business than the other two combined. Thus, from an overall economic point of view, corporations are clearly the most important form of business organization. As you study this chapter, you will learn how corporations are organized and operated, and about some of the procedures used to account for corporations.

ADVANTAGES OF THE CORPORATE FORM

LO 1

Explain the advantages, disadvantages, and organization of corporations and the differences in accounting for partnerships and corporations.

Corporations have become the dominant type of business because of the advantages created by their unique characteristics. We describe these characteristics in the following sections.

Corporations Are Separate Legal Entities

Unlike a proprietorship or partnership a corporation is a separate legal entity. Separate and distinct from its owners, a corporation conducts its affairs with the same rights, duties, and responsibilities as a person. However, because it is not a real person, a corporation can act only through its agents, who are its officers and managers.

Shareholders Are Not Liable for the Corporation's Debts

Because a corporation is a separate legal entity, it is responsible for its own acts and its own debts. Its shareholders are not liable for either. From the viewpoint of an investor, this lack of shareholders' liability is, perhaps, the most important advantage of the corporate form of business.

Ownership Rights of Corporations Are Easily Transferred

The ownership of a corporation is represented by shares that generally are easily bought or sold. Also, the transfer of shares from one shareholder to another usually has no effect on the corporation or its operations.[1] Many companies have thousands or even millions of their shares bought and sold every day through major stock exchanges located throughout the world.

---

[1] However, a transfer of ownership can create significant effects if it brings about a change in who controls the company's activities.

Corporations Have Continuity of Life

A corporation's life may continue indefinitely because it is not tied to the physical lives of its owners. In some cases, a corporation's life may be initially limited by the laws of the jurisdiction of its incorporation. However, the corporation's articles of incorporation can be renewed and its life extended when the stated time expires. Thus, a corporation may have a perpetual life as long as it continues to be successful.

Shareholders Do Not Have a Mutual Agency Relationship

The shareholders of a corporation do not have the mutual agency relationship that exists for partners. Thus, a shareholder who is not a manager does not have the power to bind the corporation to contracts. Instead, a shareholder's participation in the affairs of the corporation is limited to the right to vote in the shareholders' meetings. Therefore, if you become a shareholder in a corporation, you may not have to worry about the character of the other shareholders to the same extent that you would if the business were a partnership.

Ease of Capital Accumulation

Buying shares in a corporation often is more attractive to investors than investing in a partnership. Share investments are attractive because (1) shareholders are not liable for the corporation's actions and debts, (2) shares usually can be transferred easily, (3) the life of the corporation is not limited, and (4) shareholders do not have a relationship of mutual agency. These advantages make it possible for some corporations to accumulate large amounts of capital from the combined investments of many shareholders. In a sense, a corporation's capacity for raising capital is limited only by its ability to convince investors that it can use (and has used) their funds profitably. This situation is very different from the one faced by most partnerships, where mutual agency and unlimited liability reduce the number of investors who might be willing to become partners.

DISADVANTAGES OF THE CORPORATE FORM

Governmental Regulation

Corporations are created by fulfilling the requirements of federal or provincial incorporation laws. These laws subject a corporation to considerable regulation and control. Single proprietorships and partnerships may escape some of these regulations. In addition, they may avoid having to file some governmental reports required of corporations.

Taxation

As business units, corporations are subject to the same property and payroll taxes as single proprietorships and partnerships. In addition, corporations are subject to taxes that are not levied on either of the other two. The most burdensome of these are income taxes which may amount to 50% of a corporation's pretax income. However, the tax burden does not end there. The income of a corporation is taxed twice, first as income of the corporation and again as personal income to the shareholders when cash is distributed to them as dividends. This differs from single proprietorships and partnerships, which are not subject to income taxes as business units. Their income is taxed only as the personal income of their owners.

The tax situation of a corporation is generally viewed as a disadvantage. However, in some cases, it can work to the advantage of shareholders. Income taxes may be saved or at least delayed if a large amount of income is divided among two or more tax-paying entities. Thus, an individual who has a large personal income and pays taxes at a high rate may benefit if some of the income is earned by a corporation that person owns, as long as the corporation avoids paying dividends. By not paying dividends, the corporation's income is taxed only once at the lower corporate rate, at least temporarily until dividends are paid. Additionally, the dividend tax credit gives some relief from the effects of double taxation.

ORGANIZING A CORPORATION

A corporation is created by securing a certificate of incorporation or a charter from the federal or provincial government. The requirements that must be met to be incorporated vary among jursidictions. Under the Canada Business Corporations Act, 1975, incorporation is a matter of right. One person, over 18, of sound mind and not bankrupt, may incorporate by submitting completed articles of incorporation and other required documentation to the Director, Corporations Branch, Department of Consumer Affairs. Once the documentation is in order, the Director issues a certificate of incorporation, and a corporation comes into existence.

The newly formed corporation is authorized to issue shares, the number of which may be specified or unlimited. Authorization may also be for the issuance of more than one class of shares. If all the authorized shares have the same rights, they are usually referred to as **common**. However, if there is more than one class, the class(es) that have rights above those of the common, are preferred shares. (We discuss preferred shares later in this chapter.) The sale of shares is recorded by an entry such as

June	5	Cash	30,000.00	
		Common Shares		30,000.00
		Sold and issued 3,000 commom shares.		

The shareholders meet and elect a board of directors who are responsible for guiding the company's business affairs.

ORGANIZATION COSTS

The costs of organizing a corporation, such as legal fees, promoters' fees, and amounts paid to secure articles of incorporation, are called **organization costs**. On the corporation's books, these costs are debited on incurrence to an account called Organization costs. In a sense, this intangible asset benefits the corporation throughout its life. Thus, you could argue that organization costs should be amortized over the life of the corporation, which may be unlimited. Nevertheless, a corporation should make a reasonable estimate of the benefit period, which the CICA recommends should not exceed 40 years, and write off its organization costs over this period.

Although not necessarily related to the benefit period, income tax rules currently permit a corporation to write off 75% of organization costs as a tax-deductible expense at an annual 7% rate on a diminishing balance basis. Consequently, some corporations adopt this same tax period as the period for writing off such costs for financial statement purposes. There is no theoretical justification for this, but it is widely used in practice. Also, because organization costs are usually not material in amount, the *materiality principle* supports the arbitrarily short amortization period.

Although the organizational structures of all corporations are similar, they are not always the same. Illustration 15–1 diagrams two widely used alternatives. In all cases, the ultimate control of a corporation rests with its shareholders. However, this control is exercised only indirectly through the election of the board of directors. Individual shareholders' rights to participate in management begin and end with a vote in the shareholders' meetings, where each of them has one vote for each share owned.

Normally, a corporation holds a shareholders' meeting once each year to elect directors and transact other business as required by the corporation's bylaws. A group of shareholders that owns or controls the votes of 50% plus one share of a corporation's stock can easily elect the board and thereby control the corporation. However, in many companies, very few shareholders attend the annual meeting or even care about getting involved in the voting process. As a result, a much smaller percentage may be able to dominate the election of board members.

Shareholders who do not attend shareholders' meetings must be given an opportunity to delegate their voting rights to an agent. A shareholder does this by signing a document called a **proxy** that gives a designated agent the right to vote the shares. Prior to a shareholders' meeting, a corporation's board of directors typically mails to each shareholder an announcement of the meeting and a proxy that names the existing board chairperson as the voting agent of the shareholder. The announcement asks the shareholder to sign and return the proxy.

A corporation's board of directors is responsible for and has final authority for managing the corporation's activities. However, it can act only as a collective body. An individual director has no power to transact corporate business. Although the board has final authority, it usually limits its actions to establishing broad policy. Day-to-day direction of corporate business is delegated to executive officers appointed by the board.

Traditionally, the chief executive officer (CEO) of the corporation is the president. Under the president, there may be several vice presidents who are assigned specific areas of management responsibility, such as finance, production, and marketing. In addition, the corporate secretary keeps the minutes of the meetings of the shareholders and directors and ensures that all legal responsibilities are fulfilled. In a small corporation, the secretary is also responsible for keeping a record of the shareholders and the transfer of shares among shareholders.

As shown on the right side of Illustration 15–1, many corporations have a different structure in which the chairperson of the board of directors is also the chief executive officer. With this arrangement, the president is usually designated the chief operating officer (COO), and the rest of the structure is essentially the same.

MANAGEMENT OF A CORPORATION

When investors buy a corporation's shares, they may receive a share certificate as proof that they purchased the shares.[2] In many corporations, only one certificate is issued for each block of shares purchased. This certificate may be for any number of shares. For example, the certificate in Illustration 15–2 is for 50 shares. Corporations may use preprinted certificates, each of which represents 100 shares, plus blank certificates that may be made out for any number of shares.

SHARE CERTIFICATES AND THE TRANSFER OF SHARES

---

[2] The issuance of certificates is less common than it used to be. Instead, many shareholders maintain accounts with the corporation or their stockbrokers and never receive certificates.

Illustration 15–1
Alternative Structures
of Authority in a
Corporation

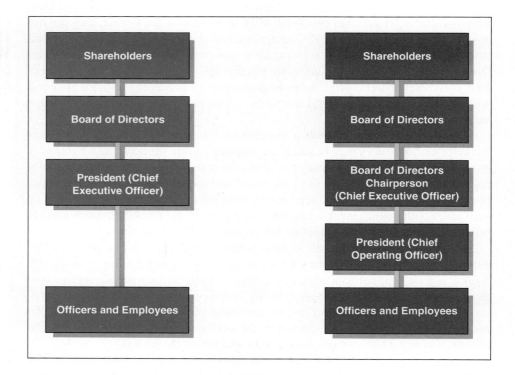

When selling shares of a corporation, a shareholder completes and signs a transfer endorsement on the back of the certificate and sends it to the corporation's secretary or the transfer agent. The secretary or agent cancels and files the old certificate, and issues a new certificate to the new shareholder. If the old certificate represents more shares than were sold, the corporation issues two new certificates. One certificate goes to the new shareholder for the sold shares and the other to the original shareholder for the remaining unsold shares.

Transfer Agent and Registrar

If a corporation's shares are traded on a major stock exchange, the corporation must have a *registrar* and a *transfer agent.* The registrar keeps the shareholder records and prepares official lists of shareholders for shareholders' meetings and for dividend payments. Registrars and transfer agents usually are large banks or trust companies that have the computer facilities and staff to carry out this kind of work.

When a corporation has a transfer agent and a shareholder wants to transfer ownership of some shares to another party, the owner completes the transfer endorsement on the back of the share certificate and sends the certificate to the transfer agent, usually with the assistance of a stockbroker. The transfer agent cancels the old certificate and issues one or more new certificates and sends them to the registrar. The registrar enters the transfer in the shareholder records and sends the new certificate or certificates to the proper owners. Millions of shares are traded each business day on exchanges such as the Toronto Stock Exchange. Illustration 15–3 is a partial list of transactions of February 15, 1995. The information was taken from the February 16, 1995, *Globe and Mail* along with an explanation of how to read the stock tables.

Illustration 15–2   A Share Certificate

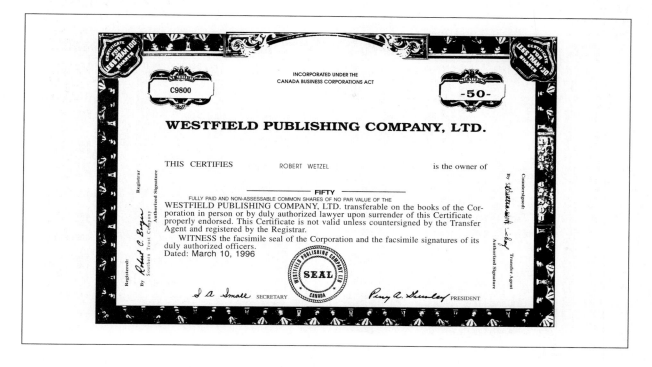

Progress Check

15–1   Which of the following is *not* a characteristic of the corporate form of business?
(a) Ease of capital accumulation.
(b) Shareholders are liable for corporate debts.
(c) Ownership rights are easily transferred.

15–2   Why is the income of a corporation said to be taxed twice?

15–3   What is a proxy?

CORPORATION ACCOUNTING

Accounting for a corporation does not differ from accounting for a proprietorship or a partnership except for transactions that directly affect the owners' equity (shareholders' equity) and recognition of corporate income tax. The shareholders' equity of a corporation is divided into contributed capital and retained earnings. The former represents consideration received by the corporation for the issued shares. The latter, retained earnings, represents the total accumulated net income from the inception of the corporation less losses, if any, and dividends. The separation of contributed capital and retained earnings is required by law.

Financial statements of a corporation consist of a balance sheet, income statement, statement of retained earnings, and a statement of changes in financial position. As indicated earlier in the chapter, corporations are legal entities subject to income tax; therefore, income tax expense is reflected in the income statement. The shareholders' equity section of a corporation's balance sheet reports share authorization, the number of shares issued, and the balance of retained earnings as reported in the statement of retained earnings.

Illustration 15–3   Record of Trades (Partial List) Toronto Stock Exchange February 15, 1995

52-week high	low	Stock	Sym	Div	High	Low	Close	Chg	Vol (1002)	Yield	P/E ratio
0.51	0.25	Amer Leduc	ARL		0.45	0.38	0.40	-0.02	307		40.0
8⅛	4.75	Anchor Lamin	AKC	0.12	6	6	6	+¼	1	2.00	10.9
18	10¾	Anderson	AXL		12¼	12	12¼	+½	8055		27.2
9½	7	Andyne Com	ADY		8⅝	8⅛	8⅝	+⅜	330		43.1
1.35	0.60	Antares Mini	ANZ		0.95	0.90	0.95	+0.02	120		
6¾	5	Anvil Range	ARO		5	5	5	-¼	51		
1.00	0.65	Apex Land	AXD.A		0.85	0.76	0.85	+0.20	20		6.1
0.95	0.06	Applied Carb	APN		.085	.085	.085		1353		
19¼	12½	Arbor Me	ABO.A	0.07	17½	17½	17½		1	0.40	19.4
23¼	9¼	Archer Res	ARC		9⅞	9¾	9⅞		647		16.5
2.70	1.60	Ariel Res	AU		2.48	2.36	2.36	-0.13	628		84.3
2.03	0.98	Arimetco j	ARX		1.10	1.01	1.01	-0.09	293		
2.70	0.80	Armbro	ARE		1.16	1.16	1.16	+0.01	10		
2.18	0.17	Arrowlink	ARK		0.18	0.17	0.18	+0.01	200		
1.00	0.61	Ascentex En	AEN		0.62	0.62	0.62	+0.01	225		62.0
3.20	0.59	Ashton Minin	ACA		0.68	0.68	0.68		20		
19	12	Astral nv	ACM.A	0.30	15⅛	15⅛	15⅛	+⅜	z 50	1.9	18.4
15⅞	12	Atco nv	ACO.X	0.28	14½	14½	14½		106	1.93	9.8
4.60	2.35	Atcor nv	AKR.A		2.50	2.45	2.45	-0.05	41		12.9
1.85	0.61	Athabaska j	AHB		1.10	1.09	1.10	-0.01	397		
5	3.05	Atlantic Coas	ATC		3.30	3.30	3.30	+0.25	8		41.3
25¾	24⅝	Atltc Sh	ATS.PR.S	2.31					18	9.16	
1.57	1.05	Audrey	AUY		1.25	1.20	1.25	+0.05	25		
19½	14¾	Ault Foods	AUL	0.66	18	17⅞	17⅞		31	3.69	15.1
7½	3.60	Aur j	AUR		4.35	4.25	4.35	+0.05	10176		
1.49	0.90	Aurex Res	AXR		0.95	0.95	0.95		40		
1.13	0.70	Aurizon j	ARZ		0.78	0.78	0.78	-0.01	53		19.5
30⅛	19⅝	Avenor	AVR		28¾	27⅜	28¼	+1¼	2069		
3.85	2.45	Azco Mining	AZC		2.50	2.45	2.45	-0.05	148		
3.35	2.00	Aztec Res	AZL		2.00	2.00	2.00	-0.10	3		8.3
11	9⅜	BAA	BAA	0.09	9⅝	9⅝	9⅝	-1¼	14	1.60	12.2
1.35	0.57	BC Bancorp	BBC		0.66	0.66	0.66	-0.01	13		
16⅛	13⅛	BC Gas	BCG	0.90	13⅝	13¾	13½	+⅛	290	6.67	13.9
25⅝	24⅝	BC Gas	BGU.PR.B	1.78	25	25	25		28	7.10	
11	7½	BC Sugar	BCS.A	0.40	7⅞	7⅝	7⅞	+¼	987	5.08	17.9
27⅜	21½	BC Telecom	BCT	1.24	24⅛	23⅞	24		102	5.17	12.8
52⅞	41⅛	BCE	B	2.72	43¾	43¼	43⅜		2512	6.27	12.3
44	41¼	BCE O	B.PR.O	2.72	41¾	41¾	41¾		9	6.51	
8⅜	0.26	BCE	B.WT		0.55	0.48	0.50	-0.04			
48⅝	35	BCE Mobile	BCY		45¾						
17¼		BGR									

52-week high	low	Stock	Sym	Div	High	Low	Close	Chg	Vol (1002)	Yield	P/E ratio
15¾	11½	Hemlo Gold	Hem	0.20	12	11¾	11⅞	+¼	536	1.68	17.7
8⅞	4.00	Hemosol	HML		6¼	6	6	-¼	167		
0.32	0.18	High Bullen	HBR		0.24	0.24	0.24	-0.01	10		
2.97	1.67	High River j	HRG		1.75	1.72	1.75	-0.03	616		
7¾	2.90	Highridge Ex	HRE		3.15	3.15	3.15	+0.05	30		15.8
1.25	0.60	Highwood j	HWD		0.65	0.65	0.65		105		5.4
2.10	1.17	Hillsborough	HLB		1.75	1.70	1.70		353		
17½	11⅝	Hollinger	HLG	0.60	12	11⅝	12	+¼	138	5.00	6.4
0.86	0.45	Hom Ca sb	HCG.B		0.50	0.50	0.50	-0.02	16		8.3
21¼	13⅞	Home Oil	HOC		14¼	13⅞	14⅛	-⅛	2179		88.3
2.10	0.85	Home Prod	HPI		0.95	0.95	0.95	+0.05	10		8.6
22⅛	16⅜	Horsham sv	HSM	A0.06	17⅞	17¾	17¾	-⅛	20	0.47	6.6
32¼	22⅞	Hudsn Bay	HBC	0.92	26½	26¼	26⅜		2076	3.49	7.9
29⅝	16¾	Hummingbir	HUM		25½	24⅞	25⅛	+⅛	104		23.5
7	3.00	Hy & Zels	HZI	0.25	3.25	3.25	3.25	+0.05	10	7.69	4.8
7⅝	4.00	Hyal j	HPC		5⅛	4.90	5⅛		181		
4.10	1.77	Hycroft Res	HYR		1.80	1.77	1.77	-0.03	25		177.0
1.10	0.55	Hydra Captl j	HYX		0.85	0.85	0.85	-0.07	10		85.0
33¼	26⅞	IPL Energy	IPL	2.00	28⅛	27¾	28⅛	+¼	4562	7.11	16.3
15	7⅞	ISG Tech	ISO		8½	8	8	+¼	38		
1.00	.175	Ican j	IMI		0.25	0.23	0.23	-.015	123		
41¾	32	Imasco	IMS	1.92	41¼	41⅜	41⅜	-⅛	532	4.64	9.9
26	21¾	Imperl Lif	IL.PR.D	2.13	24	23½	23½	-½	35	9.04	
1.70	0.55	Imperial Metl	IPM		1.10	1.05	1.05	-0.05	191		105.0
48¾	40⅛	Imperial Oil	IMO	1.80	46⅜	46	46¼	+¼	2533	3.89	25.0
3.30	0.70	Imutec Corp	IUT		1.00	1.00	1.00	-0.02	120		
43¼	29⅝	Inco	N	A0.4	38⅞	38¼	38¼	-⅜	2470	1.47	
25⅜	23½	Inco	N.PR.B	1.96	25	24½	25	+¼	9	7.85	
7⅜	4.40	Industra Svc	IND	0.08	5⅝	5½	5½	-⅛	7	1.45	78.6
3.35	2.10	Intensity	ITY		2.20	2.10	2.15	-0.01	279		15.4
4.90	2.06	Inter-City	IPR		2.50	2.35	2.40	+0.05	385		
0.75	0.30	Interaction j	INR		0.35	0.35	0.35	-0.01	79		17.5
2.80	1.75	Intl Aqua Food	IAF		2.35	2.30	2.35	+	47		
21¼	8⅜	Intl Colin j	KCN		9½	9½	9½				
1.07	0.16	Intl Contr sv	ICY.A		0.60	0.6					
1.95	1.25	Intl Curator Res									

How to read the stock tables

1 2	3	4	5	6	7	8	9	10	11	12	Reading Imperial Oil Limited Data
52-week high low	Stock	Sym	Div	High	Low	Close	Chg	Vol (100s)	Yield	P/E ratio	

1. Arrow up or down - new 52-week high or low in day's trading

2. 52-week high/low - highest and lowest inter-day price in past 52 weeks — 48¾ 40⅛

3. Stock - abbreviated company name — Imperial Oil

4. Sym - Ticker symbol assigned to issue by exchange; .PR is preferred share, .WT is warrant, .UN is unit, .S means stocks are subject to regulation of the SEC Act,. W means when issued. — IMO

5. Div - Indicated annual dividend (excluding special dividends) — 1.80

6. High - Highest inter-day trading price — 46⅜

7. Low - Lowest inter-day trading price — 46

8. Close - Closing price — 46¼

9. Chg - Change between closing price and previous closing board lot price — + ⅛

10. Vol. - Number of shares traded in 100s; z preceding figure indicates sales are reported in full — 2533

11. Yield - expressed as percentage, calculated by dividing the dividend by current market price — 3.89%

12. P/E ratio - Price/earnings ratio; current stock price divided by the company's earnings per share from continuing operations for the latest 12 months — 25

To demonstrate the use of separate accounts for contributed capital and retained earnings as found in corporation accounting and to contrast their use with the accounts used in partnership accounting, assume the following: On January 5, 1996, a partnership involving two partners and a corporation having five shareholders were formed. Also assume that $25,000 was invested in each. In the partnership, J. Olm invested $10,000 and A. Baker invested $15,000. In the corporation, each of the five shareholders bought 500 common shares at $10 per share. Without dates and explanations, General Journal entries to record the investments are:

SHAREHOLDERS' EQUITY ACCOUNTS COMPARED TO PARTNERSHIP ACCOUNTS

Partnership			Corporation		
Cash	10,000		Cash	25,000	
J. Olm, Capital		10,000	Common Shares . .		25,000
Cash	15,000				
A. Baker, Capital . .		15,000			

After the entries are posted, the owners' equity accounts of the two companies appear as follows:

Partnership
J. Olm, Capital

Date	Dr.	Cr.	Bal.
Jan. 5, 1996		10,000	10,000

Corporation
Common Shares

Date	Dr.	Cr.	Bal.
Jan. 5, 1996		25,000	25,000

A. Baker, Capital

Date	Dr.	Cr.	Bal.
Jan. 5, 1996		15,000	15,000

To continue the illustration, assume that during 1996, each company earned a net income of $8,000 and also distributed $5,000 to its owners. According to the partnership agreement, incomes are allocated 40% to Olm and 60% to Baker. The cash distribution to the partners was divided equally. The corporation declared the dividends on December 20, 1996, and both companies made the cash payments to owners on December 25, 1996. The entries to record the distribution of cash to partners and the declaration and payments of dividends to shareholders are

Partnership			Corporation		
J. Olm, Withdrawals	2,500		Dividends Declared	5,000	
A. Baker, Withdrawals . .	2,500		Dividends Payable .		5,000
Cash		5,000	Dividends Payable	5,000	
			Cash		5,000

At the end of the year, the entries to close the Income Summary accounts are

Partnership		Corporation	
Income Summary 8,000		Income Summary 8,000	
J. Olm, Capital	3,200	Retained Earnings . .	8,000
A. Baker, Capital . .	4,800		

Finally, the entries to close the withdrawals accounts and the Dividends Declared account are

Partnership		Corporation	
J. Olm, Capital 2,500		Retained Earnings 5,000	
A. Baker, Capital 2,500		Dividends Declared . .	5,000
J. Olm, Withdrawals . .	2,500		
A. Baker, Withdrawals	2,500		

After posting these entries, the owners' equity accounts of the two companies are

Partnership
J. Olm, Capital

Date	Dr.	Cr.	Bal.
5/1/96		10,000	10,000
31/12/96		3,200	13,200
31/12/96	2,500		10,700

Corporation
Common Shares

Date	Dr.	Cr.	Bal.
5/1/96		25,000	25,000

A. Baker, Capital

Date	Dr.	Cr.	Bal.
5/1/96		15,000	15,000
31/12/96		4,800	19,800
31/12/96	2,500		17,300

Retained Earnings

Date	Dr.	Cr.	Bal. (dr.)
20/12/96	5,000		5,000
31/12/96		8,000	3,000

J. Olm, Withdrawals

Date	Dr.	Cr.	Bal.
25/12/96	2,500		2,500
31/12/96		2,500	–0–

Dividends Declared

Date	Dr.	Cr.	Bal.
20/12/96	5,000		5,000
31/12/96		5,000	–0–

A. Baker, Withdrawals

Date	Dr.	Cr.	Bal.
25/12/96	2,500		2,500
31/12/96		2,500	–0–

Observe that in the partnership, after all entries have been posted, the $28,000 equity of the owners appears in the capital accounts of the partnership.

J. Olm, capital	$10,700
A. Baker, capital	17,300
Total owners' equity	$28,000

By comparison, the shareholders' equity of the corporation is divided between contributed capital and the Retained Earnings account, as follows:

Common shares	$25,000
Retained earnings	3,000
Total shareholders' equity	$28,000

Sale of Shares for Cash

When shares are sold for cash and immediately issued, an entry like the following is made to record the sale and issuance:

June	5	Cash	300,000.00	
		Common Shares		300,000.00
		Sold and issued 30,000 common shares at $10 per share.		

Exchanging Shares for Noncash Assets

A corporation may accept assets other than cash in exchange for its shares. In the process, the corporation also may assume some liabilities, such as a mortgage on some of the property. These transactions are recorded with an entry like this:

June	10	Machinery	10,000.00	
		Buildings	65,000.00	
		Land	15,000.00	
		Long-Term Notes Payable		50,000.00
		Common Shares		40,000.00
		Exchanged 4,000 common shares for machinery, buildings, and land.		

A corporation also may give shares of its share capital to its promoters in exchange for their services in organizing the company. In this case, the corporation receives the intangible asset of being organized in exchange for its shares. Record this transaction as follows:

ISSUANCE OF SHARES

LO 2
Record the issuance of common shares.

June	5	Organization Costs	5,000.00	
		Common Shares		5,000.00
		Gave the promoters 500 common shares in exchange		
		for their services in organizing the corporation.		

SALE OF SHARES THROUGH SUBSCRIPTIONS

LO 3

Record transactions involving share subscriptions and explain the effects of shares subscribed on a corporation's assets and shareholders' equity.

Usually, shares are sold for cash and immediately issued. However, corporations sometimes sell their shares through **subscriptions.** For example, when a new corporation is formed, the organizers may realize that the new business has limited immediate need for cash but will need additional cash in the future. To get the corporation started on a sound footing, the organizers may sell shares to investors who agree to contribute some cash now and to make additional contributions in the future. When shares are sold through subscriptions, the investor agrees to buy a certain number of the shares at a specified price. The agreement also states when payments are to be made. When the subscription is accepted by the corporation, it becomes a contract and the corporation acquires an asset. The asset is the right to receive payment from subscribers. At the same time, subscribers gain an equity in the corporation.

To illustrate the sale of shares through subscriptions, assume that Northgate Corporation accepted subscriptions on May 6 to 5,000 common shares at $12 per share. The subscription contracts called for a 10% down payment with the balance to be paid in two equal installments due after three and six months. Northgate records the subscriptions with the following entry:

May	6	Subscriptions Receivable, Common Shares	60,000.00	
		Common Shares Subscribed		60,000.00
		Accepted subscriptions to 5,000 common shares at . .		
		$12 per share.		

At the time that subscriptions are accepted, the firm debits the Subscriptions Receivable account for the total amount of the subscription. This is the amount the subscribers agreed to pay. Notice that the **Common Shares Subscribed** account is credited for the same amount.

The receivables are converted into cash when the subscribers pay for their shares. And when all the payments are received, the subscribed shares will be issued. Northgate records the receipt of the down payment and the two installment payments with these entries:

May	6	Cash	6,000.00	
		Subscriptions Receivable, Common Shares		6,000.00
		Collected 10% down payments on the common shares		
		subscribed.		
Aug.	6	Cash	27,000.00	
		Subscriptions Receivable, Common Shares		27,000.00
		Collected the first installment payments on the		
		common shares subscribed.		

Nov.	6	Cash	27,000.00	
		Subscriptions Receivable, Common Shares		27,000.00
		Collected the second installment payments on the common shares subscribed.		

In this case, the down payments accompanied the subscriptions. Therefore, the accountant could have combined the May 6 entries to record the receipt of the subscriptions and to record the down payments.

When shares are sold through subscriptions, the shares usually are not issued until the subscriptions are paid in full. Also, if dividends are declared before subscribed shares have been issued, the dividends go only to the holders of outstanding shares, not to the subscribers. However, as soon as the subscriptions are paid, the shares are issued. The entry to record the issuance of the Northgate common shares is

Nov.	6	Common Shares Subscribed	60,000.00	
		Common Shares		60,000.00
		Issued 5,000 common shares sold through subscriptions.		

Subscriptions are usually collected in full, but not always. Sometimes, a subscriber fails to pay the agreed amount. When this default happens, the subscription contract is canceled. If the subscriber has made a partial payment on the contract, the amount may be refunded. Or the company may issue a smaller number of shares. Or in some jurisdictions, the subscriber's partial payment may be kept by the corporation to compensate it for any damages.

Subscriptions Receivable and Subscribed Shares on the Balance Sheet

Subscriptions receivable may be reported on the balance sheet as current or long-term assets, depending on when collection is expected. If a corporation prepares a balance sheet after accepting subscriptions to its share capital but before the shares are issued, both the issued shares and the subscribed shares should be reported on the balance sheet as follows:

Common shares, unlimited number of shares authorized, 20,000 shares issued	$200,000
Common shares subscribed, 5,000 shares	60,000
Total common shares issued and subscribed ..	$260,000

Progress Check

15-4   A company issued 7,000 common shares and a $40,000, 5-year, (interest at current market) note payable in exchange for equipment valued at $105,000. The entry to record the transaction would include a credit *(a)* of $105,000 to Common Shares; *(b)* of $65,000 to Retained Earnings; *(c)* of $65,000 to Common Shares.

15-5   The costs of incorporation, such as legal costs, should be expensed in the period of incurrence. Agree?

15-6   On December 31, 1996, XPC Inc. had 100,000 common shares outstanding, issued at $10 per share. The retained earnings balance was $200,000. On January 2, 1997, XPC received confirmed subscriptions for 10,000 shares at $15 per share accompanied by a 25% down payment. XPC accepted all of the subscriptions. Determine *(a)* the number of common shares outstanding at close of January 2, 1997, and *(b)* the total shareholders' equity at close of January 2, 1997.

RIGHTS OF COMMON SHAREHOLDERS

LO 4

State the differences between common and preferred shares, and allocate dividends between common and preferred shares.

When investors buy a corporation's common shares, they acquire all the *specific* rights granted by the corporation's charter to its common shareholders. They also acquire the *general* rights granted shareholders by the laws of the jurisdiction in which the company is incorporated. The laws vary, but common shareholders usually have the following general rights:

1. The right to vote at shareholders' meetings.
2. The right to sell or otherwise dispose of their shares.
3. The right to share pro rata with other common shareholders in any dividends declared.
4. The right to share equally in any assets that remain after creditors are paid when the corporation is liquidated.

If desired, the articles of incorporation may provide additional rights. For example, the articles may specifically provide for the **preemptive right,** which holds that no shares of a class shall be issued unless the shares have first been offered to the shareholders holding shares of that class, and that those shareholders have a first opportunity to acquire the offered shares in proportion to their holdings of the shares of that class, at such a price and on such terms as those shares are offered to others.

CLASSES OF SHARES

The Canada Business Corporations Act allows corporations to issue registered no-par-value shares by class and by series of the class so long as there exists one "residual" class of shares that may vote at all meetings of shareholders (except for meetings of specified classes of shareholders) and that may receive the remaining assets of a corporation upon dissolution. The act does not use the adjectives *common* and *preferred* but simply refers to shares in general. Classes of shares may continue to be designated common, preferred, Class A, Class B, and so on. However, the act does require the articles to set out the rights, privileges, restrictions, and conditions attaching to each class and series of shares. Because of their widespread usage, the terms *common* and *preferred* are used throughout this book.

If two classes of share capital are issued, one is generally called **preferred** and the other is called *common*.

The term *preferred* is used because the preferred shares have a higher priority (or senior status) relative to common shares in one or more ways. These typically include a preference for receiving dividends and a preference in the distribution of assets if the corporation is liquidated.

In addition to the preferences it receives, preferred share capital carries all the rights of common share capital, unless they are nullified in the articles of incorporation. For example, most preferred shares do not have the right to vote. In effect, this disadvantage is accepted in return for the preferences.

PREFERRED SHARES

Preferred Dividends

A preference for dividends gives preferred shareholders the right to receive their dividends before the common shareholders receive a dividend. In other words, a dividend cannot be paid to common shareholders unless preferred shareholders also receive one. The amount of dividends that the preferred shareholders must receive is usually expressed as a dollar amount per share. For example, holders of $9 preferred shares must be paid dividends at the rate of $9 per share per year before the common shareholders can receive any dividend. A preference for dividends does not, however, grant an absolute right to dividends. If the board of directors does not declare a dividend, neither the preferred nor the common shareholders receive one.

Cumulative and Noncumulative Preferred Shares

Preferred shares can be either **cumulative** or **noncumulative**. For cumulative, any undeclared dividends accumulate each year until they are received. For noncumulative, the right to receive dividends is forfeited in any year that the dividends are not declared.

When preferred shares are cumulative and the board of directors fails to declare a dividend to the preferred shareholders, the unpaid dividend is called a **dividend in arrears**. The accumulation of dividends in arrears on cumulative preferred shares does not guarantee that they will be paid. However, the cumulative preferred shareholders must be paid both the current dividend and all dividends in arrears before any dividend can be paid to the common shareholders.

To show the difference between cumulative and noncumulative preferred shares, assume that a corporation has outstanding 1,000 of $9 preferred shares issued at $100 per share and 4,000 common shares issued at $50 per share. During 1996, the first year of the corporation's operations, the board of directors declared cash dividends of $5,000. During 1997, it declared $42,000. The allocations of the total dividends are as follows:

	Preferred	Common
Assuming noncumulative preferred:		
1996	$ 5,000	$ 0
1997:		
First: current preferred dividend	$ 9,000	
Remainder to common		$33,000
Assuming cumulative preferred:		
1996	$ 5,000	$ 0
1997:		
First: dividends in arrears	$ 4,000	
Next: current preferred dividend	9,000	
Remainder to common		$29,000
Totals	$13,000	$29,000

Notice that the allocation of the 1997 dividends depends on whether the preferred shares are noncumulative or cumulative. With noncumulative preferred shares, the preferred shareholders never receive the $4,000 that was skipped in 1996. However, when the preferred shares are cumulative, the $4,000 in arrears is paid in 1997 before the common shareholders receive a dividend.

Disclosure of Dividends in Arrears in the Financial Statements

Dividends are not like interest expense, which is incurred as time passes and therefore must be accrued. A liability for a dividend does not come into existence until the dividend is declared by the board of directors. Thus, if a preferred dividend date passes and the corporation's board fails to declare the dividend on its cumulative preferred shares, the dividend in arrears is not a liability. Accordingly, it does not appear as a liability on the balance sheet. However, when preparing the financial statements, the *full-disclosure principle* requires the corporation to report the amount of preferred dividends in arrears as of the balance sheet date. Normally, this information is given in a note. If there is no such disclosure, readers of the financial statements have the right to assume that preferred dividends are not in arrears.

WHY PREFERRED SHARES ARE ISSUED

A corporation might issue nonparticipating preferred shares for several reasons. One reason is to raise capital without sacrificing control of the corporation. For example, suppose that the organizers of a business have $100,000 cash to invest but wish to organize a corporation that needs $200,000 of capital to get off to a good start. If they sold $200,000 of common shares, they would have only 50% control and would have to negotiate extensively with the other shareholders in making policy. However, if they issue $100,000 of common shares to themselves and can sell to outsiders, at $100 per share, 1,000 shares of $8, cumulative preferred shares that have no voting rights, they can retain control of the corporation.

A second reason for issuing preferred shares is to boost the return earned by the common shareholders. Using the previous example to illustrate, suppose that the corporation's organizers expect the new company to earn an annual after-tax income of $24,000. If they sell and issue $200,000 of common shares, this income produces a 12% return on the $200,000 of common shareholders' equity. However, if they sell and issue $100,000 of each kind of shares, retaining the common for themselves, their own return increases to 16% per year, as shown here:

Net after-tax income	$24,000
Less preferred dividends at $(1,000 \times \$8)$	(8,000)
Balance to common shareholders (equal to 16% on their $100,000 investment)	$16,000

In this case, the common shareholders earn 16% because the assets contributed by the preferred shareholders are invested to earn $12,000 while the preferred dividend payments amount to only $8,000.

The use of preferred shares to increase the return to common shareholders is an example of **financial leverage**. Whenever the dividend rate on preferred shares is less than the rate that the corporation earns on its assets, the effect of issuing preferred shares is to increase (or *lever*) the rate earned by common shareholders. Financial leverage also occurs when debt is issued and paid an interest rate less than the rate earned from using the assets the creditors loaned to the corporation.

There are other reasons for issuing preferred shares. For example, a corporation's preferred shares may appeal to some investors who believe that its common shares are too risky or that the dividend rate on the common shares will be too low. Also, if a corporation's management wants to issue common shares but believes the current market price for the common shares is too low, the corporation may issue preferred shares that are convertible into common shares. If and when the price of the common shares increases, the preferred shareholders can convert their shares into common shares.

Progress Check

15-7   In what ways may preferred shares have a priority status to common shares?

15-8   Increasing the return to common shareholders by including preferred shares in the capital structure is an example of   (a) financial leverage;   (b) cumulative earnings;   (c) dividends in arrears.

15-9   MBI Corp. has 9,000 shares at $5, cumulative preferred and 27,000 common shares issued and outstanding. No dividends have been declared for the past two years, but during the current year, MBI declares a $288,000 dividend. The amount to be paid to common shareholders is   (a) $243,000;   (b) $153,000;   (c) $135,000.

As mentioned above, an issue of preferred shares can be made more attractive to some investors by giving them the right to exchange the preferred shares for a fixed number of common shares. **Convertible preferred shares** offer investors a higher potential return than do nonconvertible preferred shares. If the company prospers and its common shares increase in value, the convertible preferred shareholders can share in the prosperity by converting their preferred shares into the more valuable common shares.

CONVERTIBLE PREFERRED SHARES

LO 5

Explain convertible preferred shares and explain the meaning of the redemption, book, and market values of shares.

To see how the conversion of preferred shares is recorded, assume that a corporation's outstanding shares include 1,000 shares of $10 convertible preferred. The shares were originally issued for $103 per share. Each preferred share is convertible into four shares of common. If all of the preferred shares are converted on May 1, the entry to record the conversion is

May	1	Preferred Shares	103,000.00	
		Common Shares		103,000.00
		To record the conversion of preferred shares.		

When the preferred shares are converted into common shares, the balance in the preferred shares account is removed and replaced with an account balance related to common shares. No gain or loss is recorded.

SHARE VALUES

In addition to an average stated value, shares may have a par value, *call price*, a *market value*, and a *book value*.

The Canada Business Corporations Act, 1975, as well as the more recently passed provincial counterparts, require that all shares be of **no par** or nominal value. These acts also require the total consideration received by the corporation for each share issued must be added to the stated capital account maintained for the shares of that class or series. Some jurisdictions still permit the issuance of par value shares. **Par value** is an arbitrary value a corporation places on a share of its share capital.

In Canada, the use of par value shares has declined in recent years. As such, we have not provided examples in the text using par value shares.

Redemption Value of Callable Preferred Shares

Some issues of preferred shares are callable. This means that the issuing corporation has the right to retire the **callable preferred shares** by paying a specified amount to the preferred shareholders. The amount that must be paid to call and retire a preferred share is its **call price, or redemption value**. This amount is set at the time the shares are issued. Normally, the call price includes the issue price of the shares plus a premium that provides the shareholders with some additional return on their investment. When the issuing corporation calls and retires preferred shares, it must pay not only the call price but also any dividends in arrears.

Market Value

The market value of a share is the price at which it can be bought or sold. Market values are influenced by a wide variety of factors including expected future earnings, dividends, and events in the economy at large.

Book Value

The **book value of a share** is one share's portion of the corporation's net assets as recorded in the company's accounts. If a corporation has only common shares, the book value per share equals the total shareholders' equity divided by the number of outstanding shares. For example, if a company has 10,000 outstanding shares and total shareholders' equity of $285,000, the book value is $28.50 per share ($285,000/10,000 shares).

Computing the book values of shares is more complex when both common and preferred shares are outstanding. To calculate the book values of each class of shares, you begin by allocating the total shareholders' equity between the two classes. The preferred shareholders' portion equals the preferred share's call price (average stated value if the preferred is not callable) plus any cumulative dividends in arrears. Then allocate the remaining shareholders' equity to the common shares. To determine the book value per share of preferred, divide the portion of shareholders' equity assigned to preferred by the number of preferred shares outstanding. Similarly, the book value per share of common is the shareholders' equity assigned to common divided by the number of outstanding common shares. For example, assume a corporation has the shareholders' equity as shown in Illustration 15–4.

If the preferred shares are callable at $103 per share and two years of cumulative preferred dividends are in arrears, the book values of the corporation's shares are calculated as follows:

Total shareholders' equity		$ 447,000
Less equity applicable to preferred shares:		
Redemption value	$103,000	
Cumulative dividends in arrears ($100,000 × 7% × 2)	14,000	(117,000)
Equity applicable to common shares		$ 330,000
Book value of preferred shares ($117,000/1,000)		$117.00
Book value of common shares ($330,000/10,000)		$ 33.00

In their annual reports to shareholders, corporations sometimes report the increase in the book value of the corporation's shares that has occurred during a year. Also, book value may have significance in contracts. For example, a shareholder may enter into a contract to sell shares at their book value at some future date. However, this agreement may not be wise because book value normally does not approximate market value.

Similarly, book value should not be confused with liquidation value. If a corporation is liquidated, its assets probably will sell at prices that are quite different from the amounts at which they are carried on the books.

USING THE INFORMATION— DIVIDEND YIELD

LO 7
Calculate dividend yield and explain its meaning.

Investors buy shares of a company in anticipation of receiving a return from cash dividends and from increases in share value. Shares that pay large dividends on a regular basis are sometimes called *income shares*. They are attractive to investors who want dependable cash flows from their investments. In contrast, other shares pay few or no dividends but are still attractive to investors because they expect the market value of the shares to increase rapidly. The shares of companies that do not distribute cash but use it to finance rapid expansion are often called *growth shares*.

One way to evaluate whether a company's shares should be viewed as income or growth shares is to examine the **dividend yield.** The following formula shows that this ratio is a rate of return based on the annual cash dividends and the share's market value:

$$\text{Dividend yield} = \frac{\text{Annual cash dividends per share}}{\text{Market value per share}}$$

Illustration 15-4
Shareholders' Equity
with Preferred and
Common Shares

Shareholders' Equity	
Share capital:	
Preferred, $7, cumulative,	
2,000 shares authorized, 1,000 shares	
issued and outstanding	$105,000
Common, no par value, unlimited number of shares	
authorized, 10,000 shares issued and outstanding . .	$260,000
Total contributed capital	$365,000
Retained earnings	82,000
Total shareholders' equity	$447,000

Dividend yield may be calculated on a historical basis using the prior year's actual dividends or on an expected basis. For example, recall from the first page of this chapter the discussion of Imperial Oil and the dividend and share price information for several companies. The dividend yields for those companies were as follows:

Company	Common Dividend 1994	Share Prices Feb. 15, 1995	Current Dividend Yield
Imperial Oil Limited	$1.80*	$46 ¼	3.89%
BCE Inc.	2.72	43 ⅜	6.27
Anchor Lamina Inc.	0.12	6	2.00
Imasco Inc.	1.92	41 ⅜	4.64
Hemlo Gold Ltd.	0.20	11 ⅞	1.68

*Excludes special dividend of $3.00.

An investor can compare these dividend yields to evaluate the relative importance of dividends to the prices of the shares. Current dividends obviously have little impact on **Anchor Lamina** and **Hemlo Gold**. The values of these shares must stem from expected increases in their share prices (and the eventual dividends that may be paid).

On the other hand, **Imasco** and **BCE** pay substantial dividends to yield 4.64% and 6.27%, respectively. These are less than one would expect from investments in corporate debt securities but still high enough to conclude that dividends are a very important factor in establishing their share prices.

SUMMARY OF THE CHAPTER IN TERMS OF LEARNING OBJECTIVES

LO 1. Explain the advantages, disadvantages, and organization of corporations and the differences in accounting for partnerships and corporations. Advantages of the corporate form of business include the following: *(a)* status as separate legal entity; *(b)* lack of shareholder liability for corporate debts; *(c)* a corporation's continuity of life; and *(d)* the fact shareholders are not agents of the corporation. A disadvantage is that corporations are closely regulated by government. Also, the taxable status of corporations is often a disadvantage but sometimes may be an advantage.

A corporation is governed by the shareholders through the board of directors. Officers who manage the corporation include a president, perhaps one or more vice presidents, and a secretary. The chief executive officer may be the president or the board of directors chairperson.

LO 2. Record the issuance of no-par-value shares. When no-par-value shares are issued, the entire proceeds are credited to the share capital account.

LO 3. Record transactions involving share subscriptions and explain the effects of subscribed shares on a corporation's assets and shareholders' equity. If a corporation sells shares through subscriptions, the right to receive payment is an asset of the corporation and the subscribers' equity is recorded in contributed capital accounts. The balance of the Common Shares Subscribed account is transferred to the Common Shares account when the shares are issued, which normally occurs after all payments are received.

LO 4. State the differences between common and preferred shares and allocate dividends between the common and preferred shares. Preferred shares have a priority (or senior status) relative to common shares in one or more ways. Usually, this means that common shareholders cannot be paid dividends unless a specified amount of dividends is also paid to preferred shareholders. Preferred shares also may have a priority status if the corporation is liquidated. The dividend preference for many preferred shares is cumulative, and a few preferred shares also participate in dividends beyond the preferred amount.

LO 5. Describe convertible preferred shares and explain the meaning of the redemption, book, and market values of shares. On the conversion of convertible preferred shares into common shares, the carrying value of the preferred shares is transferred to contributed capital accounts that relate to common shares. No gain or loss is recorded. If preferred shares are callable, the amount that must be paid to retire the share is its call price plus any dividends in arrears. Market value is the price that a share commands when it is bought or sold. The book value of a preferred share is any dividends in arrears plus its stated value, or if it is callable, its redemption price. The residual shareholders' equity is divided by the number of outstanding common shares to determine the book value per share of the common.

LO 6. Calculate dividend yield and explain its meaning. The dividend yield is the ratio between a share's annual dividend and its market value. It describes the rate of return provided to the shareholders from the company's dividends. The yield can be compared with the rates of return offered by other kinds of investments to determine whether the shares should be viewed as income or growth shares.

Barton Corporation was created on January 1, 1996. The following transactions relating to shareholders' equity occurred during the first two years of the company's operations. Prepare the journal entries to record these transactions. Also prepare the balance sheet presentation of the organization costs, liabilities, and shareholders' equity as of December 31, 1996, and December 31, 1997. Include appropriate notes to the financial statements.

DEMONSTRATION PROBLEM

1996

Jan.   1   Authorized the issuance of an unlimited number of shares of no-par-value common shares and 100,000 shares of no-par-value preferred shares. The preferred shares pay a $10 annual dividend and are cumulative.

Jan. 1   Issued 200,000 common shares at $12 per share.

      1   Issued 100,000 common shares in exchange for a building valued at $820,000 and merchandise inventory valued at $380,000.

      1   Accepted subscriptions for 150,000 common shares at $12 per share. The subscribers made no down payments, and the full purchase price was due on April 1, 1996.

      1   Paid a cash reimbursement to the company's founders for $100,000 of organization costs, which are to be amortized over 10 years.

      1   Issued 12,000 preferred shares for $110 per share.

Apr. 1   Collected the full subscription price for the January 1 common shares and issued the shares.

Dec. 31   The Income Summary account for 1996 had a $125,000 credit balance before being closed to Retained Earnings; no dividends were declared on either the common or preferred shares.

1997

June 4   Issued 100,000 common shares for $15 per share.

Dec. 10   Declared dividends payable on January 10, 1998, as follows:

          To preferred shareholders for 1996 . . . . $120,000
          To preferred shareholders for 1997 120,000
          To common shareholders for 1997 300,000

     31   The Income Summary account for 1997 had a $1 million credit balance before being closed to Retained Earnings.

Planning the Solution

- Record journal entries for the events in 1996 and 1997.
- Close the accounts related to retained earnings at the end of each year.
- Determine the balances for the 1996 and 1997 balance sheets, including the following amounts to use in the balance sheet and the accompanying note:
  a. The number of shares issued.
  b. The amount of dividends in arrears.
  c. The unamortized balance of organization costs.
- Prepare the specified portions of the 1996 and 1997 balance sheets.

Solution to Demonstration Problem

1996
Jan. 1 Cash 2,400,000.00
          Common Shares 2,400,000.00
          Issued 200,000 common shares.

      1 Building 820,000.00
         Merchandise Inventory 380,000.00
          Common Shares 1,200,000.00
          Issued 100,000 common shares.

1996				
Jan.	1	Subscriptions Receivable	1,800,000.00	
		Common Shares Subscribed		1,800,000.00
		Accepted subscriptions for 150,000 common shares.		
	1	Organization Costs	100,000.00	
		Cash		100,000.00
		Reimbursed the founders for organization costs.		
	1	Cash	1,320,000.00	
		Preferred Shares		1,320,000.00
		Issued 12,000 preferred shares.		
Apr.	1	Cash	1,800,000.00	
		Subscriptions Receivable		1,800,000.00
		Collected balance due on subscribed common shares.		
	1	Common Shares Subscribed	1,800,000.00	
		Common Shares		1,800,000.00
		Issued 150,000 subscribed common shares.		
Dec.	31	Income Summary	125,000.00	
		Retained Earnings		125,000.00
		To close the Income Summary account and update Retained Earnings.		

1997				
June	4	Cash	1,500,000.00	
		Common Shares		1,500,000.00
		Issued 100,000 common shares.		
Dec.	10	Cash Dividends Declared	540,000.00	
		Dividends Payable, Common Shares		300,000.00
		Dividends Payable, Preferred Shares		240,000.00
		Declared current dividends and dividends in arrears to common and preferred shareholders, payable on January 10, 1998.		
	31	Income Summary	1,000,000.00	
		Retained Earnings		1,000,000.00
		To close the Income Summary account and update Retained Earnings.		
	31	Retained Earnings	540,000.00	
		Cash Dividends Declared		540,000.00
		To close to Retained Earnings the Cash Dividends Declared.		

Balance sheet presentations:

	As of December 31,	
	1996	1997
Assets		
Organization costs	$ 90,000	$ 80,000
Liabilities		
Dividends payable, common shares		$ 300,000
Dividends payable, preferred shares		240,000
Total liabilities		$ 540,000
Shareholders' Equity		
Share capital:		
Preferred, no par value, $10, cumulative, 100,000 shares authorized, 12,000 shares issued . . .	$1,320,000	$1,320,000
Common, no par value, unlimited number of shares authorized, 450,000 shares issued in 1996, and 550,000 shares in 1997	$5,400,000	$6,900,000
Retained Earnings (see Note 1)	125,000	585,000
Total shareholders' equity	$6,845,000	$8,805,000

Note 1: As of December 31, 1996, there were $120,000 of dividends in arrears on the preferred shares.

GLOSSARY

Book value of a share   one share's portion of the issuing corporation's share capital recorded in its accounts. pp. 702–03

Call price   another name for *redemption value.* p. 702

Callable preferred shares   preferred shares that the issuing corporation, at its option, may retire by paying a specified amount (the call price) to the preferred shareholders plus any dividends in arrears. p. 702

Common shares   shares of a corporation that has only one class of shares, or if there is more than one class, the class that has no preferences over the corporation's other classes of shares. pp. 698–99

Common Shares Subscribed   a shareholders' equity account in which a corporation records the value of unissued common shares that investors have contracted to purchase. p. 696

Convertible preferred shares   preferred shares that can be exchanged for shares of the issuing corporation's common shares at the option of the preferred shareholder. p. 701

Cumulative preferred shares   preferred shares on which undeclared dividends accumulate until they are paid; common shareholders cannot receive a dividend until all cumulative dividends have been paid. p. 699

Dividends in arrears   an unpaid dividend on cumulative preferred shares; it must be paid before any regular dividends on the preferred shares and before any dividends on the common shares. p. 699

Dividend yield   a company's annual cash dividends per share divided by the market value per share. p. 703

Financial leverage   the achievement of an increased return on common shares by paying dividends on preferred shares or interest at a rate that is less than the rate of return earned with the assets invested in the corporation by the preferred shareholders or creditors. p. 701

Noncumulative preferred shares   preferred shares on which the right to receive dividends is forfeited for any year that the dividends are not declared. p. 699

No-par shares   a class of shares that does not have a par value. p. 702

Organization costs   the costs of bringing a corporation into existence, including legal fees, promoters' fees, and amounts paid to secure incorporation. p. 688

Par value   an arbitrary value assigned to a share when the shares are authorized. p. 702

Preemptive right the right of common shareholders to protect their proportionate interest in a corporation by having the first opportunity to buy additional common shares issued by the corporation. p. 698

Preferred shares shares that give their owners a priority status over common shareholders in one or more ways, such as the payment of dividends or the distribution of assets on liquidation. pp. 699–702

Proxy a legal document that gives an agent of a shareholder the power to exercise the voting rights of that shareholder's shares. p. 689

Redemption value the amount that must be paid to call and retire a preferred share. p. 702

Subscription a contractual commitment by an investor to purchase unissued shares and become a shareholder. p. 696

SYNONYMOUS TERMS

Call price redemption value.

Preferred senior status.

Subscribers incorporators; founders; promoters.

QUESTIONS

1. Who is responsible for directing the affairs of a corporation?

2. What are organization costs? List several examples of these costs.

3. How are organization costs classified on the balance sheet?

4. What are the duties and responsibilities of a corporation's registrar and transfer agent?

5. List the general rights of common shareholders.

6. What distinguishes preferred shares from common shares?

7. What is the difference between cumulative and non-cumulative preferred shares?

8. What are the balance sheet classifications of these accounts: (a) Subscriptions Receivable, Common Shares, and (b) Common Shares Subscribed?

9. What is the difference between the market value and the book value of a share?

10. Why would an investor find convertible preferred shares attractive?

11. Laws place no limit on the amounts that partners can withdraw from a partnership. On the other hand, laws regulating corporations place definite limits on the amount of dividends that shareholders can receive from a corporation. Why do you think there is a difference?

QUICK STUDY (Five-Minute Exercises)

Of the following statements, which are true for the corporate form of business?

a. Capital is often more easily accumulated than with other forms of organization.

b. It has a limited life.

c. Owners have unlimited liability for corporate debts.

d. Distributed income is taxed twice in normal circumstances.

e. It is a separate legal entity.

f. Ownership rights cannot be easily transferred.

g. Owners are not agents of the corporation.

QS 15–1
(LO 1)

On June 1, YMI Corporation issued 25,000 common shares for $168,000 cash. Present the entry to record this transaction.

QS 15–2
(LO 2)

710   Chapter 15

QS 15–3
(LO 3)

On August 15, Retro Company accepted subscriptions to 12,000 common shares at $10 per share. A 20% down payment was made on this date with the remainder to be paid in six months. Prepare an entry to record this transaction.

QS 15–4
(LO 4)

Nosar Company's shareholders' equity includes 20,000 shares of $1, cumulative, nonparticipating preferred and 200,000 common shares. Nosar did not declare any dividends during the prior year and now declares and pays a $72,000 cash dividend. Determine the amount distributed to each class of shareholders.

QS 15–5
(LO 4)

Prepare journal entries to record the following transactions for Gruene Corporation:

June 15 Declared a $24,000 cash dividend payable to common shareholders.

July 31 Paid the dividend declared on June 15.

Dec. 31 Closed the Cash Dividends Declared account.

QS 15–6
(LO 5)

The shareholders' equity section of Roscoe Company follows:

Shareholders' Equity

Preferred shares, $0.50 cumulative, 20,000 shares authorized, issued, and outstanding	$ 200,000
Common shares, unlimited number of no par-value shares authorized, 150,000 shares issued and outstanding	750,000
Retained earnings	890,000
Total shareholders' equity	$1,840,000

QS 15–7
(LO 6)

The call price of the preferred is $45 and 1 year's dividends are in arrears. Determine the book value per common share. SOS Company expects to pay out a $4.50 per share cash dividend next year on its common shares. The current market price per share is $52.20. Calculate the expected dividend yield on SOS shares.

EXERCISES

Exercise 15–1
Recording issuances of shares
(LO 2)

Prepare General Journal entries to record the following issuances of shares by two different corporations:

1. One thousand common shares are issued for $65,000 cash.
2. Two hundred common shares are issued to promoters in exchange for their efforts in organizing the corporation. The promoters' efforts are estimated to be worth $9,000

Exercise 15–2
Comparative entries for partnership and corporation
(LO 1, 2)

Tom Seabrink and Joan Miller began a new business on February 14 when each of them invested $125,000 in the company. On December 20, it was decided that $48,000 of the company's cash would be distributed equally between the owners. Two cheques for $24,000 were prepared and given to the owners on December 23. On December 31, the company reported a $96,000 net income.

Prepare two sets of journal entries to record the investments by the owners, the distribution of cash to the owners, the closing of the Income Summary account, and the withdrawals or dividends under these alternative assumptions: *(a)* the business is a partnership, and *(b)* the business is a corporation that issued 1,000 no-par-value common shares.

On July 25 United Corporation issued 20,000 common shares for a building and land. The market value of the building and land was $300,000. A comparable land site recently sold for $60,000. Give the entry to record the acquisition.

Exercise 15–3
Accounting for issuance of shares for building and land
(LO 2)

On May 15, Sealtest Dairy Corporation accepted subscriptions to 60,000 no-par-value common shares at $39.00 per share. The subscription contracts called for one-fourth of the subscription price to accompany each contract as a down payment with the balance to be paid on November 15. Give the entries to record *(a)* the subscriptions, *(b)* the down payments, *(c)* receipt of the remaining amount due on the subscriptions, and *(d)* issuance of the shares.

Exercise 15–4
Share subscriptions
(LO 3)

The outstanding share capital of Kuker Realty Corporation includes 47,000 shares of $4 cumulative preferred and 82,000 shares no-par value of common. During its first four years of operation, the corporation declared and paid the following amounts in dividends: first year, $0; second year, $200,000; third year, $420,000; and fourth year, $200,000. Determine the total dividends paid in each year to each class of shareholders. Also determine the total dividends paid to each class over the four years.

Exercise 15–5
Allocating dividends between common and cumulative preferred shares
(LO 4)

Determine the total dividends paid in each year to each class of shareholders of the previous exercise under the assumption that the preferred shares are noncumulative. Also determine the total dividends paid to each class over the four years.

Exercise 15–6
Allocating dividends between common and noncumulative preferred shares
(LO 4)

Four individuals have agreed to begin a new business requiring a total investment of $900,000. Each of the four will contribute $150,000, and the remaining $300,000 will be raised from other investors. Two alternative plans for raising the money are being considered: (1) issue 9,000 common shares at $100 to all investors, or (2) issue 6,000 common shares at $100 to the four founders and 3,000 shares at $100, $7, cumulative preferred to the remaining investors. If the business is expected to earn an after-tax net income of $126,000, what rate of return will the founders earn under each alternative? Which of the two plans will provide the higher return to the four founders?

Exercise 15–7
Effect of preferred shares on rates of return
(LO 4)

How would your answers to Exercise 15–7 be changed if the business is expected to earn an after-tax net income of only $54,000?

Exercise 15–8
Effect of preferred shares on rates of return
(LO 4)

Lakeview Corporation has 6,400 outstanding shares of $8 preferred that is convertible into the corporation's no-par common at the rate of 4 shares of common for 1 share of preferred. The preferred shares were issued at $126 per share. Assume that all shares are presented for conversion.

Longview Manufacturing Corporation has issued 8,000 shares of $25 preferred at $250 per share. Each preferred share is convertible into 20 shares of the corporation's no-par-value common. Assume that one-fourth of the convertible preferred shares were presented for conversion.

Present entries dated March 2 to record the conversions on the books of the two corporations.

Exercise 15–9
Convertible preferred shares
(LO 5)

Exercise 15–10
Per share book value
(LO 5)

The shareholders' equity section from Micro Software Corporation's balance sheet is as follows:

Shareholders' Equity

Share capital:
Preferred share capital, $4, cumulative, $55 call price,
12,000 shares issued and outstanding . . . . $ 600,000
Common, no par value, 120,000 shares issued and outstanding . .   1,200,000
Retained earnings   780,000

Total shareholders' equity $2,580,000

Required

1. Determine the book value per share of the preferred and of the common under the assumption that there are no dividends in arrears on the preferred shares.

2. Determine the book value per share for each class of shares under the assumption that two years' dividends are in arrears on the preferred shares.

Exercise 15–11
Calculating dividend yield
(LO 6)

Calculate the dividend yield for each of these situations:

	Annual Dividend per Share	Market Price per Share
a.	$6.00	$ 64.00
b.	3.00	30.50
c.	5.50	65.00
d.	0.60	43.00
e.	1.00	25.00
f.	7.50	108.00

PROBLEMS

Problem 15–1
Share subscriptions
(LO 2, 3, 4)

Conrad Corporation is authorized to issue 50,000 shares of $8 cumulative preferred and an unlimited number of no-par-value common shares. Conrad Corporation then completed these transactions:

Apr. 4 Accepted subscriptions to 70,000 common shares at $18 per share. Down payments equal to 25% of the subscription price accompanied each subscription. The balance is due on June 3.

11 Give the corporation's promoters 1,300 common shares for their services in organizing the corporation. The board valued the services at $26,000.

May 1 Accepted subscriptions to 4,000 preferred shares at $110 per share. The subscriptions were accompanied by 40% down payments. The balance is due on July 31.

June 3 Collected the balance due on the April 4 common subscriptions and issued the shares.

July 1 Accepted subscriptions to 3,000 preferred shares at $112 per share. The subscriptions were accompanied by 40% down payments. The balance is due on August 15.

31 Collected the balance due on the May 1 preferred subscriptions and issued the shares.

Required

1. Prepare General Journal entries to record the transactions.
2. Prepare the shareholders' equity section of the corporation's balance sheet as of the close of business on July 31. Assume that retained earnings are $23,000.

Ideal Motor Company is authorized by its articles of incorporation to issue an unlimited number of common shares and 50,000 shares of $8, noncumulative convertible preferred. The company completed the following transactions:

Problem 15–2
Shareholders' equity transactions
(LO 2, 3, 4, 5)

1995

Feb. 2   Issued for cash 210,000 common shares at $1 per share.

   28   Gave the corporation's promoters 75,000 common shares for their services in organizing the corporation. The directors valued the services at $80,000.

Mar. 10   Issued 250,000 common shares in exchange for the following assets with the indicated reliable market values: land, $70,000; buildings, $130,000; and machinery, $89,000.

Dec. 31   Closed the Income Summary account. A $61,000 loss was incurred.

1996

Jan. 1   Issued for cash 6,000 preferred shares at $100 per share.

Dec. 1   Ideal Motor Company's preferred shareholders submitted 1,000 shares of their convertible preferred for conversion into common shares on this date. The convertible preferred shareholders accepted 80 common shares for each share of preferred.

   31   Closed the Income Summary account. A $196,000 net income was earned.

1997

Jan. 1   The board of directors declared an $8 cash dividend to preferred shares and $0.20 per share cash dividend to outstanding common shares, payable on January 25 to the January 15 shareholders of record.

   25   Paid the previously declared dividends.

Nov. 15   Accepted subscriptions to 30,000 common shares at $3.00 per share. Down payments of 25% accompanied the subscription contracts. The balance is due on February 15, 1998.

Dec. 31   Closed the Cash Dividends Declared and Income Summary accounts. A $262,000 net income was earned.

Required

1. Prepare General Journal entries to record the transactions.
2. Prepare the shareholders' equity section of the balance sheet as of the close of business on December 31, 1997.

Sunray Energy Company is authorized to issue an unlimited number of common shares and 200,000 shares of $5, noncumulative, convertible preferred. The company completed the following transactions:

Problem 15–3
Shareholders' equity transactions
(LO 2, 3, 4, 5)

1995

Feb. 5   Issued 140,000 common shares at $5 for cash.

   28   Gave the corporation's promoters 7,500 common shares for their services in organizing the corporation. The directors valued the services at $40,000.

Mar. 3   Issued 88,000 common shares in exchange for the following assets with the indicated reliable market values: land, $80,000; buildings, $210,000; and machinery, $155,000.

Dec. 31   Closed the Income Summary account. A $27,000 loss was incurred.

1996

Jan. 28   Issued 8,000 preferred shares at $50 for cash.

Dec. 15   Sunray Energy Company's preferred shareholders submitted 5,000 of their convertible shares for conversion into common shares on this date. The convertible preferred shareholders accepted nine common shares for each preferred share.

      31   Closed the Income Summary account. A $98,000 net income was earned.

1997

Jan. 1   The board of directors declared a $5 cash dividend to preferred shares and $0.10 per share cash dividend to outstanding common shares, payable on February 5 to the January 25 shareholders of record.

Feb. 5   Paid the previously declared dividends.

Oct. 20   Accepted subscriptions to 8,000 common shares at $7.45 per share. Down payments of 40% accompanied the subscription contracts. The balance is due on January 20, 1998.

Dec. 31   Closed the Cash Dividends Declared and Income Summary accounts. A $159,000 net income was earned.

Required

1. Prepare General Journal entries to record the transactions.
2. Prepare the shareholders' equity section of the balance sheet as of the close of business on December 31, 1997.

Problem 15–4
Calculating book values; allocating dividends between preferred and common shares
(LO 4, 5)

Part 1. The balance sheet of Fiber Filter Company includes the following information:

Shareholders' Equity

Share capital:
Preferred, $5, cumulative, 4,000 shares
    authorized and issued $200,000
Common, no-par value, 60,000 shares authorized and issued .. 600,000
Retained earnings 120,000
Total shareholders' equity $920,000

Required

Assume that the preferred shares have a call price of $55 plus any dividends in arrears. Calculate the book value per share of the preferred and common under each of the following assumptions:

a.   No dividends are in arrears on the preferred shares.

b.   One year's dividends are in arrears on the preferred shares.

c.   Three years' dividends are in arrears on the preferred shares.

Part 2. Since its organization, Newtone Corporation has had 3,200 outstanding shares of $8 preferred and 64,000 shares of no-par-value common. No dividends have been paid this year, and none were paid during either of the past two years. However, the company has recently prospered and the board of directors wants to know how much cash would be required to provide a $1.50 per share dividend on the common. The preferred was issued at $100 per share and the common at $10 per share.

Required

Prepare a schedule that shows the amounts of cash required for dividends to each class of shareholders to provide the desired $1.50 per share dividend under each of the following assumptions:

a. The preferred is noncumulative.

b. The preferred is cumulative.

c. Determine amounts in (a) and (b) if desired dividend was $2 per common share.

Part 1. The balance sheet of Instant Services Corporation includes the following information:

Problem 15–5
Calculating book values; allocating dividends between preferred and common shares
(LO 4, 5)

Shareholders' Equity

Share capital:

Preferred $8, cumulative, 5,000 shares authorized and issued	$ 500,000
Common, no-par value, 80,000 shares authorized and issued	800,000
Retained earnings	385,000
Total shareholders' equity	$1,685,000

Required

Assume that the preferred has a call price of $105 plus any dividends in arrears. Calculate the book value per share of the preferred and common under each of the following assumptions:

a. There are no dividends in arrears on the preferred.

b. One year's dividends are in arrears on the preferred.

c. Three years' dividends are in arrears on the preferred.

Part 2. Since its organization, KPO Corporation has had 14,000 outstanding shares of $11 preferred and 235,000 shares of no-par-value common. No dividends have been paid this year, and none were paid during either of the past two years. However, the company has recently prospered, and the board of directors wants to know how much cash would be required to provide a $1.00 per share dividend on the common. Preferred was issued at $100 per share and the common at $10 per share.

Required

Prepare a schedule that shows the amounts of cash required for dividends to each class of shareholders to provide the desired $1.00 per share dividend to the common shareholders under each of the following assumptions:

a. The preferred is noncumulative.

b. The preferred is cumulative.

c. Determine amounts in (a) and (b) if desired dividend was $1.50 per common share.

Problem 15–6
Allocating dividends in sequential years between preferred and common shares
(LO 4)

Axcel Bros. Company has 4,000 outstanding shares of $6 preferred and 60,000 shares of no-par-value common. During a seven-year period, the company paid out the following amounts in dividends:

1990	$ –0–
1991	54,000
1992	–0–
1993	30,000
1994	39,000
1995	48,000
1996	90,000

No dividends were in arrears for the years prior to 1990.

Required

1. Prepare two schedules with column headings as follows:

Year	Calculations	Preferred Dividend per Share	Common Dividend per Share

2. Complete a schedule under each of the following assumptions. (Round your calculations of dividends per share to the nearest cent.) The preferred was issued at $50 per share and common at $5 per share.

    a. The preferred is noncumulative.

    b. The preferred is cumulative.

Problem 15–7
Calculation of book values
(LO 5)

Essex Plastics Corporation's common shares are selling on a stock exchange today at $16.80 per share, and a just-published balance sheet shows the following information about the shareholders' equity of the corporation:

Shareholders' Equity

Share capital:	
Preferred, $5, cumulative, 15,600 shares authorized and outstanding	$ 780,000
Common, no par value, 130,000 shares authorized and outstanding	1,650,000
Retained earnings	330,000
Total shareholders' equity	$2,760,000

Required

1. What is the market value of the corporation's common shares?
2. If there are no dividends in arrears, give the book values for
    a. the preferred shares.
    b. the common shares.
3. If two years' dividends are in arrears on the preferred, give the book values for
    a. the preferred shares. (Assume that the preferred shares are not callable.)
    b. the common shares.

Problem 15–8
Analytical essay
(LO 1)

Jan Carston and Carey Glenwood want to create a new software development business. Each of them can contribute fairly large amounts of capital. However, they know that the business will need additional equity capital from other investors after its first year. With respect to their individual activities, they are both planning to devote full-time effort to getting the first products out the door within the year. They plan to hire three employees initially and expect to distribute a substantial amount of cash every year for their personal expenses. Carston has proposed organizing the business as a general partnership, but Glenwood thinks that a corporation offers more advantages. They have asked you to prepare a brief analysis that supports choosing the corporate form. What main points would you include in your analysis?

Refer to the shareholders' equity section of the balance sheet in Problem 15–4. Assume, however, that the common has an unlimited number of shares authorized instead of 60,000. Also, assume that the preferred shares are convertible into common at a rate of eight common shares for each share of preferred. If 1,000 shares of the preferred are converted into common shares, describe how this affects the shareholders' equity section of the balance sheet (immediately after the conversion). If you are a common shareholder in this company, and cash dividends of $487,000 are to be paid out, does it make any difference to you whether or not the conversion takes place? Why?

Problem 15–9
Analytical essay
(LO 4, 5)

PROVOCATIVE PROBLEMS

Jae Xu and Bob Lyle have operated a sports equipment company, X-L Sports, for a number of years as partners sharing net incomes and gains in a 3 to 2 ratio. Because the business is growing, the two partners entered into an agreement with Tom Celic to reorganize their firm into a corporation. The new corporation, X-L Sports, Inc., is authorized to issue 75,000 common shares of no-par-value. On the date of the reorganization, August 15, 1996, a trial balance of the partnership ledger appears as follows:

**Provocative Problem
15–1**
X-L Sports, Inc.
(LO 1, 2)

X-L SPORTS
Trial Balance
August 15, 1996

Cash	$ 38,255	
Accounts receivable	69,750	
Allowance for doubtful accounts		$ 2,625
Merchandise inventory	316,875	
Store equipment	73,500	
Accumulated amortization, store equipment		15,750
Buildings	375,000	
Accumulated amortization, buildings		75,000
Land	93,750	
Accounts payable		41,625
Notes payable		262,500
Jae Xu, capital		339,380
Bob Lyle, capital		230,250
Totals	$967,130	$967,130

The agreement between the partners and Celic carries these provisions:

1. The partnership assets are to be revalued as follows:
   a. The $2,250 account receivable of Blue Tigers is known to be uncollectible and is to be written off as a bad debt.
   b. After writing off the Blue Tigers account, the allowance for doubtful accounts is to be increased to 4% of the remaining accounts receivable.

    c. The merchandise inventory is to be written down to $285,000 to allow for damaged and shopworn goods.

    d. Insufficient amortization has been taken on the store equipment. Therefore, its book value is to be decreased to $48,750 by increasing the balance of the accumulated amortization account.

    e. The building is to be written up to its replacement cost, $487,500, and the balance of the accumulated amortization account is to be increased to show the building to be one-fifth amortized.

2.   After the partnership assets are revalued, the assets and liabilities are to be transferred to the corporation in exchange for its shares, with each partner accepting shares at $10 per share for his equity in the partnership.

3.   Tom Celic is to buy any remaining authorized shares for cash at $10 per share.

After reaching the agreement outlined, the three principals hired you as accountant for the new corporation. Your first task is to determine the number of shares each person should receive, and to prepare entries on the corporation's books to record the issuance of shares in exchange for the partnership's assets and liabilities and the issuance of shares to Celic for cash. In addition, prepare a balance sheet for the corporation as it should appear after all the shares are issued.

Provocative Problem 15–2
Andrews Corporation
(LO 4)

The management of Andrews Corporation is considering the expansion of its business operations to a new and exciting line of business in which newly invested assets can be expected to earn 20% per year. At present, Andrews Corporation has only 18,000 common shares of no-par-value outstanding, which were issued at $50 per share, no other contributed capital accounts, and retained earnings of $270,000. Existing operations consistently earn approximately $175,000 each year. To finance the new expansion, management is considering three alternatives: *(a)* Issue 5,000 shares of $13, cumulative preferred. The investment advisors of the company conclude that these shares could be issued at $100 per share. *(b)* Issue 2,000 shares of $13 cumulative convertible at 3 for 1, preferred. The investment advisors conclude that these shares could be sold for $250 per share. *(c)* Issue 6,250 common shares at $80 per share.

In evaluating these three alternatives, Andrews Company management asked you to calculate the dividends that would be distributed to each class of shareholder based on the assumption that each year the board of directors will declare dividends equal to the total net income earned by the corporation. Your calculations should show the distribution of dividends to preferred and common shareholders under each of the three alternative financing plans. You should also calculate dividends per share of preferred and dividends per share of common.

As a second part of your analysis, assume that you own 1,000 of the common shares outstanding prior to the expansion and that you will not acquire or purchase any of the newly issued shares. Based on your whole analysis, would you prefer that the proposed expansion in operations be rejected? If not, comment on the relative merits of each alternative from your point of view as a common shareholder.

Provocative Problem 15–3
Reinhold Corporation and Rollins Company
(LO 4, 5)

Having recently inherited $75,000, Brian Parker is thinking about investing the money in one of two securities. They are: Reinhold Corporation common shares or the preferred shares issued by Rollins Company. The companies manufacture and sell competing products, and both have been in business about the same length of time—four years in the case of Reinhold Corporation and five years for Rollins Company. Also, the two companies have about the same amounts of shareholders' equity, as the following equity sections from their latest balance sheets show:

REINHOLD CORPORATION

Common shares, no-par value, unlimited number of shares authorized, 5,000,000 shares issued	$5,000,000
Retained earnings	2,000,000
Total shareholders' equity	$7,000,000

ROLLINS COMPANY

Preferred shares, $8 cumulative unlimited number, of shares authorized, 20,000 shares issued	$2,000,000*
Common shares, no-par value, unlimited number authorized, 400,000 shares issued	4,000,000
Retained earnings	200,000
Total shareholders' equity	$6,200,000

*The current and one prior year's dividends are in arrears on the preferred shares.

Reinhold Corporation did not pay a dividend on its common shares during its first year's operations: however, since then, for the past three years, it has paid a $0.20 per share annual dividend. The shares are currently selling for $1.50 per share. The preferred shares of Rollins Company, on the other hand, are selling for $95 per share. Mr. Parker favours these shares as an investment. He feels the shares are a real bargain since they are selling $21 below book value, and as he says, "Since it is a preferred, the dividends are guaranteed." Too, he feels the common shares of Reinhold Corporation, selling at 7% above book value and 50% above its average stated value, while paying only a $0.20 per share dividend, are overpriced.

Required

a.   Are the preferred shares of Rollins Company selling at a price $21 below its book value, and are the common shares of Reinhold Corporation selling at a price 7% above book value and 50% above their average stated value?

b.   From an analysis of the shareholders' equity sections, express your opinion of the two shares as investments and describe some of the factors Mr. Parker should consider in choosing between the two securities.

Use the information provided in the financial statements of Geac Computer Corporation Limited and the notes (see Appendix I) to answer the following questions:

1.   What classes of shares have been authorized?
2.   How many shares are authorized and outstanding?
3.   Are any shares subscribed?
4.   Did the number of shares of all classes change during 1994? If so, what caused the change?
5.   Did the company pay dividends in 1994?

Provocative Problem 15–4

Financial statement analysis

ANALYTICAL AND REVIEW PROBLEMS

Until March 2 of the current year, Kay, Lace, and Moon were partners sharing losses and gains in a 5:3:2 ratio. On that date they received their certificate of incorporation of KLM Company, Limited. All the assets and liabilities of the partnership were taken over by the new corporation.

A & R Problems 15–1

The trial balance of the partnership just before the transfer and the opening trial balance of the corporation appear below:

KLM COMPANY
Post-Closing Trial Balance
March 2, 19—

Cash	$ 4,500	
Accounts receivable	20,500	
Allowance for doubtful accounts		$ 500
Merchandise inventory	33,000	
Store equipment	13,500	
Accumulated amortization, store equipment		3,500
Land	8,500	
Building	65,000	
Accumulated amortization, building		9,500
Accounts payable		15,500
Mortgage payable		12,000
Kay, capital		45,000
Lace, capital		40,000
Moon, capital		19,000
	$145,000	$145,000

KLM COMPANY, LIMITED
Trial Balance
March 2, 19—

Cash	$ 4,500	
Accounts receivable	20,500	
Allowance for doubtful accounts		$ 1,500
Merchandise inventory	25,000	
Store equipment	8,000	
Land	22,000	
Building	52,000	
Accounts payable		15,500
Mortgage payable		12,000
Share capital, common, no par value, 20,600 shares		103,000
	$132,000	$132,000

Required

How many shares did each shareholder receive? Support your answer.

A&R Problem 15–2

During the first year after incorporation, the following common share transactions were completed:

a. Immediately after incorporation sold 50,000 shares at $40 per share for cash.

b. Near mid-year received a subscription for 1,000 shares at $45 per share, collected 50% in cash, balance due in two equal installments within one year.

c. Two months later issued 500 shares for a used machine that would be used in operations. The machine had cost $30,000 new and was carried by the seller at a book value of $18,000. It was appraised at $24,000 six months previously by a reputable independent appraiser.

d. Collected half of the unpaid subscriptions in (b).

Required

Give entries for each of the above transactions.

CONCEPT TESTER

Test your understanding of the concepts introduced in this chapter by completing the following crossword puzzle.

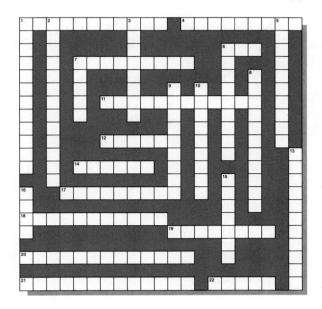

Across Clues

1. Total proceeds credited to share capital account (2 words).
4. Synonym for incorporators.
6. Arbitrary value placed on shares in some jurisdictions.
7. Shares that have senior status.
11. Costs of starting a corporation.
12. Shares with no preference over other classes of shares.
14. Value at which shares issued can be bought.
17. Possible life of a corporation.
18. Issued shares in hands of shareholders.
19. Preferred shares that the corporation has right to retire.
20. Preferred shares that forfeit claim to unpaid dividends.
21. Founders of a corporation.
22. Ratio of annual dividends to market price.

Down Clues

1. Owners of a corporation.
2. Number of shares a corporation is permitted to issue.
3. Achievement of an increased return by use of senior securities.
5. Value at which corporation can call its preferred shares.
6. CEO of a corporation.
7. Legal document that gives voting rights to another individual.
8. Capital invested by shareholders.
9. A type of leverage.
10. Redemption value of preferred shares (2 words).
13. Preferred shares that can be exchanged for common at option of owners.
15. Unpaid dividends on cumulative preferred shares.
16. A type of value of shares.

ANSWERS TO PROGRESS CHECKS

15–1　*b*

15–2　A corporation must pay taxes on its income, and its shareholders must pay personal income taxes on dividends received from the corporation.

15–3　A proxy is a legal document used to transfer a shareholder's right to vote to another person.

15–4　*c*

15–5　No. These costs should be recorded in an asset account, Organization Costs.

15–6　*(a)* $100,000. *(b)* $1,237,500.

15–7　Typically preferred shares have a preference in receiving dividends and in the distribution of assets in the case of a company's liquidation.

15–8　*a*

15–9　*b*

Total dividend	$288,000
To preferred shareholders	135,000*
Remainder to common shareholders	$153,000

*9,000 × $5 × 3 = $135,000

Additional Corporate Transactions; Reporting Income and Retained Earnings; Earnings per Share

*W*hile in the library studying the annual reports of the companies referred to in the previous chapter, Karen White came across an update on one of the companies. This was the three-month report as of November 30, 1994, of Anchor Lamina Inc. She was particularly interested in the remarks of Clare E. Winterbottom, Chairman and CEO:

> In general, we feel that the present is an appropriate time for expansion. We are very adequately financed, thanks to the equity issues placed in 1993. We have also recently concluded new banking relations and arrangements which will add greatly to our financial strength.
>
> Anchor Lamina is in an expansion mode. It is our intention to make the Company the leader in its industry—and the most profitable.

After reading the remarks, White took the following data to share with Mark Smith.

Astonishing growth of global markets is leading even small companies to customers and investors in other countries. In addition, today's complex world requires complex financial structures.

Anchor Lamina Inc.
Financial Highlights

Year Ended August 31	1994	1993	1992
Consolidated sales	$74,692,601	$59,048,537	$44,706,423
Net income	$ 8,433,081	$ 5,340,942	$ 901,899
Avg. shares outstanding	17,330,199	11,571,467	10,033,865
Earnings per share	49¢	45¢	9¢

3 Months to November 30	1994	1993
Consolidated sales	$30,315,000	$17,162,000
Net income	2,624,000	1,592,000
Avg. shares outstanding	18,096,000	16,143,789
Earnings per share	15¢	10¢

LEARNING OBJECTIVES

After studying Chapter 16, you should be able to:

1. **Record cash dividends, stock dividends, and stock splits and explain their effects on the assets and shareholders' equity of a corporation.**
2. **Record retirement of shares and describe the effect on shareholders' equity.**
3. **Describe restrictions and appropriations of retained earnings and the disclosure of such items in the financial statements.**
4. **Explain how the income effects of discontinued operations, extraordinary items, changes in accounting principles, and prior period adjustments are reported.**
5. **Calculate earnings per share for companies with simple capital structures and explain the difference between basic and fully diluted earnings per share.**
6. **Calculate the price-earnings ratio and explain its meaning.**
7. **Define or explain the words and phrases listed in the chapter glossary.**

We begin this chapter with a discussion of dividends and other transactions between a corporation and its shareholders. In this section of the chapter, you will learn about stock dividends, stock splits, and repurchases of shares by the issuing corporation. The second section of the chapter explains how income and retained earnings information is classified and reported. The third section explains how accountants report the earnings per share of a corporation. Understanding these topics will help you interpret and evaluate corporate financial statements. Note: use of the term *shares* rather than *stock* is preferred in Canada, but in the case of dividends in shares of the issuing corporation, *stock dividend* is normally used instead of *share dividend*. Also, the terms *stock split,* and *stock option,* are in common usage.

CORPORATE DIVIDENDS AND OTHER SHARE CAPITAL TRANSACTIONS

LO 1

Record cash dividends, stock dividends, and stock splits and explain their effects on the assets and shareholders' equity of a corporation.

In Chapter 3, we first described a corporation's retained earnings as the total amount of its net incomes less its net losses and dividends declared since it began operations. Years ago, retained earnings were commonly called **earned surplus**. However, the term is rarely used anymore.

Retained Earnings and Dividends

Most jurisdictions require that a corporation not pay cash dividends unless retained earnings are available. However, the payment of a cash dividend reduces both cash and shareholders' equity. Therefore, a corporation cannot pay a cash dividend simply because it has a credit balance in Retained Earnings; it also must have enough cash on hand to pay the dividend. If cash or assets that will shortly become cash are not available, the board of directors may choose to avoid a dividend declaration even though the Retained Earnings balance is adequate. Even if a corporation has a large Retained Earnings balance, the board of directors may refuse to declare a dividend because the available cash is needed in the operations of the business.

In deciding whether to declare dividends, the board of directors must recognize that operating activities are a source of cash. Perhaps some cash from operating activities should be paid out in dividends and some should be retained for emergencies. In addition, some cash may be retained to pay dividends in years when current operating activities do not generate enough cash to pay normal dividends. Furthermore, management may want to retain some cash from operating activities to finance expanded operations. See page 724 for a discussion of limitations in considering declaration and distribution of a cash dividend.

As was noted in Chapter 15, shareholders enjoy limited liability. Consequently, corporation laws provide for the protection of creditors and others dependent on the continuity of the corporation. To this end, the more recently passed corporations acts include a solvency test. For example, the Canada Business Corporation Act 1975 provides the following in section 40:

> A corporation shall not declare or pay a dividend if there are responsible grounds for believing that
>
> (a) the corporation is, or would after the payment be, unable to pay its liabilities as they become due; or
>
> (b) the realizable value of the corporation's assets would thereby be less than the aggregate of its liabilities and stated capital of all classes.

Entries for the declaration and distribution of a cash dividend were presented in Chapter 15 and need not be repeated here. It should be noted that asset distributions in excess of a credit balance in Retained Earnings are **liquidating dividends**— a return of original investment.

Stock Dividends

Sometimes, a corporation distributes its own unissued shares to its shareholders without receiving any consideration from the shareholders. This type of distribution is called a **stock dividend.** A stock dividend and a cash dividend are very different. A cash dividend transfers assets from the corporation to the shareholders. As a result, a cash dividend reduces the corporation's assets and its shareholders' equity. On the other hand, a stock dividend does not transfer assets from the corporation to the shareholders; it has no effect on assets and no effect on total shareholders' equity.

However, a stock dividend does have an effect on the components of shareholders' equity. To record a stock dividend, you must transfer some of the Retained Earnings balance to contributed capital accounts. For example, assume that Northwest Corporation's shareholders' equity is

---

Shareholders' Equity

Share capital:		
Common shares, no-par value, unlimited number of shares authorized, 10,000 shares issued and outstanding	$108,000	
Retained earnings	35,000	
Total shareholders' equity		$143,000

On December 31, the directors of Northwest Corporation declared a 10%, or 1,000-share, stock dividend distributable on January 20 to the shareholders of record on January 15.

If the market value of Northwest Corporation's shares on December 31 is $15 per share, the dividend declaration is recorded as

Dec.	31	Stock Dividends Declared	15,000.00	
		Common Stock Dividend Distributable		15,000.00
		To record the declaration of a 1,000-share common stock dividend.		

Note that the debit is to Stock Dividends Declared. In previous chapters, when we discussed cash dividends, they were debited to Dividends Declared. However, since a corporation may declare stock dividends as well as cash dividends, a convenient system of accounts would include separate Cash Dividends Declared and Stock Dividends Declared accounts.

In the year-end closing process, close the Stock Dividends Declared account to Retained Earnings as follows:

Dec.	31	Retained Earnings	15,000.00	
		Stock Dividends Declared		15,000.00

On January 20 record the distribution of the shares as follows:

Jan.	20	Common Stock Dividend Distributable	15,000.00	
		Common Shares		15,000.00
		To record the distribution of 1,000 common shares.		

Note that these entries shift $15,000 of the shareholders' equity from retained earnings to contributed capital, or in other words, $15,000 of retained earnings is *capitalized.* Note also that the amount of retained earnings capitalized is equal to the market value of the 1,000 shares issued ($15 × 1,000 shares = $15,000).[1]

As you already learned, a stock dividend does not distribute assets to the shareholders; it has no effect on the corporation's assets. Also, it has no effect on total shareholders' equity and no effect on the percentage of the company owned by each individual shareholder. To illustrate these last points, assume that Johnson owned 100 shares of Northwest Corporation's outstanding shares prior to the stock dividend. The 10% stock dividend gave each shareholder 1 new share for each 10 shares previously held. Therefore, Johnson received 10 new shares.

Illustration 16–1 shows Northwest Corporation's total contributed and retained capital and the book value of Johnson's 100 shares before the dividend and after the dividend.

---

[1]The Canada Business Corporations Act requires that the value of a stock dividend be added to the stated capital account. In other jurisdictions, for example, Ontario, the amount to be capitalized is left to the board of directors.

Before the 10% stock dividend:
Share capital:

Common shares (10,000 shares)	$108,000
Retained earnings	35,000
Total contributed and retained capital	$143,000

$143,000/10,000 shares outstanding = $14.30 per share book value.
Book value of Johnson's 100 shares: $14.30 × 100 = $1,430.

After the 10% stock dividend is distributed:
Share capital:

Common shares (11,000 shares)	$123,000
Retained earnings	20,000
Total contributed and retained capital	$143,000

$143,000/11,000 shares outstanding = $13 per share book value.
Book value of Johnson's 110 shares: $13 × 110 = $1,430.

Illustration 16-1
The Effect of Northwest
Corporation's Stock
Dividend on
Shareholders

Illustration 16–1 shows that before the stock dividend, Johnson owned 100/10,000, or 1/100, of the Northwest Corporation shares, and his holdings had a $1,430 book value. After the dividend, he owns 110/11,000, or 1/100, of the corporation, and his holdings still have a $1,430 book value. In other words, there was no effect on Johnson's investment except that it was repackaged from 100 units into 110. Also, the only effect on the corporation's capital was a transfer of $15,000 from retained earnings to contributed capital. To summarize, there was no change in the corporation's total assets, no change in its total capital or equity, and no change in the percentage of that equity owned by Johnson.

Why Stock Dividends Are Distributed

If stock dividends have no effect on corporation assets and shareholders' equities other than to repackage the equities into more units, why are such dividends declared and distributed? The primary reason for stock dividends is related to the market price of a corporation's common shares. For example, if a profitable corporation grows by retaining earnings, the price of its common shares also tends to grow. Eventually, the price of a share may become high enough to discourage some investors from buying the shares. Thus, the corporation may declare stock dividends to keep the price of its shares from increasing too much. Yet another reason normally cited by management is to preserve cash. For these reasons, some corporations declare stock dividends each year.

Some shareholders may like stock dividends for another reason. Often, corporations that declare stock dividends continue to pay the same cash dividend per share after a stock dividend as before. The result is that shareholders receive more cash each time dividends are declared.

Amount of Retained Earnings Capitalized

The Canada Business Act requires that if a corporation declares a stock dividend, it must capitalize an amount of retained earnings that equals the market value of the shares to be distributed. A requirement to capitalize a specified amount of retained earnings is without justification. If the board of directors can decide the amount of cash dividends, then the power to decide the amount of retained earnings to be capitalized should also be left to their discretion. The authors therefore believe that the provision of the Ontario Corporations Act is correct. That is, the board of directors decides the amount of retained earnings to be capitalized. In the meantime, since there is not consistency in corporate laws regarding the amount of retained earnings to be capitalized, corporations must observe the requirements of the laws of the jurisdiction of incorporation.

Stock Dividends on the Balance Sheet

Because a stock dividend is "payable" in shares rather than in assets, it is not a liability of its issuing corporation. Therefore, if a balance sheet is prepared between the declaration and distribution dates of a stock dividend, the amount of the dividend distributable should appear on the balance sheet in the shareholders' equity section:

Share Capital:
Common shares, no-par value, unlimited number of shares authorized,
    shares issued and outstanding $108,000
Common stock dividend distributable, 1,000 shares 15,000
Total common shares issued and to be issued $123,000
Retained earnings 20,000
Total shareholders' equity $143,000

STOCK SPLITS

Sometimes, when a corporation's shares are selling at a high price, the corporation calls them in and issues two, three, or more new shares in the place of each previously outstanding share. For example, a corporation that has shares selling for $375 a share may call in the old shares and issue to the shareholders 4 shares, 10 shares, or any number of shares in exchange for each share formerly held. This is known as a **stock split.** The usual purpose of a stock split is to reduce the market price of the shares and thereby facilitate trading in the shares. Less frequently, a corporation may have a **reverse stock split.** In that case the corporation calls in the old shares and issues 1 new share for each 2 shares, 3 shares, 10 shares, or any number of shares previously held. The usual purpose of a reverse stock split is to cause an increase in the per share market value.

A stock split (or reverse split) has no effect on total shareholders' equity, and no effect on the equities of the individual shareholders. Also, the balances of the Contributed Capital and Retained Earnings accounts are not changed. Thus, a stock split (or reverse split) does not require a journal entry. All that is required is a memorandum entry in the share capital account reciting the facts of the split. For example, such a memorandum might read, "Issued 10 new common shares for each old share previously outstanding." When you prepare the balance sheet, the new number of shares outstanding must be used.

As a Matter of Ethics

Falcon Corporation's board of directors and officers have been meeting to discuss and plan the agenda for the corporation's 1994 annual shareholders' meeting. The first item considered by the directors and officers was whether to report a large government contract that Falcon has just obtained. Although this contract will significantly increase income and cash flows in 1994 and beyond, management decided that there is no need to reveal the news at the shareholders' meeting. "After all," one officer said, "the meeting is intended to be the forum for describing the past year's activities, not the plans for the next year."

After concluding that the contract will not be mentioned, the group has moved on to the next topic for the shareholders' meeting. This topic is a motion for the shareholders to approve a compensation plan that will award the managers the rights to acquire large quantities of shares over the next several years. According to the plan, the managers will have a three-year option to buy shares at a fixed price that equals the market value of the shares as measured 30 days after the upcoming shareholders' meeting. In other words, the managers will be able to buy shares in 1995, 1996, or 1997 by paying the 1994 market value. Obviously, if the shares increase in value over the next several years, the managers will realize large profits without having to invest any cash. The financial vice president asks the group whether they should reconsider the decision about the government contract in light of its possible relevance to the vote on the stock option plan.

Progress Check

16–1   Which of the following statements is correct?
   a. For federally incorporated companies, a stock dividend is recorded by capitalizing retained earnings equal to the market value of the distributable shares.
   b. Stock dividends and stock splits have the same effect on total assets and retained earnings of the issuing corporation.
   c. A stock dividend does not transfer corporate assets to shareholders but does require that retained earnings be capitalized.

16–2   What distinguishes a 100% stock dividend from a 2-for-1 stock split?

16–3   When accounting for a stock dividend an Ontario corporation capitalizes what amount of retained earnings?

Under the Canada Business Corporations Act, as well as under the more recently passed provincial acts, such as the one in Ontario, a corporation may purchase and retire shares of its own outstanding share capital if it can satisfy a solvency test applicable to cash dividends and cited earlier in this chapter. For example, it was noted in the annual report of **Imasco Limited** that at December 31, 1994, 1,771,400 common shares had been repurchased. These repurchased shares were restored to the status of authorized but unissued shares.

When shares are purchased for retirement, the debit to the stated capital account is the product of the number of shares acquired multiplied by the weighted average per share invested by the shareholders. If the shares are purchased for less than the weighted average per share invested by the shareholders, the difference is credited to an account such as Contributed Capital from Retirement of Shares. On the other hand, if the shares are purchased for more than the weighted average per share invested by the shareholders, the difference is debited to contributed capital from previous credit balances of share retirement transactions to the extent of its balance with any remainder debited to Retained Earnings.

RETIREMENT OF SHARE CAPITAL

LO 2

Record retirement of shares and describe the effect on shareholders' equity.

For example, assume a corporation originally issued its no-par-value common shares at an average price of $12 per share. If the corporation later purchased and retired 1,000 of these shares at the price for which they were issued, the entry to record the retirement is

Apr.	12	Common Shares	12,000.00	
		Cash		12,000.00
		Purchased and retired 1,000 common shares at $12 per share.		

On the other hand, if the corporation paid $11 per share instead of $12, the entry for the retirement is

Apr.	12	Common Shares	12,000.00	
		Cash		11,000.00
		Contributed Capital from the Retirement of Common Shares		1,000.00
		Purchased and retired 1,000 common shares at $11 per share.		

If the corporation paid $15 per share, the entry for the purchase and retirement is

Apr.	12	Common Shares	12,000.00	
		Retained Earnings	3,000	
		Cash		15,000.00
		Purchased and retired 1,000 common shares at $15 per share.		

In jurisdictions that have par values when such shares are reaquired for cancellation, all capital items related to the shares being retired are removed from the accounts, and the difference between the purchase price and the weighted average per share invested by the shareholders is treated in a like manner to that illustrated above for no-par-value shares. In addition to the entry to record the reacquisition of shares, corporate statutes require the corporation to **restrict** or appropriate retained earnings equal to the cost of the reacquired shares. This requirement is based on a view that the reacquisition of shares has the same impact as the payment of a cash dividend. The restriction may be accomplished by a note (cross-referenced to the balance sheet) or by a journal entry such as the following:

Retained Earnings	12,000	
Resricted Retained Earnings—Reacquisition of shares		12,000

A corporation may voluntarily designate an amount of retained earnings for some special purpose as a means of explaining to shareholders why dividends are not being declared. In contrast to retained earnings, which carry binding restrictions by law or by contract, **appropriated retained earnings** result from a voluntary action by the board of directors. In earlier years, such appropriations were recorded by transferring portions of retained earnings from the Retained Earnings account to another shareholders' equity account such as Retained Earnings Appropriated for Contingencies or Retained Earnings Appropriated for Plant Expansion. When the contingency or other reason for an appropriation no longer existed, the appropriation account was eliminated by returning its balance to the Retained Earnings account. Today these retained earnings restrictions are usually explained in a letter attached to the financial statements.

VOLUNTARY APPROPRIATIONS OF RETAINED EARNINGS

LO 3

Describe restrictions and appropriations of retained earnings and the disclosure of such items in the financial statements.

REPORTING OF INCOME AND RETAINED EARNINGS INFORMATION

When the revenue and expense transactions of a company consist only of routine, continuing operations, a single-step income statement is adequate. This format shows revenues followed by a list of operating expenses and the net income. Often, however, the activities of a business include items not closely related to its continuing operations. In these cases, the income effects of such items should be separated from the revenues and expenses of continuing operations. Otherwise, the income statement fails to provide readers with clear information about the results of normal business activities.

To see how various income statement items should be classified, look at Illustration 16–2. Observe that the income statement is separated into four sections labeled 1 through 4. The first of the four portions of the income statement shows the revenues, expenses, and income generated by the company's continuing operations. This portion looks just like the single-step income statement we first discussed in Chapter 5. The next income statement section relates to discontinued operations.

INCOME STATEMENT ITEMS NOT RELATED TO CONTINUING OPERATIONS

LO 4

Explain how the income effects of discontinued operations, extraordinary items, changes in accounting principles, and prior period adjustments are reported.

Large companies often have several different lines of business operations and deal with different classes of customers. For example, **Imperial Oil Limited** not only produces and sells petroleum products but it also has a major position in the retail fertilizer industry. A company's operations that involve a particular line of business or class of customers may qualify as a **segment of the business.** To qualify as a segment of a business, the assets, activities, and financial results of operations involving a particular line of business or class of customers must be distinguished from other parts of the business.

DISCONTINUED OPERATIONS

Separating Discontinued Operations on the Income Statement

Normally, the revenues and expenses of all business segments are added together and reported as the continuing operations of the business (as in section 1 of Illustration 16–2). However, when a business sells or disposes of a business segment, the results of that segment's operations must be separated and reported as you see

Illustration 16–2 Income Statement for a Corporation

CONNELLY CORPORATION
Income Statement
For Year Ended December 31, 1996

Net sales		$8,443,000
Gain on sale of old equipment		30,000
Total		$8,473,000
Costs and expenses:		
Cost of goods sold	$5,950,000	
Amortization expense	35,000	
Other selling, general, and administrative expenses	515,000	
Interest expense	20,000	
Income taxes	792,000	(7,312,000)
Unusual loss on sale of surplus land		(45,000)
Infrequent gain on relocation of a plant		72,000
Income from continuing operations		$1,188,000
Discontinued operations:		
Income from operation of discontinued Division A		
(net of $166,000 income taxes)	$ 400,000	
Loss on disposal of Division A (net of $60,000 tax		
benefit)	(150,000)	250,000
Income before extraordinary items and cumulative		
effect of a change in accounting principle		$1,438,000
Extraordinary items:		
Gain on sale of unused land expropriated by the		
state for a highway interchange (net of $35,000		
income taxes)	$ 142,500	
Loss from earthquake damage (net of $310,000		
income taxes)	(670,000)	(527,500)
Net income		$ 910,500
Earnings per common share (250,000 shares outstanding):		
Income from continuing operations		$4.75
Discontinued operations		1.00
Extraordinary items		(2.11)
Net income		$3.64

(Section markers in left margin: 1, 2, 3, 4)

in section 2 of Illustration 16–2. In the illustration, the results of the discontinued operations are completely separated from the results of other activities. This separation makes it easier for financial statement readers to evaluate the continuing operations of the business.

Separating the Results of Operating a Segment that Is Being Discontinued from the Gain or Loss on Disposal

Within section 2 of Illustration 16–2, note that the income from *operating* Division A (the operation that is being discontinued) during the period is reported separately from the loss on the final *disposal* of Division A. Also, the income tax effects of the discontinued operations are separated from the income tax expense shown in section 1 of Illustration 16–2. Thus, the results of the discontinued operations are reported net of tax. Also, the amount of tax or tax benefit related to each item is disclosed. Similarly, unusual items, items that do not qualify as extraordinary, should be reported separately.

The above discussion summarizes the method of *reporting* the results of discontinued operations and unusual items on the income statement. The detailed requirements for *measuring* the income or losses of discontinued operations are discussed in a more advanced accounting course.

EXTRAORDINARY ITEMS

Section 3 of the income statement in Illustration 16–2 reports gains and losses that are extraordinary. The *CICA Handbook* identifies extraordinary items as items that result from transactions or events that have all of the following characteristics: *(a)* they are not expected to occur frequently over several years, *(b)* they do not typify the normal business activities of the entity, and *(c)* they do not depend primarily on decisions or determinations by management or owners.[2] Thus, the essential characteristics of extraordinary items are that they are infrequent and atypical, and they result primarily from nonmanagement decisions. Examples are government expropriation of property or natural disasters. Gains or losses resulting from the risks inherent in an entity's normal business activities, such as losses on accounts receivable or inventories and gains and losses on disposals of long-term assets, may be **unusual** but would not be considered extraordinary.

Each extraordinary item should be disclosed separately and adequately described to allow users of the financial statements to understand the nature of the transactions or events and the extent to which income has been affected.

PRIOR PERIOD ADJUSTMENTS

Prior period adjustments are accounted for and reported as direct charges (or credits, including disclosure of the applicable income tax) to Retained Earnings; they cause the opening balance of retained earnings to be restated. To qualify as prior period adjustments, items must be rare in occurrence and must meet the specific criteria set out in paragraphs 3600.02–.03 of the *CICA Handbook*. Settlement of lawsuits arising in prior periods and one-time income tax settlements are normally the only items that qualify as prior period adjustments.

ACCOUNTING CHANGES

Accounting changes (section 1506 of the *CICA Handbook*) include *(a)* accounting errors, *(b)* changes in accounting policy, and *(c)* changes in estimates. The first two types of items—accounting errors arising in prior periods and changes in accounting policy necessitated by a change in circumstances or the development of new accounting principles—receive parallel treatment to that described for prior period adjustments. That is, they are applied **retroactively** with a restatement of the opening Retained Earnings. The latter, change in estimate, is accorded **prospective** treatment. As a company gains more experience in such areas as estimating bad debts, warranty costs, and useful lives of capital assets, there is often a sound basis for revising previous estimates. Such changes affect only the present and

---

[2]*CICA Handbook,* section 3480.

Illustration 16–3
Single-Year Statement
of Retained Earnings

CONNELLY CORPORATION
Statement of Retained Earnings
For Year Ended December 31, 1997

Retained earnings, January 1, 1997	$4,745,000
Prior period adjustment for accounting error:	
Cost of the land that was incorrectly charged to expense (net of $60,000 income taxes)	130,000
Retained earnings, January 1, 1997, as restated	$4,875,000
Plus net income	937,500
Less cash dividends declared	(240,000)
Retained earnings, December 31, 1997	$5,572,500

future statements. A detailed discussion and comparative statement presentation of items that require retroactive adjustment are left to a more advanced textbook; however, a simple single-year illustration is to be found in Illustration 16–3.

STATEMENT OF CHANGES IN SHAREHOLDERS' EQUITY

In Chapter 5, we explained that some corporations do not present a separate statement of retained earnings. Instead, they present a combined statement of income and retained earnings, an example of which is shown in Illustration 16–4. Other corporations show the statement of retained earnings information in an expanded statement called a *statement of changes in shareholders' equity*. In that statement, the beginning and ending balances of each shareholders' equity account are reconciled by listing all changes that occurred during the year. For example, the annual report of **The Bank of Nova Scotia** for the year ended October 31, 1994, included the financial statement shown in Illustration 16–4.

Progress Check

16–4 Which of the following is an extraordinary item?
a. A settlement paid to a customer injured while using the company's product,
b. A loss from damages to a plant caused by a meteorite,
c. A loss from selling old equipment.

16–5 Identify the four possible major sections of the income statement that might appear below income from continuing operations.

16–6 A company that used FIFO for the past 15 years has decided to switch to LIFO. The effect of this event on past years' net income should be *(a)* reported as a prior period adjustment to retained earnings, *(b)* ignored as it is a change in an accounting estimate, *(c)* reported on the current year's income statement.

EARNINGS PER SHARE

Among the most commonly quoted statistics on the financial pages of daily newspapers is **earnings per share** of common shares. Investors use earnings per share data when they evaluate the past performance of a corporation, project its future earnings, and weigh investment opportunities.

Illustration 16–4 Statement of Shareholders' Equity

Consolidated Statement of Changes in Shareholders' Equity		
For the financial year ended October 31 ($ millions)	**1994**	**1993**
Preferred shares *(Note 10)*		
Balance at beginning of year	**$1,300**	$1,000
Proceeds of shares issued during the year	–	300
Redemption of shares during the year	**(200)**	—
Balance at end of year	**$1,100**	$1,300
Common shares *(Note 10)*		
Balance at beginning of year	**$1,429**	$1,308
Shares issued to acquire Montreal Trustco Inc. *(Note 17)*	280	—
Shareholder dividend and share purchase plan	130	121
Balance at end of year	**$1,839**	$1,429
Retained earnings		
Balance at beginning of year	**$3,175**	$2,771
Net income for the year	482	714
Dividends: Preferred	(97)	(92)
Common	(253)	(233)
Net unrealized foreign exchange gains and losses	9	20
Net costs of share issue and redemption	(14)	(5)
Balance at end of year	**$3,302**	$3,175

COMPANIES WITH SIMPLE CAPITAL STRUCTURES

LO 5

Calculate earnings per share for companies with simple capital structures and explain the difference between primary and fully diluted earnings per share.

Earnings per share calculations may be simple or complex. The calculations are not as difficult for companies that have simple capital structures. A company has a **simple capital structure** if it has only common share capital and perhaps nonconvertible preferred shares outstanding. In other words, to have a simple capital structure, the company cannot have any outstanding options or rights to purchase common shares at a specified price or any securities convertible into common shares.

Calculating Earnings per Share When the Number of Common Shares Outstanding Does Not Change

Consider a company that has only common shares and cumulative nonconvertible preferred shares outstanding.[3] If the number of common shares outstanding does not change during the period, calculate earnings per share as follows:

$$\text{Earnings per share} = \frac{\text{Net income} - \text{Preferred dividends}}{\text{Common shares outstanding}}$$

For example, assume that in 1996 Blackwell Company earned a $40,000 net income and paid its preferred dividends of $7,500. On January 1, 1996, the company

---

[3] If the preferred shares were noncumulative, the deduction from net income would be made only to the extent of the preferred dividends declared. In the case of cumulative preferred, one year's preferred dividends are deducted from net income whether declared or not.

had 5,000 common shares outstanding and this number did not change during the year. Calculate earnings per share for 1996 as follows:

$$\text{Earnings per share} = \frac{\$40,000 - \$7,500}{5,000} = \$6.50$$

However, the calculation becomes more complex if the number of common shares outstanding changes during the period. The number of common shares outstanding may change (1) because the company sells additional shares or reacquires shares or (2) because of stock dividends and stock splits.

Adjusting the Denominator for Sales or Purchases of Common Shares

If additional shares are sold or shares are reacquired during the year, earnings per share is based on the weighted-average number of shares outstanding during the year. For example, suppose that in 1997, Blackwell Company again earned $40,000 and preferred dividends were $7,500. However, on July 1, 1997, Blackwell sold 4,000 additional common shares. Also, on November 1, 1997, Blackwell reacquired 3,000 shares. In other words, 5,000 shares were outstanding for six months; then 9,000 shares were outstanding for four months; then 6,000 shares were outstanding for two months. When such changes occur, calculate the weighted-average number of shares outstanding during 1997 as follows:

Time Period	Shares Outstanding	Weighted by Portion of Year Outstanding
January–June	5,000	$(\%_2) = 2,500$
July–October	(5,000 + 4,000)	$(\%_2) = 3,000$
November–December	(9,000 − 3,000)	$(\%_2) = 1,000$
Weighted-average common shares outstanding		6,500

An alternative method of calculation is

Time Period	Number of Shares	Weighted by Number of Months Shares Outstanding
January–December	5,000	× 12 = 60,000
July–December	4,000	× 6 = 24,000
November–December	(3,000)	× 2 = (6,000)
		78,000
Weighted-average common shares outstanding 78,000/12 = 6,500		

The calculation of earnings per share for 1997 is

$$\text{Earnings per share} = \frac{\$40,000 - \$7,500}{6,500} = \$5$$

Adjusting the Denominator for Stock Splits and Stock Dividends

A stock split or stock dividend is different from a sale of shares. When shares are sold, the company receives new assets that it uses to generate additional earnings. On the other hand, stock splits and stock dividends do not provide additional assets for the company. Instead, a stock split or stock dividend simply means that the company's earnings must be allocated to a larger number of outstanding shares.

Because of the nature of stock splits and stock dividends, they are treated differently from sales of shares when calculating the weighted-average number of shares outstanding. When a stock split or stock dividend occurs, the number of shares outstanding during previous portions of the year must be retroactively restated to reflect the stock split or dividend. For example, consider the previous example of Blackwell Company. Assume that the share transactions in 1997 included a stock split, as follows:

Jan. 1: 5,000 common shares were outstanding.
July 1: Blackwell sold 4,000 additional common shares.
Nov. 1: Blackwell purchased 3,000 common shares.
Dec. 1: Outstanding common shares were split 2 for 1.

The changes in the number of common shares outstanding during 1997 is the same as in the previous example except for the 2-for-1 stock split. The calculation of the weighted average of common shares outstanding is the same except the resulting number of the former example is multiplied by 2 to arrive at 13,000 shares. The same type of restatement is required for stock dividends. If, for example, the 2-for-1 stock split on December 1 had been a 10% stock dividend, the multiplier would be 1.10 instead of 2. The calculation of Blackwell Company's earnings per share for 1997 is

$$\text{Earnings per share} = \frac{\$40,000 - \$7,500}{13,000} = \$2.50$$

Companies with **complex capital structures** have outstanding securities such as bonds or preferred shares that are convertible into common shares. Earnings per share calculations for companies with complex capital structures are more complicated. Often, such companies must present two types of earnings per share calculations. One is called **basic earnings per share**, and the other is called **fully diluted earnings per share**.

Suppose that a corporation has convertible preferred shares outstanding throughout the current year. However, consider what the effects would have been if the preferred shares had been converted at the beginning of the year. The result of this assumed conversion would have been to increase the number of common shares outstanding and to reduce preferred dividends. The net result may have been to reduce earnings per share, or to increase earnings per share. When the assumed conversion of a security reduces earnings per share, the security is said to be **dilutive**; those that increase earnings per share are **antidilutive**. Fully diluted earnings per share are calculated as if all dilutive securities (antidilutive securities are excluded

COMPANIES WITH COMPLEX CAPITAL STRUCTURES

Illustration 16–5   Reporting Basic and Fully Diluted Earnings per Share

BCE INC.
Earnings per Share

	1993	1992	1991
Earnings (loss) per share			
Continuing operations	**0.21**	4.52	3.94
Discontinued operations (note 6)	**(2.65)**	(0.31)	0.07
Net earnings (loss) per share (note 3)	**(2.44)**	4.21	4.01
Dividends declared per common share	**2.65**	261	257
Average number of common shares outstanding (millions) ..	**307.0**	307.6	307.6

ANCHOR LAMINA INC.

	1994	1993
Basic income per common share (Notes 2&15)	$0.50	$0.47
Fully diluted income per common share (Notes 2&15)	$0.49	$0.46

from the calculation) had already been converted. The complexities of fully diluted earnings per share are left for more advanced accounting courses.

PRESENTATIONS OF EARNINGS PER SHARE ON THE INCOME STATEMENT

Because of the importance attached to earnings per share data, generally accepted accounting principles require that you show this information on the face of published income statements or in the notes to the financial statements cross-referenced to the income statement. Separate earnings per share calculations are normally presented for (1) income before extraordinary items, (2) extraordinary items, and (3) net income. Some corporations provide additional calculations such as unusual items in Illustrations 16–2. Examples from published statements are presented in Illustration 16–5.

Progress Check

16-7   During 1997, FDI Co. had net income of $250,000 and paid preferred dividends of $70,000. On January 1, the company had 25,000 outstanding common shares and purchased and retired 5,000 shares on July 1. 1997 earnings per share are (a) $8.00, (b) $9.00, (c) $10.00.

16-8   How are stock splits and stock dividends treated in calculating the weighted-average number of outstanding common shares?

16-9   What two sets of earnings per share results are reported for a company with a complex capital structure?

USING THE INFORMATION— PRICE-EARNINGS RATIO

You learned in Chapter 15 that share market value is largely affected by the stream of future dividends expected to be paid out to shareholders. Market value is also affected by expected future changes in value. By comparing the company's earnings per share and its market price per share, investors and other decision makers can obtain information about the stock market's apparent expectations for growth in future earnings, dividends, and market values.

Illustration 16–6   Canadian Corporate Reports*

Abitibi-Price

3 months to Dec. 31, 1994		Year ago
Revenue	$568,000,000	$486,000,000
Prof cont ops	10,000,000	(30,000,000)
Prof disc ops	(4,000,000)	(10,000,000)
Net profit	6,000,000	(40,000,000)
Cont. ops./share	0.12	(0.39)
Disc. ops./share	(0.04)	(0.14)
Net profit/share	0.08	(0.53)

Year to Dec. 31, 1994		Year ago
Revenue	$2.11-billion	$1.87-billion
Prof cont ops	(51,000,000)	(98,000,000)
Prof disc ops	(4,000,000)	(13,000,000)
Net profit	(55,000,000)	(111,000,000)
Avg. shares	84,400,000	71,800,000
Cont. ops./share	(0.62)	(1.38)
Disc. ops./share	(0.04)	(0.18)
Net profit/share	(0.66)	(1.56)

Preferred-share dividends were nil vs nil in the quarter and $1-million vs $1-million in the year. Year-earlier results, as well as results for the first three quarters of fiscal 1994, have been restated to reflect the impact of a pact reached last December between Canadian and U.S. taxation authorities.

Accugraph Corp.

Year to Dec. 31, 1994		Year ago
Revenue	$24,806,000	$14,099,000
Net profit	5,090,000	1,075,000
Avg. shares	16,559,000	11,978,000
Net profit/share	0.31	0.09

BMTC Group

3 months to Dec. 31, 1994		Year ago
Revenue	$97,877,000	$87,958,000
Net profit	a2,276,000	3,099,000

Net profit/share	a0.25	0.31

Year to Dec. 31, 1994		Year ago
Revenue	$359,408,000	$306,770,000
Net profit	a9,209,000	7,859,000
Net profit/share	a0.97	0.79

a. Includes a $1,812,000 writedown of goodwill, and a charge of $362,000 related to a change in depreciation policy.

Bedford Capital

6 months to Dec. 31, 1994		Year ago
Revenue	$2,225,469	$782,076
Net profit	500,526	96,221
Avg. shares	6,258,700	3,600,000
Net profit/share	0.08	0.03

Bonar Inc.

Year to Dec. 3, 1994		Year ago
Revenue	$239,668,000	$201,442,000
Net profit	13,116,000	10,227,000
Net profit/share	2.68	2.10

Caribbean Utilities

9 months to Jan. 31, 1995		Year ago
Revenue	$n/a	$a/a
Net profit	7,233,810	5,874,574
Net profit/share	a0.64	0.61

a. Restated to reflect a 2-for-1 stock split in December 1994.

Co-Maxx Energy

Year to Dec. 31, 1994		Year ago
Revenue	$5,667,352	$4,607,035
Cash flow	3,164,956	2,379,108
Net profit	1,584,174	1,265,241
Avg. shares	5,680,000	4,258,000
Cash flow/share	0.56	0.56

Net profit/share	0.28	0.30

Corporate Foods

3 months to Dec. 31, 1994		Year ago
Revenue	$134,500,000	$125,300,000
Net profit	7,800,000	7,500,000
Net profit/share	0.37	0.36

Year to Dec. 31, 1994		Year ago
Revenue	$424,800,000	$360,200,000
Net profit	22,300,000	a21,400,000
Net profit/share	1.06	a1.02

a. Includes a gain of $1.3-million or 6 cents a share.

Doman Industries

3 months to Dec. 31, 1994		Year ago
Revenue	$193,953,000	$164,728,000
Net profit	a24,256,000	1,477,000
Net profit/share	a0.64	nil

Year to Dec. 31, 1994		Year ago
Revenue	$757,502,000	$661,659,000
Net profit	b55,794,000	c40,199,000
Avg. shares	35,691,000	30,498,000
Net profit/share	b1.42	c1.13

a. Includes a refund of duties of $15.2-million or 43 cents a share, and closure costs for the New Westminster sawmill of $1.7-million or 5 cents. b. Includes a refund of duties of $18.4-million or 52 cents a share, and the closure costs of $1.7-million or 5 cents. c. Includes a gain of $7.6-million or 25 cents a share from the sale of an interest.

Preferred-share dividends were $1,215,-000 vs $1,457,000 in the quarter and $5,-218,000 vs $5,803,000 for the full year.

*Globe and Mail, February 21, 1995.

Although it would be possible to make this comparison as a rate of return by dividing the earnings per share by the market price per share, the ratio has traditionally been turned upside-down and calculated as the **price-earnings ratio.** Thus, this ratio is found by dividing the share's market price by the earnings per share, as shown in this formula:

LO 6

Calculate the price-earnings ratio and explain its meaning.

$$\text{Price-earnings ratio} = \frac{\text{Market value per share}}{\text{Earnings per share}}$$

The ratio may be calculated using the earnings per share reported in the past period. However, analysts often calculate the ratio based on the expected earnings per share for the next period. Suppose, for example, that the current market price is $100 per share and that its next year's earnings are expected to be $8 per share. Its price-earnings ratio (often abbreviated as the PE ratio) is found as $100/$8, which is 12.5.

Investors normally examine the trend of earnings and the latest reported data such as presented in Illustration 16–6. Note especially the reporting of earnings per share and the detail in the footnotes, for example, Abitibi-Price and the 2-for-1 stock split of Caribbean Utilities.

As a general rule, shares with higher PE ratios (generally greater than 12 to 15) are considered more likely to be overpriced while shares with lower PE ratios (generally less than 5 to 8) are considered more likely to be underpriced. Thus, some investors prefer to sell or avoid buying shares with high PE ratios while they prefer to buy or hold shares that have low PE ratios. Investment decisions are not quite that simple, however, because shares with high PE ratios may prove to be good investments if their earnings increase rapidly. On the other hand, shares with low PE ratios may prove to be low performers. Although the price-earnings ratio is clearly important for investment decisions, it is only one piece of information that investors should consider. For example, Anchor Lamina's 12 PE may be considered as low for a growth company. Investors may have greater confidence in the strategic focus that competing companies are taking.

Progress Check

16–10 Calculate the price-earnings ratio for a company with earnings per share of $4.25 and market value of $34.00.

16–11 Two companies in the same industry face similar levels of risk, have nearly the same level of earnings, and are expected to continue their historical record of paying $1.50 annual dividends per share. Yet, one of the companies has a PE ratio of 6 while the other has a PE ratio of 10. Which company does the market apparently expect to have the highest future growth rate in earnings?

SUMMARY OF THE CHAPTER IN TERMS OF LEARNING OBJECTIVES

LO 1. Record cash dividends, stock dividends, and stock splits and explain their effects on a corporation's assets and shareholders' equity. Whereas cash dividends transfer corporate assets to the shareholders, stock dividends do not. Stock dividends and stock splits have no effect on assets, no effect on total shareholders' equity, and no effect on the equity of each shareholder. Depending on the jurisdiction, stock dividends are recorded by capitalizing retained earnings equal to the market value of the distributed shares, or capitalizing an amount set by the board of directors.

LO 2. Record retirement of shares and describe the effect on shareholders' equity. When outstanding shares are repurchased and retired, the stated capital account is debited for the weighted average per share invested by the shareholders. If the purchase price is more or less than the weighted average per share, the difference is debited to Retained Earnings (more) or credited to Contributed Capital, Share Retirements (less).

LO 3. Describe restrictions and appropriations of retained earnings and the disclosure of such items in the financial statements. In most jurisdictions, retained earnings are legally restricted by an amount equal to the cost of reacquired shares. Retained earnings also may be restricted by contract. Corporations may voluntarily appropriate retained earnings to inform shareholders why dividends are not larger in amount. More often, however, this information is expressed in a letter to the shareholders.

LO 4. **Explain how the income effects of discontinued operations, extraordinary items, changes in accounting principles, and prior period adjustments are reported.** If management has implemented a plan to discontinue a business segment, the net income or loss from operating the segment and the gain or loss on disposal are separately reported on the income statement below income from continuing operations. Next, extraordinary gains or losses are listed.

Prior period adjustments, which include the income effects of accounting errors made in prior periods and changes in accounting policy or principle, are reported on the statement of retained earnings.

Changes in accounting estimates are made because new information shows the old estimates to be invalid. When an accounting estimate is changed, the new estimate is used to calculate revenue or expense in the current and future periods.

LO 5. **Calculate earnings per share for companies with simple capital structures and explain the difference between basic and fully diluted earnings per share.** Companies with simple capital structures do not have outstanding securities convertible into common shares. For such companies, earnings per share is calculated by dividing net income less dividends to preferred shares by the weighted-average number of outstanding common shares. In calculating the weighted-average number of shares outstanding, the number of shares outstanding prior to a stock dividend or stock split must be restated to reflect the effect of the stock dividend or stock split.

Companies with complex capital structures have outstanding securities that are convertible into common shares. These companies may have to report both basic earnings per share and fully diluted earnings per share. In calculating basic earnings per share, the denominator is the weighted-average number of common shares outstanding. Fully diluted earnings per share assumes the conversion of all dilutive securities.

LO 6. **Calculate the price-earnings ratio and explain its meaning.** The price-earnings ratio of common shares is closely watched by investors and other decision makers. The ratio is calculated by dividing the current market value per share by earnings per share. A high ratio may suggest that shares are overvalued while a low ratio may suggest that shares are undervalued. However, selecting shares to buy or sell requires a great deal more information.

DEMONSTRATION PROBLEM

Part A

Maritime Corporation's books on January 31, 1996, showed the following balances (summarized):

Cash	$ 70,000
Other current assets	50,000
Capital assets (net)	470,000
Other assets	110,000
	$700,000
Current liabilities	$ 60,000
Long-term liabilities	120,000
Common, 40,000 shares	420,000
Retained earnings	100,000
	$700,000

The board of directors is considering a cash dividend, and you have been requested to provide certain assistance as the independent accountant. The following matters have been referred to you:

1. What is the maximum amount of cash dividends that can be paid at January 1? Explain.
2. What entries would be made assuming a $1 per share cash dividend is declared with the following dates specified: (*a*) declaration date, (*b*) date of record, and (*c*) date of payment.
3. Assuming a balance sheet is prepared between declared date and payment date, how would the dividend declaration be reported?

Part B

The records of South Corporation showed the following balances on November 1, 1996:

Common 27,500 shares	$770,000
Retained earnings	390,000

On November 5, 1996, the board of directors declared a stock dividend of one additional share for each five shares outstanding; issue date, January 10, 1997. The market value immediately after the declaration was $36 per share.

Required

Give entries in parallel columns for the stock dividend assuming, for problem purposes, *(a)* market value is capitalized, *(b)* $110,000 is capitalized (amount decided by the board), and *(c)* average paid in is capitalized. Assume the company records the dividend on declaration and credits a Stock Dividends Distributable account (not a liability).

Part C

Complete the following matrix:

	Method of Reflecting the Effect	
	Prospective	Retroactive
a. Change in estimate	_____	_____
b. Change in principle or method	_____	_____
c. Correction of error	_____	_____

Part D

Eastern Corporation had outstanding 10,000 no-par common shares sold initially for $20 per share. The Retained Earnings balance is $31,600. The corporation purchased and retired 500 shares of its common at $25 per share.

Required

Give entries to record the reacquired share transactions.

Part E

A company split its common shares three for one on June 30 of its fiscal year ended December 31. Before the split, there were 4,000 common shares outstanding. How many common shares should be used in computing EPS? How many common shares should be used in computing a comparative EPS amount for the preceding year?

Part A

1. The maximum cash dividend that can be paid at January 1 depends in part on the statutory provisions (i.e., solvency test); however, the *cash* available is limiting in this situation. Possible alternatives are:

   a. Limit to cash, $70,000.
   b. Limit to retained earnings, $100,000. This would require property dividends, liability dividends, or generating additional cash through borrowing or other means.

2. a. Date of declaration:

Dividends Declared (Retained Earnings)	40,000	
Dividends Payable		40,000

   b. Record date. No entry; prepare list of shareholders.
   c. Date of payment:

Dividends Payable	40,000	
Cash		40,000

3. Between declaration and payment dates, dividends payable for whatever amount is declared ($40,000) would be reported as a current liability. Retained earnings would be reported as $100,000 − $40,000 = $60,000.

Part B

	Amount Capitalized		
	(a)	**(b)**	**(c)**
	Market Value	**Decision of the Board**	**Average Paid in**
November 5, 1996:			
To record declaration:			
Retained Earnings	198,000[b]	110,000[c]	154,000[d]
Stock Dividends			
Distributable			
(5,500 shares)[a]	198,000	110,000	154,000
January 10, 1997:			
To record the share issue:			
Stock Dividend			
Distributable	198,000	110,000	154,000
Common Shares			
(5,500 shares)	198,000	110,000	154,000

Note: Alternative accounting: An equally acceptable alternative manner of accounting and reporting the stock dividend would be to disclose the November 5, 1996, stock dividend declaration in the *notes* to the 1996 financial statements. Then the entry to record the January 10, 1997, issuance of the dividend shares would be the same as the declaration entry given above, except that Common Shares would be credited instead of Stock Dividends Distributable.

[a] 27,500 shares outstanding: 27,500 ÷ 5 = 5,500 shares issued for stock dividend.
[b] Capitalize market value; 5,500 shares × $36 = $198,000.
[c] Capitalize amount decided by the board = $110,000.
[d] Capitalize average paid in: $770,000 ÷ 27,500 = $28 per share, average, 5,500 shares × $28 = $154,000.

Part C

	Method of Reflecting the Effect	
	Prospective	**Retroactive**
a. Change in estimate	√	
b. Change in principle or method		√
c. Correction of error		√

Part D

Common Shares (500 shares @ $20)	10,000		
Retained Earnings	2,500		
Cash		12,500	

Note: Restriction of Retained Earnings (required by law) for $12,500 (the cost of the reacquired shares) may be recorded by journal entry or disclosed in a note.

Part E

In computing EPS for the year, 12,000 common shares should be used. The *CICA Handbook* prescribes retroactive treatment for stock dividends and stock splits for all periods presented. Therefore, 12,000 shares would also be used to compute EPS (restated) for the preceding year as well. The two EPS amounts are therefore (a) comparable and (b) both related to the current capital structure.

GLOSSARY

Accounting changes items that can affect the evaluation or prediction of a firm's earnings. Accounting changes include (a) accounting errors, (b) changes in accounting policy, and (c) changes in accounting estimates. p 733

Antidilutive securities convertible securities, the assumed conversion of which would have the effect of increasing earnings per share. p. 737

Appropriated retained earnings retained earnings voluntarily earmarked for a special use as a way of informing shareholders that assets from earnings equal to the appropriations are not available for dividends. p. 731

Basic earnings per share earnings per share statistics that are calculated for corporations with a simple capital structure and for corporations with complex capital structures before giving effect to the dilutive securities. p. 737

Changes in accounting estimates adjustments to previously made assumptions about the future such as salvage values and the length of useful lives of buildings and equipment. p. 733

Changes in accounting policy a change in accounting data caused by a change in one generally accepted accounting principle to another generally accepted accounting principle (i.e., a change from LIFO to FIFO). p. 733

Complex capital structure a capital structure that includes outstanding rights or options to purchase common shares or securities convertible into common shares. p. 737

Dilutive securities convertible securities the assumed conversion of which would have the effect of decreasing earnings per share. p. 737

Earned surplus a synonym for retained earnings, no longer in general use. p. 724

Earnings per share the amount of net income (or components of income) that accrues to common shares divided by the weighted-average number of common shares outstanding. p. 734

Fully diluted earnings per share earnings per share statistics that are calculated as if all dilutive securities had already been converted. p. 737

Liquidating dividends asset distributions in excess of a credit balance in Retained Earnings; a return of original investment. p. 725

Price-earnings ratio the ratio between a company's current market value and its earnings per share. p. 739

Prior period adjustment items reported in the current statement of retained earnings as corrections to the beginning retained earnings balance; limited primarily to corrections of errors that were made in past years, settlement of lawsuits that originated in prior years, and one-time income tax settlements. p. 733

Prospective change affects current and future periods. p. 733

Restricted retained earnings retained earnings not available for dividends because of law or binding contract. p. 730

Retroactive change affects prior periods. p. 733

Reverse stock split the act of a corporation to call in its shares and issue one new share in the place of more than one share previously outstanding. p. 728

Segment of a business operations of a company that involve a particular line of business or class of customer, providing the assets, activities, and financial results of the operations can be distinguished from other parts of the business. p. 731

Simple capital structure a capital structure that does not include any rights or options to purchase common shares or any securities that are convertible into common shares. p. 735

Stock dividend a distribution by a corporation of its own shares to its shareholders without the receipt of any consideration in return. p. 725

Stock split the act of a corporation to issue more than one new share in the place of each share previously outstanding. p. 728

Unusual gain or loss a gain or loss (that doesn't qualify as extraordinary) that is abnormal and unrelated or only incidentally related to the ordinary activities and environment of the business. p. 733

SYNONYMOUS TERMS

Basic earnings per share earnings per common share.

Retained earnings earned surplus (no longer in use).

Statement of changes in shareholders' equity statement of shareholders' equity.

QUESTIONS

1. What effect does the declaration of a cash dividend have on the assets, liabilities, and shareholders' equity of the corporation that declares the dividend? What is the effect of the subsequent payment of the cash dividend?

2. What effect does the declaration of a stock dividend have on the assets, liabilities, and total shareholders' equity of the corporation that declares the dividend? What is the effect of the subsequent distribution of the stock dividend?

3. What is the difference between a stock dividend and a stock split?

4. If a balance sheet is prepared between the date of declaration and the date of payment or distribution of a dividend, how should the dividend be shown if it is *(a)* a cash dividend or *(b)* a stock dividend?

5. Why do laws place limitations on the reacquisition of a corporation's shares?

6. In the annual income statement of a corporation, what other sections of the statement might appear below income from continuing operations?

7. If a company operates one of its business segments at a loss during much of 1997, and then finds a buyer and disposes of that segment during November of that year, which two items concerning that segment should appear on the company's 1997 income statement?

8. Where on the income statement should a company disclose a gain that is abnormal and unrelated to the ordinary activities of the business and that is not expected to recur more often than once every several years and that occurs as a result of decisions or events outside the corporation?

9. Which of the following items would qualify as an extraordinary gain or loss: *(a)* operating losses resulting from a strike against a major supplier, *(b)* a gain from the sale of surplus equipment, or *(c)* a loss from damage to a building caused by a tornado (a type of storm that rarely occurs in the geographical region of the company's operations)?

10. In past years, Daley Company paid its sales personnel annual salaries without additional incentive payments. This year, a new policy is being instituted whereby they receive sales commissions rather than annual salaries. Does this new policy require a prior period adjustment? Explain why or why not.

11. After taking five years' straight-line amortization on an asset that was expected to have an eight-year life, a company concluded that the asset would last another six years. Does this decision involve a change in accounting principle? If not, how would you describe this change?

12. How is earnings per share calculated for a corporation with a simple capital structure?

13. In calculating the weighted-average number of common shares outstanding, how are stock splits and stock dividends treated?

14. What is the difference between basic earnings per share and fully diluted earnings per share?

15. What is the difference between simple capital structures and complex capital structures?

QUICK STUDY (Five-Minute Exercises)

QS 16–1
(LO 1)

The shareholders' equity section of Maritime Corporation's balance sheet as of June 1 follows:

Common shares, 100,000 shares issued	
and outstanding	$ 735,000
Retained earnings	422,000
Total shareholders' equity	$1,157,000

On June 1, Maritime (federally incorporated) declares and distributes a 20% stock dividend. On June 1, Maritime's shares were traded at $15 per share. Prepare the shareholders' equity section for Maritime immediately following issuance of the stock dividend.

QS 16–2
(LO 2)

On September 2, Garrett Corporation purchased 2,000 of its own shares for $18,000. The shares were retired. The average stated value per share just prior to the purchase was $5. Prepare the September 2 entry for the purchase and retirement of the shares.

QS 16–3
(LO 3)

Prepare the entry to restrict retained earnings required by law in connection with the purchase and retirement of the 2,000 shares by Garrett in 16–3 above.

QS 16–4
(LO 4)

Answer the questions about each of the following items related to a company's activities for the year:

a. After using an expected useful life of seven years and no salvage value to amortize its office equipment over the preceding three years, the company decided early this year that the equipment will last only two more years. How should the effects of this decision be reported in the current financial statements?

b. In reviewing the notes payable files, it was discovered that last year the company reported the entire amount of a payment on an installment note payable as interest expense. The mistake had a material effect on the amount of income in the prior year. How should the correction be reported in the current year financial statements?

QS 16–5
(LO 5)

On January 1, Star Company had 50,000 common shares issued and outstanding. On April 1, it issued 4,000 additional shares and on June 5, declared a 20% stock dividend. Calculate Star's weighted-average outstanding shares for the year.

QS 16–6
(LO 6)

Calculate a company's price-earnings ratio if its common shares have a market value of $62 per share and if its earnings per share are $6.

EXERCISES

Northridge Corporation's shareholders' equity appeared as follows on August 10:

Share capital:
Common shares, no-par value, unlimited number
    authorized, 80,000 shares issued $560,200
Retained earnings   235,000
Total shareholders' equity $795,200

On August 10, when the shares were selling at $9.00, the corporation's directors voted a 20% stock dividend distributable on September 2 to the August 17 shareholders of record. The shares were selling at $7.75 at the close of business on September 2.

Required

1. Prepare General Journal entries to record the declaration and distribution of the dividend.

2. Under the assumption that Cynthia McAllister owned 250 of the shares on August 10 and received her dividend shares on September 2, prepare a schedule showing the number of shares she held on August 10 and on September 2, with their total book values and total market values. Assume no change in total shareholders' equity from August 10 to September 2.

On March 31, 1996, Atlantic Management Corporation's common shares were selling for $45 and the shareholders' equity section of the corporation's balance sheet appeared as follows:

Share capital:
Common shares, no-par value, unlimited number of shares
    authorized, 15,000 shares issued $670,450
Retained earnings   298,900
Total shareholders' equity $969,350

Required

1. Assume the corporation declares and immediately issues a 50% stock dividend and capitalizes $25 per share of retained earnings. Answer the following questions about the shareholders' equity of the corporation after the new shares are issued:

   a. What is the retained earnings balance?
   b. What is the total amount of shareholders' equity?
   c. How many shares are outstanding?

2. Assume that instead of declaring a 50% stock dividend, the corporation effects a three-for-two stock split. Answer the following questions about the shareholders' equity of the corporation after the stock split takes place:

   a. What is the retained earnings balance?
   b. What is the total amount of shareholders' equity?
   c. How many shares are outstanding?

Exercise 16–3
Retirement of shares
(LO 2, 3)

On October 31, Sanborn Corporation's shareholders' equity section appeared as follows:

Shareholders' Equity

Share capital:
Common shares, no-par value, unlimited number of shares
authorized, 5,000 shares outstanding $250,000
Retained earnings   220,100
Total shareholders' equity $470,100

On October 31, the corporation purchased and retired 800 shares at $55 per share. Give the entry to record the purchase and prepare a shareholders' equity section as it would appear immediately after the purchase and retirement.

Exercise 16–4
Retirement of shares
(LO 2)

The shareholders' equity section of City Vending, Inc.'s, December 31, 1996, balance sheet is as follows:

Share capital:
Common shares, no-par value, 600,000 shares
authorized, 30,000 shares issued $540,000
Retained earnings   105,800
Total shareholders' equity $645,800

On the date of the balance sheet, the company purchased and retired 400 common shares. Prepare General Journal entries to record the purchase and retirement under each of the following independent assumptions: the shares were purchased for (*a*) $12 per share, (*b*) $18 per share, and (*c*) $24 per share.

Exercise 16–5
Income statement categories
(LO 4)

The following list of items was extracted from the December 31, 1996, trial balance of Wesson Company. Using the information contained in this listing, prepare Wesson Company's income statement for 1996. You need not complete the earnings per share calculations.

	Debit	Credit
Salaries expense	$66,700	
Income tax expense (continuing operations)	68,380	
Loss from operating segment C (net of $10,200 tax benefit)	24,000	
Sales		$700,240
Total effect on prior years' income of change from declining-balance to straight-line amortization (net of $9,600 tax)		32,400
Extraordinary gain on provincial condemnation of land owned by Wesson Company (net of $24,800 tax)		68,000
Amortization expense	62,100	
Gain on sale of segment C (net of $19,700 tax)		66,000
Cost of goods sold	420,200	

Exercise 16–6
Classifying income items not related to continuing operations
(LO 4)

In preparing the annual financial statements for Elite Electronics Company, the correct manner of reporting the following items was not clear to the company's employees. Explain where each of the following items should appear in the financial statements.

a.   After amortizing office equipment for three years based on an expected useful life of eight years, the company decided this year that the office equipment should last seven more years. As a result, the amortization for the current year is $8,000 instead of $10,000.

b. This year, the accounting department of the company discovered that last year, an installment payment on their five-year note payable had been charged entirely to interest expense. The after-tax effect of the charge to interest expense was $15,400.

c. The company keeps its repair trucks for several years before disposing of the old trucks and buying new trucks. This year, for the first time in 10 years, it sold old trucks for a gain of $19,900 and then purchased new trucks.

Carefree Footware Inc. reported $261,400 net income in 1996 and declared preferred dividends of $43,000. The following changes in common shares outstanding occurred during the year:

Exercise 16–7
Weighted-average shares outstanding and earnings per share
(LO 5)

January 1:	60,000 common shares were outstanding.
June 30:	Sold 20,000 common shares.
September 1:	Declared and issued a 20% common stock dividend, or 80,000 × 20% = 16,000 additional shares.

Calculate the weighted-average number of common shares outstanding during the year and earnings per share.

Kingsley Production Company reported $741,500 net income in 1996 and declared preferred dividends of $66,500. The following changes in common shares outstanding occurred during the year.

Exercise 16–8
Weighted-average shares outstanding and earnings per share
(LO 5)

January 1:	60,000 common shares were outstanding.
March 1:	Sold 20,000 common shares.
August 1:	Purchased and retired 4,000 shares.
December 1:	Declared and issued a two-for-one stock split.

Calculate the weighted-average number of common shares outstanding during the year and earnings per share.

Northside Corporation's 1996 income statement, excluding the earnings per share portion of the statement, was as follows:

Exercise 16–9
Reporting earnings per share
(LO 5)

Sales		$475,000
Costs and expenses:		
Amortization	$ 51,900	
Income taxes	65,100	
Other expenses	205,000	322,000
Income from continuing operations		$153,000
Loss from operating discontinued business segment (net of $23,500 tax benefit)	$ 56,000	
Loss on sale of business segment (net of $9,400 tax benefit)	22,000	(78,000)
Income before extraordinary items		$ 75,000
Extraordinary gain (net of $18,400 taxes)		43,200
Net income		$118,200

Throughout 1996, Southside had potentially dilutive securities outstanding. If these particular securities had been converted, the number of common shares outstanding would have increased but the numerators in earnings per share calculations would not have been affected. Assuming the dilutive securities had been converted at the beginning of the year, the weighted-average number of common shares outstanding during the year would have increased by 20,000 to 120,000. Present the earnings per share portion of the 1996 income statement.

Exercise 16–10
Computing the price-
earnings ratio
(LO 6)

Use the following information to calculate the price-earnings ratio for each case:

	Earnings per Share	Market Value per Share
a.	$ 4.50	$ 43.00
b.	18.00	120.00
c.	3.25	45.00
d.	0.75	18.00
e.	5.00	83.00

PROBLEMS

Problem 16–1
Cash dividend, stock
dividend, and stock split
(LO 1)

Last April 30, Fancy Foods Corporation had a $1,035,000 credit balance in its Retained Earnings account. On that date, the corporation's contributed capital consisted of 300,000 shares, which had been issued at $3 and were outstanding. It then completed the following transactions:

May   10   The board of directors declared a $1.50 per share common dividend payable on June 16 to the May 31 shareholders of record.

June   16   Paid the dividend declared on May 10.

Aug.   5   The board declared a 10% stock dividend, distributable on September 2 to the August 20 shareholders of record. The shares were selling at $10.00 per share; this amount was used to capitalize retained earnings.

Sept.   2   Distributed the stock dividend declared on August 5.

       30   Because September 30 is the end of the company's fiscal year, closed the Income Summary account, which had a credit balance of $396,000. Also closed the Cash Dividends Declared and Stock Dividends Declared accounts.

Oct.   12   The board of directors voted to split the corporation's shares two for one. The split was completed on November 17.

Required

1.   Prepare General Journal entries to record these transactions and closings.

2.   Under the assumption Phillip Bolton owned 5,000 shares on April 30 and neither bought nor sold any shares during the period of the transactions, prepare a schedule with columns for the date, supporting calculations, book value per share, and book value of Bolton's shares. Then complete the schedule by calculating the book value per share of the corporation's and of Bolton's shares at the close of business on April 30, May 10, June 16, September 2, September 30, and October 12. Assume that the only income earned by the company during these periods was the $396,000 earned and closed on September 30.

3.   Prepare three shareholders' equity sections for the corporation, the first showing the shareholders' equity on April 30, the second on September 30, and the third on October 12.

Problem 16–2
Calculating net income
from balance sheet
comparison
(LO 1, 2, 3)

The equity sections from the 1996 and 1997 balance sheets of Dylex Corporation appeared as follows:

Shareholders' Equity
(As of December 31, 1996)

Share capital:
   Common shares, no-par value, unlimited number of shares
      authorized, 96,000 shares outstanding . . . . $ 688,000
   Retained earnings   558,608
   Total shareholders' equity   1,246,608

Shareholders' Equity
(As of December 31, 1997)

Share capital:

Common shares, no-par value, unlimited number of shares
    authorized, 100,000 shares outstanding .... $ 646,000

Retained earnings, of which $144,000 is restricted—
retirement of shares   459,600

Total shareholders' equity   1,105,600

On March 16, June 25, September 5, and again on November 22, 1997, the board of directors declared $0.20 per share cash dividends on the outstanding common shares. And 20,000 shares were purchased and retired on May 14. On October 5, while the shares were selling for $7.60 per share, the corporation declared a 25% stock dividend on the outstanding shares. The new shares were issued on November 8.

Required

Under the assumption that there were no transactions affecting retained earnings other than the ones given, determine the 1997 net income of Dylex Corporation. Show your calculations. (*Hint:* Remember the impact on retained earnings of repurchase of shares at an amount greater than the per share weighted-average stated value.)

The equity sections from the 1995 and 1996 balance sheets of Henns Corporation appeared as follows:

Problem 16–3
Calculating net income
from balance sheet
comparison
(LO 1, 2, 3)

Shareholders' Equity
(As of December 31, 1995)

Share capital:

Common shares, no-par value, unlimited number of shares
    authorized, 350,000 shares issued .... $ 8,750,000

Retained earnings   1,960,720

Total shareholders' equity $10,710,720

Shareholders' Equity
(As of December 31, 1996)

Share capital:

Common shares, no-par value, unlimited number of shares
    authorized, 384,000 shares issued .... $ 9,384,000

Retained earnings of which $270,000 is restricted   1,540,640

Total shareholders' equity $10,924,640

On February 11, May 24, August 13, and again on December 12, 1996, the board of directors declared $0.25 per share cash dividends on the outstanding shares: 10,000 shares were purchased at $27 per share and retired on July 6. On November 1, while the shares were selling for $26 per share, the corporation declared a 10% stock dividend on the outstanding shares. The new shares were issued on December 5.

Required

Under the assumption that there were no transactions affecting retained earnings other than the ones given, determine the 1996 net income of Henns Corporation. Show your calculations.

Handy Supply Corporation had several unusual transactions during 1997 and has prepared the following list of trial balance items. Select the appropriate items to use in constructing the 1997 income statement for the company.

Problem 16–4
Classifying income items
in a published income
statement
(LO 4)

	Debit	Credit
Accounts payable		$ 16,600
Loss from operation of Westside Division (net of $14,000 income tax benefit)	$ 32,000	
Sales		392,500
Cost of goods sold	170,600	
Loss on sale of office equipment (an unusual transaction for the company that occurs only when administrative offices are redecorated, which happens about every eight years)	6,300	
Amortization expense, buildings	35,620	
Amortization expense, office equipment	12,450	
Income tax expense	20,950	
Payment received in November of last year on customer account receivable incorrectly recorded in Sales account (net of $4,050 income tax benefit)	16,200	
Gain on sale of investment in land (The land was originally donated to Central Supply by a shareholder. Central Supply has never held land for investment purposes before and has no intention of doing so in the future.) (Net of $7,800 income taxes)		23,400
Loss on customer breach of contract (It is not unusual for companies in this industry, to be involved in breach of contract suits. However, the problem is not expected to arise in the foreseeable future.)	48,700	
Accumulated amortization, buildings		108,000
Accumulated amortization, office equipment		20,900
Gain on sale of Westside Division (net of $3,400 income taxes)		10,750
Interest earned		2,400
Other operating expenses	55,800	
Gain on payment from supplier to compensate for late delivery of materials purchased from supplier. (In this industry, such settlements with suppliers occur quite frequently.)		12,300
Effect on prior years' income of switching from straight-line amortization to accelerated amortization (net of $5,900 income tax benefit)	20,125	

Required

Prepare Handy Supply Corporation's income statement for 1997, excluding the earnings per share statistics.

Problem 16–5
Changes in accounting principles
(LO 4)

On January 1, 1992, Fairfax Industries Inc. purchased a large piece of equipment for use in its manufacturing operations. The equipment cost $280,000 and was expected to have a salvage value of $32,000. Amortization was taken through 1995 on a declining-balance method at twice the straight-line rate, assuming an eight-year life. Early in 1996, the company concluded that given the economic conditions in the industry, a straight-line method would result in more meaningful financial statements. They argue that straight-line amortization would allow better comparisons with the financial results of other firms in the industry.

Required

1. Is Fairfax Industries allowed to change amortization methods in 1996?
2. Prepare a table that shows the amortization expense to be reported each year of the asset's life under both amortization methods and the cumulative effect of the change on prior years' incomes.

3. State the amount of amortization expense to be reported in 1996 and the cumulative effect of the change on prior years' incomes. How should the cumulative effect be reported? Does the cumulative effect increase or decrease net income?

4. Now assume that Fairfax Industries had used straight-line amortization through 1995 and justified a change to declining-balance amortization at twice the straight-line rate in 1996. What amount of amortization expense should be reported in 1996? Does the reporting of the cumulative effect of the change differ from your answer to requirement 3?

Except for the earnings per share statistics, the 1997, 1996, and 1995 income statements of Clear Printing Company were originally presented as follows:

Problem 16–6
Earnings per share calculations and presentation
(LO 5)

	1997	1996	1995
Sales	$998,900	$687,040	$466,855
Costs and expenses	383,570	234,500	157,420
Income from continuing operations	$615,330	$452,540	$309,435
Loss on discontinued operations	(107,325)	—	—
Income (loss) before extraordinary items	$508,005	$452,540	$309,435
Extraordinary gains (losses)	—	80,410	(156,191)
Net income (loss)	$508,005	$532,950	$153,244

Information on common shares:

Shares outstanding on December 31, 1994	14,400
Purchase and retirement of shares on March 1, 1995	− 1,440
Sale of shares on June 1, 1995	+ 6,240
Stock dividend of 5% on August 1, 1995	+ 960
Shares outstanding on December 31, 1995	20,160
Sale of shares on February 1, 1996	+ 2,880
Purchase and retirement of shares July 1, 1996	− 720
Shares outstanding on December 31, 1996	22,320
Sale of shares on March 1, 1997	+ 8,280
Purchase and retirement of shares on September 1, 1997	− 1,800
Stock split of 3 for 1 on October 1, 1997	+57,600
Shares outstanding on December 31, 1997	86,400

Required

1. Calculate the weighted-average number of common shares outstanding during (a) 1995, (b) 1996, and (c) 1997.

2. Present the earnings per share portions of (a) the 1995 income statement, (b) the 1996 income statement, and (c) the 1997 income statement.

The shareholders' equity section of Lang Corporation's balance sheet at September 30 is as follows:

Problem 16–7
Analytical essay
(LO 1, 2)

Share capital:
Common shares, no-par value, unlimited number of shares
authorized, 100,000 shares outstanding ... $ 650,000
Retained earnings ... 367,000
Total shareholders' equity ... $1,017,000

Assume now that an event occurs on October 1 that impacts Lang's shareholders' equity section, but does not involve net income or additional investment of capital. The following are independent cases in which Lang's shareholders' equity section has been revised to reflect that event.

	Case A	Case B	Case C
Common share capital:			
80,000 shares outstanding	$520,000		
130,000 shares outstanding		$ 800,000	
50,000 shares outstanding			$ 650,000
Retained earnings	317,000	217,000	367,000
Total shareholders' equity	$837,000	$1,017,000	$1,017,000

Required

For each case, describe the differences in the September 30 and the October 1 shareholders' equity sections and state the event that must have occurred.

Problem 16–8
Analytical essay
(LO 5)

Jaspur Company's financial statements for the year ended December 31, 1996, have been completed and submitted to you for review. The shareholders' equity section of Jaspur's balance sheet at December 31 is as follows:

Share capital:
Preferred shares, $2.80 noncumulative
10,000 shares authorized, 10,000
shares issued and outstanding . . . . $ 498,700
Common shares, no-par value, unlimited number of shares
authorized, 120,000 shares outstanding 946,900
Retained earnings 450,530
Total shareholders' equity $1,896,130

The only share transactions during 1996 were the purchase and retirement of 24,000 common shares on July 1 and the sale of 12,000 common shares on October 31. Jaspur's 1996 net income was $286,200. A cash dividend on the preferred shares was declared on December 1, but was not paid as of December 31. Earnings per share for 1996 was calculated as follows:

$$\frac{\text{Net income}}{\substack{\text{Common shares}\\ \text{outstanding on Dec. 31}}} = \frac{\$286,200}{108,000} = \$2.65$$

Required

1. Explain what is wrong with the earnings per share calculation, indicating what corrections should be made to both the numerator and the denominator.

2. Explain how your answer to requirement 1 would be different if there had not been a cash dividend declaration to preferred shares and if the purchase and retirement of 24,000 common shares had taken place on January 2, 1996.

Problem 16–9
Analytical essay
(LO 5)

Computex Corporation has tentatively prepared its financial statements for the year ended December 31, 1996, and has submitted them to you for review. The shareholders' equity section of Computex's balance sheet at December 31 is as follows:

Share capital:
Preferred shares, $2.50, cumulative,
30,000 shares authorized, 18,000
shares issued and outstanding . . . . $ 520,100
Common shares, no-par value, unlimited number of shares
authorized, 132,000 shares outstanding 777,840
Retained earnings 996,200
Total shareholders' equity $2,294,140

Computex Corporation's 1996 net income was $600,000 and no cash dividends were declared. The only share transaction that occurred during the year was the sale of 24,000 common shares on March 31, 1996. Earnings per share for 1996 was calculated as follows:

$$\frac{\text{Net income}}{\substack{\text{Common plus preferred shares} \\ \text{outstanding as of Dec. 31}}} = \frac{\$600,000}{132,000 + 18,000} = \$4.00$$

Required

1. Explain what is wrong with the earnings per share calculation, indicating what corrections should be made to both the numerator and the denominator.

2. Explain how your answer to requirement 1 would be different if the preferred shares were not cumulative and if the issuance of 24,000 shares had been a stock dividend.

PROVOCATIVE PROBLEMS

On January 1, 1994, Hal Peeks purchased 800 shares of Cornfield Corporation at $45.50 per share. On that date, the corporation had the following shareholders' equity:

Provocative Problem 16–1
Cornfield Corporation
(LO 1, 2, 3)

Common stock, no-par value, unlimited number of shares authorized, 250,000 shares issued and outstanding	$7,000,000
Retained earnings	2,500,000
Total shareholders' equity	$9,500,000

Since purchasing the 800 shares, Mr. Peeks has neither purchased nor sold any additional shares of the company. On December 31 of each year, he has received dividends on the shares held as follows: 1994, $1,408; 1995, $1,672; and 1996, $2,200.

On June 15, 1994, at a time when its shares were selling for $51.25 per share (amount capitalized), Cornfield Corporation declared a 10% stock dividend that was distributed one month later. On October 25, 1995, the corporation split its shares two for one.

Required

Assume that Cornfield Corporation's outstanding shares had a book value of $35.75 per share on December 31, 1994, a book value of $20 per share on December 31, 1995, and a book value of $22.25 on December 31, 1996. Do the following:

1. Prepare statements that show the nature of the shareholders' equity in the corporation at the end of 1994, 1995, and 1996.

2. Prepare a schedule that shows the amount of the corporation's net income each year for 1994, 1995, and 1996. Assume that the changes in the company's retained earnings during the three-year period resulted from earnings and dividends.

Byway (federal incorporation) Company's shareholders' equity on September 15 consisted of the following amounts:

Provocative Problem 16–2
Byway Company
(LO 1)

Common shares, no-par value, unlimited number of shares authorized, 50,000 shares issued and outstanding	$2,875,000
Retained earnings	1,286,000
Total shareholders' equity	$4,161,000

On September 15, when the shares were selling at $100 per share, the corporation's directors voted a 20% stock dividend, distributable on October 5 to the September 25 shareholders of record. The directors also voted a $3.45 per share annual cash dividend, payable on November 23 to the November 15 shareholders of record. The amount of the latter dividend was a disappointment to some shareholders, since the company had for a number of years paid a $4 per share annual cash dividend.

Nancy Cooper owned 1,000 Byway shares on September 25, received her stock dividend shares, and continued to hold all of her shares until after the November 23 cash dividend. She also observed that her shares had a $100 per share market value on September 15, a market value it held until the close of business on September 25, when the market value declined to $90.50 per share.

Required

Give the entries to record the declaration and distribution or payment of the dividends involved here and answer these questions:

a. What was the book value of Cooper's total shares on September 15 (after taking into consideration the cash dividend declared on that day)? What was the book value on October 5 after she received the dividend shares?

b. What fraction of the corporation did Cooper own on September 15? What fraction did she own on October 5?

c. What was the market value of Cooper's total shares on September 15? What was the market value at the close of business on September 25?

d. What did Cooper gain from the stock dividend?

**Provocative Problem
16–3
Rutland Corporation
(LO 4)**

Rutland Corporation had several rather special transactions and events in 1996 which are described below:

a. Rutland Corporation's continuing operations involve a high technology production process. Technical developments in this area occur regularly, and the production machinery becomes obsolete surprisingly often. Because such developments occurred recently, Rutland decided that it was forced to sell certain items of machinery at a loss and replace those items with a different type of machinery. The problem is how to report the loss.

b. Early last year, Rutland purchased a new type of equipment for use in its production process. Although much of the production equipment is amortized over 5 years, a careful analysis of the situation led the company to decide that the new equipment should be amortized over 10 years. Nevertheless, in the rush of year-end activities, the new equipment was included with the older equipment and amortized on a five-year basis. In preparing adjustments at the end of 1996, the accountant discovered that $90,000 amortization was taken on the new equipment last year, when only $45,000 should have been taken.

c. Rutland has a mining operation in several foreign countries, one of which has been subject to political unrest. After a sudden change in governments, the new ruling body resolved that the amount of foreign investment in the country was excessive. As a result, Rutland was forced to transfer ownership in its mines in that country to the new government. Rutland was able to continue its mining operation in a neighbouring country and was allowed to transfer much of its mining equipment to the neighbouring country. Nevertheless, the price paid to Rutland for its mines resulted in a significant loss.

d. Two years earlier, Rutland Corporation purchased some highly specialized equipment that was to be used in the operations of a new division that Rutland intended to acquire. The new division was in a separate line of business and would have been a separate segment of the business. After lengthy negotiations, the acquisition of the division was not accomplished and the company abandoned any hope of entering that line of business. Although the equipment had never been used, it was sold in 1996 at a loss. Rutland Corporation does not have a history of expanding into new lines of business and has no plans of doing so in the future.

Required

Examine Rutland Corporation's special transactions and events and describe how each one should be reported on the income statement or statement of retained earnings. Also state the specific characteristics of the item that support your decision.

Review the As a Matter of Ethics case on page 729. Discuss the ethical implications of the tentative decision to avoid announcing Falcon Corporation's new government contract. What actions would you take if you were the financial vice president?

Provocative Problem 16–4
Ethical issues essay

The financial statements and related disclosures of Geac Computer Corporation Limited are presented in Appendix I. Based on your examination of this information, answer the following:

Provocative Problem 16–5
Financial statement analysis
Geac

1. Does Geac have a simple or complex capital structure?
2. Did Geac report any extraordinary or unusual gains or losses in 1994 or in 1993?
3. What earnings per share data did Geac report?
4. How did Geac's capital structure change during 1994?
5. How many stock options were outstanding on April 30, 1994?

ANALYTICAL AND REVIEW PROBLEMS

Part 1
The more recent business corporations acts restrict the directors by the "solvency" test in the matter of declaration and payment of dividends in money or property. A similar restriction is not, however, imposed in the case of a stock dividend.

A & R Problem 16–1

Required

Discuss why a restriction is deemed necessary in the former but not in the latter situation.

Part 2
In the case of stock dividends, the Canada Business Corporations Act prescribes that the amount of retained earnings to be capitalized is the product of the number of shares issued as a stock dividend multiplied by the market value of each share. The revised Ontario Business Corporations Act does not stipulate the amount to be capitalized, simply stating that the amount to be added to the stated capital account is the amount declared by the directors.

Required

Can a case be made for either of the positions? Support your answer.

Over the last three years, Commonwealth Enterprises, Inc., has experienced the following income results (all numbers are rounded to the nearest thousand dollars):

A & R Problem 16–2

	1994	1995	1996
Revenues	$11,000	$11,900	$14,600
Expenses	(7,000)	(7,900)	(7,700)
Gains	3,200	2,400	0
Losses	(1,200)	(1,900)	(3,900)
Net income	$ 6,000	$ 4,500	$ 3,000

Part 1

Use the information to develop a general prediction of the company's net income for 1997.

Part 2

A closer analysis of the information shows that the company discontinued a segment of its operations in 1996. The company's accountant has determined that the discontinued segment produced the following amounts of income:

	1994	1995	1996
Revenues	$7,000	$2,600	$1,600
Expenses	(5,000)	(5,000)	(4,000)
Gains		400	
Losses	(1,200)	(1,500)	(900)
Loss on disposal of segment assets			(1,200)

Use the information to calculate the company's income without the discontinued segment and then develop a general prediction of the company's net income for 1997.

Part 3

A more in-depth analysis of the company's activity reveals that the company experienced these extraordinary items during the three years when it retired some of its debts before their scheduled maturity dates:

	1994	1995	1996
Extraordinary gain	$2,200	$2,000	
Extraordinary loss			$(1,700)

Use the information to calculate the company's income from continuing operations and develop a general prediction of the company's net income for 1997.

CONCEPT TESTER

Test your understanding of the concepts introduced in this chapter by completing the following crossword puzzle.

Across Clues

1. Synonym for retained earnings no longer in general use (2 words).
4. Division of shares (2 words).
6. Retained earnings not available for dividends because of contract.
8. Securities which if converted would result in lower EPS.
11. Dividend other than in cash.
13. Line of business or class of customers for which data is compiled.
14. Capital structure that includes stock options.
15. EPS before giving effect to dilutive securities.
16. Type of change resulting from updated assumptions.
17. A change that affects present and future periods.
18. Retained earnings voluntarily earmarked.
19. Dividend that is a return of original investment.

Down Clues

2. Securities which if converted would increase EPS.
3. Test for payment of cash dividend.
5. A change that affects prior periods.
7. Stock split that results in fewer shares outstanding.
9. Items that are rare in occurrence and not typical of business activity.
10. Retained earnings transferred to contributed capital account.
12. Capital structure that does not include convertible securities.
17. Ratio of EPS to market share price.

ANSWERS TO PROGRESS CHECKS

16–1 *a, c*

16–2 A 100% stock dividend doubles the number of shares outstanding and an appropriate amount of retained earnings is capitalized. A 2-for-1 stock split only doubles the number of shares outstanding.

16–3 The amount is set by the board of directors.

16–4 *b*

16–5 The four major sections are continuing operations, discontinued operations, extraordinary items, and earnings per share data.

16–6 *a*

16–7 a ($250,000 − $70,000)/22,500 = $8.00

16–8 The number of shares previously outstanding are retroactively restated to reflect the stock split or stock dividend as if it occurred at the beginning of the year.

16–9 The two sets are basic earnings per share and fully diluted earnings per share.

16–10 $34.00/$4.25 = 8

16–11 The company with the highest PE ratio.

CHAPTER 17

Installment Notes Payable and Bonds

Companies and organizations, including governments, frequently need to borrow money for large, long-term projects, such as building a stadium. Special accounting techniques are used to measure interest expense and the amount of the liabilities.

*A*s part of their next assignment, Karen White and Mark Smith have been asked to evaluate the level of debt for Imperial Oil Limited. Their instructor has provided the following information from Imperial's 1994 annual report.

Imperial's net income has been steadily increasing over the last three years. Imperial has maintained what they believe is a conservative level of debt, given the volatility of the petroleum business.

Imperial Oil Limited (in millions)	1994	1993	1992
Total revenues	$ 9,011	$ 8,903	$ 9,147
Net earnings	359	279	195
Total assets	11,928	12,861	13,192
Long-term debt	1,977	2,030	2,222
Shareholders' equity	5,955	6,566	6,636

LEARNING OBJECTIVES

After studying Chapter 17, you should be able to:

1. **Calculate the payments on an installment note payable and describe their effects on the financial statements.**

2. **Describe the various characteristics of different types of bonds and prepare entries to record bond issuances and retirements.**

3. **Estimate the price of bonds issued at a discount and describe their effects on the issuer's financial statements.**

4. **Estimate the price of bonds issued at a premium and describe their effects on the issuer's financial statements.**

5. **Calculate and describe how to use the ratio of pledged assets to secured liabilities.**

6. **Define or explain the words and phrases listed in the chapter glossary.**

In Chapter 13, you learned that some notes payable require a single payment on the date the note matures. In those cases, the single payment includes the borrowed amount plus interest. You also learned about other notes requiring a series of payments that include interest plus a part of the principal. We begin this chapter with a more complete discussion of these installment notes. Then we turn to bonds, which are securities issued by corporations and government bodies. The discussion explains the nature of long-term debt such as the notes and debentures issued by **Imperial Oil** as part of their long-term debt.

INSTALLMENT NOTES PAYABLE

LO 1

Calculate the payments on an installment note payable and describe their effects on the financial statements.

When an **installment note** is used to borrow money, the borrower records the note with an entry similar to the one used for a single-payment note. That is, the increase in cash is recorded with a debit and the increase in the liability is recorded with a credit to Notes Payable. For example, suppose that a company borrows $60,000 by signing an 8% installment note that requires six annual payments. The borrower records the note as follows:

1995					
Dec.	31	Cash	60,000.00	
		Notes Payable		60,000.00
		Borrowed $60,000 by signing an 8% installment note.		

Installment notes payable like this one require the borrower to pay back the debt with a series of periodic payments. Usually, each payment includes all interest expense that has accrued up to the date of the payment plus some portion of the original amount borrowed (the *principal*). Installment notes generally specify one of two alternative payment patterns. Some notes require payments that include interest and equal amounts of principal while other notes simply call for equal payments.

Installment Notes with Payments of Accrued Interest and Equal Amounts of Principal

Installment note agreements requiring payments of accrued interest plus equal amounts of principal create cash flows that decrease in size over the life of the note. This pattern occurs because each payment reduces the liability's principal balance, with the result that the following period's interest expense is reduced. The next payment is smaller because the amount of interest is reduced. For example, suppose the $60,000, 8% note that we just recorded requires the borrower to make six payments at the end of each year equal to the accrued interest plus $10,000 of principal.

We describe the payments, interest, and changes in the balance of this note in Illustration 17–1. Column *a* of the illustration shows the beginning balance of the note. Columns *b*, *c*, and *d* describe each cash payment and how it is divided between interest and principal. Column *b* calculates the interest expense that accrues during each year at 8% of the beginning balance. Column *c* shows the portion of the payment applied to principal. It shows that each payment reduces the liability with a $10,000 debit to the Notes Payable account. Column *d* calculates each annual payment, which consists of the interest in column *b* plus $10,000. (Notice that the credit to the Cash account equals the sum of the debits to the expense and the liability account.) Finally, column *e* shows the ending balance of the liability, which equals the beginning balance in column *a* minus the principal portion of the payment in column *c*. Over the life of the note, the table shows that the total interest expense is $16,800 and the total reduction in principal is $60,000. Thus, the total cash payments are $76,800.

The graph in the lower section of Illustration 17–1 shows these three points: (1) the total payment gets smaller as the loan balance is reduced, (2) the amount of interest included in each payment gets steadily smaller, and (3) the amount of principal in each payment remains constant at $10,000.

The borrower records the effects of the first two payments with these entries:

1996					
Dec.	31	Interest Expense	4,800.00		
		Notes Payable	10,000.00		
		Cash		14,800.00	
		To record first installment payment.			

1997					
Dec.	31	Interest Expense	4,000.00		
		Notes Payable	10,000.00		
		Cash		14,000.00	
		To record second installment payment.			

After all six payments are recorded, the balance of the Notes Payable account for the note is eliminated.

Illustration 17–1 Installment Note with Payments of Accrued Interest and Equal Amounts of Principal

	(a)	(b) Debit		(c) Debit		(d) Credit	(e)
Period Ending	**Beginning Balance** Prior (e)	**Interest Expense** 8% × (a)	+	**Notes Payable** $60,000/6	=	**Cash** (b) + (c)	**Ending Balance** (a) − (c)
Dec. 31, 1996 . . . . . $60,000		$ 4,800		$10,000		$14,800	$50,000
Dec. 31, 1997 50,000		4,000		10,000		14,000	40,000
Dec. 31, 1998 40,000		3,200		10,000		13,200	30,000
Dec. 31, 1999 30,000		2,400		10,000		12,400	20,000
Dec. 31, 2000 20,000		1,600		10,000		11,600	10,000
Dec. 31, 2001 10,000		800		10,000		10,800	0
Total		$16,800	+	$60,000	=	$76,800	

Payments on the note payable:

Payments decrease.

Interest decreases with each payment.

Each payment includes $10,000 of principal.

Interest ▪ Principal

Installment Notes with Equal Payments

In contrast to the previous pattern, many installment notes require the borrower to make a series of equal payments. These payments consist of changing amounts of interest and principal. To demonstrate this type of note, assume that a $60,000 note requires the borrower to make a series of six equal payments of $12,979 at the end of each year. Illustration 17–2 shows the effects of making the payments on this note. (The payments are $12,979 because $60,000 is the present value of an annuity of six annual payments of $12,979, discounted at 8%. We show you how to make this calculation later in this section.)

Allocating Each Payment between Interest and Principal. Each payment of $12,979 includes both interest and principal. Look at Illustration 17–2 to see how an accountant allocates the total amount of each payment between interest and principal.

Illustration 17–2 Installment Note with Equal Payments

		Payments			
		(b) Debit	(c) Debit	(d) Credit	(e)
Period Ending	(a) Beginning Balance Prior (e)	Interest Expense 6% × (a)	+ Notes Payable (d) − (b)	= Cash calculated	Ending Balance (a) − (c)
Dec. 31, 1996 . . . . . . $60,000		$ 4,800	$ 8,179	$12,979	$51,821
Dec. 31, 1997 51,821		4,146	8,833	12,979	42,988
Dec. 31, 1998 42,988		3,439	9,540	12,979	33,448
Dec. 31, 1999 33,448		2,676	10,303	12,979	23,145
Dec. 31, 2000 23,145		1,852	11,127	12,979	12,018
Dec. 31, 2001 12,018		961	12,018	12,979	0
Total		$17,874	+ $60,000	= $77,874	

Payments on the note payable:

Payments are constant.

Interest decreases with each payment.

Each payment includes an increasing amount of principal.

□ Interest   ■ Principal

The table is essentially the same as the table in Illustration 17–1. Again, column *a* shows the liability's beginning balance for each year. Column *b* presents the interest that accrues each year at 8% of the beginning balance. Column *c* calculates the change in the principal of the liability caused by each payment. The debit to the liability account in this column is the difference between the total payment in column *d* and the interest expense in column *b*. Finally, column *e* presents the ending balance after each payment is made.

Even though all six payments are equal, the amount of interest decreases each year because the balance of the liability gets smaller. Then, because the amount of interest gets smaller, the amount of the payment applied to the principal gets larger. This effect is presented graphically in Illustration 17–2. Because the tables in

Illustrations 17–1 and 17–2 show how the principal balance is reduced (or amortized) by the periodic payments, they are often referred to as *installment note amortization schedules.*[1]

The bookkeeper records the effects of the first two payments with these journal entries:

1996 Dec.	31	Interest Expense	4,800.00	
		Notes Payable	8,179.00	
		Cash		12,979.00
		To record first installment payment.		

1997 Dec.	31	Interest Expense	4,146.00	
		Notes Payable	8,833.00	
		Cash		12,979.00
		To record second installment payment.		

The amounts in these entries come from the table in Illustration 17–2. The borrower would record similar entries for each of the remaining payments. Over the six years, the Notes Payable account balance will be eliminated.

To be sure that you understand the differences between the two payment patterns, compare the numbers and graphs in Illustrations 17–1 and 17–2. Notice that the series of equal payments leads to a greater amount of interest expense over the life of the note. This result occurs because the first three payments in Illustration 17–2 are smaller and thus do not reduce the principal as quickly as the first three payments in Illustration 17–1.

Calculating the Equal Periodic Payments on an Installment Note. In the previous example, we simply gave you the size of the equal annual payments on the installment note. Now, we show you how to calculate the size of the payment.

When a note requires a series of equal payments, you can calculate the size of each payment with a present value table for an annuity such as Table 17–2 on page 788.[2] To make the calculation with the table, start with this equation:

$$\text{Payment} \times \text{Annuity table value} = \text{Present value of the annuity}$$

Then, modify the equation to get this version:

$$\text{Payment} = \frac{\text{Present value of the annuity}}{\text{Annuity table value}}$$

---

[1]Many business calculators are programmed to make these amortization calculations for annuities.

[2]Appendix F provides present value tables that include additional interest rates and additional periods (or payments). You should use them to solve the exercises and problems at the end of the chapter.

Because the balance of an installment note equals the present value of the series of payments, the equation can again be modified to become this formula:

$$\text{Payment} = \frac{\text{Note balance}}{\text{Annuity table value}}$$

For this example, the initial note balance is $60,000. The annuity table value in the formula is based on the note's interest rate and the number of payments. The interest rate is 8% and there are six payments. Therefore, enter Table 17–2 on the sixth row and go across to the 8% column, where you will find the value of 4.6229. These numbers now can be substituted into the formula to find the payment:

$$\text{Payment} = \frac{\$60,000}{4.6229} = \$12,979$$

This formula can be used for all installment notes that require equal periodic payments.[3]

Progress Check

(Answers to Progress Checks are provided at the end of the chapter.)

17-1 Which of the following is true for an installment note that requires a series of equal payments?

    a. The payments consist of an increasing amount of interest and a decreasing amount of principal.

    b. The payments consist of changing amounts of principal, but the interest portion of the payment remains constant.

    c. The payments consist of a decreasing amount of interest and an increasing amount of principal.

17-2 How is the interest portion of an installment note payment calculated?

17-3 When a borrower records an interest payment on an installment note, how are the balance sheet and income statement affected?

BORROWING BY ISSUING BONDS

LO 2

Describe the various characteristics of different types of bonds and prepare entries to record bond issuances and retirements.

Business corporations often borrow money by issuing **bonds**.[4] Bonds involve written promises to pay interest at a stated annual rate and to make a final payment of an amount identified on the bonds as the **par value of the bonds**. Most bonds require the borrower to pay the interest semiannually. The par value of the bonds (also known as the *face amount*) is paid at a specified future date called the *maturity date of the bonds*. The amount of interest that must be paid each year is determined by multiplying the par value of the bonds by the stated rate of interest established when the bonds were issued.

Differences between Notes Payable and Bonds

When a business borrows money by signing a note payable, the money is generally obtained from a single lender, such as a bank. In contrast, a group of bonds

---

[3]Business calculators can also be used to find the size of the payments.

[4]Bonds are also issued by nonprofit corporations, as well as the federal government and other governmental units, such as municipalities, provinces, and utilities. Although the examples in this chapter deal with business situations, all issuers use the same practices to account for their bonds.

(often called a *bond issue*) typically consists of a large number of bonds, usually in denominations of $1,000, that are sold to many different lenders. After bonds are originally issued, they often are bought and sold by these investors. Thus, any particular bond may actually be owned by a number of people before it matures.

Differences between Shares and Bonds

Shares and bonds are different types of securities. Shares represent an ownership right in the corporation. For example, a person who owns 1,000 of a corporation's 10,000 outstanding shares controls one-tenth of the total shareholders' equity. On the other hand, if a person owns a $1,000, 11%, 20-year bond, the bondholder has a receivable from the issuer. The bond owner has the right to receive 11% interest ($110) each year that the bond is outstanding and $1,000 when the bond matures 20 years after its issue date. The issuing company is obligated to make these payments and thus has a liability to the bondholder.

ADVANTAGES OF ISSUING BONDS

Companies that issue bonds are usually trying to increase their rate of return on equity. For example, assume a company that has $1 million of equity is considering spending $500,000 to expand its capacity. Management predicts that the $500,000 will allow the company to earn an additional $125,000 of income before paying any interest. The managers are considering three possible plans. Under Plan A, the expansion will not occur. Under Plan B, the expansion will occur, and the needed funds will be obtained from the owners. Under Plan C, the company will sell $500,000 of bonds that pay 10% annual interest ($50,000). Illustration 17–3 shows how the plans would affect the company's net income, equity, and return on equity.

Analysis of the alternatives in the illustration shows that the owners will enjoy a greater rate of return and be better off if the expansion is made and if the funds are obtained by issuing the bonds. Even though the projected net income under Plan C would be smaller than Plan B's income, the rate of return on the equity would be larger because there would be less equity. This result occurs whenever the expected rate of return from the new assets is greater than the rate of interest on the bonds. In addition, issuing bonds allows the current owner or owners of a business to remain in control of the company.

CHARACTERISTICS OF BONDS

Over the years, financial experts have created many different kinds of bonds with various characteristics. We describe some of the more common features of bonds in the following paragraphs.

Serial Bonds

Some companies issue several groups of bonds that mature at different dates. As a result, the bonds are repaid gradually over a number of years. Because these bonds mature in series, they are called **serial bonds**. For example, $1 million of serial bonds might mature at the rate of $100,000 each year from 6 to 15 years after the bonds were issued. There would be 10 groups (or series) of bonds of $100,000 each. One series would mature after six years, another after seven years, and another each successive year until the final series is repaid.

	Plan A Don't Expand	Plan B Increase Equity	Plan C Issue Bonds
Income before interest	$ 100,000	$ 225,000	$ 225,000
Interest			(50,000)
Net income	$ 100,000	$ 225,000	$ 175,000
Equity	$1,000,000	$1,500,000	$1,000,000
Return on equity	10.0%	15.0%	17.5%

Illustration 17-3
Financing with
Bonds or Shares

Sinking Fund Bonds

As an alternative to serial bonds, **sinking fund bonds** all mature on the same date. To reduce some of the risk for owners, these bonds require the issuer to create a *sinking fund*, which is a separate pool of assets used only to retire the bonds at maturity. In effect, the issuer must start to set aside the cash to pay off the bonds long before they mature.

Convertible Bonds

Some companies issue **convertible bonds** that can be exchanged by the bondholders for a fixed number of common shares of the issuing company. These bonds offer issuers the advantage that they might be settled without paying back the cash initially borrowed. Convertible bonds also offer the bondholders the potential to participate in future increases in the market value of the shares. However, if the shares do not appreciate, the bondholders continue to receive periodic interest and will receive the par value when the bond matures. In most cases, the bondholders can decide whether and when to convert the bonds to shares. However, the issuer can force conversion by exercising an option to buy the bonds back at a price less than the market value of the shares.

Registered Bonds and Bearer Bonds

A company that issues **registered bonds** keeps a record of the names and addresses of the bonds' owners. Then, over the life of the bonds, the company makes interest payments by sending cheques to these registered owners. When one investor sells a bond to another investor, the issuer must be notified of the change. Registered bonds offer the issuer the practical advantage of not having to actually issue bond certificates to the investors. This arrangement also protects investors against loss or theft of the bonds.

Unregistered bonds are called **bearer bonds**, because they are payable to whoever holds them (the *bearer*). Since there may be no record of sales or exchanges, the holder of a bearer bond is presumed to be its rightful owner. As a result, lost or stolen bonds are difficult to replace.

Many bearer bonds are also **coupon bonds**. This term reflects the fact that interest coupons are attached to each bond. Each coupon matures on a specific interest payment date. The owner detaches each coupon when it matures and presents it to a bank or broker for collection. At maturity, the owner follows the same process and presents the bond certificates to a bank or broker.

Secured Bonds and Debentures

When bonds are secured, specific assets of the issuing company are pledged (or *mortgaged*) as collateral. This arrangement gives the bondholders additional protection against default by the issuer. If the issuing company fails to pay the interest or maturity value, the secured bondholders can demand that the collateral be sold and the proceeds used to repay the debt.

In contrast to secured bonds, unsecured bonds are potentially more risky because they are supported by only the issuer's general credit standing. Unsecured bonds are also called **debentures**. Because of the greater risk of default, a company generally must be financially strong to successfully issue debentures at a favorable rate of interest.

Sometimes, companies issue debentures that rank below certain other unsecured liabilities of the company. Debentures such as this are called subordinated debentures. In a liquidation, the subordinated debentures would not be repaid until the claims of the more senior, unsecured liabilities were first satisfied.

Bond Market Values

Bonds are securities and can be easily traded between investors. Because they are bought and sold in the market, they have a market value. As a matter of convenience, bond market values are expressed as a percentage of their face value. For example, a company's bonds might be trading at $103^1/_2$, which means that they can be bought or sold for 103.5% of their par value. If other bonds are trading at 95, they can be bought or sold at 95% of their par value.

THE PROCESS OF ISSUING BONDS

When a company issues bonds, it normally sells them to an investment firm called an *underwriter*. In turn, the underwriter resells the bonds to the public. In some situations, the issuer may sell the bonds directly to investors as the cash is needed.

The legal document that identifies the rights and obligations of the bondholders and the issuer is called the **bond indenture**. In effect, the bond indenture is the legal contract between the issuer and the bondholders. Although the practice is less common today, each bondholder may receive an actual bond certificate as evidence of the company's debt. However, most companies reduce their costs by not issuing certificates to registered bondholders.

If the underwriter sells the bonds to a large number of investors, the bondholders' interests are represented and protected by a *trustee*. The trustee monitors the issuer's actions to ensure that it complies with the obligations in the bond indenture. Most trustees are large banks or trust companies.

Accounting for the Issuance of Bonds

Before bonds are issued, the terms of the indenture are drawn up and accepted by the trustee. If the bonds are to be offered to the general public by the underwriter, they must be registered with the Securities Commission (e.g., the Ontario Securities Commission, or OSC), which means that the issuer must provide extensive financial information in special reports.

For example, suppose that the Barnes Company receives authorization from the OSC to issue $800,000 of 9%, 20-year bonds dated January 1, 1995, that are due on December 31, 2014. They will pay interest semiannually on each June 30 and December 31. Most corporate or government bonds pay interest either quarterly or semiannually. After the bond indenture is accepted by the trustee on behalf of the bondholders, all or a portion of the bonds may be sold to the underwriter. If all the bonds are sold at their par value, Barnes Company makes this entry to record the sale:

1995					
Jan.	1	Cash	800,000.00	
		Bonds Payable		800,000.00
		Sold bonds at par.		

This entry reflects the fact that the company's cash and long-term liabilities are increased.

Six months later, the first semiannual interest payment is made, and Barnes records the payment with this entry:

1995					
June	30	Interest Expense	36,000.00	
		Cash		36,000.00
		Paid semiannual interest on bonds.		
		(9% × $800,000 × 1/2).		

When the bonds mature 20 years later, Barnes Company will record its payment of the maturity value with the following entry:

2014					
Dec.	31	Bonds Payable	800,000.00	
		Cash		800,000.00
		Paid bonds at maturity.		

SELLING BONDS BETWEEN INTEREST DATES

As in the previous example, many bonds are sold on their original issue date. However, circumstances may cause a company to actually sell some of the bonds later. If so, it is likely that the selling date will fall between interest payment dates. When this happens, the purchasers normally pay the issuer the purchase price plus any interest accrued since the issue date or the preceding interest payment date. This accrued interest is then refunded to the purchasers on the next interest date. For example, assume that the Fields Company sold $100,000 of its 9% bonds at par on March 1, 1996, which was two months after the original issue date. The interest on the bonds is payable semiannually on each June 30 and December 31. Because two months have passed, the issuer collects two months' interest from the buyer at the time of the sale. This amount is $1,500 ($100,000 × 9% × 2/12). This situation is represented by the following diagram:

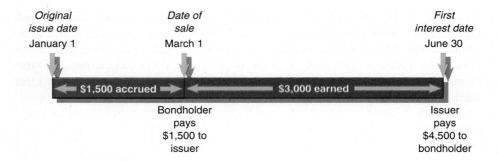

The issuer's entry to record the sale is

Mar.	1	Cash	101,500.00	
		Interest Payable		1,500.00
		Bonds Payable		100,000.00
		Sold $100,000 of bonds with two months' accrued		
		interest.		

Note that the liabilities for the interest and the bonds are recorded in separate accounts.

When the June 30 semiannual interest date arrives, the issuer pays a full six months' interest of $4,500 ($100,000 × 9% × 1/2) to the bondholder. This payment includes the four months' interest of $3,000 earned by the bondholder from March 1 to June 30 plus the refund of the two months' accrued interest collected by the issuer when the bonds were sold. The issuer's entry to record this first payment is

June	30	Interest Payable	1,500.00	
		Interest Expense	3,000.00	
		Cash		4,500.00
		Paid semiannual interest on the bonds.		

The practice of collecting and then refunding the accrued interest with the next interest payment may seem like a roundabout way to do business. However, it greatly simplifies the bond issuer's administrative efforts. To understand this point, suppose that a company sells bonds on 15 or 20 different dates between the original issue date and the first interest payment date. If the issuer did not collect the accrued interest from the buyers, it would have to pay different amounts of cash to each of them in accordance with how much time had passed since they purchased their bonds. To make the correct payments, the issuer would have to keep detailed records of the purchasers and the dates on which they bought their bonds. Issuers avoid this extra record-keeping by having each buyer pay in the accrued interest at the time of purchase. Then, the company pays a full six months' interest to all purchasers, regardless of when they bought the bonds.

The interest rate to be paid by the issuer of bonds is specified in the indenture and on the bond certificates. Because it is stated in the indenture, this rate is called the **contract rate** of the bonds. (This rate is also known as the *coupon rate*, the *stated rate*, or the *nominal rate*.) The amount of interest to be paid each year is determined by multiplying the par value of the bonds by the contract rate. The contract rate is usually stated on an annual basis, even if the interest is to be paid semiannually. For example, suppose that a company issues a $1,000, 8% bond that pays interest semiannually. As a result, the annual interest of $80 (8% $\times$ $1,000) will be paid in two semiannual payments of $40 each.

Although the contract rate sets the amount of interest that the issuer pays in *cash*, the contract rate is not necessarily the rate of interest *expense* actually incurred by the issuer. In fact, the interest expense depends on the market value of the issuer's bonds, which depends on the purchasers' opinions about the risk of lending to the issuer. This perceived risk (as well as the supply of and demand for bonds) is reflected in the **market rate** for bond interest. The market rate is the consensus rate that borrowers are willing to pay and that lenders are willing to earn at the level of risk inherent in the bonds. This rate changes often (even daily) in response to changes in the supply of and demand for bonds. The market rate tends to go up when the demand for bonds decreases or the supply increases. The rate tends to go down when the supply of bonds decreases or the demand increases.

Because many factors affect the bond market, various companies face different interest rates for their bonds. The market rate for a specific set of bonds depends on the level of risk investors assign to them. As the level of risk increases, the rate increases. Market rates also are affected by the length of the bonds' life. Long-term bonds generally have higher rates because they are more risky.

Many bond issuers offer a contract rate of interest equal to the rate they expect the market to demand as of the bonds' issuance date. If the contract and market rates are equal, the bonds sell at their par value. However, if the contract and market rates are not equal, the bonds are not sold at their par value. Instead, they are sold at a *premium* above their par value or at a *discount* below their par value. Observe the relationship between the interest rates and the issue price of the bonds' values in this table:

When the contract rate is		The bond sells
Above the market rate	$\Rightarrow$	At a premium
At the market rate	$\Rightarrow$	At par value
Below the market rate	$\Rightarrow$	At a discount

Over the last two decades, some companies have issued *zero-coupon bonds* that do not provide any periodic interest payments. Because this contract rate of 0% is always below the market rate, these bonds are always issued at prices less than their face values.

BOND INTEREST RATES

Progress Check

17-4   Unsecured bonds that are backed only by the issuer's general credit standing are called *(a)* serial bonds, *(b)* debentures, *(c)* registered bonds, *(d)* convertible bonds, *(e)* bearer bonds.

17-5   How do you calculate the amount of interest a bond issuer will pay each year?

17-6   On May 1, a company sold $500,000 of 9% bonds that pay semiannual interest on each January 1 and July 1. The bonds were sold at par value plus accrued interest since January 1. The bond issuer's entry to record the first semiannual interest payment on July 1 should include *(a)* a debit to Interest Payable for $15,000, *(b)* a debit to Interest Expense for $22,500, or *(c)* a credit to Interest Payable for $7,500.

17-7   When the contract rate is above the market rate, do the bonds sell at a premium or a discount? Do the purchasers pay more or less than the par value of the bonds?

BONDS SOLD AT A DISCOUNT

LO 3

Estimate the price of bonds issued at a discount and describe their effects on the issuer's financial statements.

As we described in the previous section, a **discount on bonds payable** arises when a company issues bonds with a contract rate less than the market rate. The expected issue price of the bonds can be found by calculating the *present value* of the expected cash flows, discounted at the market rate of interest.

To illustrate, assume that a company offers to issue bonds with a $100,000 par value, an 8% annual contract rate, and a five-year life. Also assume that the market rate of interest for this company's bonds is 10%.[5] In exchange for the purchase price received from the buyers, these bonds obligate the issuer to pay out two different future cash flows:

1. $100,000 at the end of the bonds' five-year life.
2. $4,000 (4% × $100,000) at the end of each six-month interest period throughout the five-year life of the bonds.

To estimate the bonds' issue price, use the market rate of interest to calculate the present value of the future cash flows. Using an annuity table of present values, you must work with *semiannual* compounding periods. Thus, the annual market rate of 10% is changed to the semiannual rate of 5%. Likewise, the five-year life of the bonds is changed to 10 semiannual periods.

The actual calculation requires two steps: First, you find the present value of the $100,000 maturity payment. Second, find the present value of the annuity of 10 payments of $4,000 each.

The present values can be found by using Table 17–1 (on page 788) for the single maturity payment and Table 17–2 for the annuity. To complete the first step, enter Table 17–1 on row 10 and go across to the 5% column. The table value is 0.6139. Second, enter Table 17–2 on row 10 and go across to the 5% column,

---

[5]The spread between the contract rate and the market rate of interest on a new bond issue is seldom more than a fraction of a percent. However, we use a difference of 2% here to emphasize the effects.

where the table value is 7.7217. This schedule shows the results when you multiply the cash flow amounts by the table values and add them together:

Cash Flow	Table	Table Value	Amount	Present Value
Par value	17–1	0.6139	$100,000	$61,390
Interest (annuity)	17–2	7.7217	4,000	30,887
Total				$92,277

If 5% is the appropriate semiannual interest rate for the bonds in the current market, the maximum price that informed buyers would offer for the bonds is $92,277. This amount is also the minimum price that the issuer would accept.

If the issuer accepts $92,277 cash for its bonds on the original issue date of December 31, 1996, it records the event with this entry:

1996					
Dec.	31	Cash	92,277.00	
		Discount on Bonds payable	7,723.00	
		Bonds payable		100,000.00
		Sold bonds at a discount on the original issue date.		

This entry causes the bonds to appear in the long-term liability section of the issuer's balance sheet as

Long-term liabilities:
Bonds payable, 8%, due December 31, 2001	$100,000	
Less discount	7,723	$92,277

This presentation shows that the discount is deducted from the par value of the bonds to produce the **carrying amount** of the bonds payable. As we saw in the last chapter for notes payable, the carrying amount is the net amount at which the bonds are reflected on the balance sheet.

Allocating Interest and Amortizing the Discount

In the previous example, the issuer received $92,277 for its bonds and will pay the bondholders $100,000 after five years have passed. Because the $7,723 discount is eventually paid to the bondholders at maturity, it is part of the cost of using the $92,277 for five years. This table shows that the total interest cost of $47,723 is the difference between the amount repaid and the amount borrowed:

Amount repaid:	
Ten payments of $4,000	$ 40,000
Maturity amount	100,000
Total repaid	$140,000
Less amount borrowed	(92,277)
Total interest expense	$ 47,723

The total expense also equals the sum of the 10 cash payments and the discount:

Ten payments of $4,000	$40,000
Plus discount	7,723
Total interest expense	$47,723

In describing these bonds and the interest expense, the issuer's accountant must accomplish two things. First, the total interest expense of $47,723 must be allocated among the 10 six-month periods in the bonds' life. Second, the carrying value of the bonds must be updated for each balance sheet. Two alternative methods accomplish these objectives. They are the straight-line and the interest methods of allocating interest. Because the process involves reducing the original discount on the bonds over the life of the bonds, it is also called *amortizing the bond discount.*

Straight-Line Method.　The **straight-line method** of allocating the interest is the simpler of the two methods. This method allocates an equal portion of the total interest expense to each of the six-month interest periods.

In applying the straight-line method to the present example, the accountant divides the five years' total expense of $47,723 by 10 (the number of semiannual periods in the bonds' life). The result is $4,772 per period.[6] The same number can be found by dividing the $7,723 original discount by 10. That result is $772, which is the amount of discount to be amortized in each interest period. When the $772 of amortized discount is added to the $4,000 cash payment, the total interest expense for each six-month period is $4,772.

When the semiannual cash payment is made, the issuer uses the following entry to record the interest expense and update the balance of the bond liability:

1997					
June	30	Interest Expense	4,772.00	
		Discount on Bonds payable		772.00
		Cash		4,000.00
		To record six months' interest and discount		
		amortization.		

---

[6]For simplicity, all calculations have been rounded to the nearest whole dollar. Use the same practice when solving the exercises and problems at the end of the chapter.

Illustration 17-4   Allocating Interest Expense and Amortizing the Bond Discount with the Straight-Line Method

Period Ending	(a) Beginning Balance	(b) Debit Interest Expense	(c) = Credit Discount on Bonds +	(d) Credit Cash	(e) Ending Balance
	Prior (e)	$47,723/10	$7,723/10	4% × $100,000	(a) + (c)
June 30, 1997	$92,277	$ 4,772	$ 772	$ 4,000	$ 93,049
Dec. 31, 1997	93,049	4,772	772	4,000	93,821
June 30, 1998	93,821	4,772	772	4,000	94,593
Dec. 31, 1998	94,593	4,772	772	4,000	95,365
June 30, 1999	95,365	4,772	772	4,000	96,137
Dec. 31, 1999	96,137	4,772	772	4,000	96,909
June 30, 2000	96,909	4,772	772	4,000	97,681
Dec. 31, 2000	97,681	4,772	772	4,000	98,453
June 30, 2001	98,453	4,772	772	4,000	99,225
Dec. 31, 2001	99,225	4,775*	775	4,000	100,000
Total		$47,723 =	$7,723 +	$40,000	

*Adjusted for rounding.

Note that the $772 credit to the Discount on Bonds Payable account actually *increases* the bonds' carrying value. The increase comes about by *decreasing* the balance of the contra account that is subtracted from the Bonds Payable account.

Illustration 17–4 presents a table similar to the amortization tables that you have studied for notes payable. It shows how the interest expense is allocated among the 10 six-month periods in the bonds' life. It also shows how amortizing the bond discount causes the balance of the net liability to increase until it reaches $100,000 at the end of the bonds' life. Notice the following points as you analyze Illustration 17–4:

1. The $92,277 beginning balance in column *a* equals the cash received from selling the bonds. It also equals the $100,000 face amount of the bonds less the initial $7,723 discount from selling the bonds for less than par.

2. The semiannual interest expense of $4,772 in column *b* for each row equals the amount obtained by dividing the total expense of $47,723 by 10.

3. The credit to the Discount on Bonds Payable account in column *c* equals one-tenth of the total discount of $7,723.

4. The $4,000 interest payment in column *d* is the result of multiplying the $100,000 par value of the bonds by the 4% semiannual contract rate of interest.

5. The ending balance in column *e* equals the beginning balance in column *a* plus the $772 discount amortization in column *c*. This ending balance then becomes the beginning balance on the next row in the table.

6. The balance in column *e* continues to grow each period by the $772 of discount amortization until it finally equals the par value of the bonds when they mature.

The three payment columns show that the company incurs a $4,772 interest expense each period, but pays only $4,000. The $772 unpaid portion of the expense is appropriately added to the balance of the liability. It is added to the liability by being taken from the contra account balance. This table shows you how the balance of the discount is partially amortized every six months until it is eliminated:

Period Ending	Beginning Discount Balance	Amount Amortized	Ending Discount Balance
June 30, 1997	$7,723	$ (772)	$6,951
Dec. 31, 1997	6,951	(772)	6,179
June 30, 1998	6,179	(772)	5,407
Dec. 31, 1998	5,407	(772)	4,635
June 30, 1999	4,635	(772)	3,863
Dec. 31, 1999	3,863	(772)	3,091
June 30, 2000	3,091	(772)	2,319
Dec. 31, 2000	2,319	(772)	1,547
June 30, 2001	1,547	(772)	775
Dec. 31, 2001	775	(775)*	0
Total		$(7,723)	

*Adjusted for rounding.

Interest Method.   Straight-line allocations of interest used to be widely applied in practice. However, generally accepted accounting principles now allow the straight-line method to be used only if the results do not differ materially from those obtained by using the **interest method** to allocate the interest over the life of the bonds.[7]

The interest method is exactly the same process for allocating interest that you first learned in Chapter 12 for notes payable. Interest expense for a period is found by multiplying the balance of the liability at the beginning of that period by the original market interest rate.

In Illustration 17–5, we present an amortization table for our example. The key difference between Illustrations 17–4 and 17–5 lies in the calculation of the interest expense in column b. Instead of assigning an equal amount of interest to each interest period, the interest method assigns an increasing amount of interest over the bonds' life because the balance of the liability increases over the five years. The interest expense in column b equals the original 5% market interest rate times the balance of the liability at the beginning of each period. Notice that both methods allocate the same $47,723 of total expense among the five years, but with different patterns.

The amount of discount amortized in any period is the difference between the interest expense in column b and the cash payment in column d. In effect, the accrued but unpaid portion of the interest expense in column c is added to the net liability in column a to get the ending balance in column e.

In the following table, you can see how the balance of the discount is amortized by the interest method until it reaches zero:

---

[7]FASB, *Accounting Standards—Current Text* (Norwalk, CT, 1994), sec. I69.108. First published in *APB Opinion No. 21*, par. 15. Also see *CICA Re-Exposure Draft*, "Financial Instruments," par. .170, in *CA Magazine*, April 1994, p. ED27.

Illustration 17-5 Allocating Interest Expense and Amortizing the Bond Discount with the Interest Method

	(a)	(b) Debit Interest Expense		(c) Credit Discount on Bonds		(d) Credit Cash	(e) Ending Balance
Period Ending	**Beginning Balance**		=		+		
	Prior (e)	*5% × (a)*		*(b) − (d)*		*4% × $100,000*	*(a) + (c)*
June 30, 1997	$92,277	$ 4,614		$ 614		$ 4,000	$ 93,891
Dec. 31, 1997	92,891	4,645		645		4,000	93,536
June 30, 1998	93,536	4,677		677		4,000	94,213
Dec. 31, 1998	94,213	4,711		711		4,000	94,924
June 30, 1999	94,924	4,746		746		4,000	95,670
Dec. 31, 1999	95,670	4,784		784		4,000	96,454
June 30, 2000	96,454	4,823		823		4,000	97,277
Dec. 31, 2000	97,277	4,864		864		4,000	98,141
June 30, 2001	98,141	4,907		907		4,000	99,048
Dec. 31, 2001	99,048	4,952		952		4,000	100,000
Total		$47,723	=	$7,723	+	$40,000	

Period Ending	**Beginning Discount Balance**	**Amount Amortized**	**Ending Discount Balance**
June 30, 1997 . .	$7,723	$ (614)	$7,109
Dec. 31, 1997	7,109	(645)	6,464
June 30, 1998	6,464	(677)	5,787
Dec. 31, 1998	5,787	(711)	5,076
June 30, 1999	5,076	(746)	4,330
Dec. 31, 1999	4,330	(784)	3,546
June 30, 2000	3,546	(823)	2,723
Dec. 31, 2000	2,723	(864)	1,859
June 30, 2001	1,859	(907)	952
Dec. 31, 2001	952	(952)*	0
Total		$(7,723)	

*Adjusted for rounding.

Except for the differences in the amounts, journal entries that record the expense and update the liability balance are the same under the interest method and the straight-line method. For example, the entry to record the interest payment at the end of the first interest period is

1997					
June	30	Interest Expense	4,614.00		
		Discount on Bonds payable		614.00	
		Cash		4,000.00	
		To record six months' interest and discount amortization.			

Illustration 17-6   Comparing the Straight-Line and Interest Methods of Allocating Interest on a Bond Sold at a Discount

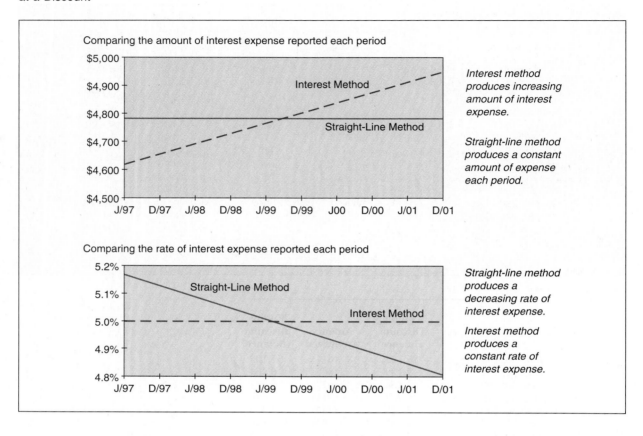

The accountant uses the numbers in Illustration 17–5 to make similar entries throughout the five-year life of the bonds.

Comparing the Straight-Line and Interest Methods. With this background in place, we can now look more closely at the differences between the straight-line and interest methods of allocating interest among the periods in the bonds' life. In Illustration 17–6, the two graphs illustrate the differences for bonds issued at a discount.

The horizontal line in the first graph in Illustration 17–6 represents the amounts of interest expense reported each period under straight-line. The upward sloping line represents the increasing amounts of interest reported under the interest method. The amounts increase because the constant 5% rate is applied to the growing balance of the liability.

The horizontal line in the second graph represents the constant rate of 5% that the interest method uses to determine the interest expense for every six-month period. The downward sloping line represents the changing interest rates produced by the straight-line method when the bond is issued at a discount. The interest rates decrease each period because the amount of interest expense remains constant while the balance of the liability increases.

The interest method is preferred over the straight-line method because it provides a more reasonable description of the growth of the liability and the amount of interest expense incurred each period. As we mentioned, the straight-line method can be used only if the results do not differ materially from those obtained by using the interest method.

Progress Check

A company recently issued a group of five-year, 6% bonds with a $100,000 par value. The interest is to be paid semiannually, and the market interest rate was 8% on the issue date. Use this information to answer the following questions:

17-8   What is the bonds' selling price? (a) $100,000; (b) $92,393; (c) $91,893; (d) $100,321; (e) $92,016.

17-9   What is the journal entry to record the sale?

17-10   What is the amount of interest expense recorded at the time of the first semi-annual cash payment using (a) the straight-line method of allocating interest and (b) the interest method of allocating interest?

When bonds carry a contract interest rate that is greater than the market rate, the bonds sell at a price greater than the par value and the difference between the par and market values is called the **premium**. In effect, buyers bid up the price of the bonds until it reaches the level that creates the current market rate of interest. As we explained for the discount situation, this premium market price can be estimated by finding the present value of the expected cash flows from the bonds at the market interest rate.

For example, assume that a company decides to issue bonds with a $100,000 par value, a 12% annual contract rate, and a five-year life. On the issue date, the market interest rate for the bonds is only 10%. Thus, potential buyers of these bonds bid up their market price until the effective rate equals the market rate. To estimate this price, we use the 5% semiannual market rate to find the present value of the expected cash flows. The cash flows consist of:

1. $100,000 at the end of the bonds' five-year life.
2. $6,000 (6% × $100,000) at the end of each six-month interest period throughout the five-year life of the bonds.

The present values can be found by using Table 17–1 (page 788) for the single maturity payment and Table 17–2 for the annuity. To complete the first step, enter Table 17–1 on row 10 and go across to the 5% column. The table value is 0.6139. Second, enter Table 17–2 on row 10 and go across to the 5% column, where the table value is 7.7217. Finally, use these table values to reduce the future cash flows to their present value. This schedule shows the results when you multiply the cash flow amounts by the table values and add them together:

BONDS SOLD AT A PREMIUM

LO 4

Estimate the price of bonds issued at a premium and describe their effects on the issuer's financial statements.

Cash Flow	Table	Table Value	Amount	Present Value
Par value	17–1	0.6139	$100,000	$ 61,390
Interest (annuity)	17–2	7.7217	6,000	46,330
Total				$107,720

If 5% is the appropriate semiannual interest rate for the bonds in the current market, the maximum price that informed buyers would offer for the bonds is $107,720. This amount is also the minimum price that the issuer would accept.

If the issuer does accept $107,720 cash for its bonds on the original issue date of December 31, 1996, it records the event with this entry:

1996				
Dec.	31	Cash	107,720.00	
		Premium on Bonds Payable		7,720.00
		Bonds Payable		100,000.00
		Sold bonds at a premium on the original issue date.		

This entry causes the bonds to appear in the long-term liability section of the issuer's balance sheet as follows:

Long-term liabilities:		
Bonds payable, 8%, due December 31, 2001	$100,000	
Plus premium	7,720	$107,720

This presentation shows that the premium is added to the par value of the bonds to produce their carrying amount.

Allocating Interest Expense and Amortizing the Premium

Over the life of these premium bonds, the issuer pays back $160,000, which consists of the 10 periodic interest payments of $6,000 plus the $100,000 par value. Because it borrowed $107,720, the total interest expense will be $52,280. This table shows the calculation:

Amount repaid:	
Ten payments of $6,000	$ 60,000
Maturity amount	100,000
Total repaid	$160,000
Less amount borrowed	(107,720)
Total interest expense	$ 52,280

The following calculation confirms that the total expense also equals the difference between the 10 cash payments and the premium:

Ten payments of $6,000	$ 60,000
Less premium	(7,720)
Total interest expense	$ 52,280

The premium is subtracted because it will not be paid to the bondholders when the bonds mature.

This total interest expense can be allocated over the 10 semiannual periods with either the straight-line or the interest method. Because the interest method is preferred, it is the only one illustrated for these bonds. Illustration 17–7 shows an amortization schedule for the bonds using this method.

Again, column *a* of the illustration shows the beginning balance, and column *b* shows the amount of expense at 5% of the beginning balance. But, the amount of cash paid out in column *d* is larger than the expense because the payment is based on the higher 6% contract rate. As a result, the excess payment over the expense reduces the principal. These amounts are shown in column *c*. Finally, column *e* shows the new ending balance after the amortized premium in column *c* is deducted from the beginning balance in column *a*.

The following table shows how the premium is reduced by the amortization process over the life of the bonds:

Period Ending	Beginning Discount Balance	Amount Amortized	Ending Premium Balance
June 30, 1997	$7,720	$ (614)	$7,106
Dec. 31, 1997	7,106	(645)	6,461
June 30, 1998	6,461	(677)	5,784
Dec. 31, 1998	5,784	(711)	5,073
June 30, 1999	5,073	(746)	4,327
Dec. 31, 1999	4,327	(784)	3,543
June 30, 2000	3,543	(823)	2,720
Dec. 31, 2000	2,720	(864)	1,856
June 30, 2001	1,856	(907)	949
Dec. 31, 2001	949	(949)*	0
Total		$(7,720)	

*Adjusted for rounding.

The effect of premium amortization on interest expense and on the liability can be seen in this journal entry on June 30, 1997, when the issuer makes the first semiannual interest payment:

Illustration 17-7   Allocating Interest Expense and Amortizing the Bond Premium with the Interest Method

		Payments			
	(a)	(b) Debit Interest Expense	(c) Debit Premium on Bonds	(d) Credit Cash	(e) Ending Balance
Period Ending	Beginning Balance		+ =		
	Prior (e)	5% × (a)	(d) − (b)	6% × $100,000	(a) − (c)
June 30, 1997	$107,720	$ 5,386	$ 614	$ 6,000	$107,106
Dec. 31, 1997	107,106	5,355	645	6,000	106,461
June 30, 1998	106,461	5,323	677	6,000	105,784
Dec. 31, 1998	105,784	5,289	711	6,000	105,073
June 30, 1999	105,073	5,254	746	6,000	104,327
Dec. 31, 1999	104,327	5,216	784	6,000	103,543
June 30, 2000	103,543	5,177	823	6,000	102,720
Dec. 31, 2000	102,720	5,136	864	6,000	101,856
June 30, 2001	101,856	5,093	907	6,000	100,949
Dec. 31, 2001	100,949	5,051*	949	6,000	100,000
Total		$52,280	+ $7,720 =	$60,000	

*Adjusted for rounding.

1997					
June	30	Interest Expense	5,386.00		
		Premium on Bonds Payable		614.00	
		Cash			6,000.00
		To record six months' interest and premium amortization.			

Similar entries are recorded at each payment date until the bonds mature at the end of 2001. However, the interest method causes the company to report decreasing amounts of interest expense and increasing amounts of premium amortization.

ACCOUNTING FOR ACCRUED INTEREST EXPENSE

If a bond's interest period does not coincide with the issuing company's accounting period, an adjusting entry is necessary to recognize the interest expense that has accrued since the most recent interest payment. For example, assume that the bonds described in Illustration 17–7 were issued on September 1, 1996, instead of December 31, 1996. As a result, four months' interest (and premium amortization) accrue before the end of the 1996 calendar year. Because the reporting period ends on that date, an adjusting entry is needed to capture this information about the bonds.

Interest for the four months ended December 31, 1996, equals $3,591, which is 4/6 of the first six months' interest of $5,386. The premium amortization is $409, which is 4/6 of the first six months' amortization of $614. The sum of the interest expense and the amortization is $4,000 ($3,591 + $409), which also equals 4/6 of the $6,000 cash payment that is due on March 1, 1997. The accountant records these effects with this adjusting entry:

1996				
Dec.	31	Interest Expense	3,591.00	
		Premium on Bonds Payable	409.00	
		Interest Payable		4,000.00
		To record four months' accrued interest and		
		premium amortization.		

Similar entries are made on each December 31 throughout the five-year life of the bonds.

When the $6,000 cash payment occurs on the next interest date, the journal entry recognizes the interest expense and amortization for January and February of 1997 and eliminates the interest payable liability created by the adjusting entry. For this example, the accountant makes the following entry to record the payment on March 1, 1997:

1997				
Mar.	1	Interest Payable	4,000.00	
		Interest Expense ($5,386 × 2/6)	1,795.00	
		Premium on Bonds Payable ($614 × 2/6)	205.00	
		Cash		6,000.00
		To record two months' interest and amortization		
		and eliminate the accrued interest liability.		

The interest payments made each September are recorded normally because the entire six-month interest period is included within a single fiscal year.

Progress Check

On December 31, 1996, Cello Corporation issued 16%, 10-year bonds with a par value of $100,000. Interest is paid on June 30 and December 31. The bonds were sold to yield a 14% annual market rate of interest. Use this information to solve the following:

17-11 What is the selling price of the bonds?

17-12 Using the interest method of allocating interest expense, Cello would record the second interest payment (on December 31, 1997) with a debit to Premium on Bonds Payable in the amount of *(a)* $7,470; *(b)* $7,741; *(c)* $259; *(d)* $530; or *(e)* $277.

17-13 How would the bonds appear in the long-term liability section of Cello's balance sheet as of December 31, 1997?

RETIRING BONDS PAYABLE

For various reasons, companies may want to retire some or all of their bonds prior to maturity. For example, if market interest rates decline significantly, a company may wish to replace old high-interest debt obligations with new lower-interest debt. Many companies reserve the right to retire bonds early by issuing **callable bonds**. This means the bond indenture gives the issuing company an option to *call* the bonds before they mature by paying the par value plus a *call premium* to the bondholders. When interest rates were high in the 1980s, **Nova Corporation** and

LO 2

Describe the various
characteristics of different
types of bonds and pre-
pare entries to record
bond issuances and
retirements.

many other companies issued callable bonds. When market rates dropped dramat-
ically in the early 1990s, many of these bonds were called and retired.

Even if a specific bond issue is not callable, the issuer may be able to retire its
bonds by repurchasing them on the open market at the current market price.
Whether bonds are called or repurchased, the issuer is unlikely to pay a price that
equals the bonds' carrying value. In the case of a repurchase, this is because a bond's
market value changes as the market interest rate changes.

If there is a difference between the bonds' carrying value and the amount paid in
a bond retirement transaction, the issuer must record a gain or loss equal to the difference. For example, assume that a company issued callable bonds with a par value
of $100,000. The call option required the issuer to pay a call premium of $3,000
to the bondholders in addition to the par value. Also assume that immediately after a June 30 interest payment, the bonds had a carrying value of $104,500. Then,
on July 1, the issuer called all of the bonds and paid $103,000 to the bondholders.
The issuer must recognize a $1,500 gain as a result of the difference between the
bonds' carrying value of $104,500 and the retirement price of $103,000. This entry records the bond retirement:

July	1	Bonds Payable	100,000.00	
		Premium on Bonds Payable	4,500.00	
		Gain on Retirement of Bonds		1,500.00
		Cash		103,000.00
		To record the retirement of bonds.		

Although a company generally must call all of its bonds when it exercises a call
option, it may retire as many or as few bonds as it desires through open market
transactions. If it retires less than the entire set of bonds, it recognizes a gain or
loss for the difference between the carrying value of those bonds and the amount
paid to acquire them.

MORTGAGES AS SECURITY FOR BONDS AND NOTES

Earlier in this chapter, we said that some bonds are secured by collateral agreements, while others, called *debentures*, are not secured. These risk-reducing
arrangements also are widely used for notes payable, including car and home loans.
Unsecured bonds and notes are more risky because the issuer's obligation to pay
interest and principal has the same priority as all other unsecured liabilities in the
event of bankruptcy. If the company's financial troubles leave it unable to pay its
debts in full, the unsecured creditors (including the holders of debentures) lose a
proportion or all of their balances.

Thus, a company's ability to borrow money with or without collateral agreements depends on its credit rating. In many cases, debt financing is simply un-
available if the borrower cannot provide security to the creditors with a collateral
agreement. Even if unsecured loans are available, the creditors are likely to charge
a higher rate of interest to compensate for the additional risk. To borrow the funds
at a more economical rate, many notes payable and bonds are secured by collateral agreements called *mortgages*.

A **mortgage** is a legal agreement that helps protect a lender if a borrower fails to
make the required payments on a note payable or on bonds payable. A mortgage

gives the lender the right to be paid out of the cash proceeds from the sale of the borrower's specific assets identified in the mortgage.

A separate legal document, called the *mortgage contract*, describes the terms of a mortgage. The mortgage contract is given to the lender who accepts a note payable or to the trustee for the bondholders. Mortgage contracts usually require a borrower to pay all property taxes on the mortgaged assets, to maintain them properly, and to carry adequate insurance against fire and other types of losses. These requirements are designed to keep the property from losing value and thus avoid diminishing the lender's security. Importantly, mortgage contracts grant the lender the right to *foreclose* on the property if the borrower fails to pay in accordance with the terms of the debt agreement. If a foreclosure occurs, a court either orders the property to be sold or simply grants legal title of the mortgaged property to the lender. If the property is sold, the proceeds are first applied to court costs and then to the claims of the mortgage holder. If there are any additional proceeds, the borrower is entitled to receive them. However, this cash is subject to any claims from the company's unsecured creditors.

Given the relevance of information about a company's security agreements with its lenders, the notes to the financial statements may describe the amounts of assets pledged as security against liabilities. The next section describes a ratio that can be used to assess a borrower's situation with respect to its security agreements.

Progress Check

17-14   Six years ago, a company issued $500,000 of 6%, 8-year bonds at a price of 95. The current carrying value is $493,750. The company retired 50% of the bonds by buying them on the open market at a price of 102 1/2. What is the amount of gain or loss on retirement of the bonds?

17-15   A mortgage is
a. A promissory note that requires the borrower to make a series of payments consisting of interest and principal.
b. A legal agreement that protects a lender by giving the lender the right to be paid out of the cash proceeds from the sale of specific assets owned by the borrower.
c. A company's long-term liability that requires periodic payments of interest and a final payment of its par value when it matures.

USING THE INFORMATION— PLEDGED ASSETS TO SECURED LIABILITIES

LO 5

Calculate and describe how to use the ratio of pledged assets to secured liabilities.

As you have learned in this chapter, creditors can reduce their risk with agreements that can force borrowers to sell specific assets to settle overdue debts. Investors who consider buying a company's secured debt obligations need to determine whether the pledged assets of the debtor provide adequate security. One method of evaluating this is to calculate the ratio of **pledged assets to secured liabilities**. This is calculated by dividing the book value of the company's assets pledged as collateral by the book value of the liabilities secured by these collateral agreements:

$$\text{Pledged assets to secured liabilities} = \frac{\text{Book value of pledged assets}}{\text{Book value of secured liabilities}}$$

For example, suppose that a company has assets with a book value of $2,300,000 pledged against loans with a balance of $1,000,000. The ratio is

$2,300,000/\$1,000,000 = 2.3$ to 1. Although there are no hard and fast guidelines for interpreting the values of this ratio, 2.3 to 1 may be sufficiently high to provide the existing secured creditors with some comfort that the debts are safely covered by the assets.

The pledging of assets for the benefit of secured creditors also affects unsecured creditors. As an increasing portion of the assets are pledged, the unsecured creditors are less likely to receive a full repayment. In evaluating their position, unsecured creditors may gain some information from the ratio of pledged assets to secured creditors. For two reasons, an unusually large ratio may suggest that the unsecured creditors are at risk. First, secured creditors may have demanded an unusually large ratio because the value of the assets in liquidation is low. Second, the secured creditors may perceive that the ability of the company to meet its obligations from operating cash flows is weak.

In using this ratio, a creditor must be aware that the reported book value of the company's assets is unlikely to reflect their fair value. Thus, creditors would have better information if they could determine the assets' current market value and then use it in the ratio instead of book value. Major creditors may be able to get this information directly by asking the borrower to provide recent appraisals or other evidence of the assets' fair value. Other creditors may not have this option. In addition, using the ratio requires knowledge about the amounts of secured liabilities and pledged assets. This information may or may not be clearly identified in the financial statements.

Progress Check

17-16 At the end of 1996, A to Z Company has $350,000 of unsecured liabilities and $575,000 of secured liabilities. The book value of pledged assets is $1,265,000. Calculate the ratio of pledged assets to secured liabilities.

17-17 Would the secured creditors or the unsecured creditors be more concerned if A to Z's ratio of pledged assets to secured liabilities was 1.7 to 1 the previous year?

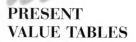

PRESENT VALUE TABLES

Table 17-1
Present Value of $1

				Rate				
Periods	**3%**	**4%**	**5%**	**6%**	**7%**	**8%**	**10%**	**12%**
1	0.9709	0.9615	0.9524	0.9434	0.9346	0.9259	0.9091	0.8929
2	0.9426	0.9246	0.9070	0.8900	0.8734	0.8573	0.8264	0.7972
3	0.9151	0.8890	0.8638	0.8396	0.8163	0.7938	0.7513	0.7118
4	0.8885	0.8548	0.8227	0.7921	0.7629	0.7350	0.6830	0.6355
5	0.8626	0.8219	0.7835	0.7473	0.7130	0.6806	0.6209	0.5674
6	0.8375	0.7903	0.7462	0.7050	0.6663	0.6302	0.5645	0.5066
7	0.8131	0.7599	0.7107	0.6651	0.6227	0.5835	0.5132	0.4523
8	0.7894	0.7307	0.6768	0.6274	0.5820	0.5403	0.4665	0.4039
9	0.7664	0.7026	0.6446	0.5919	0.5439	0.5002	0.4241	0.3606
10	0.7441	0.6756	0.6139	0.5584	0.5083	0.4632	0.3855	0.3220
20	0.5537	0.4564	0.3769	0.3118	0.2584	0.2145	0.1486	0.1037
30	0.4120	0.3083	0.2314	0.1741	0.1314	0.0994	0.0573	0.0334

Table 17-2   Present Value of an Annuity of $1

Payments	Rate							
	3%	4%	5%	6%	7%	8%	10%	12%
1	0.9709	0.9615	0.9524	0.9434	0.9346	0.9259	0.9091	0.8929
2	1.9135	1.8861	1.8594	1.8334	1.8080	1.7833	1.7355	1.6901
3	2.8286	2.7751	2.7232	2.6730	2.6243	2.5771	2.4869	2.4018
4	3.7171	3.6299	3.5460	3.4651	3.3872	3.3121	3.1699	3.0373
5	4.5797	4.4518	4.3295	4.2124	4.1002	3.9927	3.7908	3.6048
6	5.4172	5.2421	5.0757	4.9173	4.7665	4.6229	4.3553	4.1114
7	6.2303	6.0021	5.7864	5.5824	5.3893	5.2064	4.8684	4.5638
8	7.0197	6.7327	6.4632	6.2098	5.9713	5.7466	5.3349	4.9676
9	7.7861	7.4353	7.1078	6.8017	6.5152	6.2469	5.7590	5.3282
10	8.5302	8.1109	7.7217	7.3601	7.0236	6.7101	6.1446	5.6502
20	14.8775	13.5903	12.4622	11.4699	10.5940	9.8181	8.5136	7.4694
30	19.6004	17.2920	15.3725	13.7648	12.4090	11.2578	9.4269	8.0552

SUMMARY OF THE CHAPTER IN TERMS OF LEARNING OBJECTIVES

LO 1.   Calculate the payments on an installment note payable and describe their effects on the financial statements. Typical installment notes require one of two alternative payment patterns: *(a)* payments that include interest plus equal amounts of principal or *(b)* equal payments. In either case, interest is allocated to each period in a note's life by multiplying the carrying value by the original interest rate. If a note is repaid with equal payments, the payment's size is found by dividing the borrowed amount by the annuity table value for the interest rate and the number of payments.

LO 2.   Describe the various characteristics of different types of bonds and prepare entries to record bond issuances and retirements. Bonds usually are issued to many investors. Serial bonds mature at different points in time. Companies that issue sinking fund bonds must accumulate a fund of assets to use to pay out the par value of the bonds at the maturity date. Convertible bonds can be exchanged by the bondholders for shares of the issuing company. When bonds are registered, each bondholder's name and address is recorded by the issuing company. In contrast, bearer bonds are payable to whoever holds the bonds.

Some bonds are secured by mortgages on the issuer's assets while other bonds, called debentures, are unsecured. When bonds are sold between interest dates, the accrued interest is collected from the purchasers, who are then refunded that amount on the next interest payment date. Bonds can be retired early by the issuer by exercising a call option or by purchases on the open market. The issuer must recognize a gain or loss for the difference between the amount paid out and the bonds' carrying value.

LO 3.   Estimate the price of bonds issued at a discount and describe their effects on the issuer's financial statements. The cash paid to bondholders on semiannual interest payment dates is calculated as one-half of the result of multiplying the par value of the bonds by their contract interest rate. The market value of a bond can be estimated by using the market interest rate to find the present values of the interest payments and the par value. Bonds are issued at a discount when the contract rate is less than the market rate. Then, the issuer records the issuance with a credit to the Bonds Payable account for the par value and a debit to Discount on Bonds Payable. The amount of interest assigned to each interest period can be allocated with the straight-line method if the result is not materially different from the results of applying the interest method. The interest method assigns interest to a period by multiplying the beginning carrying value by the original market interest rate.

LO 4. Estimate the price of bonds issued at a premium and describe their effects on the issuer's financial statements. Bonds are issued at a premium when the contract rate is higher than the market interest rate. The issuer records the premium as a credit to Premium on Bonds Payable. The balance of this account is reduced over the life of the bonds through the interest allocation process.

LO 5. Calculate and describe how to use the ratio of pledged assets to secured liabilities. Secured and unsecured creditors are both concerned about the relationship between the amounts of assets owned by the debtor and the amounts of secured liabilities. The secured creditors are safer when the ratio of pledged assets to secured liabilities is larger, while the risks of unsecured creditors may be increased in this circumstance.

DEMONSTRATION PROBLEM

The Staley Tile Company patented and successfully test-marketed a new product. However, to expand its ability to produce and market the product, the company needed to raise $800,000 of additional financing. On January 1, 1996, the company borrowed the money under these arrangements:

a. Staley signed a $400,000, 10% installment note that will be repaid with five equal annual installments. The payments will be made on December 31 of 1996 through 2000.

b. Staley issued five-year bonds with a par value of $400,000. The bonds have a 12% annual contract rate and pay interest on June 30 and December 31. The annual market interest rate for the bonds was 10% on January 1, 1996.

Required

1. For the installment note, *(a)* calculate the size of each payment, *(b)* prepare an amortization table, and *(c)* present the entry for the first payment.

2. For the bonds, *(a)* estimate the issue price of the bonds; *(b)* present the January 1, 1996, entry to record issuing the bonds; *(c)* prepare an amortization table using the interest method; *(d)* present the June 30, 1996, entry to record the first payment of interest; and *(e)* present an entry to record retiring the bonds at the call price of $416,000 on January 1, 1998.

Planning the Solution

• For the installment note, divide the borrowed amount by the annuity table factor (from Table 17–2 on page 788) for 10% and five payments. Prepare a table similar to Illustration 17–2 and use the numbers in the first line for the entry.

• For the bonds, estimate the issue price by using the market rate to find the present values of the bonds' cash flows. Then, use this result to record issuing the bonds. Next, develop an amortization table like Illustration 17–7, and use it to get the numbers that you need for the journal entry. Finally, use the table to find the carrying value as of the date of the retirement of the bonds that you need for the journal entry.

Part 1:

Payment = Note balance/Table value = $400,000/3.7908 = $105,519

Table value is for 5 payments and an interest rate of 10%.

Table:

	(a)	Payments			(e)
		(b)	(c)	(d)	
Period Ending	Beginning Balance	Debit Interest Expense	Debit Notes Payable	Credit Cash	Ending Balance
			+	=	
1996	$400,000	$ 40,000	$ 65,519	$105,519	$334,481
1997	334,481	33,448	72,071	105,519	262,410
1998	262,410	26,241	79,278	105,519	183,132
1999	183,132	18,313	87,206	105,519	95,926
2000	95,926	9,593	95,926	105,519	0
Total		$127,595	$400,000	$527,595	

Journal entry:

1996				
Dec.	31	Interest Expense	40,000.00	
		Notes Payable	65,519.00	
		Cash		105,519.00
		To record first installment payment.		

Part 2:

Estimated issue price of the bonds:

Cash Flow	Table	Table Value	Amount	Present Value
Par value	17–1	0.6139	$400,000	$245,560
Interest (annuity)	17–2	7.7217	24,000	185,321
Total				$430,881

Table value is for 10 payments and an interest rate of 5%.

Journal entry:

1996				
Jan.	1	Cash	430,881.00	
		Premium on Bonds Payable		30,881.00
		Bonds Payable		400,000.00
		Sold bonds at a premium.		

Table:

Period Ending	(a) Beginning Balance *Prior (e)*	Payments		(d) Credit Cash *6% × $400,000*	(e) Ending Balance *(a) − (c)*
		(b) Debit Interest Expense *5% × (a)* +	(c) Debit Premium on Bonds *(d) − (b)* =		
June 30, 1996	$430,881	$ 21,544	$ 2,456	$ 24,000	$428,425
Dec. 31, 1996	428,425	21,421	2,579	24,000	425,846
June 30, 1997	425,846	21,292	2,708	24,000	423,138
Dec. 31, 1997	423,138	21,157	2,843	24,000	420,295
June 30, 1998	420,295	21,015	2,985	24,000	417,310
Dec. 31, 1998	417,310	20,866	3,134	24,000	414,176
June 30, 1999	414,176	20,709	3,291	24,000	410,885
Dec. 31, 1999	410,885	20,544	3,456	24,000	407,429
June 30, 2000	407,429	20,371	3,629	24,000	403,800
Dec. 31, 2000	403,800	20,200*	3,800	24,000	400,000
Total		$209,119	$30,881	$240,000	

*Adjusted for rounding.

Journal entries:

1996					
June	30	Interest Expense	21,544.00		
		Premium on Bonds Payable	2,456.00		
		Cash		24,000.00	
		Paid semiannual interest on the bonds.			
1998					
Jan.	1	Bonds Payable	400,000.00		
		Premium on Bonds Payable	20,295.00		
		Cash		416,000.00	
		Gain on Retirement of Bonds		4,295.00	
		To record the retirement of bonds (carrying value			
		determined as of December 31, 1997).			

GLOSSARY

Bearer bonds bonds that are made payable to whoever holds them (called the bearer); these bonds are not registered. p. 769

Bond a company's long-term liability that requires periodic payments of interest and final payment of its par value when it matures; usually issued in denominations of $1,769. p. 767

Bond indenture the contract between the bond issuer and the bondholders; it identifies the rights and obligations of the parties. p. 770

Callable bonds bonds that give the issuer an option of retiring them before they mature. p. 785

Carrying amount the net amount at which bonds are reflected on the balance sheet; equals the par value of the bonds less any unamortized discount or plus any unamortized premium. p. 775

Contract rate the interest rate specified in the bond indenture; it is multiplied by the par value of the bonds to determine the amount of interest to be paid each year. p. 773

Convertible bonds bonds that can be exchanged by the bondholders for a fixed number of shares of the issuing company's common shares. p. 769

Coupon bonds bonds that have interest coupons attached to their certificates; the bondholders detach the coupons when they mature and present them to a bank for collection. p. 769

Debentures unsecured bonds that are supported by only the general credit standing of the issuer. p. 770

Discount on bonds payable the difference between the par value of a bond and its lower issue price or paying amount; arises when the contract rate is lower than the market rate. p. 774

Installment notes promissory notes that require the borrower to make a series of payments consisting of interest and principal. p. 762

Interest method (interest allocation) a method that allocates interest expense to a reporting period by multiplying the beginning carrying value by the original market interest rate. p. 778

Market rate the consensus interest rate that borrowers are willing to pay and that lenders are willing to earn at the level of risk inherent in the bonds. p. 773

Mortgage a legal agreement that protects a lender by giving the lender the right to be paid out of the cash proceeds from the sale of the borrower's specific assets identified in the mortgage. p. 786

Par value of a bond the amount that the bond issuer agrees to pay at maturity and the amount on which interest payments are based; also called the *face amount*. p. 767

Pledged assets to secured liabilities the ratio of the book value of a company's pledged assets to the book value of its secured liabilities. p. 787

Premium on bonds payable the difference between the par value of a bond and its higher issue price or paying amount; arises when the contract rate is higher than the market rate. p. 781

Registered bonds bonds owned by investors whose names and addresses are recorded by the issuing company; the interest payments are made with checks to the bondholders. p. 769

Serial bonds bonds that mature at different dates with the result that the entire debt is repaid gradually over a number of years. p. 768

Sinking fund bonds bonds that require the issuing company to make deposits to a separate pool of assets; the bondholders are repaid at maturity from the assets in this pool. p. 768

Straight-line method (interest allocation) a method that allocates an equal amount of interest to each accounting period in the life of bonds. p. 776

SYNONYMOUS TERMS

Contract interest rate coupon rate; stated rate; nominal rate.

Principal of a bond par value; face value.

QUESTIONS

1. Describe two alternative payment patterns for installment notes.
2. What is the difference between notes payable and bonds payable?
3. What is the primary difference between a share and a bond?
4. What is the main advantage of issuing bonds instead of obtaining funds from the company's owners?
5. What is a bond indenture? What provisions are usually included in an indenture?
6. What are the duties of a trustee for bondholders?
7. Why does a company that issues bonds between interest dates collect accrued interest from the bonds' purchasers?
8. What are the *contract* and *market interest rates* for bonds?
9. What factors affect the market interest rates for bonds?
10. If you know the par value of bonds, the contract rate, and the market interest rate, how can you estimate the market value of the bonds?
11. Does the straight-line or interest method produce an allocation of interest that creates a constant rate of interest over a bond's life? Explain your answer.

12. What is the cash price of a $2,000 bond that is sold at 98¼? What is the cash price of a $6,000 bond that is sold at 101½?

13. Explain why unsecured creditors should be alarmed when the pledged assets to secured liabilities ratio for a borrower has grown substantially.

14. Refer to the financial statements for Geac Computer Corporation Ltd., presented in Appendix I. Is there any indication in the balance sheet that the company has issued bonds?

QUICK STUDY (Five-Minute Exercises)

QS 17–1
(LO 1)

The owner of Ripley's Restaurant borrowed $80,000 from a bank and signed an installment note that calls for eight annual payments of equal size, with the first payment due one year after the note was signed. Use Table 17–2 on page 789 to calculate the size of the annual payment for each of the following annual interest rates: *a.* 5%, *b.* 7%, *c.* 10%

QS 17–2
(LO 2)

Match the following terms and phrases by entering the letter of the phrase that best describes each term in the blank next to the term.

_____ serial bonds   _____ bearer bonds
_____ sinking fund bonds   _____ secured bonds
_____ convertible bonds   _____ debentures
_____ registered bonds   _____ bond indenture

a. Issuer records the bondholders' names and addresses.

b. Unsecured; backed only by the issuer's general credit standing.

c. Varying maturity dates.

d. Identifies the rights and responsibilities of the issuer and bondholders.

e. Can be exchanged for the issuer's common shares.

f. Unregistered; interest is paid to whoever possesses them.

g. Issuer maintains a separate pool of assets from which bondholders are paid at maturity.

h. Specific assets of the issuer are mortgaged as collateral.

QS 17–3
(LO 3)

The Carraway Co. issued 10%, 10-year bonds with a par value of $200,000. On the issue date, the annual market rate of interest for the bonds was 12%, and they sold for $177,059. The straight-line method is used to allocate the interest.

a. What is the total amount of interest expense that will be recognized over the life of the bonds?

b. What is the amount of interest expense recorded on the first interest payment date?

QS 17–4
(LO 4)

The Downhome Co. issued 12%, 10-year bonds with a par value of $60,000 and semiannual interest payments. On the issue date, the annual market rate of interest for the bonds was 10%, and they were sold for $67,478. The interest method is used to allocate the interest.

a. What is the total amount of interest expense that will be recognized over the life of the bonds?

b. What is the amount of interest expense recorded on the first interest payment date?

Use the following information to compute the ratio of pledged assets to secured liabilities for both companies:

	Red Co.	Blue Co.
Pledged assets	$155,000	$ 87,000
Total assets	180,000	300,000
Secured liabilities	90,000	66,000
Unsecured liabilities	140,000	160,000

EXERCISES

When solving the following exercises, round all dollar amounts to the nearest whole dollar. Also assume that none of the companies uses reversing entries.

On December 31, 1996, Acorn Co. borrowed $16,000 by signing a four-year, 5% installment note. The note requires annual payments of accrued interest and equal amounts of principal on December 31 of each year from 1997 through 2000.

a. How much principal will be included in each of the four payments?

b. Prepare an amortization table for this installment note like the one presented in Illustration 17–1 on page 764.

Exercise 17–1
Installment note with
payments of accrued
interest and equal
amounts of principal
(LO 1)

Use the data in Exercise 17–1 to prepare journal entries that Acorn Co. would make to record the loan on December 31, 1996, and the four payments starting on December 31, 1997, through the final payment on December 31, 2000.

Exercise 17–2
Journal entries for an
installment note with
payments of accrued
interest and equal
amounts of principal
(LO 1)

On December 31, 1996, Gates Co. borrowed $10,000 by signing a four-year, 5% installment note. The note requires four equal payments of accrued interest and principal on December 31 of each year from 1997 through 2000.

a. Calculate the size of each of the four equal payments.

b. Prepare an amortization table for this installment note like the one presented in Illustration 17–2 on page 765.

Use the data in Exercise 17–3 to prepare journal entries that Gates Co. would make to record the loan on December 31, 1996, and the four payments starting on December 31, 1997, through the final payment on December 31, 2000.

Exercise 17–4
Journal entries for an
installment note with
equal payments
(LO 1)

On January 1, 1996, the Tennyson Co. issued $300,000 of 20-year bonds that pay 8% interest semiannually on June 30 and December 31. The bonds were sold to investors at their par value.

a. How much interest will the issuer pay to the holders of these bonds every six months?

Exercise 17–5
Journal entries for bond
issuance and interest
payments
(LO 2)

b.   Show the journal entries that the issuer would make to record (1) the issuance of the bonds on January 1, 1996, (2) the first interest payment on June 30, 1996, and (3) the second interest payment on December 31, 1996.

Exercise 17–6
Journal entries for bond issuance with accrued interest
(LO 2)

On March 1, 1996, the Tennyson Co. issued $300,000 of 20-year bonds dated January 1, 1996. The bonds pay 8% interest semiannually on June 30 and December 31. The bonds were sold to investors at their par value plus the two months' interest that had accrued since the original issue date.

a.   How much accrued interest was paid to the issuer by the purchasers of these bonds on March 1, 1996?

b.   Show the journal entries that the issuer would make to record (1) the issuance of the bonds on March 1, 1996; (2) the first interest payment on June 30, 1996; and (3) the second interest payment on December 31, 1996.

Exercise 17–7
Calculating the present value of a bond and recording the issuance
(LO 3)

The Sesame Co. issued bonds with a par value of $150,000 on their initial issue date. The bonds mature in 15 years and pay 8% annual interest in two semiannual payments. On the issue date, the annual market rate of interest for the bonds turned out to be 10%.

a.   What is the size of the semiannual interest payment for these bonds?

b.   How many semiannual interest payments will be made on these bonds over their life?

c.   Use the information about the interest rates to decide whether the bonds were issued at par, a discount, or a premium.

d.   Estimate the market value of the bonds as of the date they were issued.

e.   Present the journal entry that would be made to record the bonds' issuance.

Exercise 17–8
Straight-line allocation of interest for bonds sold at a discount
(LO 3)

The Columbia Company issued bonds with a par value of $50,000 on January 1, 1997. The annual contract rate on the bonds is 8%, and the interest is paid semiannually. The bonds mature after three years. The annual market interest rate at the date of issuance was 12%, and the bonds were sold for $45,085.

a.   What is the amount of the original discount on these bonds?

b.   How much total interest expense will be recognized over the life of these bonds?

c.   Present an amortization table like Illustration 17–4 on page 777 for these bonds; use the straight-line method of allocating the interest and amortizing the discount.

Exercise 17–-9
Interest method allocation of interest for bonds sold at a discount
(LO 3)

The Chatham Company issued bonds with a par value of $30,000 on January 1, 1997. The annual contract rate on the bonds is 8%, and the interest is paid semiannually. The bonds mature after three years. The annual market interest rate at the date of issuance was 10%, and the bonds were sold for $28,477.

a.   What is the amount of the original discount on these bonds?

b.   How much total interest expense will be recognized over the life of these bonds?

c.   Present an amortization table like Illustration 17–5 on page 779 for these bonds; use the interest method of allocating the interest and amortizing the discount.

Exercise 17–10
Calculating the present value of a bond and recording the issuance
(LO 3)

The Allan Co. issued bonds with a par value of $25,000 on their initial issue date. The bonds mature in 15 years and pay 8% annual interest in two semiannual payments. On the issue date, the annual market rate of interest for the bonds turned out to be 6%.

a. What is the size of the semiannual interest payment for these bonds?

b. How many semiannual interest payments will be made on these bonds over their life?

c. Use the information about the interest rates to decide whether the bonds were issued at par, a discount, or a premium.

d. Estimate the market value of the bonds as of the date they were issued.

e. Present the journal entry that would be made to record the bonds' issuance.

The Cypress Company issued bonds with a par value of $40,000 on January 1, 1997. The annual contract rate on the bonds was 12%, and the interest is paid semiannually. The bonds mature after three years. The annual market interest rate at the date of issuance was 10%, and the bonds were sold for $42,030.

Exercise 17–11
Interest method allocation of interest for bonds sold at a premium
(LO 3)

a. What is the amount of the original premium on these bonds?

b. How much total interest expense will be recognized over the life of these bonds?

c. Present an amortization table like Illustration 17–7 on page 000 for these bonds; use the interest method of allocating the interest and amortizing the premium.

On January 1, 1996, the Amsterdam Co. issued $700,000 of its 10%, 15-year bonds at the price of 95½. Three years later, on January 1, 1999, the company retired 30% of these bonds by buying them on the open market at 105¾. All interest had been properly accounted for and paid through December 31, 1998, the day before the purchase. The company used the straight-line method to allocate the interest and amortize the original discount.

Exercise 17–12
Retiring bonds payable
(LO 2)

a. How much money did the company receive when it first issued the entire group of bonds?

b. How large was the original discount on the entire group of bonds?

c. How much amortization did the company record on the entire group of bonds between January 1, 1996, and December 31, 1998?

d. What was the carrying value of the entire group of bonds as of the close of business on December 31, 1998? What was the carrying value of the retired bonds on this date?

e. How much money did the company pay on January 1, 1999, to purchase the bonds that it retired?

f. What is the amount of the gain or loss from retiring the bonds?

g. Provide the general journal entry that the company would make to record the retirement of the bonds.

The Schaffner Co. issued bonds with a par value of $100,000 and a five–year life on May 1, 1996. The contract interest rate is 7%. The bonds pay interest on October 31 and April 30. They were issued at a price of $95,948.

Exercise 17–13
Straight-line amortization table and accrued interest
(LO 3, 4, 5)

a. Prepare an amortization table for these bonds that covers their entire life. Use the straight-line method of allocating interest.

b. Show the journal entries that the issuer would make to record the first two interest payments and to accrue interest as of December 31, 1996.

PROBLEMS

When solving the following problems, round all dollar amounts to the nearest whole dollar. Also assume that none of the companies uses reversing entries.

Problem 17–1
Installment notes
(LO 1)

On November 30, 1996, the Stanley Company borrowed $50,000 from a bank by signing a four-year installment note bearing interest at 12%. The terms of the note require equal payments each year on November 30.

Required

1. Calculate the size of each installment payment. (Use Table 17–2 on page 789.)
2. Complete an installment note amortization schedule for this note similar to Illustration 17–2 on page 000.
3. Present the journal entries that the borrower would make to record accrued interest as of December 31, 1996 (the end of the annual reporting period) and the first payment on the note.
4. Now assume that the note does not require equal payments but does require four payments that include accrued interest and an equal amount of principal in each payment. Complete an installment note amortization schedule for this note similar to Illustration 17–1 on page 764. Present the journal entries that the borrower would make to record accrued interest as of December 31, 1996 (the end of the annual reporting period) and the first payment on the note.

Problem 17–2
Calculating bond prices and recording issuances with journal entries
(LO 2, 3, 4)

Helmer Co. issued a group of bonds on January 1, 1996, that pay interest semiannually on June 30 and December 31. The par value of the bonds is $40,000, the annual contract rate is 8%, and the bonds mature in 10 years.

Required

For each of these three situations, *(a)* determine the issue price of the bonds and *(b)* show the journal entry that would record the issuance.

1. The market interest rate at the date of issuance was 6%.
2. The market interest rate at the date of issuance was 8%.
3. The market interest rate at the date of issuance was 10%.

Problem 17–3
Straight-line method of allocating interest and amortizing a bond discount
(LO 3)

Abbot Company issued $125,000 of bonds that pay 6% annual interest with two semiannual payments. The date of issuance was January 1, 1996, and the interest is paid on June 30 and December 31. The bonds mature after 10 years and were issued at the price of $108,014.

Required

1. Prepare a general journal entry to record the issuance of the bonds.
2. Determine the total interest expense that will be recognized over the life of these bonds.
3. Prepare the first four lines of an amortization table like Illustration 17–4 based on the straight-line method of allocating the interest.
4. Prepare the first four lines of a separate table that shows the beginning balance of the discount, the amount of straight-line amortization of the discount, and the ending balance.
5. Present the journal entries that the bond issuer would make to record the first two interest payments.

The Martin Company issued $50,000 of bonds that pay 4% annual interest with two semi-annual payments. The date of issuance was January 1, 1996, and the interest is paid on June 30 and December 31. The bonds mature after three years and were issued at the price of $47,292. The market interest rate was 6%.

Problem 17–4
Interest method of allocating bond interest and amortizing a discount
(LO 2, 3)

Required

Preparation component:

1. Prepare a general journal entry to record the issuance of the bonds.
2. Determine the total interest expense that will be recognized over the life of these bonds.
3. Prepare the first four lines of an amortization table like Illustration 17–5 based on the interest method.
4. Prepare the first four lines of a separate table that shows the beginning balance of the discount, the amount of interest method amortization of the discount, and the ending balance.
5. Present the journal entries that the bond issuer would make to record the first two interest payments.

Analysis component:

6. Instead of the facts described in the problem, assume that the market interest rate on January 1, 1996, was 3% instead of 6%. Without presenting any specific numbers, describe how this change would affect the amounts presented on the company's financial statements.

The Jones Company issued $100,000 of bonds that pay 9% annual interest with two semi-annual payments. The date of issuance was January 1, 1996, and the interest is paid on June 30 and December 31. The bonds mature after three years and were issued at the price of $102,619. The market interest rate was 8%.

Problem 17–5
Interest method of amortizing bond premium and retiring bonds
(LO 2, 4)

Required

1. Prepare a general journal entry to record the issuance of the bonds.
2. Determine the total interest expense that will be recognized over the life of these bonds.
3. Prepare the first four lines of an amortization table like Illustration 17–7 based on the interest method.
4. Prepare the first four lines of a separate table that shows the beginning balance of the premium, the amount of interest method amortization of the premium, and the ending balance.
5. Present the journal entries that the bond issuer would make to record the first two interest payments.
6. Present the journal entry that would be made to record the retirement of these bonds on December 31, 1997, at the price of 98.

The Briggs Company issued bonds with a par value of $80,000 and a five–year life on January 1, 1996. The bonds pay interest on June 30 and December 31. The contract interest rate is 8.5%. The bonds were issued at a price of $81,625. The market interest rate was 8% on the original issue date.

Problem 17–6
Bond premium amortization and finding the present value of remaining cash flows
(LO 3, 4)

Required

1. Prepare an amortization table for these bonds that covers their entire life. Use the interest method.

2. Show the journal entries that the issuer would make to record the first two interest payments.

3. Use the original market interest rate to calculate the present value of the remaining cash flows for these bonds as of December 31, 1998. Compare your answer with the amount shown on the amortization table as the balance for that date, and explain your findings.

Problem 17–7
Computing and analyzing ratio of pledged assets to secured liabilities
(LO 5)

On January 1, 1997, Alpha Company issued $45,000 of 10%, five-year bonds secured by a mortgage that specifies assets totaling $75,000 as collateral. On the same date, Beta Company isssued 10%, five-year bonds with a par value of $20,000. Beta is securing its bonds with a mortgage that includes $50,000 of pledged assets. Following is December 31, 1996, balance sheet information for both companies:

	Alpha Co.	Beta Co.
Total assets	$300,000*	$150,000†
Liabilities:		
Secured	$ 70,000	$ 25,000
Unsecured	50,000	55,000
Owners' equity	180,000	70,000
Total liabilities and owners' equity	$300,000	$150,000

*33% pledged
†42% pledged

Required

Preparation component:

1. Calculate the ratio of pledged assets to secured liabilities for each company after January 1, 1997.

Analysis component:

2. Which company's bonds appear to offer the best security? What other information might be helpful in evaluating the risk of the bonds?

Problem 17–8
Analytical essay
(LO 5)

An unsecured major creditor of the Hawkins Company has been monitoring the company's financing activities. Two years before, the ratio of its pledged assets to secured liabilities had been 1.4. One year ago, the ratio had climbed to 2.0, and the most recent financial report shows that the ratio value is now 3.1. Briefly describe what this trend may indicate about the company's activities, specifically from the point of view of this creditor.

Problem 17–9
Installment notes
(LO 1)

Bisk Hardware Manufacturing Company financed a major expansion of its production capacity by borrowing $220,000 from a bank and signing an installment note. The four-year, 14%, $220,000 note is dated April 30, 1996, and requires equal semiannual payments beginning on November 30, 1996

Required

1. Calculate the size of the installment payments. (Use Table 17–2 on page 789.)
2. Complete an installment note amortization schedule for the Bisk Hardware Manufacturing Company note similar to Illustration 17–2.
3. Prepare General Journal entries to record the first and last payments on the note.
4. Now assume that the note requires payments of accrued interest plus equal amounts of principal. Prepare General Journal entries to record the first and last payments on the note.

On December 31, 1996, SONOS Corporation sold $3.7 million of its own 12.9%, 10-year bonds. The bonds are dated December 31, 1996, with interest payable on each June 30 and December 31, and were sold to yield the buyers a 12% annual return. The corporation uses the straight-line method of amortizing the premium.

Problem 17–10
Straight-line method of amortizing bond premium
(LO 4)

Required

1. Calculate the price at which the bonds were sold. (Use present value Tables 17–1 and 17–2, pages 788 and 789.)
2. Prepare a bond premium amortization table similar to Illustration 17–7 but complete only the first two lines.
3. Prepare General Journal entries to record the sale of the bonds and the first two interest payments.

JBC Corporation sold $800,000 of its own 9.7%, five-year bonds on their date of issue, December 31, 1996. Interest is payable on each June 30 and December 31, and the bonds were sold at a price to yield the buyers a 10% annual return. The corporation uses the interest method of amortizing the discount.

Problem 17–11
Interest method of amortizing bond discount
(LO 3)

Required

1. Calculate the price at which the bonds were sold. (Use present value Tables 17–1 and 17–2, page 788.)
2. Prepare a bond discount amortization table similar to Illustration 17–5 but complete only the first two lines.
3. Prepare General Journal entries to record the sale of the bonds and the first two interest payments.

Prepare General Journal entries to record the following bond transactions of Eco Paper Corporation:

Problem 17–12
Interest method of amortizing bond premium; retirement of bonds
(LO 4, 5)

1996

Oct. 1 Sold $2.8 million par value of its own 10.7%, five-year bonds at a price to yield the buyers a 10% annual return. The bonds were dated October 1, 1996, with interest payable on each April 1 and October 1.

Dec. 31 Accrued interest on the bonds and amortized the premium for October through December 1996. The interest method was used to amortize the premium.

1997

Apr. 1 Paid the semiannual interest on the bonds.

Oct. 1 Paid the semiannual interest on the bonds.

1998

Oct. 1   After paying the semiannual interest on the bonds on this date, Eco Paper Corporation purchased one fourth of the bonds at 101¾ and retired them. (Present only the entry to record the purchase and retirement of the bonds.)

Problem 17–13
Comparison of straight-line and interest methods
(LO 3, 4)

On December 31, 1996, Trask Chemical Company sold $7 million of 10-year, 12.5% bonds payable at a price that reflected a 12% market rate of bond interest. The bonds pay interest on June 30 and December 31. Use present value Tables 17–1 and 17–2 (page 788) as needed in calculating your answers.

Required

1. Present a General Journal entry to record the sale of the bonds.

2. Present General Journal entries to record the first and second payments of interest on June 30, 1997, and on December 31, 1997, using the straight-line method to amortize the premium or discount.

3. Present General Journal entries to record the first and second payments of interest on June 30, 1997, and on December 31, 1997, using the interest method to amortize the premium or discount.

4. Prepare a schedule similar to the table in Illustration 17–6 on page 780. It should have columns for the beginning-of-period carrying amount, interest expense to be recorded, and interest expense as a percentage of carrying amount, as calculated under (*a*) the interest method, and (*b*) the straight-line method. In completing the schedule, present the amounts for the six-month periods ending on June 30, 1997, and December 31, 1997.

Problem 17–14
Analytical essay
(LO 3, 4, 5)

Review the transactions presented in Problem 17–12 for Eco Paper Corporation. Assume now that on October 1, 1996, the market rate of bond interest was 13% instead of 10%. Describe how the entries to record the sale of the bonds and the December 31, 1996, accrual of interest are different as a result of this change in the facts.

Problem 17–15
Analytical essay
(LO 4, 5)

Review the transactions presented in Problem 17–12 for Eco Paper Corporation. Assume now that on October 1, 1996, Eco sold $2.8 million of its own 10%, 10-year bonds instead of 10.7%, 5-year bonds. Describe how the entries to record the sale of the bonds and the December 31, 1996, accrual of interest are different as a result of this change in the facts.

PROVOCATIVE PROBLEMS

Provocative Problem 17–1
Management decision case
(LO 2, 3, 4)

Star Manufacturing Company is planning major additions to its operating capacity and needs approximately $400,000 to finance the expansion. The company has been considering three alternative proposals for issuing bonds that pay annual interest over the eight years in their lives. The alternatives are:

Plan A: Issue $400,000 of 8% bonds.
Plan B: Issue $450,000 of 6% bonds.
Plan C: Issue $360,000 of 10% bonds.

The market rate of interest for all of these bonds is expected to be 8%.

Required

1. For each plan, calculate:

   a. The expected cash proceeds from issuing the bonds.

   b. The expected annual cash outflow for interest.

   c. The expected interest expense for the first year. (Use the interest method to amortize bond premium or discount.)

   d. The amount that must be paid at maturity.

2. Which plans have the smallest and largest cash demands on the company prior to the final payment at maturity? Which plans require the smallest and largest payment at maturity?

The Angela Company issued $500,000 of zero-coupon bonds on January 1, 1996. These bonds are scheduled to mature seven years later on December 31, 2002. Under the terms of the bond agreement, the company will pay out $500,000 to the bondholders on the maturity date without making any periodic interest payments. The market rate of interest for these bonds was 10% when they were issued.

Provocative Problem 17–2
Financial reporting problem
(LO 3)

Required

1. Estimate the amount of cash that Angela received when it issued these bonds (assume annual compounding).

2. Present the journal entry that Angela's accountant would use to record the issuance of these bonds.

3. Calculate the total amount of interest expense that will be incurred over the life of the bonds.

4. Prepare an amortization table that shows the amount of interest expense that will be allocated to each year in the bonds' life with the interest method.

5. Present the journal entry that Angela's accountant would use to record the interest expense from these bonds for the year ended December 31, 1996.

The following information is taken from the 1995 annual report of The Oshawa Group Limited for the year ended January 28, 1995.

Provocative Problem 17–3
Financial statement analysis case
(LO 1)

Notes to Consolidated Financial Statements (millions)
4. Long-Term Debt

	1995	1994
Series "A" Debentures	$100.0	$100.0
Mortgages and loans payable	23.9	24.5
	123.9	124.5
Less current portion	0.4	0.3
	$123.5	$124.2

The unsecured Series "A" debentures due June 30, 2003, bear interest at a rate of 8.25% per annum and are redeemable in whole or in part, at any time, at the greater of par and a formula price based upon yields at the time of redemption.

   The mortgages and loans payable bear interest at an average rate of 9.5% per annum with repayments of less than $2.5 in each of the four years commencing in 1997.

6. Interest

	1995 **(53 weeks)**	1994 (52 weeks)
Interest on long-term debt	**$ 9.8**	$6.4
Other interest	**1.3**	3.0
	$11.1	$9.4

Required

1. Are the debentures secured or unsecured?
2. What is the average interest rate on the mortgages and loans payable?
3. When do the debentures mature?

ANALYTICAL AND REVIEW PROBLEMS

A & R Problem 17–1   On June 30, 1996, Gorge Company issued $500,000 par value 8%, 10-year bonds convertible at the rate of a $1,000 bond for 50 common shares. The bonds were dated June 30, 1996, and were sold at a price to yield investors 10%. Interest was payable annually.

Required

1. Prepare entries on the following dates (Gorge uses straight-line to amortize discounts or premiums): June 30, 1996; December 31, 1996 (year-end); June 30, 1997; and June 30, 1998, to record conversion of 40 of the bonds.

2. On the assumption that Gorge used the interest method for amortization of discounts and premiums prepare entries on the following dates:

   a. December 31, 1996.
   b. June 30, 1997.
   c. June 30, 1998.

A & R Problem 17–2   On May 1, 1996, Tania Torres purchased as a long-term investment 20, $1,000 par value, 10% bonds, due 5½ years from date of purchase. Interest on the bonds is due and payable annually on November 1. Torres does not use discount or premium accounts related to investments of this nature and uses straight-line amortization.

Required

1. On the assumption that Torres' *total* cash outlay for the bonds was $17,040, prepare entries on the following 1996 dates:

   a. May 1, 1996.
   b. November 1, 1996.
   c. December 31, 1996 (year-end).

2. On the assumption that Torres' total cash outlay for the bonds was $22,520 prepare the entries on the following dates:

   a. May 1, 1996.
   b. November 1, 1996.
      December 31, 1996 (year-end).

CONCEPT TESTER

Test your understanding of the concepts introduced in this chapter by completing the following crossword puzzle.

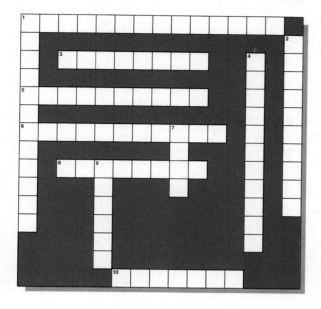

Across Clues

1. The net value of the bonds on the balance sheet (2 words).

3. Type of loan that protects the lender with specific assets of the borrower.

5. Bonds where the names and addresses of the investor are recorded by the issuing company.

6. Bonds that can be exchanged for shares.

8. The difference between the par value of the bonds and the lower issue price.

10. The difference between the par value of the bonds and the higher issue price.

Down Clues

1. The interest charge specified in the bond indenture (2 words).

2. The interest that borrowers are willing to pay and lenders willing to accept (2 words).

4. Bonds that require the borrower to make a series of principal payments.

7. A long-term liability requiring periodic interest payments and payment of principal on maturity.

9. Bonds that mature at different dates.

ANSWERS TO PROGRESS CHECKS

17–1 c

17–2 The interest portion of an installment payment equals the beginning balance for the period multiplied by the original interest rate.

17–3 On the balance sheet, the balances of the liability and cash are decreased. On the income statement, interest expense is increased.

17–4 b

17–5 Multiply the par value of the bonds by the contract rate of interest.

17–6 a

17–7 The bonds sell at a premium, and the purchasers pay more than the par value of the bonds.

17–8 c. (Present values of $100,000 and a semiannual annuity of $3,000, both at 4% for 10 semiannual periods.)

17–9
Cash	91,893.00	
Discount on Bonds Payable	8,107.00	
Bonds Payable		100,000.00

17–10 a. $3,811 (Total interest equal to $38,107, or 10 payments of $3,000 plus the $8,107 discount, divided by 10 periods.)
       b. $3,676 (Beginning balance of $91,893 times 4% market interest rate.)

17–11 $110,592 (Present value of $100,000 plus the semiannual annuity of $8,000, both at 7% for 20 semiannual periods.)

17–12 e. (On June 30/97: $110,592 × 7% = $7,741 interest expense; $8,000 − $7,741 = $259 premium amortization; $110,592 − $259 = $110,333 ending balance. On Dec 31/97: $110,333 × 7% = $7,723 interest expense; $8,000 − $7,723 = $277 premium amortization.)

17–13
Bonds payable, 16%, due December 31, 1997	$100,000	
Plus premium	10,056*	$110,056

*Beginning premium balance of $10,592 less $259 and $277 amortized on June 30/97 and Dec 31/97.

17–14 $9,375 loss (Difference between repurchase price of $256,250 [50% of ($500,000 × 102.5%)] and carrying value of $246,875 [50% of $493,750].)

17–15 b

17–16 2.2 to 1 ($1,265,000/$575,000)

17–17 Unsecured creditors. They may be less likely to receive full repayment if the portion of assets pledged increases.

CHAPTER 18

Statement of Changes in Financial Position

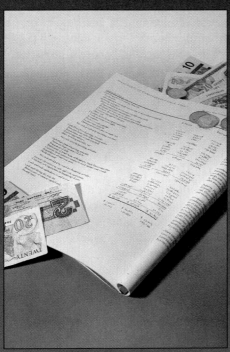

Cash flows in and out of a company as the company makes sales, collects receivables, pays expenses, buys and sells assets, borrows cash, issues stock, repays debt, and pays dividends. Information about the cash generated and spent is useful for evaluating the past and predicting the future.

*I*n continuing their study of Imperial Oil Limited's financial statements, Karen White and Mark Smith examined Imperial's Statement of Cash Flows. The excerpt from the statement shows the changing levels of Imperial's cash balances over the last five years. The statement also shows that although Imperial's operating activities provided cash of $783 million, there was a net decrease in cash due to the payment of $930 million in dividends during 1994 and repayment of long-term debt.

It is extremely important that management monitor the levels of cash and its sources and uses. The statement of changes in financial position enables both managers and investors to evaluate how a company has used its cash resources.

IMPERIAL OIL LIMITED—CONSOLIDATED STATEMENT OF CASH FLOWS
(in millions)

Year Ended December 31	1994	1993	1992	1991	1990
Cash: Increase (decrease)	$(196)	$340	$ (21)	$352	$ 34
At beginning of year	605	265	286	(66)	(100)
At end of year	$ 409	$605	$265	$286	(66)

LEARNING OBJECTIVES

After studying Chapter 18, you should be able to:

1. **Explain why cash flow information is important to decision making and describe the information in a statement of changes in financial position (SCFP) and the method used to disclose noncash investing and financing activities.**

2. **Calculate cash inflows and outflows by inspecting the noncash account balances and prepare an SCFP.**

3. **Prepare a working paper for an SCFP.**

4. **Define or explain the words or phrases listed in the chapter glossary.**

Up to this point in your study of accounting, profitability may have seemed to be the sole focus of business managers. Profits certainly are important to business success. However, a business cannot achieve or maintain profitability without carefully managing its cash. Cash is the lifeblood of a business enterprise. In a sense, cash is the fuel that keeps a business moving forward.

Managers and external parties such as investors and creditors pay close attention to a company's cash position and the events and transactions causing that position to change. Information about these events and transactions is reported in a financial statement called the **statement of changes in financial position** or statement of changes in financial position. By studying this chapter, you will learn how to prepare and interpret an SCFP. You will also begin to appreciate the importance of cash flow information as the basis for projecting future cash flows and making a variety of decisions.

WHY CASH FLOW INFORMATION IS IMPORTANT

LO 1

Explain why cash flow information is important to decision making and describe the information in a statement of changes in financial position and the method used to disclose noncash investing and financing activities.

Information about cash flows can influence decision makers in many ways. For example, if a company's regular operations bring in more cash than they use, investors will value the company higher than if property and equipment must be sold to finance operations. Information about cash flows can help creditors decide whether a company will have enough cash to pay its existing debts as they mature. And investors, creditors, managers, and other users of financial statements use cash flow information to evaluate a company's ability to meet unexpected obligations. Cash flow information is used by decision makers outside as well as inside the firm to evaluate a company's ability to take advantage of new business opportunities that may arise. Managers within a company use cash flow information to plan day-to-day operating activities and make long-term investment decisions.

The story of W. T. Grant Co. is a classic example of why cash flow information should be considered in predicting a firm's future stability and performance. From 1970 to 1973, Grant was reporting net income of more than $40 million per year. At the same time, it was experiencing an alarming decrease in cash provided by operations. Net cash *outflow* exceeded $90 million by 1973.[1] In spite of its earnings performance, Grant went bankrupt within a few years.

---

[1]James Largay and Clyde Stickney, "Cash Flow, Ratio Analysis and the W. T. Grant Company Bankruptcy," *Financial Analysts Journal,* July–August 1980, pp. 51–56.

As a Matter of Opinion

Mrs. Hagarty earned a BBA degree with a major in finance and marketing at Wilfrid Laurier University in Waterloo. Upon graduation, she joined the Commercial Banking Group at CIBC where she began her career as an Account Officer. She has also held regional office positions in Quality Management, Project Re-engineering and Marketing Management. Presently, she is a Commercial Account Manager in CIBC's Kitchener office where she manages a lending and investment portfolio of local small businesses.

When I entered the banking industry, there was much talk of "cash flow analysis" but at the end of the day, loan officers focused primarily on profitability and debt/equity ratio when reviewing financial statements. However, in the past few years, the analysis of cash flow has become increasingly important.

We now recognize that a lender must have a complete understanding of a borrower's cash flow in order to better assess borrowing needs and repayment sources. This requires historical and projected information about the major types of cash inflows and outflows.

The bottom line is that cash, and only cash, can repay loans. Accordingly, my job is to determine if a company can generate sufficient cash to service their debt. Over the years I have seen many companies, whose financial statements indicated good profitability, end up experiencing severe financial problems because the owners or managers lacked a good understanding of the company's cash flow. It is my challenge to help my clients properly understand and manage cash flow to their advantage.

Leanne L. Hagarty, BBA

The W. T. Grant investors who relied solely on earnings per share figures in the early 1970s were unpleasantly surprised. In more recent years, investors generally have learned to evaluate cash flows as well as income statement and balance sheet information as they make their investment decisions.[2]

The importance of cash flow information to decision makers has directly influenced the thinking of accounting authorities. For example, the CICA's *Financial Statement Concepts* clearly reflect the importance of cash flow information. The CICA stated that a business's financial statements should include information about

- How it obtains and spends cash.
- Its borrowing and repayment activities.
- The sale and repurchase of its ownership securities.
- Dividend payments and other distributions to its owners.
- Other factors affecting its liquidity or solvency.[3]

To accomplish these objectives, a financial statement is needed to summarize, classify, and report the periodic cash inflows and outflows of a business. This information is provided in a statement of changes in financial position.

---

[2]Marc J. Epstein and Moses L. Pava, "How Useful Is the Statement of Cash Flows," *Management Accounting,* July 1992.

[3]*CICA Handbook,* section 1540, "Statement of Changes in Financial Position," par. .01.

Illustration 18–1   Categories of Information in the Statement of Changes in Financial Position

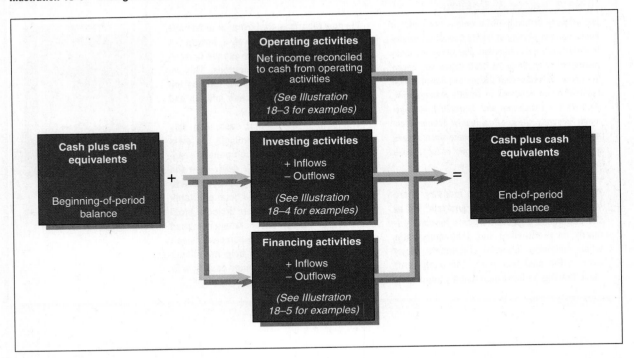

STATEMENT OF CHANGES IN FINANCIAL POSITION

In September 1985, the CICA's Accounting Standards Board revised section 1540 of the *Handbook*. This recommendation requires businesses to include a statement of changes in financial position (SCFP) in all financial reports that contain both a balance sheet and an income statement. The purpose of this statement is to present information about a company's cash receipts and disbursements during the reporting period.

Illustration 18–1 is a diagram of the information reported in an SCFP. The illustration shows three categories of cash flows: cash flows from operating activities, cash flows from investing activities, and cash flows from financing activities. Both inflows and outflows are included within each category. Because all cash inflows and outflows are reported, the statement reconciles the beginning-of-period and end-of-period balances of cash plus cash equivalents.

Direct Method of Presenting Cash Flows from Operating Activities

When preparing a statement of changes in financial position, you can calculate the net cash provided (or used) by operating activities two different ways. One is the *direct method of calculating net cash provided (or used) by operating activities.* The other is the indirect method. When using the direct method, you separately list each major class of operating cash receipts (for example, cash received from customers) and each major class of cash payments (such as payments for merchandise). Then, you subtract the payments from the receipts to determine the net cash provided (or used) by operating activities.

Indirect Method of Presenting Cash Flows from Operating Activities

The indirect method of calculating **net cash provided (or used) by operating activities** is the preferred method in Canada because the *Handbook* indicates that the amount of cash from operations should be reconciled to the income statement.[4] Thus we explain the indirect method.

When using the indirect method, list net income first. Next, adjust it for items that are necessary to reconcile net income to the net cash provided (or used) by operating activities. For example, in the calculation of net income, we subtract amortization expense. However, amortization expense does not involve a current cash payment. Therefore, add amortization expense back to net income in the process of reconciling net income to the net cash provided (or used) by operating activities.

The Format of the Statement of Changes in Financial Position

Illustration 18–2 shows the SCFP for Grover Company calculated using the indirect method. Notice that net income is listed first. It is then adjusted to reconcile its amount to the net amount of cash provided (or used) by operating activities.

Also observe in Illustration 18–2 the other two categories of cash flows reported on the SCFP. In both categories—investing activities and financing activities—we subtract the cash outflows from the cash inflows to determine the net cash provided (or used).

Compare the statement in Illustration 18–2 with the chart in Illustration 18–1. Notice that the beginning and ending balances are called *cash plus cash equivalents* in Illustration 18–1. However, in Illustration 18–2, the beginning and ending balances refer only to *cash*. The balances in Illustration 18–2 are called *cash* because Grover Company does not own any cash equivalents, such as Treasury Bills.

Cash and Cash Equivalents

In section 1540 of the *CICA Handbook,* the Accounting Standards Board concluded that a statement of changes in financial position should explain the difference between the beginning and ending balances of cash and cash equivalents. Prior to this standard, cash equivalents were generally understood to be short-term, temporary investments of cash. As you learned in Chapter 7, however, a *cash equivalent* must satisfy these two criteria:

1. The investment must be readily convertible to a known amount of cash.
2. The investment must be sufficiently close to its maturity date so that its market value is relatively insensitive to interest rate changes.

---

[4]Ibid., par. 1540.12.

Illustration 18–2
Statement of Changes
in Financial Position

GROVER COMPANY		
Statement of Changes in Financial Position		
For Year Ended December 31, 1997		
Cash flows from operating activities:		
Net income	$ 38,000	
Adjustments to reconcile net income to net		
cash provided by operating activities:		
(1) Increase in accounts receivable	(20,000)	
Increase in merchandise inventory ...	(14,000)	
Increase in prepaid expenses	(2,000)	
Decrease in accounts payable	(5,000)	
Decrease in interest payable	(1,000)	
Increase in income taxes payable	10,000	
(2) Amortization expense	24,000	
(3) Loss on sale of plant assets	6,000	
Gain on retirement of bonds	(16,000)	
Net cash provided by operating activities		$ 20,000
Cash flows from investing activities:		
Cash received from sale of plant assets ...	$ 12,000	
Cash paid for purchase of plant assets	(10,000)	
Net cash provided by investing activities ..		2,000
Cash flows from financing activities:		
Cash received from issuing shares	$ 15,000	
Cash paid to retire bonds	(18,000)	
Cash paid for dividends	(14,000)	
Net cash used in financing activities		(17,000)
Net increase in cash		$ 5,000
Cash balance at beginning of 1997		12,000
Cash balance at end of 1997		$ 17,000

The idea of classifying short-term, highly liquid investments as cash equivalents is based on the assumption that companies make these investments to earn a return on idle cash balances. Sometimes, however, items that meet the criteria of cash equivalents are not held as temporary investments of idle cash balances. For example, an investment company that specializes in the purchase and sale of securities may buy cash equivalents as part of its investing strategy. Companies that have such investments are allowed to exclude them from the cash equivalents category. However, the companies must develop a clear policy for determining which items to include and which to exclude. These policies must be disclosed in the notes to the financial statements and must be followed consistently from period to period.

CLASSIFYING CASH TRANSACTIONS

On an SCFP, cash and cash equivalents are treated as a single item. In other words, the statement reports the changes in cash plus cash equivalents. Therefore, cash payments to purchase cash equivalents and cash receipts from selling cash equivalents do not appear on the statement. All other cash receipts and payments are classified and reported on the statement as operating, investing, or financing activities. Within each category, individual cash receipts and payments are summarized in a manner that clearly describes the general nature of the company's cash transactions. Then, the summarized cash receipts and payments within each category are netted against each other. A category provides a net cash inflow if the receipts in the category exceed the payments. And, if the payments in a category exceed the receipts, the category is a net use of cash (outflow) during the period.

Operating Activities

Look at the cash flows classified as **operating activities** in Illustration 18–2. Notice that the cash provided by operating activities is $20,000. Net income of $38,000 was modified to exclude those amounts included in the determination of net income but not involved in operating cash inflows or outflows during the period. Net income was also modified to include operating cash inflows and outflows not recorded as revenues and expenses, such as collections of accounts receivable and payments of accounts payable.

Illustration 18–2 shows three types of adjustments to net income. The adjustments grouped under section (1) are for changes in noncash current assets and current liabilities that relate to operating activities. Adjustment (2) is for an income statement item that relates to operating activities but that did not involve a cash inflow or outflow during the period. The adjustments grouped under (3) eliminate gains and losses that resulted from investing and financing activities. These gains and losses do not relate to operating activities.

Adjustments for Changes in Current Assets and Current Liabilities

To help you understand why adjustments for changes in noncash current assets and current liabilities are part of the reconciliation process, we use the transactions of a very simple company as an example. Assume that Simple Company's income statement shows only two items, as follows:

Sales	$20,000
Operating expenses.	(12,000)
Net income	$ 8,000

For a moment, assume that all of Simple Company's sales and operating expenses are for cash. The company has no current assets other than cash and has no current liabilities. Given these assumptions, the net cash provided by operating activities during the period is $8,000, which is the cash received from customers less the cash paid for operating expenses.

Adjustments for Changes in Noncash Current Assets

Now assume that Simple Company's sales are on account. Also assume that its Accounts Receivable balance was $2,000 at the beginning of the year and $2,500 at the end of the year. Under these assumptions, cash receipts from customers equal sales of $20,000 minus the $500 increase in Accounts Receivable, or $19,500. Therefore, the net cash provided by operating activities is $7,500 ($19,500 − $12,000).

When we calculate the net cash flow, net income of $8,000 is adjusted for the $500 increase in Accounts Receivable to get $7,500 as the net amount of cash provided by operating activities. The calculations are:

Receipts from customers ($20,000 − $500)	$19,500
Payments for operating expenses	(12,000)
Cash provided (or used) by operating activities	$ 7,500
Net income.	$8,000
Less the increase in accounts receivable	(500)
Cash provided (or used) by operating activities	$7,500

Notice that the increase in Accounts Receivable is subtracted from net income to determine cash provided.

As another example, assume instead that the Accounts Receivable balance decreased from $2,000 to $1,200. Under this assumption, cash receipts from customers equal sales of $20,000 plus the $800 decrease in Accounts Receivable, or $20,800. The net cash provided by operating activities is $8,800 ($20,800 − $12,000). And the $800 decrease in Accounts Receivable is *added* to the $8,000 net income to get $8,800 net cash provided by operating activities.

Adjustments like those for Accounts Receivable are required for all noncash current assets related to operating activities. When a noncash current asset increases, part of the assets derived from operating activities goes into the increase. This leaves a smaller amount as the net cash inflow. Therefore, when you calculate the net cash inflow, subtract the noncash current asset increase from net income. But, when a noncash current asset decreases, additional cash is produced, and you should add this amount to net income. These modifications of income for changes in current assets related to operating activities are

Net income
Add: Decreases in current assets
Subtract: Increases in current assets
Net cash provided (or used) by operating activities

Adjustments for Changes in Current Liabilities

To illustrate the adjustments for changes in current liabilities, return to the original assumptions about Simple Company. Sales of $20,000 are for cash, and operating expenses are $12,000. However, assume now that Simple Company has Interest Payable as its only current liability. Also assume that the beginning-of-year balance in Interest Payable was $500 and the end-of-year balance was $900. This increase means that the operating expenses of $12,000 were $400 larger than the amount paid in cash during the period. Therefore, the cash payments for operating expenses were only $11,600, or ($12,000 − $400). Under these assumptions, the calculation of net cash provided by operating activities is $8,400, or $20,000 receipts from customers less $11,600 payments for expenses. The calculation of $8,400 is net income of $8,000 plus the $400 increase in Interest Payable.

Alternatively, if the Interest Payable balance decreased, for example by $300, the cash outflow for operating expenses would have been the $12,000 expense plus the $300 liability decrease, or $12,300. Then, the calculation of net cash flow is $20,000 − $12,300 = $7,700. Or, the reconciliation is $8,000 − $300 = $7,700. In other words, subtract a *decrease* in Interest Payable from net income.

Adjustments like those for Interest Payable are required for all current liabilities related to operating activities. When a current liability decreases, part of the cash derived from operating activities pays for the decrease. Therefore, subtract the decrease from net income to determine the remaining net cash inflow. And, when a current liability increases, it finances some operating expenses. In other words, cash was not used to pay for the expense and the liability increase must be *added* to net income when you calculate cash provided by operating activities. These adjustments for changes in current liabilities related to operating activities are

---

Net income
Add: Increases in current liabilities
Subtract: Decreases in current liabilities
Net cash provided (or used) by operating activities

One way to remember how to make these modifications to net income is to observe that a *debit* change in a noncash current asset or a current liability is *subtracted* from net income. And, a *credit* change in a noncash current asset or a current liability is *added* to net income.

Adjustments for Operating Items that Do Not Provide or Use Cash

Some operating items that appear on an income statement do not provide or use cash during the current period. One example is amortization, such as amortization of intangible assets, depreciation, or depletion of natural resources. Another example is bad debts expense.

These expenses are recorded with debits to expense accounts and credits to noncash accounts. They reduce net income but do not require cash outflows during the period. Therefore, when adjustments to net income are made, add these noncash expenses back to net income.

In addition to noncash expenses such as amortization, net income may include some revenues that do not provide cash inflows during the current period. An example is equity method earnings from a share investment in another entity (see Chapter 12). If net income includes revenues that do not provide cash inflows, subtract the revenues from net income in the process of reconciling net income to the net cash provided by operating activities.

The adjustments for expenses and revenues that do not provide or use cash during the current period are

---

Net income
Add: Expenses that do not use cash
Subtract: Revenues that do not provide cash
Net cash provided (or used) by operating activities

Adjustments for Nonoperating Items

Some income statement items are not related to the operating activities of the company. These gains and losses result from investing and financing activities. Examples are gains or losses on the sale of plant assets and gains or losses on the retirement of bonds payable.

Remember that net income is reconciled to the net cash provided (or used) by operating activities. Therefore, net income must be modified to exclude gains and losses created by investing and financing activities. In making these modifications, subtract gains from financing and investing activities from net income and add losses back to net income:

Net income
Add: Losses from investing or financing activities
Subtract: Gains from investing or financing activities
Net cash provided (or used) by operating activities

Illustration 18-3 summarizes the adjustments to net income or net loss required to determine net cash flows from operating activities.

Investing Activities

Transactions that involve making and collecting loans or that involve purchasing and selling capital assets, other productive assets, or investments (other than cash equivalents) are called **investing activities.** Usually, investing activities involve the purchase or sale of assets classified on the balance sheet as plant and equipment, intangible assets, or long-term investments. However, the purchase and sale of short-term investments other than cash equivalents are also investing activities. Illustration 18–4 shows examples of cash flows from investing activities.

The fourth type of receipt listed in Illustration 18–4 involves proceeds from collecting the principal amount of loans. Regarding this item, carefully examine any cash receipts that relate to notes receivable. If the notes resulted from sales to customers, classify the cash receipts as operating activities. Use this classification even if the notes are long-term notes. But, if a company loans money to other parties, classify the cash receipts from collecting the principal of the loans as inflows from investing activities. Nevertheless, the CICA concluded that collections of interest are not investing activities. Instead, they are included in operating activities.

Net Income or Net Loss	
Plus	**Minus**
Decreases in noncash current assets.	Increases in noncash current assets.
Increases in current liabilities.	Decreases in current liabilities.
Expenses which do not require a cash outflow during the period.	Income which did not result in a cash inflow during the period.
Losses for investing and financing activities.	Gains from investing and financing activities.

Illustration 18-4
Cash Flows from
Investing Activities

Cash Inflows	**Cash Outflows**
Proceeds from selling productive assets (for example, land, buildings, equipment, natural resources, and intangible assets).	Payments to purchase property, plant, and equipment or other productive assets (excluding merchandise inventory).
Proceeds from selling investments in the equity securities of other companies.	Payments to acquire equity securities of other companies, except cash equivalents.
Proceeds from selling investments in the debt securities of other entities, except cash equivalents.	Payments to acquire debt securities of other entities, except cash equivalents.
Proceeds from collecting the principal amount of loans.	Payments in the form of loans made to other parties.
Proceeds from the sale (discounting) of loans made by the enterprise.	

Financing Activities

The **financing activities** of a business include transactions with its owners and transactions with creditors to borrow money or to repay the principal amounts of loans. Financing activities include borrowing and repaying both short-term loans and long-term debt. However, cash payments to settle credit purchases of merchandise, whether on account or by note, are operating activities. Payments of interest expense are also operating activities. Illustration 18–5 shows examples of cash flows from financing activities.

Some important investing and financing activities do not involve cash receipts or payments during the current period. For example, a company might purchase land and buildings and finance 100% of the purchase by giving a long-term note payable. Because this transaction clearly involves both investing and financing activities, it must be reported in both sections of the SCFP even though no cash was received or paid. That is, the transaction is treated as if two cash transactions occurred simultaneously.

**NONCASH
INVESTING
AND
FINANCING
ACTIVITIES**

Illustration 18–5
Cash Flows from
Financing Activities

Cash Inflows	Cash Outflows
Proceeds from issuing equity securities (e.g., common and preferred shares).	Payments of dividends and other distributions to owners.*
Proceeds from issuing bonds and notes payable.	Repayments of cash loans.
Proceeds from other short- or long-term borrowing transactions.	Payments of the principal amounts involved in long-term credit arrangements.

*Some companies treat dividends as an operating activity outflow, while others disclose them in a separate category. Section 1540 of the *CICA Handbook* requires that dividends be disclosed but does not offer any guidance as to their category in the SCFP.

Other investing and financing activities may involve some cash receipt or payment as well as giving or receiving other types of consideration. For example, suppose that you purchase machinery for $12,000 by paying cash of $5,000 and trading in old machinery that has a market value of $7,000. In this case, the SCFP reports a $7,000 cash inflow from the sale of the old machines and a $12,000 cash outflow for the purchase of machinery. Illustration 18–6 shows an example of how a company might disclose its noncash investing and financing activities.

Examples of transactions that must be disclosed as noncash investing and financing activities include the following:

- The retirement of debt securities by issuing equity securities.
- The conversion of preferred shares to common shares.
- The leasing of assets in a transaction that qualifies as a capital lease.
- The purchase of long-term assets by issuing a note payable to the seller.
- The exchange of a noncash asset for other noncash assets.
- The purchase of noncash assets by issuing equity or debt securities.

Progress Check
(Answers to Progress Checks are provided at the end of the chapter.)

18–1   Does an SCFP disclose payments of cash to purchase cash equivalents? Does it disclose receipts of cash from the liquidation of cash equivalents?

18–2   What are the categories of cash flows reported separately on the SCFP?

18–3   Identify the category for each of the following cash flow activities: *(a)* purchase of equipment for cash; *(b)* payment of wages; *(c)* sale of common shares; *(d)* receipt of cash dividends on equity investment; *(e)* collection from customers; *(f)* issuance of bonds for cash.

PREPARING A STATEMENT OF CHANGES IN FINANCIAL POSITION

The information you need to prepare a statement of changes in financial position comes from a variety of sources. These include comparative balance sheets at the beginning and the end of the accounting period, an income statement for the period, and a careful analysis of each noncash balance sheet account in the general ledger. However, because cash inflows and cash outflows are to be reported, you

The company issued 1,000 common shares for the purchase of land and buildings with fair values of $5,000 and $15,000, respectively.

> Investing activity (outflow): Purchase of property for $20,000.
> Financing activity (inflow): Issue of common shares for $20,000.

The company entered into a capital lease obligation of $12,000 for new computer equipment.

> Investing activity (outflow): Acquisition of capital lease assets for $12,000.
> Financing activity (inflow): Capital lease obligation assumed for $12,000.

The company exchanged old machinery with a fair value of $7,000 and a book value of $8,000 for new machinery valued at $12,000. The balance of $5,000 was paid in cash.

> Investing activity (outflow): Acquisition of new machinery for $12,000.
> Investing activity (inflow): Disposal of old machinery for $7,000.

might wonder why we do not focus our attention on the Cash account. For the moment, we should at least consider this approach.

Analyzing the Cash Account

All of a company's cash receipts and cash payments are recorded in the Cash account in the General Ledger. Therefore, the Cash account would seem to be the logical place to look for information about cash flows from operating, investing, and financing activities. To demonstrate, review this summarized Cash account of Grover Company:

LO 2

Calculate cash inflows and outflows by inspecting the noncash account balances and prepare an SCFP.

Summarized Cash Account

Balance, Dec. 31, 1996	12,000		
Receipts from customers	570,000	Payments for merchandise	319,000
Proceeds from sale of plant		Payments for wages and other	
assets	12,000	operating expenses	218,000
Proceeds from issue of shares	15,000	Interest payments	8,000
		Tax payments	5,000
		Payments for purchase of	
		plant assets	10,000
		Payments to retire bonds	18,000
		Dividend payments	14,000
Balance, Dec. 31, 1997	17,000		

In this account, the individual cash transactions are already summarized in terms of major types of receipts and payments. For example, the account has only one debit entry for the total receipts from all customers. All that remains is to determine whether each type of cash inflow or outflow is an operating, investing, or financing activity and then place it in its proper category on the SCFP. The completed SCFP appears in Illustration 18–2 on page 812.

While an analysis of the Cash account may appear to be an easy way to prepare an SCFP, it has two serious drawbacks. First, most companies have so many individual cash receipts and disbursements that it is not practical to review them all. Imagine what a problem this analysis would present for **Stelco, INCO, Loblaw,**

Illustration 18-7   Why an Analysis of the Noncash Accounts Explains the Change in Cash

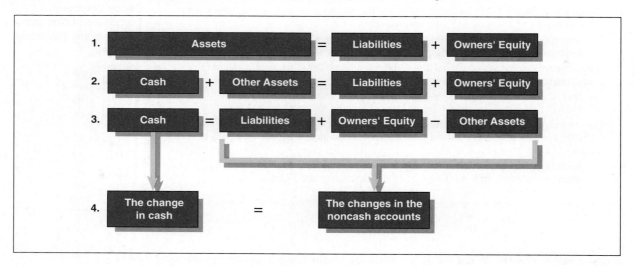

or **Corel,** or even for a relatively small business. Second, the Cash account usually does not contain a description of each cash transaction. Therefore, even though the Cash account shows the periodic postings of debits and credits, you generally cannot determine the type of transaction by looking at the Cash account. Thus, the Cash account does not readily provide the information you need to prepare a statement of cash flows. To obtain the necessary information, you must analyze the changes in the noncash accounts.

Analyzing Noncash Accounts to Determine Cash Flows

When a company records cash inflows and outflows with debits and credits to the Cash account, it also records credits and debits in other accounts. Some of these accounts are balance sheet accounts. Others are revenue and expense accounts that are closed to Retained Earnings, a balance sheet account. As a result, all cash transactions eventually affect noncash balance sheet accounts. Therefore, we can determine the nature of the cash inflows and outflows by examining the changes in the noncash balance sheet accounts. Illustration 18–7 shows this important relationship between the Cash account and the noncash balance sheet accounts.

In Illustration 18–7, notice that the balance sheet equation labeled (1) is expanded in (2) so that cash is separated from the other assets. Then, the equation is rearranged in (3) so that cash is set equal to the sum of the liability and equity accounts less the noncash asset accounts. The illustration then points out in (4) that changes in one side of the equation (cash) must be equal to the changes in the other side (noncash accounts). Part (4) shows that you can fully explain the changes in cash by analyzing the changes in liabilities, owners' equity, and noncash assets.

This overall process has another advantage. The examination of each noncash account also identifies any noncash investing and financing activities that occurred during the period. As you learned earlier, these noncash items must also be disclosed on the SCFP.

Illustration 18–8   Analysis of the Noncash Accounts Explains the Change in Cash

Income Statement Items	Related Balance Sheet Accounts	Possible Cash Flow Effects
Sales	Accounts receivable	Cash receipts from customers
Cost of goods sold	Merchandise inventory, accounts payable	Cash payments to suppliers
Amortization expense	Accumulated amortization	None
Operating expense	Prepaid expenses, accrued liabilities	Cash payments for operating expenses
Gain or loss on sale of capital assets	Capital assets, accumulated amortization, notes receivable	Cash receipts from sale of capital assets
Gain or loss on retirement of bonds payable	Bonds payable, premium or discount on bonds payable	Cash payments for retirement of bonds

When beginning to analyze the changes in the noncash balance sheet accounts, recall that Retained Earnings is affected by revenues, expenses, and dividend declarations. Therefore, look at the income statement accounts to help explain the change in Retained Earnings. In fact, the income statement accounts provide important information that relates to the changes in several balance sheet accounts.

Illustration 18–8 summarizes some of these relationships between income statement accounts, balance sheet accounts, and possible cash flows. For example, to determine the cash receipts from customers during a period, adjust the amount of sales revenue for the increase or decrease in Accounts Receivable.[5] If the Accounts

---

[5]This introductory explanation assumes that there is no bad debts expense. However, if bad debts occur and are written off directly to Accounts Receivable, the change in the Accounts Receivable balance will be due in part to the write-off. The remaining change results from credit sales and from cash receipts. This chapter does not discuss the allowance method of accounting for bad debts since it would make the analysis unnecessarily complex at this time.

Receivable balance did not change, the cash collected from customers is equal to sales revenue. On the other hand, if the Accounts Receivable balance decreased, cash collections must have been equal to sales revenue *plus* the reduction in Accounts Receivable. And, if the Accounts Receivable balance increased, the cash collected from customers must have been equal to Sales *less* the increase in Accounts Receivable.

By analyzing all noncash balance sheet accounts and related income statement accounts in this fashion, you can obtain the necessary information for a statement of changes in financial position. Next, we illustrate this process by examining the noncash accounts of Grover Company.

GROVER COMPANY—A COMPREHENSIVE EXAMPLE

Grover Company's December 31, 1996, and 1997 balance sheets and its 1997 income statement are presented in Illustration 18–9. Our objective is to prepare an SCFP that explains the $5,000 increase in cash, based on these financial statements and this additional information about the 1997 transactions:

a. Net income was $38,000.

b. Accounts receivable increased by $20,000.

c. Merchandise inventory increased by $14,000.

d. Prepaid expenses increased by $2,000.

e. Accounts payable decreased by $5,000.

f. Interest payable decreased by $1,000.

g. Income taxes payable increased by $10,000.

h. Amortization expense was $24,000.

i. Loss on sale of plant assets was $6,000; assets that cost $30,000 with accumulated amortization of $12,000 were sold for $12,000 cash.

j. Gain on retirement of bonds was $16,000; bonds with a book value of $34,000 were retired with a cash payment of $18,000.

k. Plant assets that cost $70,000 were purchased; the payment consisted of $10,000 cash and issuing $60,000 of bonds payable.

l. Sold 3,000 common shares for $15,000.

m. Paid cash dividends of $14,000.

PREPARATION OF THE SCFP

Intuitive Approach

The intuitive approach uses the comparative balance sheets, the income statement, and supplementary data to clarify certain transactions. To illustrate the intuitive approach, we use the financial statements in Illustration 18–9 and the information listed above. The comparative balance sheets show that cash increased by $5,000 during 1997. Therefore, $5,000 must be the amount on the last line before the cash balance at the beginning of 1997 on the SCFP (Illustration 18–2). This change is explained by examining and identifying the causes of the cash inflows and out flows.

Illustration 18-9
Financial Statements

GROVER COMPANY
Balance Sheet
December 31, 1997 and 1996

Assets		1997		1996
Current assets:				
Cash		$ 17,000		$ 12,000
Accounts receivable		60,000		40,000
Merchandise inventory		84,000		70,000
Prepaid expenses		6,000		4,000
Total current assets		$167,000		$126,000
Long-term assets:				
Plant assets	$250,000		$210,000	
Less accumulated amortization	60,000	190,000	48,000	162,000
Total assets		$357,000		$288,000
Liabilities				
Current liabilities:				
Accounts payable		$ 35,000		$ 40,000
Interest payable		3,000		4,000
Income taxes payable		22,000		12,000
Total current liabilities		$ 60,000		$ 56,000
Long-term liabilities:				
Bonds payable		90,000		64,000
Total liabilities		$150,000		$120,000
Shareholders' Equity				
Contributed capital:				
Common shares, no par value	$ 95,000		$ 80,000	
Retained earnings	112,000		88,000	
Total shareholders' equity		207,000		168,000
Total liabilities and shareholders' equity		$357,000		$288,000

GROVER COMPANY
Income Statement
For Year Ended December 31, 1997

Sales		$ 590,000
Cost of goods sold	$300,000	
Wages and other operating expenses . .	216,000	
Interest expense	7,000	
Income taxes expense	15,000	
Amortization expense	24,000	(562,000)
Loss on sale of plant assets		(6,000)
Gain on retirement of debt		16,000
Net income		$ 38,000

Illustration 18-10

GROVER COMPANY
Statement of Changes in Financial Position
For Year Ended December 31, 1997

	Increase (Decrease)
Cash flows from operating activities:	
Net income for 1997 *(a)*	$ 38,000
Adjustments to reconcile net income to cash provided by operating activities:	
1. Accounts receivable *(b)*	(20,000)
Merchandise inventory *(c)*	(14,000)
Prepaid expenses *(d)*	(2,000)
Accounts payable *(e)*	(5,000)
Interest payable *(f)*	(1,000)
Income taxes payable *(g)*	10,000
2. Amortization expense *(h)*	24,000
3. Loss on sale of plant assets *(i)*	6,000
Gain on retirement of debt *(j)*	(16,000)
Net adjustments	(18,000)
Cash provided by operating activities	20,000
Cash flows from investing activities:	
Cash received from sale of plant assets *(i)*	12,000
Cash paid for purchase plant assets *(k)*	(70,000)
Net cash provided by investing activities . .	(58,000)
Cash flows from financing activities:	
Cash received from share issue *(l)*	15,000
Cash received from bond issue *(k)*	60,000
Cash paid to retire bonds *(j)*	(18,000)
Cash paid for dividends *(m)*	(15,000)
Net cash used in financing activities	43,000
Net increase in cash	$ 5,000
Cash balance at beginning of 1997	12,000
Cash balance at end of 1997	$ 17,000

Analysis of Cash Flows

In order to determine the cash flows from operations, we must adjust the net income figure from Illustration 18–9. First, we add or subtract the changes in the noncash current asset and current liability accounts as shown in Illustration 18–10.

Second, we adjust for the other operating items that do not provide or use cash. From the income statement we can determine that only amortization expense fits into this category. Therefore, we add back the amortization expense.

Third, we adjust for nonoperating items. In Illustration 18–10 these are the loss on sale of plant assets and the gain on retirement of debt.

The net cash provided by financing activities and by investing activities is taken from the additional information. Each item is identified with the corresponding letter from the above list of 1997 transactions, denoted *a* through *m*.

Although the intuitive approach technique may be adequate when doing relatively simple SCFPs, in many cases a more formal method is desirable. This is known as the *working paper approach,* which is illustrated and discussed next.

When a company has a large number of accounts and many operating, investing, and financing transactions, the analysis of noncash accounts can be difficult and confusing. In these situations, a working paper can help organize the information needed to prepare an SCFP. A working paper also makes it easier to check the accuracy of your work.

Illustration 18–11 shows the working paper for Grover Company. Notice that the beginning and ending balance sheets are recorded on the working paper. Following the balance sheets, we enter information in the Analysis of Changes columns about cash flows from operating, investing, and financing activities and about noncash investing and financing activities. Note that the working paper does not reconstruct the income statement. Instead, net income is entered as the first item used in computing the amount of cash flows from operating activities.

Entering the Analysis of Changes on the Working Paper

After the balance sheets are entered, we recommend using the following sequence of procedures to complete the working paper:

1. Enter net income as an operating cash inflow (a debit) and as a credit to Retained Earnings (*a1*) and the change in cash as a debit and credit (*a2*).
2. In the Statement of Changes in Financial Position section, adjustments to net income are entered as debits if they increase cash inflows and as credits if they decrease cash inflows. Following this rule, adjust net income for the change in each noncash current asset and current liability related to operating activities. For each adjustment to net income, the offsetting debit or credit should reconcile the beginning and ending balances of a current asset or current liability.
3. Enter the adjustments to net income for income statement items, such as amortization, that did not provide or use cash during the period. For each adjustment, the offsetting debit or credit should help reconcile a noncash balance sheet account.
4. Adjust net income to eliminate any gains or losses from investing and financing activities. Because the cash associated with a gain must be excluded from operating activities, the gain is entered as a credit in the operating activities section. On the other hand, losses are entered with debits. For each of these adjustments, the related debits and/or credits help reconcile balance sheet accounts and also involve entries to show the cash flow from investing or financing activities.

PREPARING
A WORKING
PAPER FOR
AN SCFP

LO 3
Prepare a working paper
for an SCFP.

Illustration 18–11

GROVER COMPANY
Working Paper for Statement of Changes in Financial Position
For Year Ended December 31, 1997

	December 31, 1996	Analysis of Changes Debit	Analysis of Changes Credit	December 31, 1997
Balance sheet—debits:				
Cash	12,000	(a2) 5,000		17,000
Accounts receivable	40,000	(b) 20,000		60,000
Merchandise inventory	70,000	(c) 14,000		84,000
Prepaid expenses	4,000	(d) 2,000		6,000
Plant assets	210,000	(k1) 70,000	(i) 30,000	250,000
	336,000			417,000
Balance sheet—credits:				
Accumulated amortization	48,000	(i) 12,000	(h) 24,000	60,000
Accounts payable	40,000	(e) 5,000		35,000
Interest payable	4,000	(f) 1,000		3,000
Income taxes payable	12,000		(g) 10,000	22,000
Bonds payable	64,000	(j) 34,000	(k2) 60,000	90,000
Common stock, no par value	80,000		(l) 15,000	95,000
Retained earnings	88,000	(m) 14,000	(a1) 38,000	112,000
	336,000			417,000
Statement of changes in financial position:				
Operating activities:				
Net income		(a1) 38,000		
Increase in accounts receivable			(b) 20,000	
Increase in merchandise inventory			(c) 14,000	
Increase in prepaid expenses			(d) 2,000	
Decrease in accounts payable			(e) 5,000	
Decrease in interest payable			(f) 1,000	20,000
Increase in income taxes payable		(g) 10,000		
Amortization expense		(h) 24,000		
Loss on sale of plant assets		(i) 6,000		
Gain on retirement of bonds			(j) 16,000	
Investing activities:				
Receipts from sale of plant assets		(i) 12,000		(58,000)
Purchase of plant assets			(k1) 70,000	
Financing activities:				
Payments to retire bonds			(j) 18,000	
Receipts from issuance of shares		(l) 15,000		43,000
Payments of dividends			(m) 14,000	
Receipts from issuance of bonds		(k2) 60,000		
Increase in cash balance			(a2) 5,000	5,000
		342,000	342,000	

5. After reviewing any unreconciled balance sheet accounts and related information, enter the reconciling entries for all remaining investing and financing activities. These include items such as purchases of plant assets, issuances of long-term debt, sales of shares, and dividend payments.

6. Confirm the accuracy of your work by totaling the Analysis of Changes columns and by determining that the change in each balance sheet account has been explained.

For Grover Company, these steps were performed in Illustration 18–11:

Step	Entries
1	(a)
2	(b) through (g)
3	(h)
4	(i) through (j)
5	(k) through (m)

Because adjustments *i, j,* and *k* are more complex, we show them in the following debit and credit format. This format is similar to the one used for general journal entries, except that the changes in the Cash account are identified as sources or uses of cash. Note that these are only used on the SCFP working papers and are not entered in the books of Grover.

		Debit	Credit
i.	Loss from Sale of Plant Assets	6,000.00	
	Accumulated Amortization	12,000.00	
	Receipt from Sale of Plant Assets	12,000.00	
	Plant Assets		30,000.00
	To describe the sale of plant assets.		
j.	Bonds Payable	34,000.00	
	Payments to Retire Bonds		18,000.00
	Gain on Retirement of Bonds		16,000.00
	To describe the retirement of bonds.		
k1.	Plant Assets	70,000.00	
	Purchase of Plant Assets Financed by Bonds		70,000.00
	To describe the purchase of plant assets, the cash payment, and the use of noncash financing.		
k2.	Proceeds of Bonds Used to Purchase Plant Assets	60,000.00	
	Bonds Payable		60,000.00
	To show the issuance of bonds payable to finance the purchase of plant assets.		

Progress Check

18–4 **In preparing a working paper for an SCFP, which of the following is true?**
  a. **A decrease in accounts receivable is analyzed with a debit in the statement of cash flows section and a credit in the balance sheet section.**

b. **A cash dividend paid is analyzed with a debit to retained earnings and a credit in the investing activities section.**

c. **The analysis of a cash payment to retire bonds payable at a loss would require one debit and two credits.**

d. **Amortization expense would not require analysis on the working paper because there is no cash inflow or outflow.**

18–5   **Determine the net cash provided (or used) by operating activities based on the following data:**

Net income	$74,900
Decrease in accounts receivable	4,600
Increase in inventory	11,700
Decrease in accounts payable	1,000
Loss on sale of equipment	3,400
Payment of dividends	21,500

18–6   **Why are expenses such as amortization of equipment and amortization of goodwill added to net income when cash flow from operating activities is calculated by the indirect method?**

18–7   **A company reports a net income of $15,000 that includes a $3,000 gain on the sale of plant assets. Why is this gain subtracted from net income in calculating cash flow from operating activities according to the indirect method?**

USING THE INFORMATION— CASH FLOWS

LO 1

Explain why cash flow information is important to decision making and describe the information in an SCFP and the methods used to disclose noncash investing and financing activities.

Numerous ratios are used to analyze income statement and balance sheet data. By comparison, ratios related to the statement of changes in financial position are not widely used.[6] Only one ratio of that nature, cash flow per share, has received much attention. Some financial analysts use that ratio, usually calculated as net income adjusted for noncash items such as amortization. Currently, however, the GAAP does not require reporting cash flow per share, apparently because it might be misinterpreted as a measure of earnings performance.

Leanne Hagarty (As a Matter of Opinion, page 809) typifies the attitude of most managers when she emphasizes the importance of understanding and predicting cash flows. Many business decisions are based on cash flow evaluations. For example, creditors evaluate a company's ability to generate cash before deciding whether to loan money to the company. Investors often make similar evaluations before they buy a company's shares. In making these evaluations, cash flows from investing and financing activities are considered. However, special attention is given to the company's ability to generate cash flows from its operations. The cash flows statement facilitates this by separating the investing and financing activity cash flows from the operating cash flows.

To see the importance of identifying cash flows as operating, investing, and financing activities, consider the following three companies. Assume they operate in the same industry and have been in business for several years.

---

[6]To consider some suggested cash flow ratios, see Don E. Giacomino and David E. Mielke, "Cash Flows: Another Approach to Ratio Analysis," *Journal of Accountancy,* March 1993.

	First Company	Second Company	Third Company
Cash provided (used) by operating activities	$ 90,000	$ 40,000	$(24,000)
Cash provided (used) by investing activities:			
Proceeds from sale of operating assets			26,000
Purchase of operating assets	(48,000)	(25,000)	
Cash provided (used) by financing activities:			
Proceeds from issuance of debt			13,000
Repayment of debt	(27,000)		
Net increase (decrease) in cash	$ 15,000	$ 15,000	$ 15,000

Each of the three companies generated a $15,000 net increase in cash. Their means of accomplishing this, however, were very different. First Company's operating activities provided $90,000, which allowed the company to purchase additional operating assets for $48,000 and repay $27,000 of debt. By comparison, Second Company's operating activities provided only $40,000, enabling it to purchase only $25,000 of operating assets. By comparison, Third Company's net cash increase was obtained only by selling operating assets and incurring additional debt; operating activities resulted in a net cash outflow of $24,000.

The implication of this comparison is that First Company is more capable of generating cash to meet its future obligations than is Second Company; and Third Company is least capable. This evaluation is, of course, tentative and may be contradicted by other information.

Managers analyze cash flows in making a variety of short-term decisions. In deciding whether borrowing will be necessary, managers use the procedures you learned in this chapter to predict cash flows for the next period or periods. These short-term planning situations also may lead to decisions about investing idle cash balances. Another example is deciding whether a customer's offer to buy a product at a reduced price should be accepted or rejected.

Long-term decisions involving new investments usually require detailed cash flow predictions. Companies must estimate cash inflows and outflows over the life of the investment, often extending many years into the future. Other decisions that require cash flow information include deciding whether a product should be manufactured by the company or purchased from an outside supplier, and deciding whether a product or a department should be eliminated or retained.

Progress Check

18-8   Refer to the consolidated statements of changes in financial position for Geac Computer Corporation, in Appendix I. What type and amount of investing activities took place during the year ended April 30, 1994? What was the largest source of cash to finance these activities?

SUMMARY OF THE CHAPTER IN TERMS OF LEARNING OBJECTIVES

LO 1. Explain why cash flow information is important to decision making and describe the information in a statement of changes in financial position and the methods used to disclose noncash investing and financing activities. Many decisions involve evaluating cash flows. Examples are investor and creditor decisions to invest in or loan money to a company. The evaluations include paying attention to the activities that provide or use cash. Managers evaluate cash flows in deciding whether borrowing is necessary, whether cash balances should be invested, and in a variety of other short-term and long-term decisions.

The SCFP reports cash receipts and disbursements as operating, investing, or financing activities. Operating activities include transactions related to producing or purchasing merchandise, selling goods and services to customers, and performing administrative functions. Investing activities include purchases and sales of noncurrent assets and short-term investments that are not cash equivalents. Financing activities include transactions with owners and transactions to borrow or repay the principal amounts of long-term and short-term debt.

LO 2. Calculate cash inflows and outflows by inspecting the noncash account balances and prepare an SCFP. To identify the cash receipts and cash payments, analyze the changes in the noncash balance sheet accounts created by income statement transactions and other events. To calculate the net cash provided (or used) by operating activities, first list the net income and then modify it for these three types of events: (a) changes in noncash current assets and current liabilities related to operating activities, (b) revenues and expenses that did not provide or use cash, and (c) gains and losses from investing and financing activities.

LO 3. Prepare a working paper for an SCFP. To prepare a working paper, first enter the beginning and ending balances of the balance sheet accounts in columns 1 and 4. Then, establish the three sections of the SCFP. Net income is entered as the first item in the operating activities section. Then, adjust the net income for events (a) through (c) identified in the preceding paragraph. This process reconciles the changes in the noncash current assets and current liabilities related to operations. Reconcile any remaining balance sheet account changes and report their cash effects in the appropriate sections.

DEMONSTRATION PROBLEM

Given the following condensed income statement and a partial list of account balances, calculate the cash provided by operating activities:

BUTTERFIELD COMPANY
Income Statement
For the Year Ended December 31, 1997

Sales		$225,000
Cost of goods sold		130,000
Gross profit from sales		$ 95,000
Operating expenses:		
Salaries and wages	$31,250	
Amortization expense	3,750	
Rent expense	9,000	
Amortization of patents	750	
Office expense	1,000	
Bond interest expense	3,375	49,125
Net income		$ 45,875

Butterfield Company's partial list of comparative account balances as of December 31, 1997 and 1996:

	1997	1996
Cash	$ 2,600	$ 2,200
Accounts receivable (net)	23,200	21,800
Inventory	17,900	19,300
Prepaid expenses	1,200	1,400
Accounts payable	11,400	12,100
Salaries and wages payable	250	650
Interest payable	1,500	750
Unamortized bond discount	500	875

- Prepare a blank section of an SCFP for operating activities.
- Insert the net income figure at the beginning of the schedule.
- Examine each account balance to determine if it has increased or decreased during 1997.
- Adjust net income for increases and decreases in current assets and liabilities.
- Adjust net income for expenses which are not a decrease in cash.
- Compare your answer to the solution.

Planning the Solution

BUTTERFIELD COMPANY
Cash Provided by Operating Activities
For the Year Ended December 31, 1997

Solution to Demonstration Problem

Cash provided by operating activities:		
Net income		$45,875
Adjustments to reconcile net income to		
cash provided by operations:		
Increase in accounts receivable	$(1,400)	
Decrease in inventory	1,400	
Decrease in prepaid expenses	200	
Decrease in accounts payable	(700)	
Decrease in salaries and wages payable	(400)	
Increase in interest payable	750	
Amortization expense	3,750	
Amortization of patents	750	
Amortization of bond discount	375	4,725
Cash provided by operating activities		$50,600

GLOSSARY

Financing activities transactions with the owners of a business or transactions with its creditors to borrow money or to repay the principal amounts of loans. p. 817

Investing activities transactions that involve making and collecting loans or that involve purchasing and selling capital assets, other productive assets, or investments other than cash equivalents. p. 816

Net cash provided (or used) by operating activities a calculation that begins with net income and then adjusts the net income amount by adding and subtracting items

that are necessary to reconcile net income to the net cash provided or used by operating activities. p. 811

Operating activities activities that involve the production or purchase of merchandise and the sale of goods and services to customers, including expenditures related to administering the business. p. 813

Statement of changes in financial position a financial statement that reports the cash inflows and outflows for an accounting period, and that classifies those cash flows as operating activities, investing activities, and financing activities. p. 808

SYNOMYMOUS TERMS

Cash inflow   source of cash.

Cash outflow   use of cash.

Statement of Changes in Financial Position   statement of cash flows.

QUESTIONS

1. What are some examples of items reported on an SCFP as investing activities?

2. What are some examples of items reported on an SCFP as financing activities?

3. What are some examples of items in the reconciliation for cash flows from operating activities?

4. If a corporation pays cash dividends, where on the corporation's SCFP should the payment be reported?

5. A company purchases land for $100,000, paying $20,000 cash and borrowing the remainder on a long-term note payable. How should this transaction be reported on an SCFP?

6. What is the direct method of reporting cash flows from operating activities?

7. What is the indirect method of reporting cash flows from operating activities?

8. Is amortization a source of cash?

9. On June 3, a company borrowed $50,000 by giving its bank a 60-day, interest-bearing note. On the SCFP, where should this item be reported?

10. If a company reports a net income for the year, is it possible for the company to show a net cash outflow from operating activities? Explain your answer.

11. Refer to Geac Computer Corporation's consolidated statement of changes in financial position shown in Appendix I. What does the change in "non-cash working capital components" represent?

QUICK STUDY (Five-Minute Exercises)

QS 18–1
(LO 1)

Describe the content of a statement of changes in financial position.

QS 18–2
(LO 1)

Classify the following cash flows as operating, investing, or financing activities:

1. Purchased merchandise for cash.
2. Paid interest on outstanding bonds.
3. Sold delivery equipment at a loss.
4. Paid property taxes on the company offices.
5. Collected proceeds from sale of long-term investments.
6. Issued common shares for cash.
7. Received payments from customers.
8. Paid wages.
9. Paid dividends.
10. Received interest on investment.

List three examples of transactions that are noncash financing and investing transactions.

QS 18–3
(LO 1)

Use the following information in QS 18–4 through QS 18–9.

QS 18–4
(LO 2)

KUNG ATTIRE, INC.
Comparative Balance Sheet

Assets	1997	1996
Cash	$ 47,900	$ 12,500
Accounts receivable (net)	21,000	26,000
Inventory	43,400	48,400
Prepaid expenses	3,200	2,600
Furniture	55,000	60,000
Accumulated amortization, furniture	(9,000)	(5,000)
Total assets	$161,500	$144,500

Liabilities and Shareholders' Equity		
Accounts payable	$ 8,000	$ 11,000
Wages payable	5,000	3,000
Income taxes payable	1,200	1,800
Notes payable (long-term)	15,000	35,000
Common shares, n.p.v. par value	115,000	90,000
Retained earnings	17,300	3,700
Total liabilities and shareholders' equity	$161,500	$144,500

KUNG ATTIRE, INC.
Income Statement
For Year Ended June 30, 1997

Sales		$234,000
Cost of goods sold		156,000
Gross profit		$ 78,000
Operating expenses:		
Amortization expense	$19,300	
Other expenses	28,500	
Total operating expenses		47,800
Net income from operations		$ 30,200
Income taxes		12,300
Net income		$ 17,900

How much cash was received from customers during Year 2?

Refer to the facts in QS 18–4. How much cash was paid for merchandise during 1997?

QS 18–5
(LO 2)

Refer to the facts in QS 18–4. How much cash was paid for operating expenses during 1997?

QS 18–6
(LO 2)

QS 18–7 **(LO 2)**	Refer to the facts in QS 18–4 and assume furniture that cost $27,000 was sold at its book value and all furniture acquisitions were for cash. What was the cash inflow related to the sale of furniture?
QS 18–8 **(LO 2)**	Refer to the facts in QS 18–4 and assume that all shares were issued for cash. How much cash was disbursed for dividends?
QS 18–9 **(LO 2)**	Refer to the facts in QS 18–4. Calculate cash provided or used from operating activities.
QS 18–10 **(LO 3)**	When a working paper for an SCFP is prepared, all changes in noncash balance sheet accounts are accounted for on the working paper. Explain why this occurs.

EXERCISES

Exercise 18–1
Classifying transactions
on an SCFP
(LO 1)

The following events occurred during the year. Indicate the proper accounting treatment for each event by placing an *x* in the appropriate column. If the item should appear in more than one section, place an *x* in the appropriate columns.

	Statement of Changes in Financial Position		
	Operating Activities	**Investing Activities**	**Financing Activities**
a. Long-term bonds payable were retired by issuing common shares.	_____	_____	_____
b. Surplus merchandise inventory was sold for cash.	_____	_____	_____
c. Borrowed cash from the bank by signing a nine-month note payable.	_____	_____	_____
d. Paid cash to purchase a patent.	_____	_____	_____
e. A six-month note receivable was accepted in exchange for a building that had been used in operations.	_____	_____	_____
f. Recorded amortization expense on all plant assets.	_____	_____	_____
g. A cash dividend that was declared in a previous period was paid in the current period.	_____	_____	_____

Exercise 18–2
Organizing the SCFP and
supporting schedule
(LO 2)

Use the following information about the 1997 cash flows of Forrest Company to prepare an SCFP.

Cash and cash equivalents balance, December 31, 1996 . . . $ 50,000
Cash and cash equivalents balance, December 31, 1997 . . .   140,000
Cash received as interest   5,000
Decrease in salaries payable   35,000
Bonds payable retired by issuing common shares
    (there was no gain or loss on the retirement)   375,000
Cash paid to retire long-term notes payable   250,000
Cash received from sale of equipment   122,500
Cash borrowed on six-month note payable   50,000
Land purchased and financed by long-term note payable . .   212,500
Cash paid for store equipment   47,500
Cash dividends paid   30,000
Increase in accounts payable   40,000
Increase in acounts receivable   80,000
Increase in merchandise inventory   90,000
Net income   265,000
Amortization expense   145,000

In each of the following cases, use the information provided about the 1996 operations of Benzar Company to calculate the indicated cash flow:

Exercise 18–3
Calculating cash flows
(LO 2)

Case A: Calculate cash received from customers:
         Sales revenue $255,000
         Accounts receivable, January 1   12,600
         Accounts receivable, December 31   17,400

Case B: Calculate cash paid for insurance:
         Insurance expense . . . . $ 34,200
         Prepaid insurance, January 1   5,700
         Prepaid insurance, December 31   8,550

Case C: Calculate cash paid for salaries:
         Salaries expense $102,000
         Salaries payable, January 1   6,300
         Salaries payable, December 31   7,500

In each of the following cases, use the information provided about the 1996 operations of CNA Company to calculate the indicated cash flow:

Exercise 18–4
Calculating cash flows
(LO 2)

Case A: Calculate cash paid for rent:
         Rent expense . . . . $ 20,400
         Rent payable, January 1   4,400
         Rent payable, December 31   3,600

Case B: Calculate cash received from interest:
         Interest revenue . . . . $ 68,000
         Interest receivable, January 1   6,000
         Interest receivable, December 31   7,200

Case C: Calculate cash paid for merchandise:
         Cost of goods sold $352,000
         Merchandise inventory, January 1   106,400
         Accounts payable, January 1   45,200
         Merchandise inventory, December 31   87,600
         Accounts payable, December 31   56,000

Exercise 18–5
Cash flows from
operating activities
(LO 2)

Use the following income statement and information about changes in noncash current assets and current liabilities to present the cash flows from operating activities:

ALAMO DATA COMPANY
Income Statement
For Year Ended December 31, 1996

Sales		$606,000
Cost of goods sold		297,000
Gross profit from sales		$309,000
Operating expenses:		
Salaries expense	$82,845	
Depreciation expense	14,400	
Rent expense	16,200	
Amortization expense, patents	1,800	
Utilities expense	6,375	121,620
Total		$187,380
Gain on sale of equipment		2,400
Net income		$189,780

Changes in current asset and current liability accounts during the year, all of which related to operating activities, were as follows:

Accounts receivable	$13,500 increase
Merchandise inventory	9,000 increase
Accounts payable	4,500 decrease
Salaries payable	1,500 decrease

Exercise 18–6
Cash flows from
operating activities
(LO 2)

Trador Company's 1996 income statement showed the following: net income, $728,000; depreciation expense, $90,000; amortization expense, $16,400; and gain on sale of plant assets, $14,000. An examination of the company's current assets and current liabilities showed that the following changes occurred because of operating activities: accounts receivable decreased $36,200; merchandise inventory decreased $104,000; prepaid expenses increased $7,400; accounts payable decreased $18,400; other payables increased $2,800. Calculate the cash flow from operating activities.

Exercise 18–7
Classifying transactions
on an SCFP
(LO 1, 2)

The following events occurred during the year. Indicate the proper accounting treatment for each event listed below by placing an x in the appropriate column.

		Statement of Changes in Financial Position		
		Operating Activities	Investing Activities	Financing Activities
a.	Land for a new plant was purchased by issuing common shares.	_____	_____	_____
b.	Recorded amortization expense.	_____	_____	_____
c.	Income taxes payable increased by 15% from prior year.	_____	_____	_____
d.	Declared and paid a cash dividend.	_____	_____	_____
e.	Merchandise inventory increased.	_____	_____	_____
f.	Sold plant equipment at a loss.	_____	_____	_____
g.	Accounts receivable decreased during the year.	_____	_____	_____

PROBLEMS

Helix Corporation's 1996 and 1995 balance sheets carried the following items:

Problem 18–1
Statement of changes in financial position
(LO 1, 3)

	December 31	
Debits	**1996**	**1995**
Cash	$116,000	$ 78,000
Accounts receivable	62,000	54,000
Merchandise inventory	406,000	356,000
Equipment.	222,000	198,000
Totals	$806,000	$686,000

Credits		
Accumulated amortization, equipment	$104,000	$ 68,000
Accounts payable.	46,000	64,000
Income taxes payable	18,000	16,000
Common shares, no par value	520,000	480,000
Retained earnings.	118,000	58,000
Totals	$806,000	$686,000

An examination of the company's activities during 1996, including the income statement, shows the following:

a.	Sales		$1,328,000
b.	Cost of goods sold	$796,000	
c.	Amortization expense	36,000	
d.	Other operating expenses	334,000	
e.	Income taxes expense	28,000	1,194,000
f.	Net income		$ 134,000

g. Equipment was purchased for $24,000 cash.
h. Eight thousand common shares were issued for cash at $5 per share.
i. The company declared and paid $74,000 of cash dividends during the year.

Required

Prepare an SCFP working paper.

Refer to the facts about Helix Corporation presented in Problem 18–1. Prepare an SCFP directly from your examination of the financial statements and the other data provided. Do not prepare a working paper.

Problem 18–2
SCFP
(LO 2)

Purcell Company's 1996 and 1995 balance sheets included the following items:

Problem 18–3
SCFP working paper
(LO 1, 3)

	December 31	
Debits	**1996**	**1995**
Cash	$ 107,750	$153,250
Accounts receivable	130,000	99,250
Merchandise inventory	547,500	505,000
Prepaid expenses	10,750	12,500
Equipment	319,000	220,000
Totals	$1,115,000	$990,000

Credits	December 31	
	1996	1995
Accumulated amortization, equipment .	$ 69,250	$ 88,000
Accounts payable	176,250	233,250
Short-term notes payable	20,000	12,500
Long-term notes payable	187,500	107,500
Common shares, no par value	402,500	312,500
Retained earnings	259,500	236,250
Totals	$1,115,000	$990,000

Additional information about the 1996 activities of the company follows:

a.	Sales revenue		$992,500
b.	Cost of goods sold	$500,000	
c.	Amortization expense	37,500	
d.	Other expenses	273,000	
e.	Income taxes expense (paid with cash)	24,250	
f.	Loss on sale of equipment	10,250	845,000

The equipment cost $93,750, was amortized by
$56,250, and was sold for $27,250.

g.	Net income	$147,500

h. Equipment that cost $192,750 was purchased by paying cash of
   $50,000 and by signing a long-term note payable for the balance.
i. Borrowed $7,500 by signing a short-term note payable.
j. Paid $62,750 to reduce a long-term note payable.
k. Issued 5,000 common shares for cash at $18 per share.
l. Declared and paid cash dividends of $124,250.

Required

Preparation component:

1. Prepare an SCFP working paper.

Analysis component:

2. Analyze and discuss the information contained in your answer to requirement 1, giv-
    ing special attention to the wisdom of the dividend payment.

Problem 18–4
Statement of changes
in financial position
(LO 2)

Refer to the facts about Purcell Company presented in Problem 18–3. Prepare an SCFP directly from your examination of the financial statements and the other data provided. Do
not prepare a working paper.

Problem 18–5
Analytical essay
(LO 2)

Write a brief essay explaining why, in preparing an SCFP, it is generally better to determine
the changes in cash by analyzing the changes in the noncash accounts rather than by examining the Cash account directly. You should include in your essay an explanation of why the
changes in cash for the period equal the changes in the noncash balance sheet accounts.

The following items might be found on a working paper for an SCFP. Write a brief essay describing where each item appears on a working paper for an SCFP. Also describe the nature of any debits and/or credits that should be entered in the Analysis of Changes columns next to each item, and any balancing entries.

Problem 18–6
Analytical essay
(LO 3)

a.   Accounts receivable.

b.   Depreciation expense.

c.   Payment for purchase of plant assets.

Cemco Corporation's 1996 and 1995 balance sheets carried the following items:

Problem 18–7
SCFP
(LO 1, 3)

	December 31	
Debits	**1996**	**1995**
Cash	$ 50,400	$ 19,200
Accounts receivable	38,400	43,200
Merchandise inventory	100,800	86,400
Equipment	88,800	72,000
Totals	$278,400	$220,800
Credits		
Accumulated amortization, equipment	$ 21,600	$ 14,400
Accounts payable	40,800	24,000
Income taxes payable	4,800	9,600
Common shares	158,400	144,000
Retained earnings	52,800	28,800
Totals	$278,400	$220,800

Additional information about the company's activities during 1996 follows:

a.   Net income was $48,000.

b.   Accounts receivable decreased.

c.   Merchandise inventory increased.

d.   Accounts payable increased.

e.   Income taxes payable decreased.

f.   Amortization expense was $7,200.

g.   Equipment was purchased for $16,800 cash.

h.   Twelve hundred shares were issued for cash at $12 per share.

i.   The company declared and paid $24,000 of cash dividends during the year.

Required

Prepare an SCFP working paper.

Problem 18–8
SCFP working paper
(LO 3)

Refer to the material in Problem 18–7.

Required

Prepare an SCFP directly from your examination of the balance sheets and the additional information provided about the income statement and other transactions of the company. Do not prepare a working paper.

Problem 18–9
Reconciling net income
to cash flows from
operating activities
(LO 1, 2)

Columbus Corporation's 1996 and 1995 balance sheets included the following items:

Debits	December 31 1996	1995
Cash	$146,700	$ 38,700
Accounts receivable	72,000	90,000
Merchandise inventory	283,500	288,000
Prepaid expenses	9,000	10,800
Equipment	330,900	231,000
Totals	$842,100	$658,500

Credits	1996	1995
Accumulated amortization, equipment	$ 54,900	$ 49,200
Accounts payable	193,500	161,100
Short-term notes payable	22,500	13,500
Long-term notes payable	114,000	90,000
Common shares	292,500	225,000
Retained earnings	164,700	119,700
Totals	$842,100	$658,500

Additional information about the 1996 activities of the company follows:

a. Net income was $72,000.
b. Accounts receivable decreased.
c. Merchandise inventory decreased.
d. Prepaid expenses decreased.
e. Accounts payable increased.
f. Amortization expense was $18,900.
g. Equipment that cost $22,200 and was amortized $13,200 was sold for $6,300 cash, which caused a loss of $2,700.
h. Equipment that cost $112,100 was purchased by paying cash of $62,100 and by signing a long-term note payable for the balance.
i. Borrowed $9,000 by signing a short-term note payable.
j. Paid $36,000 to reduce a long-term note payable.
k. Issued 500 common shares for cash at $135 per share.
l. Declared and paid cash dividends of $27,000.

Required

Prepare a schedule that reconciles net income to the net cash provided or used by operating activities.

Problem 18–10
SCFP
(LO 2)

Refer to the information about Columbus Corporation presented in Problem 18–9.

Required

Prepare an SCFP. Do not prepare a working paper. Instead, prepare the statement directly from your examination of the balance sheets and the additional information provided about the income statement and other transactions of the company. Show your supporting calculations.

PROVOCATIVE PROBLEMS

Yaupon, Inc.'s 1996 statement of changes in financial position appeared as follows:

Cash flows from operating activities:

Net income		$111,100
Accounts receivable increase	$(14,700)	
Inventory decrease	47,600	
Prepaid expense increase	(4,600)	
Accounts payable decrease	(16,300)	
Income tax payable increase	4,400	
Amortization expense	12,000	
Loss on disposal of equipment	13,400	
Gain on bond retirement	(7,700)	34,100
Net cash provided by operating activities		$145,200
Cash flows from investing activities:		
Receipt from sale of office equipment	$ 5,100	
Purchase of store equipment	(33,000)	
Net cash used by investing activities		(27,900)
Cash flows from financing activities:		
Payment to retire bonds payable	$(42,300)	
Payment of dividends	(30,000)	
Net cash used by financing activities		(72,300)
Net increase in cash		$ 45,000
Cash balance at beginning of year		45,400
Cash balance at end of year		$ 90,400

Yaupon, Inc.'s beginning and ending balance sheets were as follows:

	December 31	
Debits	**1996**	**1995**
Cash	$ 90,400	$ 45,400
Accounts receivable	114,900	100,200
Merchandise inventory	212,700	260,300
Prepaid expenses	9,000	4,400
Equipment	99,100	108,600
Totals	$526,100	$518,900
Credits		
Accumulated amortization, equipment	$ 18,200	$ 30,200
Accounts payable	58,500	74,800
Income taxes payable	10,900	6,500
Dividends payable	–0–	7,500
Bonds payable	–0–	50,000
Common shares	300,000	300,000
Retained earnings	138,500	49,900
Totals	$526,100	$518,900

An examination of the company's statements and accounts showed:

a.   All sales were made on credit.

b.   All merchandise purchases were on credit.

c.   Accounts Payable balances resulted from merchandise purchases.

d.   Prepaid expenses relate to other operating expenses.

e.   Equipment that cost $42,500 and was amortized $24,000 was sold for cash.

f.   Equipment was purchased for cash.

g.   The change in the balance of Accumulated Amortization resulted from amortization expense and from the sale of equipment.

h.   The change in the balance of Retained Earnings resulted from dividend declarations and net income.

i.   Cash receipts from customers were $772,800.

j.   Cash payments for merchandise inventory amounted to $425,400.

k.   Cash payments for other operating expenses were $169,800.

l.   Income taxes paid were $32,400.

Required

Present Yaupon, Inc.'s income statement for 1996. Show your supporting calculations.

**Provocative Problem
18–2
James Company
(LO 1, 3)**

The following items include the 1996 and 1995 balance sheets and the 1996 income statement of the James Company. Additional information about the company's 1996 transactions is presented after the financial statements.

JAMES COMPANY
Balance Sheet
December 31, 1996 and 1995

	1996		1995	
Assets				
Current assets:				
Cash and cash equivalents	$ 1,000		$ 800	
Accounts receivable	4,500		3,100	
Merchandise inventory	19,000		16,000	
Prepaid expenses	700		600	
Total current assets		$25,200		$20,500
Long-term investments:				
Icahn Corporation common shares		10,000		12,000
Plant assets:				
Land		9,000		4,000
Buildings	$60,000		$60,000	
Less accumulated amortization	38,000	22,000	36,000	24,000
Equipment	$21,000		$16,000	
Less accumulated amortization	6,000	15,000	4,000	12,000
Total assets		$81,200		$72,500

Liabilities

Current liabilities:

Notes payable	$ 5,000	$ 3,500
Accounts payable	9,000	10,000
Other accrued liabilities	5,300	4,200
Interest payable	400	300
Taxes payable	300	500
Total current liabilities	$20,000	$18,500

Long-term liabilities:

Bonds payable, due in 2004	25,000	22,000
Total liabilities	$45,000	$40,500

Shareholders' Equity

Contributed capital:

Common shares	$16,000	$14,000
Retained earnings	20,200	18,000
Total shareholders' equity	36,200	32,000
Total liabilities and shareholders' equity	$81,200	$72,500

JAMES COMPANY
Income Statement
For Year Ended December 31, 1996

Revenues:

Sales	$120,000	
Gain on sale of equity investment	3,000	
Dividend income	500	
Interest income	400	$123,900

Expenses and losses:

Cost of goods sold	$ 50,000	
Other expenses	54,800	
Interest expense	2,000	
Income tax expense	2,500	
Amortization expense, buildings	2,000	
Amortization expense, equipment	4,000	
Loss on sale of equipment	600	
Total expenses and losses		115,900
Net income		$ 8,000

Additional Information

1. Received $5,000 from the sale of Icahn Corporation common shares that originally cost $2,000.

2. Received a cash dividend of $500 from the Icahn Corporation.

3. Received $400 cash from the First National Bank on December 31, 1996, as interest income.

4. Sold old equipment for $1,400. The old equipment originally cost $4,000 and had accumulated amortization of $2,000.

5. Purchased land costing $5,000 on December 31, 1996, in exchange for a note payable. Both principal and interest are due on June 30, 1997.

6. Purchased new equipment for $9,000 cash.

7. Paid $3,500 of notes payable.
8. Sold additional bonds payable at par of $3,000 on January 1, 1996.
9. Issued 1,000 common shares for cash at $2 per share.
10. Declared and paid a $5,800 cash dividend on October 1, 1996.

(The working papers that accompany the text include forms for this problem.)

Required

a. Prepare a working paper for James Company's 1996 SCFP.
b. Prepare the SCFP for 1996.

Provocative Problem 18–3
Financial statement analysis case
(LO 1)

Geac

Look in Appendix I at the end of the book to find Geac Computer Corporation Ltd.'s statement of changes in financial position. Based on your examination of that statement, answer the following questions:

1. During each of the fiscal years 1994 and 1993, was the cash provided by operating activities more or less than the cash paid for dividends?
2. What was the major reason for the difference between net income and cash flow from operating activities?
3. Describe the major cash inflows and outflows during 1994.
4. Describe the major differences in Geac's 1994 cash flows compared to its 1993 cash flows.

ANALYTICAL AND REVIEW PROBLEMS

A & R Problem 18–1

Barrie Company earned $168,000 net income during 1996. Machinery was sold for $232,000, and a $48,000 loss on the sale was recorded. Machinery purchases totaled $660,000 including a July purchase for which a $160,000 promissory note was issued. Bonds were retired at their face value, and the issuance of new common shares produced an infusion of cash. Barrie's comparative balance sheets were as follows (in thousands):

	December 31	
	1996	1995
Cash	$ 208	$ 168
Receivables	392	444
Inventory	648	620
Machinery	2,700	2,520
Accumulated amortization	(380)	(420)
Total assets	$3,568	3,332
Accounts payable	$ 476	$ 572
Notes payable	544	420
Dividends payable	64	40
Bonds payable	456	640
Common shares	1,400	1,120
Retained earnings	628	540
Total liabilities and shareholders' equity	$3,568	$3,332

a. What was Barrie's amortization expense in 1996?

b. What was the amount of cash flow from operations?

c. What was the amount of cash flow from investing activities?

d. What was the amount of the cash dividend declared? Paid?

e. By what amount would you expect the total sources of cash to differ from the total uses of cash?

f. What was the amount of cash flow from financing activities?

The data below refer to the activities of Banff Limited.

A & R Problem 18–2

Required

For each item, identify both the dollar amount and its classification—that is, whether it would appear as a positive or a negative adjustment to net income in the measurement of cash flow from operations or as some other source or use of cash.

1. Declared a $22,000 cash dividend; paid $19,000 during the year.
2. Sold for $120,000 cash land that had cost $95,000 two years earlier.
3. Sold for cash 2,000 shares for $14 a share.
4. Bought machinery for $37,000 in exchange for a note due in eight months.
5. Bought a computer that had a fair value of $140,000 by giving in exchange real estate that had cost $95,000 in an earlier period.
6. Equipment amortization, $56,000.
7. Issued for cash on December 31, 1993, 10-year, 10% $500,000 no-par-value bonds at $24,000 discount.
8. Bought its own shares for $12,500 and immediately canceled them.
9. Paid a lawyer $13,500 for services performed, billed, and recorded correctly in 1995.
10. Reported net income of $86,000 for the year ended December 31, 1996.

Adjustments to derive cash flow from operations:

A & R Problem 18–3

Income Element	Adjust By Adding	Subtracting
1. Changes in current assets:		
a. Increases		
b. Decreases		
2. Changes in current liabilities		
a. Increases		
b. Decreases		
3. Amortization of plant assets		
4. Amortization of intangible assets		
5. Interest expense:		
a. Premium amortized		
b. Discount amortized		
6. Sale of noncurrent asset:		
a. Gain		
b. Loss		

Required

Indicate by an x in the appropriate column whether an item is added or subtracted to derive cash flow from operations.

CONCEPT TESTER

Test your understanding of the concepts introduced in this chapter by completing the following crossword puzzle.

Across Clues

1. Transactions to borrow money or repay debit (1st of 2 words; also see 5 across).

3. The statement that reports the cash inflows and outflows for the period (abbreviation).

4. Transactions that involve the purchase and sale of goods and services in the ordinary course of business (1st of 2 words; also see 5 across).

5. See 1 across, 2 down and 4 across for clues (2nd of 2 words).

Down Clues

2. Transactions that involve the purchase or sale of capital assets (1st of 2 words; also see 5 across).

ANSWERS TO PROGRESS CHECKS

18–1 No. The SCFP reports changes in the sum of cash plus cash equivalents. It does not report transfers between cash and cash equivalents.

18–2 The three categories of cash inflows and outflows are operating activities, investing activities, and financing activities.

18–3
a. Investing
b. Operating
c. Financing
d. Operating
e. Operating
f. Financing

18–4 a

18–5 $74,900 + $4,600 − $11,700 − $1,000 + $3,400 = $70,200

18–6 In the calculation of net income, expenses such as amortization are subtracted. However, these expenses do not require current cash outflows. Therefore, adding these expenses back to net income eliminates noncash items from the net income number, converting it to a cash basis.

18–7 In the process of reconciling net income to net cash provided or used by operating activities, a gain on sale of plant assets is subtracted from net income because a sale of plant assets is not an operating activity; it is an investing activity.

18–8 Investing activities during the year ended April 30, 1994, used net cash of $14,866 ($ in thousands). Cash outflows that contributed to this include net additions to fixed assets for $5,435, additions to capitalized software development of $5,385, and acquisitions of $5,572. The foreign exchange adjustment provided $1,526. The largest source of cash to finance these activities was a common share issue for $2,245.

Financial reports are highly summarized descriptions of complex organizations. Analyzing and understanding the information they present requires a lot of effort; the people who prepare reports need to know what their readers are looking for and how to help them find it.

Analyzing Financial Statements

Karen White and Mark Smith were given an article about a group of hi-tech wizards who have a vision and a desire to create a computer software corporation. In their enthusiasm, they have told a few potential investors that their proposed company was likely to be so successful it would rival the current companies in the industry. Corel corporation was named as an example of what the new venture was likely to become. The investors were quite familiar with the history of Corel and suggested that the wizards might be wise to be a little more moderate in their expectations. When the wizards disagreed, the investors pointed out that Corel was formed in 1985 and by 1994 had revenues of $67.5 million. It ships its products through a network of more than 160 distributors in 60 countries worldwide.

In concluding the conversation, the investors gave the wizards a copy of Corel's 1994 annual report and suggested that they study it carefully to see if it really represented a goal they could achieve. Karen and Mark prepared the following schedule:

COREL CORPORATION
Growth percentages—increases

	Year Ended November 30			
	1994	1993	1992	1991
Sales	56%	56%	29%	79%
Net income	56%	149%	-26%	62%
Earnings per share	40%	105%	-77%	50%
Book value per share	32%	-37%	-9%	37%

LEARNING OBJECTIVES

After studying Chapter 19, you should be able to:

1. Explain the relationship between financial reporting and general purpose financial statements.
2. Describe, prepare, and interpret comparative financial statements and common-size comparative statements.
3. Calculate and explain the interpretation of the ratios, turnovers, and rates of return used to evaluate (a) short-term liquidity, (b) long-term risk and capital structure, and (c) operating efficiency and profitability.
4. State the limitations associated with using financial statement ratios and the sources from which standards for comparison may be obtained.
5. Define or explain the words and phrases listed in the chapter glossary.

Chapter 19 demonstrates how to use the information in financial statements to evaluate the activities and financial status of a business. By explaining how you can relate the numbers in financial statements to each other, this chapter expands your ability to interpret the ratios we described in previous chapters.

FINANCIAL REPORTING

LO 1

Explain the relationship between financial reporting and general purpose financial statements.

Many people receive and analyze financial information about business firms. These people include managers, employees, directors, customers, suppliers, current and potential owners, current and potential lenders, brokers, regulatory authorities, lawyers, economists, labour unions, financial advisors, and financial analysts. Some of these, such as managers and some regulatory agencies, are able to gain access to specialized financial reports that meet their specific interests. However, the others must rely on the **general purpose financial statements** that companies publish periodically. General purpose financial statements include the (1) income statement, (2) balance sheet, (3) statement of changes in shareholders' equity (or statement of retained earnings), (4) statement of changes in financial position, and (5) notes related to the statements.

Financial reporting is intended to provide useful information to investors, creditors, and others for making investment, credit, and similar decisions. The information should help the users assess the amounts, timing, and uncertainty of prospective cash inflows and outflows.

Financial reporting includes communicating through a variety of means in addition to the financial statements. Some examples are reports filed with the Securities Commissions, news releases, and management letters or analyses included in annual reports. For an example, in Appendix I look at the section of **Geac Computer Corporation's** annual report called Management Discussion and Analysis of Financial Condition and Results of Operations.

Progress Check

19-1 Who are the intended users of general purpose financial statements?

19-2 What statements are usually included in the general purpose financial statements published by corporations?

In analyzing financial information, individual items usually are not very revealing. However, important relationships exist between items and groups of items. As a result, financial statement analysis involves identifying and describing relationships between items and groups of items and changes in those items.

You can see changes in financial statement items more clearly when amounts for two or more successive accounting periods are placed side by side in columns on a single statement.[1] Statements prepared in this manner are called **comparative statements.** Each financial statement can be presented in this comparative format.

In its simplest form, a comparative balance sheet consists of the amounts from two or more successive balance sheet dates arranged side by side. However, the usefulness of the statement can be improved by also showing each item's dollar amount of change and percentage change. When this is done, large dollar or percentage changes are more readily apparent. Illustration 19–1 shows this type of comparative balance sheet for Corel Corporation.

A comparative income statement is prepared in the same way. Amounts for two or more successive periods are placed side by side, with dollar and percentage changes in additional columns. Look at Illustration 19–2 to see **Corel Corporation's** comparative income statement.

Calculating Percentage Increases and Decreases

To calculate the percentage increases and decreases on comparative statements, divide the dollar increase or decrease of an item by the amount shown for the item in the base year. If no amount is shown in the base year, or if the base year amount is negative (such as a net loss), a percentage increase or decrease cannot be calculated.

In this text, percentages and ratios typically are rounded to one or two decimal places. However, there is no uniform practice on this matter. In general, percentages should be carried out far enough to be meaningful. They should not be carried out so far that the important relationships become lost in the length of the numbers.

Analyzing and Interpreting Comparative Statements

In analyzing comparative data, study any items that show significant dollar or percentage changes. Then, try to identify the reasons for each change and, if possible, determine whether they are favorable or unfavorable. For example, in Illustration 19–1, the first item, Cash and short-term investments, shows a $28.6 million increase (50.2%). To a large extent, this may be explained by the increase in two other items: the $21.6 million increase in share capital and the $32.5 million increase in Retained earnings.

Note that **Corel's** liabilities increased by $5.4 million. In light of this, the $28.6 million increase in Cash and short-term investments might appear to be an excessive investment in highly liquid assets that usually earn a low return. However, the

[1] *CICA Handbook,* section 1500, "General Standards of Financial Statement Presentation," par. .09.

COMPARATIVE STATEMENTS

LO 2

Describe, prepare, and interpret comparative financial statements and common-size comparative statements.

Illustration 19–1

			Amount of	Percent of
	November 30		**Increase or**	**Increase or**
	1994	**1993**	**(Decrease)**	**(Decrease)**
	(in thousands)		**in 1994**	**in 1994**

COREL CORPORATION
Consolidated Balance Sheets
November 30, 1994, and November 30, 1993

	1994	1993	Amount of Increase or (Decrease) in 1994	Percent of Increase or (Decrease) in 1994
Assets				
Current assets:				
Cash and short-term investments	$ 85,618	$ 57,000	$28,618	50.2
Accounts receivable				
Trade	50,586	36,327	14,259	39.3
Other	2,264	2,185	79	3.6
Inventory	13,417	7,361	6,056	82.3
Prepaid expenses	1,348	812	536	66.0
Total current assets	153,233	103,685	49,548	47.8
Capital assets	38,189	28,605	9,584	33.5
Total assets	$191,422	$132,290	$59,132	44.7
Liabilities and shareholders' equity				
Current liabilities:				
Accounts payable	$ 8,487	$ 5,391	$ 3,096	57.4
Accrued liabilities	10,722	6,073	4,649	76.6
Income taxes payable	4,930	7,400	(2,470)	(33.4)
Total current liabilities	24,139	18,864	5,275	28.0
Deferred income taxes	2,330	2,192	$ 138	6.3
Total liabilities	26,469	21,056	5,413	25.7
Shareholders' equity:				
Common share capital	89,380	67,792	21,588	31.8
Contributed surplus	352	352	0	0.0
Foreign currency adjustment		372	(372)	(100.0)
Retained earnings	75,221	42,718	32,503	76.1
Total shareholders' equity	164,953	111,234	53,719	48.3
Total liabilities and				
shareholders' equity	$191,422	$132,290	$59,132	44.7

company's very strong and liquid financial position indicates an outstanding ability to respond to new opportunities such as the acquisition of other companies.

Now look at the comparative income statement for Corel in Illustration 19–2. Corel's rapid growth is reflected by its 56.4% increase in sales. In fact, we should point out that the growth in 1994 continued a very strong trend established in prior years. (Later, we present data showing that sales in 1994 were 562% of sales in 1990.) Perhaps the most fundamental reason for this is the company's commitment to research and development. Note that research and development expenses were $10.9 million in 1994, up $4.6 million from 1993.

Illustration 19–2

COREL CORPORATION
Consolidated Statements of Income
For Years Ended November 30, 1994, and 1993

	Years Ended November 30		Amount of Increase or (Decrease) in 1994	Percent of Increase or (Decrease) in 1994
	1994	1993		
	(in thousands)			
Sales	$164,313	$105,027	$59,286	56.4
Cost of sales	35,940	24,310	11,630	47.8
Gross profit	128,373	80,717	47,656	59.0
Expenses:				
Advertising	34,390	20,579	13,811	67.1
Selling, general and administrative	30,833	18,005	12,828	71.2
Research and development	10,888	6,256	4,632	74.0
Depreciation and amortization ...	6,137	4,079	2,058	50.5
Loss (gain) on foreign exchange ..	1,546	(480)	2,026	422.1
Total expenses	83,794	48,439	35,355	73.0
Income from continuing operations	44,579	32,278	12,301	38.1
Interest income	2,861	2,389	472	19.8
Income from continuing operations before income taxes	47,440	34,667	12,773	36.8
Income taxes	14,937	13,814	1,123	8.1
Net income	$ 32,503	$ 20,853	$11,650	55.9

All of the income statement items (except foreign exchange) reflect the company's rapid growth. The increases ranged from 67.1 to 19.8%. Especially note the large $13.8 million or 67.1% increase in Advertising. This suggests the company's leadership and strong response to competition in the software industry. Although the dollar increase in Interest income was only $.5 million, this amounted to a 19.8% increase. This is consistent with the increase in Cash and short-term investments reported on the balance sheet.

Trend Percentages

Trend percentages (also known as *index numbers*) can be used to describe changes that have occurred from one period to the next. They are also used to compare data that cover a number of years. To calculate trend percentages:

1. Select a base year and assign each item on the base year statement a weight of 100%.

2. Express each item from the statements for the other years as a percentage of its base year amount. To determine these percentages, divide the amounts in the nonbase years by the amount of the item in the base year.

For example, consider the following data for Corel Corporation:

	1994	1993	1992	1991	1990
Sales	$164,313	$105,027	$67,515	$52,242	$29,230
Cost of sales	35,940	24,310	19,459	7,735	6,015
Gross profit	$128,373	$ 80,717	$48,056	$44,507	$23,215

Using 1990 as the base year, we calculate the trend percentages for each year by dividing the dollar amounts in each year by the 1990 dollar amounts. When the percentages are calculated, the trends for these items appear as follows:

	1994	1993	1992	1991	1990
Sales	562.1%	359.3%	231.0%	178.7%	100.0%
Cost of sales	597.5	404.2	323.5	128.6	100.0
Gross profit	553.0	347.7	207.0	191.7	100.0

Illustration 19–3 presents the same data in a graph. A graph can help you identify trends and detect changes in their strength or direction. For example, note that the gross profit line was bending upward from 1990 to 1991 but was essentially flat from 1991 to 1992. The gross profit increased at a lower rate from 1991 to 1992 but then parallels the sales line from 1992 to 1994.

A graph also may help you identify and understand the relationships between items. For example, the graph in Illustration 19–3 shows that through 1993, cost of sales increased at a rate that was somewhat more than the increase in sales. Further, the differing trends in these two items had a clear effect on the percentage changes in gross profit. That is, gross profit increased each year at a somewhat slower rate than sales.

The analysis of financial statement items also may include the relationships between items on different financial statements. For example, note the following comparison of Corel's total assets and sales:

	1994	1990	1994 Amount as a Percentage of 1990
Sales	$164.3	$29.2	562.7%
Total assets (fiscal year-end)	191.4	41.9	456.8

The rate of increase in total assets was not quite as large as the increase in sales. Was this change favourable? We cannot say for sure. It might suggest that the company is no longer able to use its assets as efficiently as in earlier years. On the other hand, it might mean that the company can expect slower growth in future years. Financial statement analysis often leads the analyst to ask questions, without providing one clear answer.

Illustration 19-3 Trend Lines Showing Percentage Changes in Net Revenues, Cost of Revenues, and Gross Profit

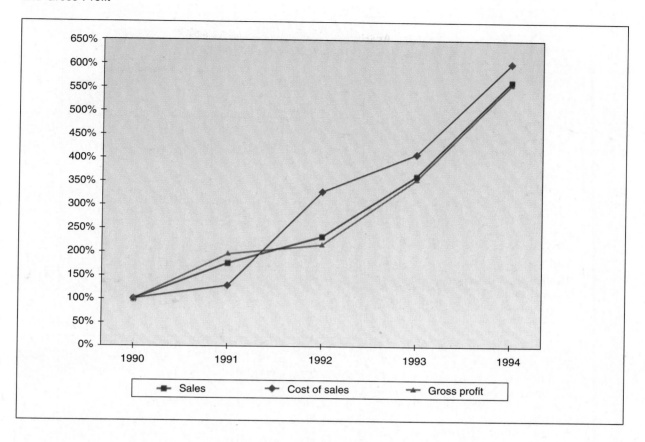

Common-Size Comparative Statements

Although the comparative statements illustrated so far show how each item has changed over time, they do not emphasize the relative importance of each item. Changes in the relative importance of each financial statement item are shown more clearly by **common-size comparative statements.**

In common-size statements, each item is expressed as a percentage of a *base amount*. For a common-size balance sheet, the base amount is usually the amount of total assets. This total is assigned a value of 100%. (Of course, the total amount of liabilities plus owners' equity also equals 100%.) Then, each asset, liability, and owners' equity item is shown as a percentage of total assets (or total liabilities plus owners' equity). If you present a company's successive balance sheets in this way, changes in the mixture of the assets or liabilities and equity are more readily apparent.

For example, look at the common-size comparative balance sheet for Corel in Illustration 19–4. Note that Cash and short-term investments amounted to 43.1% of total assets at the end of the 1993 fiscal year. By comparison, they were 44.7% of total assets at the end of 1994.

Illustration 19–4

COREL CORPORATION **Common-Size Comparative Balance Sheet** **November 30, 1994, and November 30, 1993**				
	November 30		**Common-Size Percentages**	
	1994	**1993**	**1994**	**1993**
	(in thousands)			
Assets				
Current assets:				
Cash and short-term investments	$ 85,618	$57,000	44.7	43.1
Accounts receivable				
Trade	50,586	36,327	26.4	27.4
Other	2,264	2,185	1.2	1.7
Inventory	13,417	7,361	7.0	5.6
Prepaid expenses	1,348	812	0.7	0.6
Total current assets	153,233	103,685	80.0	78.4
Capital assets	38,189	28,605	20.0	21.6
Total assets	$191,422	$132,290	100.0	100.0
Liabilities and shareholders' equity				
Current liabilities:				
Accounts payable	$8,487	$5,391	4.4	4.1
Accrued liabilities	10,722	6,073	5.6	4.6
Income taxes payable	4,930	7,400	2.6	5.6
Total current liabilities	24,139	18,864	12.6	14.3
Deferred income taxes	2,330	2,192	1.2	1.6
Total liabilities	26,469	21,056	13.8	15.9
Shareholders' equity				
Common share capital	89,380	67,792	46.7	51.2
Contributed surplus	352	352	0.2	0.3
Foreign currency adjustment		372		0.3
Retained earnings	75,221	42,718	39.3	32.3
Total shareholders' equity	164,953	111,234	86.2	84.1
Total liabilities and shareholders' equity	$191,422	$132,290	100.0	100.0

In producing a common-size income statement, the amount of net sales is usually the base amount and is assigned a value of 100%. Then, each statement item appears as a percentage of net sales. If you think of the 100% sales amount as representing one sales dollar, the remaining items show how each sales dollar was distributed among costs, expenses, and profit. For example, the comparative income statement in Illustration 19–5 shows that for each dollar of sales during 1994, research and development expenses amounted to 6.6 cents. In 1993, research and development consumed 6.0 cents of each sales dollar.

Common-size percentages help the analyst see any potentially important changes in a company's expenses. For Corel, the relative size of each expense changed very little from 1993 to 1994. A common problem with the percentages is that the totals do not foot because of rounding. However, these slight errors, which are 0.1%, do not usually cause serious difficulties.

Illustration 19–5

COREL CORPORATION
Common-Size Comparative Income Statement
For Years Ended November 30, 1994 and 1993

	Years Ended November 30		Common-Size Percentage	
	1994	1993	1994	1993
	(in thousands)			
Sales	$164,313	$105,027	100.0	100.0
Cost of sales	35,940	24,310	21.9	23.1
Gross profit	128,373	80,717	78.1	76.9
Expenses:				
Advertising	34,390	20,579	20.9	19.6
Selling, general and administrative	30,833	18,005	18.8	17.1
Research and development	10,888	6,256	6.6	6.0
Depreciation and amortization	6,137	4,079	3.7	3.9
Loss (gain) on foreign exchange	1,546	(480)	0.9	(0.5)
Total expenses	83,794	48,439	51.0	46.1
Income from continuing operations	44,579	32,278	27.1	30.7
Interest income	2,861	2,389	1.7	2.3
Income from continuing operations before income taxes	47,440	34,667	28.9	33.0
Income taxes	14,937	13,814	9.1	13.2
Net income	$ 32,503	$ 20,853	19.8	19.9
Earnings per share	$ 0.63	$ 0.45		
Weighted-average shares outstanding	51,768	46,146		

Many corporate annual reports include graphic presentations such as those in Illustration 19–6 from Corel's 1994 Annual Report. The pie chart on the left side of the illustration shows the sales generated by each of the company's geographic regions in 1993. The pie chart on the right shows the revenues by sales channel. In that chart, OEM refers to original equipment manufacturers. In the annual report, the data for these charts did not appear in the financial statements. Instead, they were included as part of the discussion and analysis by management.

Progress Check

19–3 On common-size comparative statements, which of the following is true? *(a)* Each item is expressed as a percentage of a base amount. *(b)* Total assets is assigned a value of 100%. *(c)* Amounts from two or more successive periods are placed side by side. *(d)* All of the above are true.

19–4 What is the difference between the percentages shown on a comparative income statement and those shown on a common-size comparative income statement?

19–5 Trend percentages *(a)* are shown on the comparative income statement and balance sheet; *(b)* are shown on common-size comparative statements; or *(c)* are also known as index numbers.

Illustration 19–6   Pie-Chart Presentations, Corel Corporation

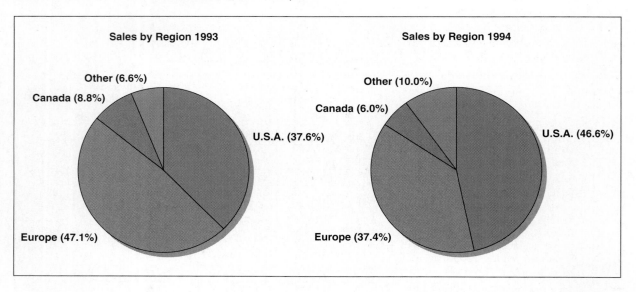

ANALYSIS OF SHORT-TERM LIQUIDITY

LO 3

Calculate and explain the interpretation of the ratios, turnovers, and rates of return used to evaluate *(a)* short-term liquidity, *(b)* long-term risk and capital structure, and *(c)* operating efficiency and profitability.

The amount of current assets less current liabilities is called the **working capital** or *net working capital* of a business. A business must maintain an adequate amount of working capital to meet current debts, carry sufficient inventories, and take advantage of cash discounts. Indeed, a business that runs out of working capital cannot meet its current obligations or continue operations.

Current Ratio

When evaluating the working capital of a business, you must look beyond the dollar amount of current assets less current liabilities. Also consider the relationship between the amounts of current assets and current liabilities. Recall from Chapter 3 that the *current ratio* describes a company's ability to pay its short-term obligations. The current ratio relates current assets to current liabilities, as follows:

$$\text{Current ratio} = \frac{\text{Current assets}}{\text{Current liabilities}}$$

For example, using the information in Illustration 19–1, Corel's working capital positions and current ratios at the end of its 1994 and 1993 years were:

	November 30, 1994	November 30, 1993
(In millions)		
Current assets	$153,233	$103,685
Current liabilities	24,139	18,864
Working capital	$129,094	$84,821
Current ratio:		
$153,233/$24,139 . .	6.35 to 1	
$103,685/$18,864 . .		5.50 to 1

A high current ratio generally indicates a strong position because a high ratio suggests the company is capable of meeting its current obligations. On the other hand, a company might have a current ratio that is too high. This condition means that the company has invested too much in current assets compared to its needs. Normally, current assets do not generate very much additional revenue. Therefore, if a company invests too much in current assets, the investment is not being used efficiently.

Years ago, bankers and other creditors often used a current ratio of 2 to 1 as a rule of thumb in evaluating the debt-paying ability of a credit-seeking company. A company with a 2 to 1 current ratio was generally thought to be a good credit risk in the short run. However, most lenders realize that the 2 to 1 rule of thumb is not a good test of debt-paying ability. Whether a company's current ratio is good or bad depends on at least three factors:

1. The nature of the company's business.
2. The composition of its current assets.
3. The turnover rate for some of its current assets.

Whether a company's current ratio is adequate depends on the nature of its business. A service company that has no inventories other than supplies and that grants little or no credit may be able to operate on a current ratio of less than 1 to 1 if its sales generate enough cash to pay its current liabilities on time. On the other hand, a company that sells high-fashion clothing or furniture may occasionally misjudge customer demand. If this happens, the company's inventory may not generate as much cash as expected. A company that faces risks like these may need a current ratio of much more than 2 to 1 to protect its liquidity.

Therefore, when you study the adequacy of working capital, consider the type of business under review. Before you decide that a company's current ratio is too low or too high, compare the company's current ratio with ratios of other successful companies in the same industry. Another important source of insight is to observe how the ratio has changed over time.

Keep in mind that the current ratio can be affected by a company's choice of an inventory flow assumption. For example, a company that uses LIFO tends to report a smaller amount of current assets than if it uses FIFO. Therefore, consider the underlying factors before deciding that a given current ratio is acceptable.

Also consider the composition of a company's current assets when you evaluate its working capital position. Cash and short-term investments are more liquid than accounts and notes receivable. And, short-term receivables normally are more liquid than merchandise inventory. Cash can be used to pay current debts at once. But, accounts receivable and merchandise inventory must be converted into cash before payments can be made. Therefore, an excessive amount of receivables and inventory could weaken the company's ability to pay its current liabilities.

One way to take the composition of current assets into account is to evaluate the acid-test ratio. We discuss this next; then, we examine the turnover rates for receivables and inventories.

Acid-Test Ratio

Recall from Chapter 5 that an easily calculated check on current asset composition is the *acid-test ratio,* also called the *quick ratio.* Quick assets are cash, short-term investments, accounts receivable, and notes receivable. These are the most liquid types of current assets. Calculate the ratio as follows:

$$\text{Acid-test ratio} = \frac{\text{Quick assets}}{\text{Current liabilities}}$$

Using the information in Illustration 19–1, we calculate Corel's acid-test ratios as follows:

(In millions)	November 30, 1994	November 30, 1993
Cash and short-term investments	$ 85,618	$ 57,000
Accounts receivable, trade	50,586	36,327
Total quick assets	$136,102	$ 93,327
Current liabilities	$ 24,139	$ 18,864
Acid-test ratio:		
$136,102/$24,139	5.64 to 1	
$93,327/$18,864		4.95 to 1

A traditional rule of thumb for an acceptable acid-test ratio is 1 to 1. However, as is true for all financial ratios, you should be skeptical about rules of thumb. The working capital requirements of a company are also affected by how frequently the company converts its current assets into cash. Thus, a careful analysis of a company's short-term liquidity should include additional analyses of its receivables and inventories.

Accounts Receivable Turnover

One way to measure how frequently a company converts its receivables into cash is to calculate the accounts receivable turnover. As you learned in Chapter 8, this is calculated as follows:

$$\text{Accounts receivable turnover} = \frac{\text{Net sales}}{\text{Average accounts receivable}}$$

Although this ratio is widely known as accounts receivable turnover, all short-term receivables from customers normally are included in the denominator. Thus, if a company has short-term notes receivable, those balances should be included with the accounts receivable. In the numerator, the calculation would be more precise if credit sales were used. Usually, however, net sales is used because information about credit sales is not available.

Applying the formula to Corel's 1994 fiscal year results, the company's accounts receivable turnover was

$$\frac{\$164,313}{(\$50,586 + \$36,327)/2} = 3.78 \text{ times}$$

If accounts receivable are collected quickly, the accounts receivable turnover is high. In general, this is favorable because it means that the company does not have to commit large amounts of capital to accounts receivable. However, an accounts receivable turnover may be too high. This might occur when credit terms are so restrictive they negatively affect sales volume.

Sometimes, the ending accounts receivable balance can substitute for the average balance in calculating accounts receivable turnover. This is acceptable if the effect is not significant. Also, some analysts prefer using gross accounts receivable before subtracting the allowance for doubtful accounts. However, balance sheets may report only the net amount of accounts receivable.

Days' Sales Uncollected

Accounts receivable turnover is only one way to measure how frequently a company collects its accounts. Another method is to calculate the days' sales uncollected, which we defined in Chapter 7 as

$$\text{Days' sales uncollected} = \frac{\text{Accounts receivable}}{\text{Net sales}} \times 365$$

Although this formula takes the usual approach of placing accounts receivable in the numerator, short-term notes receivable from customers should be included. To illustrate, we refer to the information about Corel in Illustrations 19–1 and 19–2. The days' sales uncollected on November 30, 1994, was

$$\frac{\$50,586}{\$164,313} \times 365 = 112.4 \text{ days}$$

Days' sales uncollected has more meaning if you know the credit terms. A rule of thumb is that days' sales uncollected: *(a)* should not exceed one and one-third times the days in the credit period, if discounts are not offered; *(b)* should not exceed one and one-third times the days in its discount period, if discounts are offered.

Turnover of Merchandise Inventory

Working capital requirements are also affected by how long a company holds merchandise inventory before selling it. This effect can be measured by calculating merchandise turnover, which we defined in Chapter 9 as:

$$\text{Merchandise turnover} = \frac{\text{Cost of goods sold}}{\text{Average merchandise inventory}}$$

Using the cost of revenues and inventories information in Illustrations 19–1 and 19–2, we calculate Corel's merchandise turnover during 1994 as follows (cost of goods sold is called *cost of sales* on Corel's income statement):

$$\frac{\$35,940}{(\$13,417 + \$7,361)/2} = 3.46 \text{ times}$$

In this calculation, the average inventory was estimated by averaging the beginning and the ending inventories for 1994. In case the beginning and ending inventories do not represent the amount normally on hand, an average of the quarterly inventories may be used, if that is available.

From a working capital point of view, a company with a high turnover requires a smaller investment in inventory than one that produces the same sales with a low turnover. On the other hand, the merchandise turnover may be too high if a company keeps such a small inventory that sales volume is restricted.

Days' Stock on Hand

Recall from Chapter 9 that days' stock on hand is another means of evaluating the liquidity of a company's inventory. It relates to inventory in a similar fashion as day's sales uncollected relates to receivables. The calculation is

$$\text{Days' stock on hand} = \frac{\text{Ending inventory}}{\text{Cost of goods sold}} \times 365$$

Applying the formula to Corel's 1994 information, we calculate days' stock on hand as:

$$\frac{\$13,417}{\$35,940} \times 365 = 136.3 \text{ days}$$

Assuming the particular products in inventory are those customers demand, the formula estimates that the inventory will be converted into receivables (or cash) in 136.3 days. If all of Corel's sales were credit sales, the conversion of inventory to receivables in 136.3 days plus the conversion of receivables to cash in 112.4 days would suggest that the inventory would be converted into cash in about 249 days $(136.3 + 112.4 = 248.7)$.

Progress Check

19–6   The following is taken from the December 31, 1996, balance sheet of Paff Company: cash, $820,000; accounts receivable, $240,000; inventories, $470,000; plant and equipment, $910,000; accounts payable, $350,000; and income taxes payable, $180,000. Calculate the [a] current ratio and [b] acid-test ratio.

19–7   On December 31, 1995, Paff Company (see 19–6) had accounts receivable of $290,000 and inventories of $530,000. Also, during 1996, net sales amounted to $2,500,000 and cost of goods sold was $750,000. Calculate the [a] accounts receivable turnover, [b] days' sales uncollected, [c] merchandise turnover, and [d] days' stock on hand.

ANALYSIS OF LONG-TERM RISK AND CAPITAL STRUCTURE

LO 3

Calculate and explain the interpretation of the ratios, turnovers, and rates of return used to evaluate (*a*) short-term liquidity, (*b*) long-term risk and capital structure, and (*c*) operating efficiency and profitability.

An analysis of working capital evaluates the short-term liquidity of the company. However, analysts are also interested in a company's ability to meet its obligations and provide security to its creditors over the long run. Indicators of this ability include *debt* and *equity* ratios, the relationship between *pledged assets* and *secured liabilities,* and the company's capacity to earn *sufficient income to pay its fixed interest charges.*

Debt and Equity Ratios

Financial analysts are always interested in the portion of a company's assets contributed by its owners and the portion contributed by creditors. This relationship is described by the debt ratio you learned about in Chapter 2. Recall that the debt ratio expresses total liabilities as a percentage of total assets. The **equity ratio** provides complementary information by expressing total shareholders' equity as a percentage of total assets.

We calculate the debt and equity ratios of Corel Corporation as follows:

	1994	1993
a. Total liabilities	$ 26,469	$ 21,056
b. Total shareholders' equity	164,953	111,234
c. Total liabilities and shareholders' equity	$191,422	$132,290
Percentages provided by creditors: (a/c)	13.8%	15.9%
Percentages provided by shareholders: (b/c)	86.2%	84.1%

Corel's financial statements reflect very little debt compared to most companies. It has only one long-term liability and, at the end of the 1994 year, its current liabilities provide only 13.8% of the total assets. In general, a company is less risky if it has only a small amount of debt in its capital structure. The larger the portion provided by shareholders, the more losses can be absorbed by shareholders before the remaining assets become inadequate to satisfy the claims of creditors.

From the shareholders' point of view, however, including debt in the capital structure of a company may be desirable, so long as the risk is not too great. If a business can earn a return on borrowed capital that is higher than the cost of borrowing, the difference represents increased income to shareholders. Because debt can have the effect of increasing the return to shareholders, the inclusion of debt is sometimes described as financial leverage. Companies are said to be highly leveraged if a large portion of their assets is financed by debt.

Pledged Assets to Secured Liabilities

In Chapter 17, we explained how to use the ratio of pledged assets to secured liabilities to evaluate the risk of nonpayment faced by secured creditors. Recall that the ratio also may provide information of interest to unsecured creditors. The ratio is calculated as follows:

$$\text{Pledged assets to secured liabilities} = \frac{\text{Book value of pledged assets}}{\text{Secured liabilities}}$$

Regardless of how helpful this ratio might be in evaluating the risk faced by creditors, the information needed to calculate the ratio is seldom presented in published financial statements. Thus, it is used primarily by persons who have the ability to obtain the information directly from the company managers.

The usual rule-of-thumb minimum value for this ratio is 2 to 1. However, the ratio needs careful interpretation because it is based on the book value of the pledged assets. As you know, book values are not intended to reflect the amount that would be received for the assets in a liquidation sale. Also, the long-term earning ability of the company with pledged assets may be more important than the value of the pledged assets. Creditors prefer that a debtor be able to pay with cash generated by operating activities rather than with cash obtained by liquidating assets.

Times Fixed Interest Charges Earned

As you learned in Chapter 13, the times fixed interest charges earned ratio is often calculated to describe the security of the return offered to creditors. The amount of income before the deduction of interest charges and income taxes is the amount available to pay the interest charges. Calculate the ratio as follows:

$$\text{Times fixed interest charges earned} = \frac{\text{Income before interest and income taxes}}{\text{Interest expense}}$$

The larger this ratio, the greater the security for the lenders. A rule of thumb for this statistic is that creditors are reasonably safe if the company earns its fixed interest charges two or more times each year. Look in Illustration 19–2 and observe that Corel did not report interest expense as a separate item. Apparently interest expense is not material; probably it is offset against interest income. Also recall from Illustration 19–1 that Corel did not have any long-term debt. Furthermore, few if any of the company's current liabilities would be likely to generate interest expense. As a result, we are not able to calculate a times fixed interest charges earned ratio for Corel. Yet, we should again recognize that there appears to be little risk for Corel's creditors.

ANALYSIS OF OPERATING EFFICIENCY AND PROFITABILITY

Financial analysts are especially interested in the ability of a company to use its assets efficiently to produce profits for its owners and thus provide cash flows to them. Several ratios are available to help you evaluate operating efficiency and profitability.

Profit Margin

The operating efficiency of a company can be expressed in two components. The first is the company's *profit margin*. As you learned in Chapter 4, this ratio describes a company's ability to earn a net income from sales. It is measured by expressing net income as a percentage of net sales. For example, we can use the information in Illustration 19–2 to calculate **Corel's** 1994 profit margin as follows:

$$\text{Profit margin} = \frac{\text{Net income}}{\text{Revenues}} = \frac{\$32,503}{\$164,313} = 19.8\%$$

To evaluate the profit margin of a company, consider the nature of the industry in which the company operates. For example, a publishing company might be expected to have a profit margin between 10 and 15%, while a retail supermarket might have a normal profit margin of 1 or 2%. Low margin businesses rely on high sales volume to be successful.

Total Asset Turnover

The second component of operating efficiency is *total asset turnover,* which describes the ability of the company to use its assets to generate sales. In Chapter 11, you learned to calculate this ratio as follows:

$$\text{Total asset turnover} = \frac{\text{Net sales}}{\text{Average total assets}}$$

In calculating Corel's total asset turnover for 1994, we follow the usual practice of averaging the total assets at the beginning and the end of the year. Taking the information from Illustrations 19–1 and 19–2, the calculation is:

$$\frac{\$164,313}{(\$191,422 + \$132,290)/2} = 1.015 \text{ times*}$$

*Carried to three decimal places to avoid later rounding error.

Both profit margin and total asset turnover describe the two basic components of operating efficiency. However, they also evaluate management performance because the management of a company is fundamentally responsible for its operating efficiency.

Return on Total Assets

Because operating efficiency has two basic components (profit margin and total asset turnover), analysts frequently calculate a summary measure of these components. This summary measure is the *return on total assets* that we discussed in Chapter 12. Recall that the calculation is:

$$\text{Return on total assets} = \frac{\text{Net income}}{\text{Average total assets}}$$

Applying this to Corel's 1994 year, we calculate return on total assets as

$$\frac{\$32,503}{(\$191,422 + \$132,290)/2} = 20.1\%$$

Corel's 20.1% return on total assets appears very favourable compared to most businesses. However, you should make comparisons with competing companies and alternative investment opportunities before reaching a final conclusion. Also, you should evaluate the trend in the rates of return earned by the company in recent years.

Earlier, we said that the return on total assets summarizes the two components of operating efficiency—profit margin and total asset turnover. The following calculation shows the relationship between these three measures. Notice that both profit margin and total asset turnover contribute to overall operating efficiency, as measured by return on total assets.

Profit margin	$\times$	Total asset turnover	$=$	Return on total assets
$\dfrac{\text{Net income}}{\text{Net sales}}$	$\times$	$\dfrac{\text{Net sales}}{\text{Average total assets}}$	$=$	$\dfrac{\text{Net income}}{\text{Average total assets}}$
For Corel Corporation:				
19.8%	$\times$	1.015	$=$	20.1%

Return on Common Shareholders' Equity

Perhaps the most important reason for operating a business is to earn a net income for its owners. The *return on common shareholders' equity* measures the success of a business in reaching this goal. In Chapter 1, we simplified this calculation by basing it on the beginning balance of owners' equity. However, many companies have frequent transactions that involve issuing and perhaps repurchasing stock during each year. Thus, you should allow for these events by calculating the return based on the average shareholders' equity, as follows:

$$\text{Return on common shareholders' equity} = \frac{\text{Net income} - \text{Preferred dividends}}{\text{Average common shareholders' equity}}$$

Recall from Illustration 19–1 that Corel did not have any preferred shares outstanding. As a result, we determine Corel's 1994 return as follows:

$$\frac{\$32,503}{(\$164,953 + \$111,234)/2} = 23.5\%$$

When preferred shares are outstanding, the denominator in the calculation should be the book value of the common shares. In the numerator, the dividends on cumulative preferred shares must be subtracted whether they were declared or are in arrears. If the preferred is not cumulative, the dividends are subtracted only if declared.

Price Earnings Ratio

Don't Do -

Recall from Chapter 16 that the price earnings ratio is calculated as follows:

$$\text{Price earnings ratio} = \frac{\text{Market price per share}}{\text{Earnings per share}}$$

Sometimes, the predicted earnings per share for the next period is used in the denominator of the calculation. Other times, the reported earnings per share for the most recent period is used. In either case, the ratio is an indicator of the future growth of and risk related to the company's earnings as perceived by investors who establish the market price of the shares.

During the last three months of Corel's 1994 year, the market price of its common shares ranged from a low of $14.50 to a high of $23.25. Using the $0.63 earnings per share that was reported after the year-end, the price earnings ratios for the low and the high were

$$\text{Low: } \frac{\$14.50}{\$0.63} = 23.0 \qquad \text{High: } \frac{\$23.25}{\$0.63} = 36.9$$

In its 1994 annual report, Corel's management reported that it did not expect the 1995 revenue growth rates to be as high as those for 1994. Management also indicated that operating expenses as a percentage of revenues might increase. Nevertheless, the price earnings ratios are much higher than for most companies. No doubt, Corel's high ratios reflect the expectation of investors that the company would continue to grow at a much higher rate than most companies.

Dividend Yield

Don't

As you learned in Chapter 15, *dividend yield* is a statistic used to compare the dividend-paying performance of different investment alternatives. The formula is

$$\text{Dividend yield} = \frac{\text{Annual dividends per share}}{\text{Market price per share}}$$

Some companies may not declare dividends because they need the cash in the business. For example, Corel's 1994 annual report stated that the company had not declared any dividends.

Progress Check

19-8 Which ratio describes the security of the return offered to creditors? *(a)* Debt ratio; *(b)* Equity ratio; *(c)* Times fixed interest charges earned; *(d)* Pledged assets to secured liabilities.

19-9 Which ratio measures the success of a business in earning net income for its owners? *(a)* Profit margin; *(b)* Return on common shareholders' equity; *(c)* Price earnings ratio; *(d)* Dividend yield.

19-10 If BK Company has net sales of $8,500,000, net income of $945,000, and total asset turnover of 1.8 times, what is BK's return on total assets?

Ratio will be given on exa

To evaluate short-term liquidity, use these ratios:

$$\text{Current ratio} = \frac{\text{Current assets}}{\text{Current liabilities}}$$

$$\text{Acid-test ratio} = \frac{\text{Cash} + \text{Short-term investments} + \text{Current receivables}}{\text{Current liabilities}}$$

$$\text{Accounts receivable turnover} = \frac{\text{Net sales}}{\text{Average accounts receivable}}$$

$$\text{Days' sales uncollected} = \frac{\text{Accounts receivable}}{\text{Net sales}} \times 365$$

$$\text{Merchandise turnover} = \frac{\text{Cost of goods sold}}{\text{Average merchandise inventory}}$$

$$\text{Days' stock on hand} = \frac{\text{Ending inventory}}{\text{Cost of goods sold}} \times 365$$

To evaluate long-term risk and capital structure, use these ratios:

$$\text{Debt ratio} = \frac{\text{Total liabilities}}{\text{Total assets}}$$

$$\text{Equity ratio} = \frac{\text{Total shareholders' equity}}{\text{Total assets}}$$

$$\text{Pledged assets to secured liabilities} = \frac{\text{Book value of pledged assets}}{\text{Secured liabilities}}$$

$$\text{Times fixed interest charges earned} = \frac{\text{Income before interest and taxes}}{\text{Interest expense}}$$

To evaluate operating efficiency and profitability, use these ratios:

$$\text{Profit margin} = \frac{\text{Net income}}{\text{Net sales}}$$

$$\text{Total asset turnover} = \frac{\text{Net sales}}{\text{Average total assets}}$$

$$\text{Return on total assets} = \frac{\text{Net income}}{\text{Average total assets}}$$

REVIEW OF FINANCIAL STATEMENT RATIOS AND STATISTICS FOR ANALYSIS

$$\text{Return on common} \atop \text{shareholders' equity} = \frac{\text{Net income} - \text{Preferred dividends}}{\text{Average common shareholders' equity}}$$

$$\text{Price earnings ratio} = \frac{\text{Market price per common share}}{\text{Earnings per share}}$$

$$\text{Dividend yield} = \frac{\text{Annual dividends per share}}{\text{Market price per share}}$$

STANDARDS OF COMPARISON

LO 4

State the limitations associated with using financial statement ratios and the sources from which standards for comparison may be obtained.

After computing ratios and turnovers in the process of analyzing financial statements, you have to decide whether the calculated amounts suggest good, bad, or merely average performance by the company. To make these judgments, you must have some bases for comparison. The following are possibilities:

1. An experienced analyst may compare the ratios and turnovers of the company under review with *subjective* standards acquired from past experiences.
2. For purposes of comparison, an analyst may calculate the ratios and turnovers of a selected group of competing companies in the same *industry*.
3. *Published* ratios and turnovers (such as those provided by Dun & Bradstreet) may be used for comparison.
4. Some local and national trade associations gather data from their members and publish *standard* or *average* ratios for their trade or industry. When available, these data can give the analyst a useful basis for comparison.
5. *Rule-of-thumb* standards can be used as a basis for comparison.

Of these five standards, the ratios and turnovers of a selected group of competing companies normally are the best bases for comparison. Rule-of-thumb standards should be applied with great care and then only if they seem reasonable in light of past experience and the industry's norms.

Progress Check

19-11   Which of the following would not be used as a basis for comparison when analyzing ratios and turnovers?
   a. Companies in different industries.
   b. Subjective standards from past experience.
   c. Rule-of-thumb standards.
   d. Averages within a trade or industry.

19-12   Which of the typical bases of comparison is usually best?

SUMMARY OF THE CHAPTER IN TERMS OF LEARNING OBJECTIVES

LO 1. Explain the relationship between financial reporting and general purpose financial statements. Financial reporting is intended to provide information that is useful to investors, creditors, and others in making investment, credit, and similar decisions. The information is communicated in a variety of ways, including general purpose financial statements. These statements normally include an income statement, balance sheet, statement of changes in shareholders' equity or statement of retained earnings, statement of changes in financial position, and the related notes.

LO 2. Describe, prepare, and interpret comparative financial statements and common-size comparative statements. Comparative financial statements show amounts for two or more successive periods, sometimes with the changes in the items disclosed in absolute and percentage terms. In common-size statements, each item is expressed as a percentage of a base amount. The base amount for the balance sheet is usually total assets, and the base amount for the income statement is usually net sales.

LO 3. Calculate and explain the interpretation of the ratios, turnovers, and rates of return used to evaluate (*a*) short-term liquidity, (*b*) long-term risk and capital structure, and (*c*) operating efficiency and profitability. To evaluate the short-term liquidity of a company, calculate a current ratio, an acid-test ratio, the accounts receivable turnover, the days' sales uncollected, the merchandise turnover, and the days' stock on hand.

In evaluating the long-term risk and capital structure of a company, calculate debt and equity ratios, pledged assets to secured liabilities, and the number of times fixed interest charges were earned.

In evaluating operating efficiency and profitability, calculate profit margin, total asset turnover, return on total assets, and return on common shareholders' equity. Other statistics used to evaluate the profitability of alternative investments include the price earnings ratio and the dividend yield.

LO 4. State the limitations associated with using financial statement ratios and the sources from which standards for comparison may be obtained. In deciding whether financial statement ratio values are satisfactory, too high, or too low, you must have some bases for comparison. These bases may come from past experience and personal judgment, from ratios of similar companies, or from ratios published by trade associations or other public sources. Traditional rules of thumb should be applied with great care and only if they seem reasonable in light of past experience.

DEMONSTRATION PROBLEM

Use the financial statements of Precision Co. to satisfy the following requirements:

1. Prepare a comparative income statement showing the percentage increase or decrease for 1996 over 1995.
2. Prepare a common-size comparative balance sheet for 1996 and 1995.
3. Compute the following ratios as of December 31, 1996, or for the year ended December 31, 1996:
   a. Current ratio.
   b. Acid-test ratio.
   c. Accounts receivable turnover.
   d. Days' sales uncollected.
   e. Merchandise turnover.
   f. Debt ratio
   g. Pledged assets to secured liabilities.
   h. Times fixed interest charges earned.
   i. Profit margin.
   j. Total asset turnover.
   k. Return on total assets.
   l. Return on common shareholders' equity.

PRECISION COMPANY
Comparative Income Statement
For Years Ended December 31, 1996 and 1995

	1996	1995
Sales	$2,486,000	$2,075,000
Cost of goods sold	1,523,000	1,222,00
Gross profit from sales	$ 963,000	$ 853,000
Operating expenses:		
Advertising expense	$ 145,000	$ 100,000
Sales salaries expense	240,000	280,000
Office salaries expense	165,000	200,000
Insurance expense	100,000	45,000
Supplies expense	26,000	35,000
Amortization expenses	85,000	75,000
Miscellaneous expense	17,000	15,000
Total operating expenses	$ 778,000	$ 750,000
Operating income	$ 185,000	$ 103,000
Less interest expense	44,000	46,000
Income before taxes	$ 141,000	$ 57,000
Income taxes	47,000	19,000
Net income	$ 94,000	$ 38,000
Earnings per share	$ 0.99	$ 0.40

PRECISION COMPANY
Comparative Balance Sheet
December 31, 1996, and December 31, 1995

	1996	1995
Assets		
Current assets:		
Cash	$ 79,000	$ 42,000
Short-term investments	65,000	96,000
Accounts receivable (net)	120,000	100,000
Merchandise inventory	250,000	265,000
Total current assets	$ 514,000	$ 503,000
Capital assets:		
Store equipment (net)	$ 400,000	$ 350,000
Office equipment (net)	45,000	50,000
Buildings (net)	625,000	675,000
Land	100,000	100,000
Total plant and equipment	$1,170,000	$1,175,000
Total assets	$1,684,000	$1,678,000
Liabilities		
Current liabilities:		
Accounts payable	$ 164,000	$ 190,000
Short-term notes payable	75,000	90,000
Taxes payable	26,000	12,000
Total current liabilities	$ 265,000	$ 292,000
Long-term liabilities:		
Notes payable (secured by mortgage on building and land)	400,000	420,000
Total liabilities	$ 665,000	$ 712,000

Shareholders' Equity

Contributed capital:

Common share, no par value	$ 475,000	$ 475,000
Retained earnings	544,000	491,000
Total shareholders' equity	$1,019,000	$ 966,000
Total liabilities and shareholders' equity	$1,684,000	$1,678,000

- Set up a four-column income statement; enter the 1996 and 1995 amounts in the first two columns, and then enter the dollar change in the third column and the percentage change from 1995 in the fourth column.

- Set up a four-column balance sheet; enter the 1996 and 1995 amounts in the first two columns, and then compute and enter the amount of each item as a percent of total assets.

- Compute the given ratios using the provided numbers; be sure to use the average of the beginning and ending amounts where appropriate.

Planning the Solution

1.

PRECISION COMPANY
Comparative Income Statement
For Years Ended December 31, 1996 and 1995

Solution to Demonstration Problem

	1996	1995	Increase (Decrease) in 1996 Amount	Percent
Sales	$2,486,000	$2,075,000	$411,000	19.8
Cost of goods sold	1,523,000	1,222,000	301,000	24.6
Gross profit from sales	$ 963,000	$ 853,000	$110,000	12.9
Operating expenses:				
Advertising expense	$ 145,000	$ 100,000	$ 45,000	45.0
Sales salaries expense	240,000	280,000	(40,000)	(14.3)
Office salaries expense	165,000	200,000	(35,000)	(17.5)
Insurance expense	100,000	45,000	55,000	122.2
Supplies expense	26,000	35,000	(9,000)	(25.7)
Amortization expense	85,000	75,000	10,000	13.3
Miscellaneous expenses	17,000	15,000	2,000	13.3
Total operating expenses	$ 778,000	$ 750,000	$ 28,000	3.7
Operating income	$ 185,000	$ 103,000	$ 82,000	79.6
Less interest expense	44,000	46,000	(2,000)	(4.3)
Income before taxes	$ 141,000	$ 57,000	$ 84,000	147.4
Income taxes	47,000	19,000	28,000	147.4
Net income	$ 94,000	$ 38,000	$ 56,000	147.4
Earnings per share	$ 0.99	$ 0.40	$ 0.59	147.5

2.

PRECISION COMPANY
Common-Size Comparative Balance Sheet
December 31, 1996, and December 31, 1995

	December 31		Common-Size Percentages	
	1996	**1995**	**1996***	**1995***
Assets				
Current assets:				
Cash	$ 79,000	$ 42,000	4.7	2.5
Short-term investments	65,000	96,000	3.9	5.7
Accounts receivable (net)	120,000	100,000	7.1	6.0
Merchandise inventory	250,000	265,000	14.8	15.8
Total current assets	$ 514,000	$ 503,000	30.5	30.0
Capital assets:				
Store equipment (net)	$ 400,000	$ 350,000	23.8	20.9
Office equipment (net)	45,000	50,000	2.7	3.0
Buildings (net)	625,000	675,000	37.1	40.2
Land	100,000	100,000	5.9	6.0
Total plant and equipment	$1,170,000	$1,175,000	69.5	70.0
Total assets	$1,684,000	$1,678,000	100.0	100.0

	December 31		Common-size Percentages	
	1996	**1995**	**1996***	**1995***
Liabilities				
Current liabilities:				
Accounts payable	$ 164,000	$ 190,000	9.7	11.3
Short-term notes payable	75,000	90,000	4.5	5.4
Taxes payable	26,000	12,000	1.5	0.7
Total current liabilities	$ 265,000	$ 292,000	15.7	17.4
Long-term liabilities:				
Notes payable (secured by mortgage on building and land)	400,000	420,000	23.8	25.0
Total liabilities	$ 665,000	$ 712,000	39.4	42.4
Shareholders' Equity				
Contributed capital:				
Common share, no par value	$ 475,000	$ 475,000	28.2	28.3
Retailed earnings	544,000	491,000	32.3	29.3
Total shareholders' equity	$1,019,000	$ 966,000	60.5	57.6
Total liabilities and equity	$1,684,000	$1,678,000	100.0	100.0

*Columns may not foot due to rounding.

3. Ratios for 1996:

a. Current ratio: $514,000/$265,000 = 1.9 to 1

b. Acid-test ratio: ($79,000 + $65,000 + $120,000)/$265,000 = 1.0 to 1

c. Average receivables: ($120,000 + $100,000)/2 = $110,000
   Accounts receivable turnover: $2,486,000/$110,000 = 22.6 times

d. Days' sales uncollected: ($120,000/$2,486,000) × 365 = 17.6 days

e. Average inventory: ($250,000 + $265,000)/2 = $257,500
   Merchandise turnover: $1,523,000/$257,500 = 5.9 times

f. Debt ratio: $665,000/$1,684,000 = 39.5%

g. Pledged assets to secured liabilities:
($625,000 + $100,000)/$400,000 = 1.8 to 1

h. Times fixed interest charges earned: $185,000/$44,000 = 4.2 times

i. Profit margin: $94,000/$2,486,000 = 3.8%

j. Average total assets: ($1,684,000 + $1,678,000)/2 = $1,681,000
Total asset turnover: $2,486,000/$1,681,000 = 1.48 times

k. Return on total assets: $94,000/$1,681,000 = 5.6% or 3.8% × 1.48 = 5.6%

l. Average total equity: ($1,019,000 = $966,000)/2 = $992,500
Return on common shareholders' equity: $94,000/$992,500 = 9.5%

GLOSSARY

Common-size comparative statements comparative financial statements in which each amount is expressed as a percentage of a base amount. In the balance sheet, the amount of total assets is usually selected as the base amount and is expressed as 100%. In the income statement, net sales is usually selected as the base amount. p. 855

Comparative statement a financial statement with data for two or more successive accounting periods placed in columns side by side, sometimes with changes shown in dollar amounts and percentages. p. 851

Equity ratio the portion of total assets provided by shareholders' equity, calculated as shareholders' equity divided by total assets. p. 862

Financial reporting the process of providing information that is useful to investors, creditors, and others in making investment, credit, and similar decisions. p. 850

General purpose financial statements statements published periodically for use by a wide variety of interested parties; include the income statement, balance sheet, statement of changes in shareholders' equity (or statement of retained earnings), statement of changes in financial position, and related notes. p. 850

Working capital current assets minus current liabilities. p. 858

QUESTIONS

1. Explain the difference between financial reporting and financial statements.
2. What is the difference between comparative financial statements and common-size comparative statements?
3. Which items are usually assigned a value of 100% on a common-size comparative balance sheet and a common-size comparative income statement?
4. Why is working capital given special attention in the process of analyzing balance sheets?
5. What are three factors that would influence your decision as to whether a company's current ratio is good or bad?
6. Suggest several reasons why a 2 to 1 current ratio may not be adequate for a particular company.
7. What does a relatively high accounts receivable turnover indicate about a company's short-term liquidity?
8. What is the significance of the number of days' sales uncollected?
9. Why does merchandise turnover provide information about a company's short-term liquidity?
10. Why is the capital structure of a company, as measured by debt and equity ratios, of importance to financial statement analysts?
11. Why must the ratio of pledged assets to secured liabilities be interpreted with caution?
12. Why would a company's return on total assets be different from its return on common shareholders' equity?

13. What ratios would you calculate for the purpose of evaluating management performance?

14. Using the financial statements for Geac Corpora-

tion in Appendix I, calculate Geac's return on total assets for the fiscal year ended April 30, 1994.

QUICK STUDY (Five-Minute Exercises)

QS 19–1
(LO 1)

Which of the following items are means of accomplishing the objective of financial reporting but are not included within general purpose financial statements? *(a)* Income statements; *(b)* Company news releases; *(c)* Balance sheets; *(d)* Certain reports filed with the Securities Commission; *(e)* Statements of changes in financial position; *(f)* Management discussions and analyses of financial performance.

QS 19–2
(LO 2)

Given the following information for Moyers Corporation, determine *(a)* the common-size percentages for gross profit from sales, and *(b)* the trend percentages for net sales, using 1995 as the base year.

	1995	1996
Net sales	$134,400	$114,800
Cost of goods sold	72,800	60,200

QS 19–3
(LO 3)

a. Which two terms describe the difference between current assets and current liabilities?

b. Which two short-term liquidity ratios measure how frequently a company collects its accounts?

c. Which two ratios are the basic components in measuring a company's operating efficiency? Which ratio is the summary of these two components?

QS 19–4
(LO 4)

What are five possible bases of comparison you can use when analyzing financial statement ratios? Which of these is generally considered to be the most useful? Which one is least likely to provide a good basis for comparison?

EXERCISES

Exercise 19–1
Calculating trend percentages
(LO 2)

Calculate trend percentages for the following items, using 1993 as the base year. Then, state whether the situation shown by the trends appears to be favourable or unfavourable.

	1997	1996	1995	1994	1993
Sales	$377,600	$362,400	$338,240	$314,080	$302,000
Cost of goods sold	172,720	164,560	155,040	142,800	136,000
Accounts receivable	25,400	24,400	23,200	21,600	20,000

Where possible, calculate percentages of increase and decrease for the following:

Exercise 19–2
Reporting percentage changes
(LO 2)

	1995	1994
Short-term investments	$145,200	$110,000
Accounts receivable	28,080	32,000
Notes payable	38,000	–0–

Express the following income statement information in common-size percentages and assess whether the situation is favourable or unfavourable:

Exercise 19–3
Calculating common-size percentages
(LO 2)

CLEARWATER CORPORATION
Comparative Income Statement
For Years Ended December 31, 1995 and 1994

	1995	1994
Sales	$960,000	$735,000
Cost of goods sold	576,000	382,200
Gross profit from sales	$384,000	$352,800
Operating expenses	216,000	148,470
Net income	$168,000	$204,330

TGA Company's December 31 balance sheets included the following data:

Exercise 19–4
Evaluating short-term liquidity
(LO 3)

	1996	1995	1994
Cash	$ 61,600	$ 71,250	$ 73,600
Accounts receivable, net	177,000	125,000	98,400
Merchandise inventory	223,000	165,000	106,000
Prepaid expenses	19,400	18,750	8,000
Plant assets, net	555,000	510,000	459,000
Total assets	$1,036,000	$890,000	$745,000
Accounts payable	$ 257,800	$150,500	$ 98,500
Long-term notes payable secured by mortgages on plant assets	195,000	205,000	165,000
Common shares, no par value (32,500 shares issued) ..	325,000	325,000	325,000
Retained earnings	258,200	209,500	156,500
Total liabilities and shareholders' equity	$1,036,000	$890,000	$745,000

Required

Compare the short-term liquidity positions of the company at the end of 1996, 1995, and 1994 by calculating: (a) the current ratio and (b) the acid-test ratio. Comment on any changes that occurred.

Refer to the information in Exercise 19–4 about TGA Company. The company's income statements for the years ended December 31, 1996, and 1995 included the following data:

Exercise 19–5
Evaluating short-term liquidity
(LO 3)

	1996	1995
Sales	$1,345,000	$1,060,000
Cost of goods sold	$ 820,450	$ 689,000
Other operating expenses	417,100	267,960
Interest expense	22,200	24,600
Income taxes	17,050	15,690
Total costs and expenses	$1,276,800	$ 997,250
Net income	$ 68,200	$ 62,750
Earnings per share	$ 2.10	$ 1.93

Required

For the years ended December 31, 1996, and 1995, assume all sales were on credit and calculate the following: (a) days' sales uncollected, (b) accounts receivable turnover, (c) merchandise turnover, and (d) days' stock on hand. Comment on any changes that occurred from 1995 to 1996.

Exercise 19–6
Evaluating long-term risk and capital structure
(LO 3)

Refer to the information in Exercises 19–4 and 19–5 about TGA Company. Compare the long-term risk and capital structure positions of the company at the end of 1996 and 1995 by calculating the following ratios: (a) debt and equity ratios, (b) pledged assets to secured liabilities, and (c) times fixed interest charges earned. Comment on any changes that occurred.

Exercise 19–7
Evaluating operating efficiency and profitability
(LO 3)

Refer to the financial statements of TGA Company presented in Exercises 19–4 and 19–5. Evaluate the operating efficiency and profitability of the company by calculating the following: (a) profit margin, (b) total asset turnover, and (c) return on total assets. Comment on any changes that occurred.

Exercise 19–8
Evaluating profitability
(LO 3)

Refer to the financial statements of TGA Company presented in Exercises 19–4 and 19–5. This additional information about the company is known:

Common share market price, December 31, 1996	$30.00
Common share market price, December 31, 1995	28.00
Annual cash dividends per share in 1996	.60
Annual cash dividends per share in 1995	.30

Required

To evaluate the profitability of the company, calculate the following for 1996 and 1995: (a) return on common shareholders' equity, (b) price earnings ratio on December 31, and (c) dividend yield.

Exercise 19–9
Determining income effects from common-size and trend percentages
(LO 2)

Common-size and trend percentages for a company's sales, cost of goods sold, and expenses follow:

	Common-Size Percentages			Trend Percentages		
	1996	1995	1994	1996	1995	1994
Sales	100.0%	100.0%	100.0%	106.5%	105.3%	100.0%
Cost of goods sold	64.5	63.0	60.2	104.1	102.3	100.0
Expenses	16.4	15.9	16.2	96.0	94.1	100.0

Required

Determine whether the company's net income increased, decreased, or remained unchanged during this three-year period.

PROBLEMS

The condensed statements of Stellar Company follow:

Problem 19–1
Calculating ratios and
percentages
(LO 2, 3)

STELLAR COMPANY
Comparative Income Statement
For Years Ended December 31, 1996, 1995, and 1994
($000)

	1996	1995	1994
Sales	$148,000	$136,000	$118,000
Cost of goods sold	89,096	85,000	75,520
Gross profit from sales	$ 58,904	$ 51,000	$ 42,480
Selling expenses	$ 20,898	$ 18,768	$ 15,576
Administrative expenses	13,379	11,968	9,735
Total expenses	$ 34,277	$ 30,736	$ 25,311
Income before taxes	$ 24,627	$ 20,264	$ 17,169
Income taxes	4,588	4,148	3,481
Net income	$ 20,039	$ 16,116	$ 13,688

STELLAR COMPANY
Comparative Balance Sheet
December 31, 1996, 1995, and 1994
($000)

	1996	1995	1994
Assets			
Current assets	$24,240	$18,962	$25,324
Long-term investments	–0–	250	1,860
Plant and equipment	45,000	48,000	28,500
Total assets	$69,240	$67,212	$55,684
Liabilities and Shareholders' Equity			
Current liabilities	$10,100	$ 9,980	$ 9,740
Common shares	36,000	36,000	27,000
Other contributed capital	4,500	4,500	3,000
Retained earnings	18,640	16,732	15,944
Total liabilities and shareholders' equity	$69,240	$67,212	$55,684

Required

Preparation component:

1. Calculate each year's current ratio.
2. Express the income statement data in common-size percentages.
3. Express the balance sheet data in trend percentages with 1994 as the base year.

Analysis component:

4. Comment on any significant relationships revealed by the ratios and percentages.

Problem 19–2
Calculation and analysis
of trend percentages
(LO 2)

The condensed comparative statements of Jasper Company follow:

JASPER COMPANY
Comparative Income Statement
For Years Ended December 31, 1997–1991
($000)

	1997	1996	1995	1994	1993	1992	1991
Sales	$797	$698	$635	$582	$543	$505	$420
Cost of goods sold	573	466	401	351	326	305	250
Gross profit from sales	$224	$232	$234	$231	$217	$200	$170
Operating expenses	170	133	122	90	78	77	65
Net income	$ 54	$ 99	$112	$141	$139	$123	$105

JASPER COMPANY
Comparative Balance Sheet
December 31, 1997–1991
($000)

	1997	1996	1995	1994	1993	1992	1991
Assets							
Cash	$ 34	$ 44	$ 46	$ 47	$ 49	$ 48	$ 50
Accounts receivable, net	240	252	228	175	154	146	102
Merchandise inventory	869	632	552	466	418	355	260
Other current assets	23	21	12	22	19	19	10
Long-term investments	0	0	0	68	68	68	68
Plant and equipment, net	1,060	1,057	926	522	539	480	412
Total assets	$2,226	$2,006	$1,764	$1,300	$1,247	$1,116	$902
Liabilities and Equity							
Current liabilities	$ 560	$ 471	$ 309	$ 257	$ 223	$ 211	$136
Long-term liabilities	597	520	506	235	240	260	198
Common shares	500	500	500	420	420	320	320
Other contributed capital	125	125	125	90	90	80	80
Retained earnings	444	390	324	298	274	245	168
Total liabilities and equity	$2,226	$2,006	$1,764	$1,300	$1,247	$1,116	$902

Required

Preparation component:

1. Calculate trend percentages for the items of the statements using 1991 as the base year.

Analysis component:

2. Analyze and comment on the situation shown in the statements.

The 1996 financial statements of Oltorf Corporation follow:

Problem 19–3
Calculation of financial
statement ratios
(LO 3)

OLTORF CORPORATION
Income Statement
For Year Ended December 31, 1996

Sales		$697,200
Cost of goods sold:		
Merchandise inventory, December 31, 1995	$ 64,800	
Purchases	455,800	
Goods available for sale	$520,600	
Merchandise inventory, December 31, 1996	62,300	
Cost of goods sold		458,300
Gross profit from sales		$238,900
Operating expenses		122,700
Operating income		$116,200
Interest expense		7,100
Income before taxes		$109,100
Income taxes		17,800
Net income		$ 91,300

OLTORF CORPORATION
Balance Sheet
December 31, 1996

Assets		Liabilities and Shareholders' Equity	
Cash	$ 18,000	Accounts payable	$ 32,600
Temporary investments	14,700	Accrued wages payable	4,200
Accounts receivable, net	55,800	Income taxes payable	4,800
Notes receivable (trade)	6,200	Long-term note payable,	
Merchandise inventory	62,300	secured by mortgage on	
Prepaid expenses	2,800	plant assets	125,000
Plant assets, net	306,300	Common shares, no par value	180,000
		Retained earnings	119,500
		Total liabilities and	
Total assets	$466,100	shareholders' equity	$466,100

Assume that all sales were on credit. On the December 31, 1995, balance sheet, the assets totaled $367,500, common shares were $180,000, and retained earnings were $86,700.

Required

Calculate the following: (*a*) current ratio, (*b*) acid-test ratio, (*c*) days' sales uncollected, (*d*) merchandise turnover, (*e*) days' stock on hand, (*f*) ratio of pledged assets to secured liabilities, (*g*) times fixed interest charges earned, (*h*) profit margin, (*i*) total asset turnover, (*j*) return on total assets, and (*k*) return on common shareholders' equity.

Problem 19–4
Comparative analysis of
financial statement ratios
(LO 3)

Two companies that compete in the same industry are being evaluated by a bank that can lend money to only one of them. Summary information from the financial statements of the two companies follows:

	Payless Company	Capital Company
Data from the current year-end balance sheets:		
Assets		
Cash	$ 37,400	$ 66,000
Accounts receivable	73,450	112,900
Notes receivable (trade)	16,200	13,100
Merchandise inventory	167,340	263,100
Prepaid expenses	8,000	11,900
Plant and equipment, net	568,900	606,400
Total assets	$ 871,290	$1,073,400
Liabilities and Shareholders' Equity:		
Current liabilities	$ 120,200	$ 184,600
Long-term notes payable	159,800	210,000
Common shares, no par value	350,000	410,000
Retained earnings	241,290	268,800
Total liabilities and shareholders' equity	$871,290	$1,073,400
Data from the current year's income statements:		
Sales	$1,325,000	$1,561,200
Cost of goods sold	970,500	1,065,000
Interest expense	14,400	23,000
Income tax expense	24,840	38,700
Net income	135,540	210,400
Beginning-of-year data:		
Accounts receivable, net	$ 57,800	$ 106,200
Notes receivable	0	0
Merchandise inventory	109,600	212,400
Total assets	776,400	745,100
Common shares, no par value	350,000	410,000
Retained earnings	189,300	181,200

Required

1. Calculate the current ratio, acid-test ratio, accounts (including notes) receivable turnover, merchandise turnover, days' stock on hand, and days' sales uncollected for the two companies. Then, identify the company that you consider to be the better short-term credit risk and explain why.

2. Calculate the profit margin, total asset turnover, return on total assets, and return on common shareholders' equity for the two companies. Assuming that each company paid cash dividends of $2.00 per share and each company's shares can be purchased at $25 per share, calculate their price earnings ratios and dividend yields. Payless has 70,000 shares and Capital has 82,000 shares outstanding. Also, identify which company's shares you would recommend as the better investment and explain why.

Metro Corporation began the month of March with $750,000 of current assets, a current ratio of 2.5 to 1, and an acid-test ratio of 1.1 to 1. During the month, it completed the following transactions:

Problem 19–5
Analysis of working capital
(LO 3)

Mar. 4 Bought $85,000 of merchandise on account. (The company uses a perpetual inventory system.)

10 Sold merchandise that cost $68,000 for $113,000.

12 Collected a $29,000 account receivable.

17 Paid a $31,000 account payable.

19 Wrote off a $13,000 bad debt against the Allowance for Doubtful Accounts account.

24 Declared a $1.25 per share cash dividend on the 40,000 outstanding common shares.

28 Paid the dividend declared on March 24.

29 Borrowed $85,000 by giving the bank a 30-day, 10% note.

30 Borrowed $100,000 by signing a long-term secured note.

31 Used the $185,000 proceeds of the notes to buy additional machinery.

Required

Prepare a schedule showing Metro's current ratio, acid-test ratio, and working capital after each of the transactions. Round calculations to two decimal places.

The condensed statements of Tradent Corporation follow:

Problem 19–6
Calculating ratios and percentages
(LO 2, 3)

TRADENT CORPORATION
Comparative Income Statement
For Years Ended December 31, 1996, 1995, and 1994
($000)

	1996	1995	1994
Sales	$98,000	$82,400	$71,000
Cost of goods sold	54,500	43,300	33,800
Gross profit from sales	43,500	39,100	37,200
Selling expenses	13,100	10,350	10,900
Administrative expenses	9,800	10,450	9,500
Total expenses	22,900	20,800	20,400
Income before taxes	20,600	18,300	16,800
Income taxes	7,210	6,405	5,880
Net income	$13,390	$11,895	$10,920

TRADENT CORPORATION
Comparative Balance Sheet
December 31, 1996, 1995, and 1994
($000)

	1996	1995	1994
Assets			
Current assets	$22,600	$12,500	$14,900
Long-term investments		700	5,700
Plant and equipment	51,000	53,000	39,200
Total assets	$73,600	$66,200	$59,800

Liabilities and Capital

	1996	1995	1994
Current liabilities	$11,000	$ 9,200	$ 7,700
Common shares	19,600	19,600	16,000
Retained earnings	43,000	37,400	36,100
Total liabilities and capital	$73,600	$66,200	$59,800

Required

1. Calculate each year's current ratio.

2. Express the income statement data in common-size percentages.

3. Express the balance sheet data in trend percentages with 1994 as the base year.

4. Comment on any significant relationships revealed by the ratios and percentages.

Problem 19–7
Calculation and analysis
of trend percentages
(LO 2)

The condensed comparative statements of Clear River Company, Ltd., follow:

CLEAR RIVER COMPANY, LTD.
Comparative Income Statement
For Years Ended December 31, 1996–1990
($000)

	1996	1995	1994	1993	1992	1991	1990
Sales	$450	$470	$460	$490	$530	$520	$560
Cost of goods sold	190	197	194	208	219	212	214
Gross profit from sales	$260	$273	$266	$282	$311	$308	$346
Operating expenses	200	207	205	224	231	235	255
Income before taxes	$ 60	$ 66	$ 61	$ 58	$ 80	$ 73	$ 91

CLEAR RIVER COMPANY, LTD.
Comparative Balance Sheet
December 31, 1996–1990
($000)

	1996	1995	1994	1993	1992	1991	1990
Assets							
Cash	$ 30	$ 33	$ 32	$ 36	$ 45	$ 42	$ 46
Accounts receivable, net	92	103	99	101	112	110	118
Merchandise inventory	143	149	147	156	159	169	162
Other current assets	20	21	22	24	23	26	28
Long-term investments	80	60	40	87	87	87	90
Plant and equipment, net	362	368	372	287	292	297	302
Total assets	$727	$734	$712	$691	$718	$731	$746
Liabilities and Capital							
Current liabilities	$162	$169	$152	$121	$143	$171	$216
Long-term liabilities	130	145	160	175	190	205	220
Common shares	205	205	205	205	205	205	205
Retained earnings	230	215	195	190	180	150	105
Total liabilities and capital	$727	$734	$712	$691	$718	$731	$746

Required

1. Calculate trend percentages for the items of the statements using 1990 as the base year.

2. Analyze and comment on the situation shown in the statements.

The year-end statements of Tooner Corporation follow:

Problem 19–8
Financial statement ratios
(LO 3)

TOONER CORPORATION
Income Statement
For Year Ended December 31, 1996

Sales		$805,000
Cost of goods sold:		
Merchandise inventory, December 31, 1995	$ 62,800	
Purchases	500,700	
Goods available for sale	$563,500	
Merchandise inventory, December 31, 1996	48,200	
Cost of goods sold		515,300
Gross profit from sales		$289,700
Operating expenses		227,800
Operating income		$ 61,900
Interest expense		9,500
Income before taxes		$ 52,400
Income taxes		15,720
Net income		$ 36,680

TOONER CORPORATION
Balance Sheet
December 31, 1996

Assets		Liabilities and Shareholders' Equity	
Cash	$ 18,500	Accounts payable	$ 40,700
Temporary investments	20,400	Accrued wages payable	5,200
Accounts receivable, net	43,400	Income taxes payable	5,800
Notes receivable	8,800	Long-term note payable,	
Merchandise inventory	49,200	secured by mortgage	
Prepaid expenses	4,800	on plant assets	95,000
Plant assets, net	272,100	Common shares, 160,000 shares	160,000
		Retained earnings	110,500
		Total liabilities and	
Total assets	$417,200	shareholders' equity	$417,200

Assume all sales were on credit. On the December 31, 1995, balance sheet, the assets totaled $360,600, common shares were $160,000, and retained earnings was $89,700.

Required

Calculate the following: (a) current ratio, (b) acid-test ratio, (c) days' sales uncollected, (d) merchandise turnover, (e) ratio of pledged plant assets to secured liabilities, (f) times fixed interest charges earned, (g) profit margin, (h) total asset turnover, (i) return on total assets employed, and (j) return on common shareholders' equity.

Two companies that operate in the same industry as competitors are being evaluated by a bank that may lend money to each one. Summary information from the financial statements of the two companies is provided below:

Problem 19–9
Comparative analysis of
financial statement ratios
(LO 3)

Data from the Current Year-End Balance Sheets

	Zesta Corporation	Festa Corporation
Assets		
Cash	$ 30,200	$ 57,100
Accounts receivable	105,500	118,500
Notes receivable	18,000	16,500
Merchandise inventory	98,700	133,300
Prepaid expenses	15,700	17,900
Plant and equipment, net	332,900	340,100
Total assets	$601,000	683,400
Liabilities and Capital		
Current liabilities	$113,400	$141,800
Long-term notes payable	120,000	135,000
Common shares*	182,000	212,000
Retained earnings	185,600	194,600
Total liabilities and capital . . .	$601,000	$683,400

Data from the Current Year's Income Statements

Sales	$703,500	$992,100
Cost of goods sold	518,000	708,200
Interest expense	14,100	17,800
Income tax expense	22,500	42,700
Net income	54,200	74,700

Beginning-of-Year Data

Accounts receivable, net	$ 98,000	$100,500
Notes receivable	–0–	–0–
Merchandise inventory	118,200	93,900
Total assets	514,300	600,000
Common shares*	182,000	212,000
Retained earnings	158,700	151,700

*All shares were issued at $20 per share.

Required

1. Calculate current ratios, acid-test ratios, accounts (and notes) receivable turnovers, merchandise turnovers, and days' sales uncollected for the two companies. Then state which company you think is the better short-term credit risk and why.

2. Calculate profit margins, total asset turnovers, returns on total asset employed, and returns on common shareholders' equity. Assuming that each company paid cash dividends of $3 per share and each company's shares can be purchased at $45 per share, calculate price earnings ratio and dividend yield. Also state which company's shares you would recommend as the better investment and why.

Problem 19–10
Analysis of working capital
(LO 3)

Ft. Mason Corporation began the month of March with $286,000 of current assets, a current ratio of 2.2 to 1, and an acid-test ratio of 0.9 to 1. During the month, it completed the following transactions:

Mar. 3   Sold for $55,000 merchandise that cost $36,000.

5   Collected a $35,000 account receivable.

10   Bought $56,000 of merchandise on account. (The company uses a perpetual inventory system.)

12   Borrowed $60,000 by giving the bank a 60-day, 12% note.

15 Borrowed $90,000 by signing a long-term secured note.

22 Used the $150,000 proceeds of the notes to buy additional machinery.

24 Declared a $1.75 per share cash dividend on the 40,000 shares of outstanding common shares.

26 Wrote off a $14,000 bad debt against Allowance for Doubtful Accounts.

28 Paid a $45,000 account payable.

30 Paid the dividend declared on March 24.

Required

Prepare a schedule showing the company's current ratio, acid-test ratio, and working capital after each of the foregoing transactions. Round to two decimal places.

PROVOCATIVE PROBLEMS

Kerbey Company and Telcom Company are similar firms that operate within the same industry. The following information is available:

Provocative Problem 19–1
Analytical essay
(LO 3)

	Kerbey			Telcom		
	1996	1995	1994	1996	1995	1994
Current ratio	1.8	1.9	2.2	3.3	2.8	2.0
Acid-test ratio	1.1	1.2	1.3	2.9	2.6	1.7
Accounts receivable turnover	30.5	25.2	29.2	16.4	15.2	16.0
Merchandise turnover ...	24.2	21.9	17.1	14.5	13.0	12.6
Working capital	$65,000	$53,000	$47,000	$126,000	$98,000	$73,000

Required

Write a brief essay comparing Kerbey and Telcom based on the preceding information. Your discussion should include their relative ability to meet current obligations and to use current assets efficiently.

Snowden Company and Comet Company are similar firms that operate within the same industry. Comet began operations in 1994 and Snowden in 1988. In 1996, both companies paid 7% interest to creditors. The following information is available:

Provocative Problem 19–2
Analytical essay
(LO 3)

	Snowden			Comet		
	1996	1995	1994	1996	1995	1994
Total asset turnover	3.3	3.0	3.2	1.9	1.7	1.4
Return on total assets ..	9.2	9.8	9.0	6.1	5.8	5.5
Profit margin	2.6	2.7	2.5	3.0	3.2	3.1
Sales	$800,000	$740,000	$772,000	$400,000	$320,000	$200,000

Required

Write a brief essay comparing Snowden and Comet based on the preceding information. Your discussion should include their relative ability to use assets efficiently to produce profits. Also comment on their relative success in employing financial leverage in 1996.

**Provocative Problem
19–3**
Financial statement
analysis case
(LO 2, 3)

In your position as controller of Skinner Company, you are responsible for keeping the board of directors informed about the financial activities and status of the company. In preparing for the next board meeting, you have calculated the following ratios, turnovers, and percentages to enable you to answer questions:

	1996	1995	1994
Sales trend	137.00	125.00	100.00
Selling expenses to net sales	9.8%	13.7%	15.3%
Sales to plant assets	3.5 to 1	3.3 to 1	3.0 to 1
Current ratio	2.6 to 1	2.4 to 1	2.1 to 1
Acid-test ratio	0.8 to 1	1.1 to 1	1.2 to 1
Merchandise turnover	7.5 times	8.7 times	9.9 times
Accounts receivable turnover	6.7 times	7.4 times	8.2 times
Total asset turnover	2.6 times	2.6 times	3.0 times
Return on total assets	8.8%	9.4%	10.1%
Return on shareholders' equity . .	9.75%	11.50%	12.25%
Profit margin	3.3%	3.5%	3.7%

Required

Using the preceding data, answer each of the following questions and explain your answers:

a. Is it becoming easier for the company to meet its current debts on time and to take advantage of cash discounts?

b. Is the company collecting its accounts receivable more rapidly?

c. Is the company's investment in accounts receivable decreasing?

d. Are dollars invested in inventory increasing?

e. Is the company's investment in plant assets increasing?

f. Is the shareholders' investment becoming more profitable?

g. Is the company using its assets efficiently?

h. Did the dollar amount of selling expenses decrease during the three-year period?

**Provocative Problem
19–4**
Financial statement
analysis
(LO 2, 3)

Refer to the financial statements of Geac Computer Corporation, Ltd., in Appendix I, to answer the following questions:

a. Calculate common-size percentages for 1994 and 1993 for the following categories of assets: total current assets; fixed assets; and other assets.

b. Calculate the 1994 and 1993 common-size percentages for sales, total expenses, and net income.

c. Calculate the high and low price earnings ratio for 1994. Geac's share prices were 18⅞ high and 11⅞ low.

d. Calculate the debt and equity ratios for 1994.

ANALYTICAL AND REVIEW PROBLEMS

On the basis of the information given, complete the balance sheet.

VIDIO COMPANY LIMITED
December 31, 1996

Assets		Liabilities and Capital	
Cash	$_____	Current liabilities	$_____
Accounts receivable	_____	8% bonds payable	_____
Inventory	_____	Common shares	15,000
Plant and equipment	_____	Retained earnings	_____
. . . .		Total liabilities and	
Total assets	$_____	capital	$_____

Sales (all credit)	$40,000
Cost of goods sold	24,000
Expenses	13,000
Income taxes	1,000
Net income	2,000
Net income/shareholders' equity	10%
Bonds payable/shareholders' equity	1 to 4
Inventory turnover	4 times
Accounts receivable collection period (360-day year) . .	45 days
Current ratio	2 to 1
Total asset turnover	1.25 times

A & R Problem 19–2   A company began the month of May with $200,000 of current assets, a 2-to-1 current ratio, and a 1-to-1 acid-test (quick) ratio. During the month it completed the following transactions:

		Current Ratio			Acid-Test Ratio		
		Inc.	Dcr.	No Change	Inc.	Dcr.	No Change
a.	Bought $20,000 of merchandise on account (the company uses a perpetual inventory system)						
b.	Sold for $25,000 merchandise that cost $15,000						
c.	Collected an $8,500 account receivable						
d.	Paid a $12,000 account payable						
e.	Wrote off a $1,000 bad debt against the allowance for doubtful accounts						
f.	Declared a $1 per share cash dividend on the 10,000 shares of outstanding common shares						
g.	Paid the dividend declared in (f)						
h.	Borrowed $12,000 by giving the bank a 60-day, 10% note						
i.	Borrowed $30,000 by placing a 10-year mortgage on the plant						
j.	Used $20,000 of proceeds of the mortgage to buy additional machinery						

Required

1. Indicate the affect on (a) current ratio and (b) working capital of each transaction. Set up a chart in your answer similar to that shown above and use check marks to indicate your answers. (Working capital is defined as "current assets minus current liabilities.")

2. For the end of May, calculate the

    a.   Current ratio.

    b.   Acid-test ratio.

    c.   Working capital.

CONCEPT TESTER

Test your understanding of the concepts introduced in this chapter by completing the following crossword puzzle:

Across Clues

1. When data is presented for two or more accounting periods (1st of 2 words; also see 7 down).

9. The process of providing information that is useful to the users of statements (1st of 2 words; also see 3 down).

10. Cost of goods sold divided by average inventory (2nd of 2 words; also see 5 down).

11. Dividends per share divided by market price per share (2 words).

Down Clues

1. Ratio of current assets to current liabilities.

2. Net income divided by net sales (2 words).

3. The process of providing information that is useful to the users of statements (2nd of 2 words; also see 9 across).

4. Ratio of market price per share to earnings per share (2 words).

5. Cost of goods sold divided by average inventory (1st of 2 words; also see 10 across).

6. The proportion of total assets provided by shareholders' equity (2 words).

7. When data are presented for two or more successive accounting periods (2nd of 2 words; also see 1 across).

8. Ratio of total liabilities to total assets.

ANSWERS TO PROGRESS CHECKS

19–1 General purpose financial statements are intended for the large variety of users who are interested in receiving financial information about a business but who do not have the ability to require the company to prepare specialized financial reports designed to meet their specific interests.

19–2 General purpose financial statements include the income statement, balance sheet, statement of changes in shareholders' equity (or statement of retained earnings), and statement of changes in financial position, plus notes related to the statements.

19–3 *d*

19–4 Percentages on a comparative income statement show the increase or decrease in each item from one period to the next. On a common-size comparative income statement, each item is shown as a percentage of net sales for a specific period.

19–5 *c*

19–6 (*a*) ($820,000 + $240,000 + $470,000)/($350,000 + $180,000) = 2.9 to 1
(*b*) ($820,000 + $240,000)/($350,000 + $180,000) = 2 to 1

19–7 (*a*) $2,500,000/[($290,000 + $240,000)/2] = 9.43 times
(*b*) ($240,000/$2,500,000) × 365 = 35 days
(*c*) $750,000/[($530,000 + $470,000)/2] = 1.5 times
(*d*) ($470,000/$750,000) × 365 = 228.7 days

19–8 *c*

19–9 *b*

19–10 Profit margin × Total asset turnover = Return on total assets ($945,000/$8,500,000) × 1.8 = 20%

19–11 *a*

19–12 The ratios and turnovers of a selected group of competing companies.

Present and Future Values: An Expansion

After studying Appendix F, you should be able to:

1. Explain what is meant by the present value of a single amount and the present value of an annuity and be able to use tables to solve present value problems.
2. Explain what is meant by the future value of a single amount and the future value of an annuity and be able to use tables to solve future value problems.

The concept of present value is introduced and applied to accounting problems in Chapters 13 and 18 (Volume II). This appendix supplements those presentations with additional discussion, more complete tables, and additional homework exercises. In studying this appendix, you also learn about the concept of future value.

The present value of a single amount to be received or paid at some future date may be expressed as:

$$p = \frac{f}{(1 + i)^n}$$

where

    p = Present value
    f = Future value
    i = Rate of interest per period
    n = Number of periods

PRESENT VALUE OF A SINGLE AMOUNT

LO 1

Explain what is meant by the present value of a single amount and the present value of an annuity, and be able to use tables to solve present value problems.

For example, assume that $2.20 is to be received one period from now. It would be useful to know how much must be invested now, for one period, at an interest rate of 10% to provide $2.20. We can calculate that amount with this formula:

$$p = \frac{f}{(1 + i)^n} = \frac{\$2.20}{(1 + .10)^1} = \$2.00$$

Alternatively, we can use the formula to find how much must be invested for two periods at 10% to provide $2.42:

$$p = \frac{f}{(1 + i)^n} = \frac{\$2.42}{(1 + .10)^2} = \$2.00$$

Note that the number of periods (n) does not have to be expressed in years. Any period of time such as a day, a month, a quarter, or a year may be used. However, whatever period is used, the interest rate (i) must be compounded for the same period. Thus, if a problem expresses n in months, and i equals 12% per year, then 1% of the amount invested at the beginning of each month is earned during that month and added to the investment. Thus, the interest is compounded monthly.

A present value table shows present values for a variety of interest rates (i) and a variety of numbers of periods (n). Each present value is based on the assumption that the future value (f) is 1. The following formula is used to construct a table of present values of a single future amount:

$$p = \frac{1}{(1 + i)^n}$$

Table F–1 on page AP–8 is a table of present values of a single future amount and often is called a *present value of 1* table.

Progress Check

F–1   **Lamar Company is considering an investment that will yield $70,000 after six years. If Lamar requires an 8% return, how much should it be willing to pay for the investment?**

FUTURE VALUE OF A SINGLE AMOUNT

LO 2

Explain what is meant by the future value of a single amount and the future value of an annuity, and be able to use tables to solve future value problems.

The following formula for the present value of a single amount can be modified to become the formula for the future value of a single amount with a simple step:

$$p = \frac{f}{(1 + i)^n}$$

By multiplying both sides of the equation by $(1 + i)^n$, the result is:

$$f = p \times (1 + i)^n$$

For example, we can use this formula to determine that $2.00 invested for one period at an interest rate of 10% will increase to a future value of $2.20:

$$f = p \times (1 + i)^n$$
$$= \$2.00 \times (1 + .10)^1$$
$$= \$2.20$$

Alternatively, assume that $2.00 will remain invested for three periods at 10%. The $2.662 amount that will be received after three periods is calculated with the formula as follows:

$$f = p \times (1 + i)^n$$
$$= \$2.00 \times (1 + .10)^3$$
$$= \$2.662$$

A future value table shows future values for a variety of interest rates (i) and a variety of numbers of periods (n). Each future value is based on the assumption that the present value (p) is 1. Thus, the formula used to construct a table of future values of a single amount is:

$$f = (1 + i)^n$$

Table F–2 on page AP–9 is a table of future values of a single amount and often is called a *future value of 1* table.

In Table F–2, look at the row where $n = 0$ and observe that the future value is 1 for all interest rates because no interest is earned.

Observe that a table showing the present values of 1 and a table showing the future values of 1 contain exactly the same information because both tables are based on the same equation:

$$p = \frac{f}{(1 + i)^n}$$

This equation is nothing more than a reformulation of:

$$f = p \times (1 + i)^n$$

Both tables reflect the same four variables, p, f, i, and n. Therefore, any problem that can be solved with one of the two tables can also be solved with the other table.

For example, suppose that a person invests $100 for five years and expects to earn 12% per year. How much should the person receive after five years? To solve the problem using Table F–2, find the future value of 1, five periods from now, compounded at 12%. In the table, $f = 1.7623$. Thus, the amount to be accumulated over five years is $176.23 ($100 $\times$ 1.7623).

Table F–1 shows that the present value of 1, discounted five periods at 12% is 0.5674. Recall that the relationship between present value and future value may be expressed as:

$$p = \frac{f}{(1 + i)^n}$$

This formula can be restated as:

$$p = f \times \frac{1}{(1 + i)^n}$$

In turn, it can be restated as:

$$f = \frac{p}{\dfrac{1}{(1 + i)^n}}$$

Because we know from Table F–1 that $1/(1 + i)^n$ equals 0.5674, the future value of $100 invested for five periods at 12% is:

$$f = \frac{\$100}{0.5674} = \$176.24$$

In summary, the future value can be found two ways. First, we can multiply the amount invested by the future value found in Table F–2. Second, we can divide the amount invested by the present value found in Table F–1. As you can see in this problem, immaterial differences can occur between these two methods through rounding.

F–2   On May 9, Cindy Huber was notified that she had won $150,000 in a sweepstakes. She decided to deposit the money in a savings account that yields an 8% annual rate of interest and plans on quitting her job when the account equals $299,850. How many years will it be before Cindy is able to quit working? *(a)* 2; *(b)* 8; *(c)* 9.

PRESENT VALUE OF AN ANNUITY

LO 3

Explain what is meant by the present value of a single amount and the present value of an annuity, and be able to use tables to solve present value problems.

An annuity is a series of equal payments occurring at equal intervals, such as three annual payments of $100 each. The present value of an annuity is defined as the present value of the payments one period prior to the first payment. Graphically, this annuity and its present value (p) may be represented as follows:

One way to calculate the present value of this annuity finds the present value of each payment with the formula and adds them together. For this example, assuming an interest rate of 15%, the calculation is:

$$p = \frac{\$100}{(1 + .15)^1} + \frac{\$100}{(1 + .15)^2} + \frac{\$100}{(1 + .15)^3} = \$228.32$$

Another way calculates the present value of the annuity by using Table F–1 to compute the present value of each payment then taking their sum:

First payment:	$p = \$100 \times 0.8696 =$	$ 86.96
Second payment:	$p = \$100 \times 0.7561 =$	75.61
Third payment:	$p = \$100 \times 0.6575 =$	65.75
Total:		$p = $228.32

We can also use Table F–1 to solve the problem by first adding the table values for the three payments and then multiplying this sum by the $100 amount of each payment:

From Table F–1:	$i = 15\%, n = 1, p =$ 0.8696
	$i = 15\%, n = 2, p =$ 0.7561
	$i = 15\%, n = 3, p =$ 0.6575
	2.2832

$$2.2832 \times \$100 = \$228.32$$

An easier way to solve the problem uses a different table that shows the present values of annuities like Table F–3 on page AP–10, which often is called a *present value of an annuity of 1* table. Look in Table F–3 on the row where $n = 3$ and $i = 15\%$ and observe that the present value is 2.2832. Thus, the present value of an annuity of 1 for three periods, discounted at 15%, is 2.2832.

Although a formula is used to construct a table showing the present values of an annuity, you can construct one by adding the amounts in a present value of 1 table.[1] Examine Table F–1 and Table F–3 to confirm that the following numbers were drawn from those tables:

From Table F–1		From Table F–3	
$i = 8\%, n = 1$	0.9259		
$i = 8\%, n = 2$	0.8573		
$i = 8\%, n = 3$	0.7938		
$i = 8\%, n = 4$	0.7350		
Total	3.3120	$i = 8\%, n = 4$	3.3121

The minor difference in the results occurs only because the numbers in the tables have been rounded.

In addition to the preceding methods, you can use preprogrammed business calculators and spreadsheet computer programs to find the present value of annuities.

Progress Check

F–3   Smith & Company is considering an investment that would pay $10,000 every six months for three years. The first payment would be received in six months. If Smith & Company requires an annual return of 8%, they should be willing to invest no more than: *(a)* $25,771; *(b)* $46,229; *(c)* $52,421.

FUTURE VALUE OF AN ANNUITY

Just as an annuity has a present value, it also has a future value. The future value of an annuity is the accumulated value of the annuity payments and interest as of the date of the final payment. Consider the earlier annuity of three annual payments of $100. These are the points in time at which the present value (p) and the future value (f) occur:

Note that the first payment is made two periods prior to the point at which the future value is determined. Therefore, for the first payment, $n = 2$. For the second payment, $n = 1$. Since the third payment occurs on the future value date, $n = 0$.

One way to calculate the future value of this annuity uses the formula to find the future value of each payment and adds them together. Assuming an interest rate of 15%, the calculation is:

$$f = \$100 \times (1 + .15)^2 + \$100 \times (1 + .15)^1 + \$100 \times (1 + .15)^0 = \$347.25$$

---

[1]The formula for the present value of an annuity of 1 is:

$$p = \frac{1 - \frac{1}{(1 + i)^n}}{i}$$

Another way calculates the future value of the annuity by using Table F–2 to find the sum of the future values of each payment:

First payment:	$f = \$100 \times 1.3225 = \$132.25$	
Second payment:	$f = \$100 \times 1.1500 =$	115.00
Third payment:	$f = \$100 \times 1.0000 =$	100.00
Total:	$f = \$347.25$	

A third approach adds the future values of three payments of 1 and multiplies the sum by $100:

From Table F–1: $i = 15\%, n = 2, f =$ 1.3225
$i = 15\%, n = 1, f =$ 1.1500
$i = 15\%, n = 0, f =$ 1.0000
Sum = 3.4725

Future value = $3.4725 \times \$100 = \$347.25$

A fourth and easier way to solve the problem uses a table that shows the future values of annuities, often called a *future value of an annuity of 1* table. Table F–4 on page AP–11 is such a table. Note in Table F–4 that when $n = 1$, the future values are equal to 1 ($f = 1$) for all rates of interest because the annuity consists of only one payment and the future value is determined on the date of the payment. Thus, the future value equals the payment.

Although a formula is used to construct a table showing the future values of an annuity of 1, you can construct one by adding together the amount in a future value of 1 table like Table F–2.[2] Examine Table F–2 and Table F–4 to confirm that the following numbers were drawn from those tables:

From Table F–2		From Table F–4	
$i = 8\%, n = 0$	1.0000		
$i = 8\%, n = 1$	1.0800		
$i = 8\%, n = 2$	1.1664		
$i = 8\%, n = 3$	1.2597		
Total	4.5061	$i = 8\%, n = 4$	4.5061

Minor differences may occur because the numbers in the tables have been rounded.

You can also use business calculators and spreadsheet computer programs to find the future values of annuities.

Observe that the future value in Table F–2 is 1.0000 when $n = 0$ but the future value in Table F–4 is 1.0000 when $n = 1$. Why does this apparent contradiction arise? When $n = 0$ in Table F–2, the future value is determined on the date that the single payment occurs. Thus, no interest is earned and the future value equals the payment. However, Table F–4 describes annuities with equal payments occurring

---

[2]The formula for the future value of an annuity of 1 is:

$$f = \frac{(1 + i)^n - 1}{i}$$

each period. When $n = 1$, the annuity has only one payment, and its future value also equals 1 on the date of its final and only payment.

Progress Check

F–4   **Syntel Company invests $45,000 per year for five years at 12%. Calculate the value of the investment at the end of five years.**

LO 1. **Explain what is meant by the present value of a single amount and the present value of an annuity, and be able to use tables to solve present value problems.** The present value of a single amount to be received at a future date is the amount that could be invested now at the specified interest rate to yield that future value. The present value of an annuity is the amount that could be invested now at the specified interest rate to yield that series of equal periodic payments. Present value tables and business calculators simplify calculating present values.

LO 2. **Explain what is meant by the future value of a single amount and the future value of an annuity, and be able to use tables to solve future value problems.** The future value of a single amount invested at a specified rate of interest is the amount that would accumulate at a future date. The future value of an annuity to be invested at a specified rate of interest is the amount that would accumulate at the date of the final equal periodic payment. Future value tables and business calculators simplify calculating future values.

SUMMARY OF THE APPENDIX IN TERMS OF LEARNING OBJECTIVES

Table F-1 Present Value of 1 Due in *n* Periods

							Rate						
Periods	1%	2%	3%	4%	5%	6%	7%	8%	9%	10%	12%	15%
1	0.9901	0.9804	0.9709	0.9615	0.9524	0.9434	0.9346	0.9259	0.9174	0.9091	0.8929	0.8696
2	0.9803	0.9612	0.9426	0.9246	0.9070	0.8900	0.8734	0.8573	0.8417	0.8264	0.7972	0.7561
3	0.9706	0.9423	0.9151	0.8890	0.8638	0.8396	0.8163	0.7938	0.7722	0.7513	0.7118	0.6575
4	0.9610	0.9238	0.8885	0.8548	0.8227	0.7921	0.7629	0.7350	0.7084	0.6830	0.6355	0.5718
5	0.9515	0.9057	0.8626	0.8219	0.7835	0.7473	0.7130	0.6806	0.6499	0.6209	0.5674	0.4972
6	0.9420	0.8880	0.8375	0.7903	0.7462	0.7050	0.6663	0.6302	0.5963	0.5645	0.5066	0.4323
7	0.9327	0.8706	0.8131	0.7599	0.7107	0.6651	0.6227	0.5835	0.5470	0.5132	0.4523	0.3759
8	0.9235	0.8535	0.7894	0.7307	0.6768	0.6274	0.5820	0.5403	0.5019	0.4665	0.4039	0.3269
9	0.9143	0.8368	0.7664	0.7026	0.6446	0.5919	0.5439	0.5002	0.4604	0.4241	0.3606	0.2843
10	0.9053	0.8203	0.7441	0.6756	0.6139	0.5584	0.5083	0.4632	0.4224	0.3855	0.3220	0.2472
11	0.8963	0.8043	0.7224	0.6496	0.5847	0.5268	0.4751	0.4289	0.3875	0.3505	0.2875	0.2149
12	0.8874	0.7885	0.7014	0.6246	0.5568	0.4970	0.4440	0.3971	0.3555	0.3186	0.2567	0.1869
13	0.8787	0.7730	0.6810	0.6006	0.5303	0.4688	0.4150	0.3677	0.3262	0.2897	0.2292	0.1625
14	0.8700	0.7579	0.6611	0.5775	0.5051	0.4423	0.3878	0.3405	0.2992	0.2633	0.2046	0.1413
15	0.8613	0.7430	0.6419	0.5553	0.4810	0.4173	0.3624	0.3152	0.2745	0.2394	0.1827	0.1229
16	0.8528	0.7284	0.6232	0.5339	0.4581	0.3936	0.3387	0.2919	0.2519	0.2176	0.1631	0.1069
17	0.8444	0.7142	0.6050	0.5134	0.4363	0.3714	0.3166	0.2703	0.2311	0.1978	0.1456	0.0929
18	0.8360	0.7002	0.5874	0.4936	0.4155	0.3505	0.2959	0.2502	0.2120	0.1799	0.1300	0.0808
19	0.8277	0.6864	0.5703	0.4746	0.3957	0.3305	0.2765	0.2317	0.1945	0.1635	0.1161	0.0703
20	0.8195	0.6730	0.5537	0.4564	0.3769	0.3118	0.2584	0.2145	0.1784	0.1486	0.1037	0.0611
25	0.7798	0.6095	0.4776	0.3751	0.2953	0.2330	0.1842	0.1460	0.1160	0.0923	0.0588	0.0304
30	0.7419	0.5521	0.4120	0.3083	0.2314	0.1741	0.1314	0.0994	0.0754	0.0573	0.0334	0.0151
35	0.7059	0.5000	0.3554	0.2534	0.1813	0.1301	0.0937	0.0676	0.0490	0.0356	0.0189	0.0075
40	0.6717	0.4529	0.3066	0.2083	0.1420	0.0972	0.0668	0.0460	0.0318	0.0221	0.0107	0.0037

Table F-2 Future Value of 1 Due in *n* Periods

Periods	1%	2%	3%	4%	5%	6%	7%	8%	9%	10%	12%	15%
0	1.0000	1.0000	1.0000	1.0000	1.0000	1.0000	1.0000	1.0000	1.0000	1.0000	1.0000	1.0000
1	1.0100	1.0200	1.0300	1.0400	1.0500	1.0600	1.0700	1.0800	1.0900	1.1000	1.1200	1.1500
2	1.0201	1.0404	1.0609	1.0816	1.1025	1.1236	1.1449	1.1664	1.1881	1.2100	1.2544	1.3225
3	1.0303	1.0612	1.0927	1.1249	1.1576	1.1910	1.2250	1.2597	1.2950	1.3310	1.4049	1.5209
4	1.0406	1.0824	1.1255	1.1699	1.2155	1.2625	1.3108	1.3605	1.4116	1.4641	1.5735	1.7490
5	1.0510	1.1041	1.1593	1.2167	1.2763	1.3382	1.4026	1.4693	1.5386	1.6105	1.7623	2.0114
6	1.0615	1.1262	1.1941	1.2653	1.3401	1.4185	1.5007	1.5869	1.6771	1.7716	1.9738	2.3131
7	1.0721	1.1487	1.2299	1.3159	1.4071	1.5036	1.6058	1.7138	1.8280	1.9487	2.2107	2.6600
8	1.0829	1.1717	1.2668	1.3686	1.4775	1.5938	1.7182	1.8509	1.9926	2.1436	2.4760	3.0590
9	1.0937	1.1951	1.3048	1.4233	1.5513	1.6895	1.8385	1.9990	2.1719	2.3579	2.7731	3.5179
10	1.1046	1.2190	1.3439	1.4802	1.6289	1.7908	1.9672	2.1589	2.3674	2.5937	3.1058	4.0456
11	1.1157	1.2434	1.3842	1.5395	1.7103	1.8983	2.1049	2.3316	2.5804	2.8531	3.4785	4.6524
12	1.1268	1.2682	1.4258	1.6010	1.7959	2.0122	2.2522	2.5182	2.8127	3.1384	3.8960	5.3503
13	1.1381	1.2936	1.4685	1.6651	1.8856	2.1329	2.4098	2.7196	3.0658	3.4523	4.3635	6.1528
14	1.1495	1.3195	1.5126	1.7317	1.9799	2.2609	2.5785	2.9372	3.3417	3.7975	4.8871	7.0757
15	1.1610	1.3459	1.5580	1.8009	2.0789	2.3966	2.7590	3.1722	3.6425	4.1772	5.4736	8.1371
16	1.1726	1.3728	1.6047	1.8730	2.1829	2.5404	2.9522	3.4259	3.9703	4.5950	6.1304	9.3576
17	1.1843	1.4002	1.6528	1.9479	2.2920	2.6928	3.1588	3.7000	4.3276	5.0545	6.8660	10.7613
18	1.1961	1.4282	1.7024	2.0258	2.4066	2.8543	3.3799	3.9960	4.7171	5.5599	7.6900	12.3755
19	1.2081	1.4568	1.7535	2.1068	2.5270	3.0256	3.6165	4.3157	5.1417	6.1159	8.6128	14.2318
20	1.2202	1.4859	1.8061	2.1911	2.6533	3.2071	3.8697	4.6610	5.6044	6.7275	9.6463	16.3665
25	1.2824	1.6406	2.0938	2.6658	3.3864	4.2919	5.4274	6.8485	8.6231	10.8347	17.0001	32.9190
30	1.3478	1.8114	2.4273	3.2434	4.3219	5.7435	7.6123	10.0627	13.2677	17.4494	29.9599	66.2118
35	1.4166	1.9999	2.8139	3.9461	5.5160	7.6861	10.6766	14.7853	20.4140	28.1024	52.7996	133.176
40	1.4889	2.2080	3.2620	4.8010	7.0400	10.2857	14.9745	21.7245	31.4094	45.2593	93.0510	267.864

Rate

Table F-3 Present Value of an Annuity of 1 per Period

Periods	1%	2%	3%	4%	5%	6%	7%	8%	9%	10%	12%	15%
1	0.9901	0.9804	0.9709	0.9615	0.9524	0.9434	0.9346	0.9259	0.9174	0.9091	0.8929	0.8696
2	1.9704	1.9416	1.9135	1.8861	1.8594	1.8334	1.8080	1.7833	1.7591	1.7355	1.6901	1.6257
3	2.9410	2.8839	2.8286	2.7751	2.7232	2.6730	2.6243	2.5771	2.5313	2.4869	2.4018	2.2832
4	3.9020	3.8077	3.7171	3.6299	3.5460	3.4651	3.3872	3.3121	3.2397	3.1699	3.0373	2.8550
5	4.8534	4.7135	4.5797	4.4518	4.3295	4.2124	4.1002	3.9927	3.8897	3.7908	3.6048	3.3522
6	5.7955	5.6014	5.4172	5.2421	5.0757	4.9173	4.7665	4.6229	4.4859	4.3553	4.1114	3.7845
7	6.7282	6.4720	6.2303	6.0021	5.7864	5.5824	5.3893	5.2064	5.0330	4.8684	4.5638	4.1604
8	7.6517	7.3255	7.0197	6.7327	6.4632	6.2098	5.9713	5.7466	5.5348	5.3349	4.9676	4.4873
9	8.5660	8.1622	7.7861	7.4353	7.1078	6.8017	6.5152	6.2469	5.9952	5.7590	5.3282	4.7716
10	9.4713	8.9826	8.5302	8.1109	7.7217	7.3601	7.0236	6.7101	6.4177	6.1446	5.6502	5.0188
11	10.3676	9.7868	9.2526	8.7605	8.3064	7.8869	7.4987	7.1390	6.8052	6.4951	5.9377	5.2337
12	11.2551	10.5753	9.9540	9.3851	8.8633	8.3838	7.9427	7.5361	7.1607	6.8137	6.1944	5.4206
13	12.1337	11.3484	10.6350	9.9856	9.3936	8.8527	8.3577	7.9038	7.4869	7.1034	6.4235	5.5831
14	13.0037	12.1062	11.2961	10.5631	9.8986	9.2950	8.7455	8.2442	7.7862	7.3667	6.6282	5.7245
15	13.8651	12.8493	11.9379	11.1184	10.3797	9.7122	9.1079	8.5595	8.0607	7.6061	6.8109	5.8474
16	14.7179	13.5777	12.5611	11.6523	10.8378	10.1059	9.4466	8.8514	8.3126	7.8237	6.9740	5.9542
17	15.5623	14.2919	13.1661	12.1657	11.2741	10.4773	9.7632	9.1216	8.5436	8.0216	7.1196	6.0472
18	16.3983	14.9920	13.7535	12.6593	11.6896	10.8276	10.0591	9.3719	8.7556	8.2014	7.2497	6.1280
19	17.2260	15.6785	14.3238	13.1339	12.0853	11.1581	10.3356	9.6036	8.9501	8.3649	7.3658	6.1982
20	18.0456	16.3514	14.8775	13.5903	12.4622	11.4699	10.5940	9.8181	9.1285	8.5136	7.4694	6.2593
25	22.0232	19.5235	17.4131	15.6221	14.0939	12.7834	11.6536	10.6748	9.8226	9.0770	7.8431	6.4641
30	25.8077	22.3965	19.6004	17.2920	15.3725	13.7648	12.4090	11.2578	10.2737	9.4269	8.0552	6.5660
35	29.4086	24.9986	21.4872	18.6646	16.3742	14.4982	12.9477	11.6546	10.5668	9.6442	8.1755	6.6166
40	32.8437	27.3555	23.1148	19.7928	17.1591	15.0463	13.3317	11.9246	10.7574	9.7791	8.2438	6.6418

Rate

Table F-4 Future Value of an Annuity of 1 per Period

Periods	1%	2%	3%	4%	5%	6%	7%	8%	9%	10%	12%	15%
							Rate					
1	1.0000	1.0000	1.0000	1.0000	1.0000	1.0000	1.0000	1.0000	1.0000	1.0000	1.0000	1.0000
2	2.0100	2.0200	2.0300	2.0400	2.0500	2.0600	2.0700	2.0800	2.0900	2.1000	2.1200	2.1500
3	3.0301	3.0604	3.0909	3.1216	3.1525	3.1836	3.2149	3.2464	3.2781	3.3100	3.3744	3.4725
4	4.0604	4.1216	4.1836	4.2465	4.3101	4.3746	4.4399	4.5061	4.5731	4.6410	4.7793	4.9934
5	5.1010	5.2040	5.3091	5.4163	5.5256	5.6371	5.7507	5.8666	5.9847	6.1051	6.3528	6.7424
6	6.1520	6.3081	6.4684	6.6330	6.8019	6.9753	7.1533	7.3359	7.5233	7.7156	8.1152	8.7537
7	7.2135	7.4343	7.6625	7.8983	8.1420	8.3938	8.6540	8.9228	9.2004	9.4872	10.0890	11.0668
8	8.2857	8.5830	8.8923	9.2142	9.5491	9.8975	10.2598	10.6366	11.0285	11.4359	12.2997	13.7268
9	9.3685	9.7546	10.1591	10.5828	11.0266	11.4913	11.9780	12.4876	13.0210	13.5795	14.7757	16.7858
10	10.4622	10.9497	11.4639	12.0061	12.5779	13.1808	13.8164	14.4866	15.1929	15.9374	17.5487	20.3037
11	11.5668	12.1687	12.8078	13.4864	14.2068	14.9716	15.7836	16.6455	17.5603	18.5312	20.6546	24.3493
12	12.6825	13.4121	14.1920	15.0258	15.9171	16.8699	17.8885	18.9771	20.1407	21.3843	24.1331	29.0017
13	13.8093	14.6803	15.6178	16.6268	17.7130	18.8821	20.1406	21.4953	22.9534	24.5227	28.0291	34.3519
14	14.9474	15.9739	17.0863	18.2919	19.5986	21.0151	22.5505	24.2149	26.0192	27.9750	32.3926	40.5047
15	16.0969	17.2934	18.5989	20.0236	21.5786	23.2760	25.1290	27.1521	29.3609	31.7725	37.2797	47.5804
16	17.2579	18.6393	20.1569	21.8245	23.6575	25.6725	27.8881	30.3243	33.0034	35.9497	42.7533	55.7175
17	18.4304	20.0121	21.7616	23.6975	25.8404	28.2129	30.8402	33.7502	36.9737	40.5447	48.8837	65.0751
18	19.6147	21.4123	23.4144	25.6454	28.1324	30.9057	33.9990	37.4502	41.3013	45.5992	55.7497	75.8364
19	20.8109	22.8406	25.1169	27.6712	30.5390	33.7600	37.3790	41.4463	46.0185	51.1591	63.4397	88.2118
20	22.0190	24.2974	26.8704	29.7781	33.0660	36.7856	40.9955	45.7620	51.1601	57.2750	72.0524	102.444
25	28.2432	32.0303	36.4593	41.6459	47.7271	54.8645	63.2490	73.1059	84.7009	98.3471	133.334	212.793
30	34.7849	40.5681	47.5754	56.0849	66.4388	79.0582	94.4608	113.283	136.308	164.494	241.333	434.745
35	41.6603	49.9945	60.4621	73.6522	90.3203	111.435	138.237	172.317	215.711	271.024	431.663	881.170
40	48.8864	60.4020	75.4013	95.0255	120.800	154.762	199.635	259.057	337.882	442.593	767.091	1,779.09

EXERCISES

Exercise F–1
Present value of an amount
(LO 1)

Jasper Company is considering an investment which, if paid for immediately, is expected to return $172,500 five years hence. If Jasper demands a 9% return, how much will it be willing to pay for this investment?

Exercise F–2
Future value of an amount
(LO 2)

LCV Company invested $529,000 in a project expected to earn a 12% annual rate of return. The earnings will be reinvested in the project each year until the entire investment is liquidated 10 years hence. What will the cash proceeds be when the project is liquidated?

Exercise F–3
Present value of an annuity
(LO 1)

Cornblue Distributing is considering a contract that will return $200,400 annually at the end of each year for six years. If Cornblue demands an annual return of 7% and pays for the investment immediately, how much should it be willing to pay?

Exercise F–4
Future value of an annuity
(LO 2)

Sarah Oliver is planning to begin an individual retirement program in which she will invest $1,200 annually at the end of each year. Oliver plans to retire after making 30 annual investments in a program that earns a return of 10%. What will be the value of the program on the date of the last investment?

Exercise F–5
Interest rate on an investment
(LO 1)

Kevin Smith has been offered the possibility of investing $0.3152 for 15 years, after which he will be paid $1. What annual rate of interest will Smith earn? (Use Table F–1 to find the answer.)

Exercise F–6
Number of periods of an investment
(LO 1)

Laura Veralli has been offered the possibility of investing $0.5268. The investment will earn 6% per year and will return Veralli $1 at the end of the investment. How many years must Veralli wait to receive the $1? (Use Table F–1 to find the answer.)

Exercise F–7
Number of periods of an investment
(LO 2)

Tom Albertson expects to invest $1 at 15% and, at the end of the investment, receive $66.2118. How many years will elapse before Albertson receives the payment? (Use Table F–2 to find the answer.)

Exercise F–8
Interest rate on an investment
(LO 2)

Ed Teller expects to invest $1 for 35 years, after which he will receive $20.4140. What rate of interest will Teller earn? (Use Table F–2 to find the answer.)

Exercise F–9
Interest rate on an investment
(LO 1)

Helen Fanshawe expects an immediate investment of $9.3936 to return $1 annually for 13 years, with the first payment to be received in one year. What rate of interest will Fanshawe earn? (Use Table F–3 to find the answer.)

Exercise F–10
Number of periods of an investment
(LO 1)

Ken Priggin expects an investment of $7.6061 to return $1 annually for several years. If Priggin is to earn a return of 10%, how many annual payments must he receive? (Use Table F–3 to find the answer.)

Steve Church expects to invest $1 annually for 40 years and have an accumulated value of $95.0255 on the date of the last investment. If this occurs, what rate of interest will Church earn? (Use Table F–4 to find the answer.)

Exercise F–11
Interest rate on an investment
(LO 2)

Bitsy Brennon expects to invest $1 annually in a fund that will earn 8%. How many annual investments must Brennon make to accumulate $45.7620 on the date of the last investment? (Use Table F–4 to find the answer.)

Exercise F–12
Number of periods of an investment
(LO 2)

Bill Lenehan financed a new automobile by paying $3,100 cash and agreeing to make 20 monthly payments of $450 each, the first payment to be made one month after the purchase. The loan was said to bear interest at an annual rate of 12%. What was the cost of the automobile?

Exercise F–13
Present value of an annuity
(LO 1)

Stephanie Powell deposited $4,900 in a savings account that earns interest at an annual rate of 8%, compounded quarterly. The $4,900 plus earned interest must remain in the account 10 years before it can be withdrawn. How much money will be in the account at the end of the 10 years?

Exercise F–14
Future value of an amount
(LO 2)

Sally Sayer plans to have $90 withheld from her monthly paycheque and deposited in a savings account that earns 12% annually, compounded monthly. If Sayer continues with her plan for 2½ years, how much will be accumulated in the account on the date of the last deposit?

Exercise F–15
Future value of an annuity
(LO 2)

Stellar Company plans to issue 12%, 15-year, $500,000 par value bonds payable that pay interest semiannually on June 30 and December 31. The bonds are dated December 31, 1996, and are to be issued on that date. If the market rate of interest for the bonds is 10% on the date of issue, what will be the cash proceeds from the bond issue?

Exercise F–16
Present value of bonds
(LO 1)

Travis Company has decided to establish a fund that will be used 10 years hence to replace an aging productive facility. The company makes an initial contribution of $150,000 to the fund and plans to make quarterly contributions of $60,000 beginning in three months. The fund is expected to earn 12%, compounded quarterly. What will be the value of the fund 10 years hence?

Exercise F–17
Future value of an amount plus an annuity
(LO 2)

McCoy Company expects to earn 10% per year on an investment that will pay $756,400 six years hence. Use Table F–2 to calculate the present value of the investment.

Exercise F–18
Present value of an amount
(LO 1)

Comet Company invests $216,000 at 7% per year for nine years. Use Table F–1 to calculate the future value of the investment nine years hence.

Exercise F–19
Future value of an amount
(LO 2)

ANSWERS TO PROGRESS CHECKS

F–1 $70,000 × 0.6302 = $44,114

F–2 *c* $299,850/$150,000 = 1.9990
        Table F–2 shows this value for nine years at 8%.

F–3 *c* $10,000 × 5.2421 = $52,421

F–4 $45,000 × 6.3528 = $285,876

Accounting Principles and Conceptual Framework

After studying Appendix G, you should be able to:

1. Explain the difference between descriptive concepts and prescriptive concepts.
2. Explain the difference between bottom-up and top-down approaches to the development of accounting concepts.
3. Describe the major components in the Accounting Standards Board's "Financial Statement Concepts."

Accounting principles or concepts are not laws of nature. They are broad ideas developed as a way of *describing* current accounting practices and *prescribing* new and improved practices. In studying Appendix G, you will learn about some new accounting concepts that the Accounting Standards Board (AcSB) developed in an effort to guide future changes and improvements in accounting.

ACCOUNTING PRINCIPLES AND CONCEPTUAL FRAMEWORK

To fully understand the importance of financial accounting concepts or principles, you must realize that they serve two purposes. First, they provide general descriptions of existing accounting practices. In doing this, concepts and principles serve as guidelines that help you learn about accounting. Thus, after learning how the concepts or principles are applied in a few situations, you develop the ability to apply them in different situations. This is easier and more effective than memorizing a very long list of specific practices.

Second, these concepts or principles help accountants analyze unfamiliar situations and develop procedures to account for those situations. This purpose is especially important for the Accounting Standards Board, which is charged with developing uniform practices for financial reporting in Canada and with improving the quality of such reporting.

In prior chapters, we defined and illustrated several important accounting principles. These principles, listed together here for convenience, describe in general terms the practices currently used by accountants.

DESCRIPTIVE AND PRESCRIPTIVE ACCOUNTING CONCEPTS

LO 1

Explain the difference between descriptive concepts and prescriptive concepts.

Generally Accepted Principles

Business entity principle	Going-concern principle	Revenue recognition
Conservatism principle	Matching principle	principle
Consistency principle	Materiality principle	Time-period principle
Cost principle	Objectivity principle	Unit of measure
Full-disclosure principle		assumption

The listed principles (defined on pages 20–23) are useful for teaching and learning about accounting practice and are helpful for dealing with some unfamiliar transactions. As business practices have evolved in recent years, however, these principles have become less useful as guides for accountants to follow in dealing with new and different types of transactions. This problem has occurred because the principles are intended to provide general descriptions of current accounting practices. In other words, they describe what accountants currently do; they do not necessarily describe what accountants should do. Also, since these principles do not identify weaknesses in accounting practices, they do not lead to major changes or improvements in accounting practices.

In order to improve accounting practices, principles or concepts should not merely *describe* what was being done, they should *prescribe* what ought to be done to make things better.

Before we examine the concepts enunciated in the conceptual framework, we need to look more closely at the differences between descriptive and prescriptive uses of accounting concepts.

THE PROCESSES OF DEVELOPING DESCRIPTIVE AND PRESCRIPTIVE ACCOUNTING CONCEPTS

LO 2

Explain the difference between bottom-up and top-down approaches to the development of accounting concepts.

Sets of concepts differ in how they are developed and used. In general, when concepts are intended to describe current practice, they are developed by looking at accepted specific practices and then making some general rules to encompass them. This bottom-up approach is diagrammed in Illustration G–1 which shows the arrows going from the practices to the concepts. The outcome of the process is a set of general rules that summarize practice and that can be used for education and for solving some new problems. For example, this approach leads to the concept that asset purchases are recorded at cost. However, these kinds of concepts often fail to show how new problems should be solved. To continue the example, the concept that assets are recorded at cost does not provide much direct guidance for situations in which assets have no cost because they are donated to a company by a local government. Further, because these concepts are based on the presumption that current practices are adequate, they do not lead to the development of new and improved accounting methods. To continue the example, the concept that assets are initially recorded at cost does not encourage asking the question of whether they should always be carried at that amount.

In contrast, if concepts are intended to *prescribe* improvements in accounting practices, they are likely to be designed by a top-down approach (Illustration G–2). Note that the top-down approach starts with broad accounting objectives. The process then generates broad concepts about the types of information that should be reported. Finally, these concepts should lead to specific practices that ought to be used. The advantage of this approach is that the concepts are good for solving

Illustration G-1 A Bottom-Up Process of Developing Descriptive Accounting Concepts

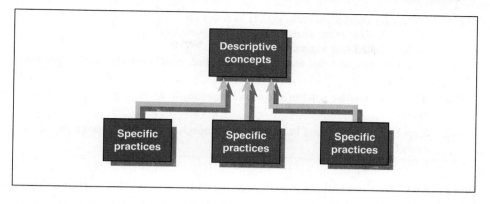

Illustration G-2 A Top-Down Process of Developing Prescriptive Accounting Concepts

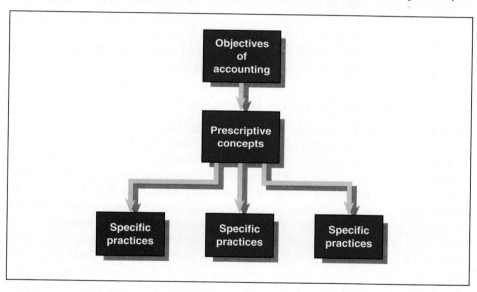

new problems and evaluating old answers; its disadvantage is that the concepts may not be very descriptive of current practice. In fact, the suggested practices may not be in current use.

Since the AcSB uses accounting concepts to prescribe accounting practices, the Board used a top-down approach to develop its conceptual framework. The Board's concepts are not necessarily more correct than the previously developed concepts. However, the new concepts are intended to provide better guidelines for developing new and improved accounting practices. The Board has stated that it will use them as a basis for its future actions and already has used them to justify important changes in financial reporting.

Progress Check

G–1   **The AcSB's conceptual framework is intended to:**
       a. **provide a historical analysis of accounting practice.**
       b. **describe current accounting practice.**
       c. **provide concepts that are prescriptive of what should be done in accounting practice.**

G–2   **What is the starting point in a top-down approach to developing accounting concepts?**

G–3   **What is the starting point in a bottom-up approach to developing accounting concepts?**

THE CONCEPTUAL FRAMEWORK

LO 3

Describe the major components in the Accounting Standards Board's "Financial Statement Concepts."

During the 1970s the accounting profession in both Canada and the United States turned its attention to the apparent need for improvement in financial reporting. In 1980 *Corporate Reporting: Its Future Evolution,* a research study, was published by the Canadian Institute of Chartered Accountants, and in 1989 "Financial Statement Concepts," section 1000 of the *CICA Handbook,* was approved. In the United States the Financial Accounting Standards Board (FASB) published, in the 1978–85 period, six statements regarded as the most comprehensive pronouncement of the conceptual framework of accounting. FASB *(SFAC 1)* and Accounting Standards Board *(CICA Handbook,* section 1000) identified the broad objectives of financial reporting.

The Objectives of Financial Reporting

"Financial Statement Concepts" identified the broad objectives of financial reporting. The most general objective stated in the *CICA Handbook,* par. 1000.12, is to "communicate information that is useful to investors, creditors, and other users in making resource allocation decisions and/or assessing management stewardship." From this beginning point the Accounting Standards Board (AcSB) expressed other, more specific objectives. These objectives recognize that (1) financial reporting should help users predict future cash flow and (2) in making such predictions, information about a company's resources and obligations is useful if it possesses certain qualities. All of the concepts in the "Financial Statement Concepts" are intended to be consistent with these general objectives. Of course, present accounting practice already provides information about a company's resources and obligations. Thus, although the conceptual framework is intended to be prescriptive of new and improved practices, the concepts in the framework are also descriptive of many current practices.

The Qualities of Useful Information

The AcSB discussed the fact that information can be useful only if it is understandable to users. However, the users are assumed to have the training, experience, and motivation to analyze financial reports. With this decision, the Board indicated that financial reporting should not try to meet the needs of unsophisticated or other casual report users.

The AcSB said that information is useful if it is (1) relevant, (2) reliable, and (3) comparable. Information is *relevant* if it can make a difference in a decision.

As a Matter of Opinion

Ms. Gordon received a B.A. in economics and commerce and both an M.A. and a Ph.D. in economics at Simon Fraser University, where she has been a member of the faculty of business administration since 1981. Ms. Gordon teaches financial accounting and is engaged in research in the areas of positive accounting theory, the accounting-economics interface, social responsibility accounting, and issues in accounting education. She has been a member of CGA-Canada Research Committee since 1984 and was president of the Canadian Academic Accounting Association for 1988–1989.

While my university degrees all carry economics in the title, my Ph.D. courses, thesis, and subsequent research have heavily emphasized accounting issues ranging from pensions to internal control to accounting theory.

Accounting research is fundamentally interdisciplinary in character. It is this breadth of character that initially sparked my interest and has held it over time. Additionally, in a world where accounting standard setters' decisions are made which have an effect on differing cultures, societies, economic systems, and individuals, this interdisciplinary emphasis is vital. The link between the research of individual accounting academics and standard setting is both important and a "two-way street." Without continuing accounting research, the standard setting process might lack the background or new ways to view our rapidly changing world. As well this linkage gives a purpose to much of the ongoing accounting research.

Irene M. Gordon, CGA

Information has this quality when it helps users predict the future or evaluate the past, and when it is received in time to affect their decisions.

Information is *reliable* if users can depend on it to be free from bias and error. Reliable information is verifiable and faithfully represents what is supposed to be described. In addition, users can depend on information only if it is neutral. This means that the rules used to produce information should not be designed to lead users to accept or reject any specific decision alternative.

Information is *comparable* if users can use it to identify differences and similarities between companies. Comparability is possible only if companies follow uniform practices. However, even if all companies uniformly follow the same practices, comparable reports do not result if the practices are not appropriate. For example, comparable information would not be provided if all companies were to ignore the useful lives of their assets and amortize all assets over two years.

Comparability also requires consistency, which means that a company should not change its accounting practices unless the change is justified as a reporting improvement. Another important concept discussed is materiality.

Elements of Financial Statements

Another important step in developing the conceptual framework was to determine the elements of financial statements. This involved defining the categories of information that should be contained in financial reports. The AcSB's discussion of financial statement elements includes definitions of important elements such as assets, liabilities, equity, revenues, expenses, gains, and losses. In earlier chapters, we referred to many of these definitions when we explained various accounting procedures.

Recognition and Measurement

The AcSB, in paragraphs 36-47 of section 1000, established concepts for deciding (1) when items should be presented (or recognized) in the financial statements, and (2) how to assign numbers to (or measure) those items. In general, the Board concluded that items should be recognized in the financial statements if they meet the following criteria:

- Definitions. The item meets the definition of an element of financial statements.
- Measurability. It has a relevant attribute measurable with sufficient reliability.
- Relevance. The information about it is capable of making a difference in user decisions.
- Reliability. The information is representationally faithful, verifiable, and neutral.

The question of how items should be measured raises the fundamental question of whether financial statements should be based on cost or on value. Since this question is quite controversial, the AcSB's discussion of this issue is more descriptive of current practice than it is prescriptive of new measurement methods. However, before we consider alternative accounting valuation systems, let us review and expand upon the accounting concepts or principles.

ACCOUNTING PRINCIPLES

An understanding of accounting principles begins with the recognition of the broad concepts as to the nature of the economic setting in which accounting operates.

The Business Entity Principle

Every business unit or enterprise is treated in accounting as a separate entity, with the affairs of the business and those of the owner or owners being kept entirely separate.

The Going-Concern Principle

Unless there is strong evidence to the contrary, it is assumed that a business will continue to operate as a going concern, earning a reasonable profit for a period longer than the life expectancy of any of its assets.

The Time-Period Principle

The environment in which accounting operates—the business community and the government—requires that the life of a business be divided into relatively short periods and that changes be measured over these short periods. Yet, it is generally agreed that earnings cannot be measured precisely over a short period and that it is impossible to learn the exact earnings of a business until it has completed its last transaction and converted all its assets to cash.

Cost Principle

The cost principle specifies that cash-equivalent cost is the most useful basis for the initial accounting of the elements that are recorded in the accounts and reported on the financial statements. It is important to note that the cost principle applies to the initial recording of transactions and events.

The cost principle is supported by the fact that at the time of a completed arm's-length business transaction, the market value of the resources given up in the transaction provides reliable evidence of the valuation of the item acquired in the transaction.

When a noncash consideration is involved, cost is measured as the market value of the resources given or the market value of the item received, whichever is more reliably determinable. For example, an asset may be acquired with a debt given as settlement. Cost in this instance is the present value of the amount of cash to be paid in the future, as specified by the terms of the debt. The cost principle applies to all of the elements of financial statements, including liabilities.

The cost principle provides guidance at the original recognition date. However, the original cost of some items acquired is subject to depreciation, depletion, amortization, and write-down in conformity with the matching principle and the conservatism constraint (discussed in the sections that follow).

Revenue Recognition Principle

The revenue recognition principle specifies when revenue should be recognized in the accounts and reported in the financial statements. Revenue is measured as the market value of the resources received or the product or service given, whichever is the more reliably determinable.

Under the revenue recognition principle, revenue from the sale of goods is recognized according to the sales method (i.e., at the time of sale) because the earning process usually is complete at the time of sale. At that time, the relevant information about the asset inflows to the seller would be known with reliability.

Under revenue recognition principle, revenue from the sale of services is recognized on the basis of performance because performance determines the extent to which the earning process is complete.

The revenue recognition principle requires accrual basis accounting rather than cash basis accounting for revenues. For example, completed transactions for the sale of goods or services on credit usually are recognized as revenue in the period in which the sale or service occurred rather than in the period in which the cash is eventually collected.

Matching Principle

A major objective of accounting is the determination of periodic net income by matching appropriate costs against revenues. The principle recognizes that streams of revenues continually flow into a business, and it requires (1) that there be a precise cutoff in these streams at the end of an accounting period, (2) that the inflows of the period be measured, (3) that the costs incurred in securing the inflows be determined, and (4) that the sum of the costs be deducted from the sum of the inflows to determine the period's net income.

The Objectivity Principle

The objectivity principle holds that changes in account balances should be supported to the fullest extent possible by objective evidence.

Bargained transactions supported by verifiable business documents originating outside the business are the best objective evidence obtainable, and whenever possible, accounting data should be supported by such documents.

Full-Disclosure Principle

The full-disclosure principle requires that the financial statements of a business clearly report all of the relevant information about the economic affairs of the enterprise. This principle rests upon the primary characteristic of relevance. Full disclosure requires (a) reporting of all information that can make a difference in a decision and (b) that the accounting information reported must be understandable (i.e., not susceptible to misleading inferences). Full disclosure also requires that the major accounting policies and any special accounting policies used by the company be explained in the notes to the financial statements.

The Consistency Principle

In many cases two or more methods or procedures have been derived in accounting practice to accomplish a particular accounting objective. While recognizing the validity of different methods under varying circumstances, it is still necessary, in order to ensure a high degree of comparability in any concern's accounting data, to insist on a consistent application in the company of any given accounting method, period after period. It is also necessary to insist that any departures from this doctrine of consistency be fully disclosed in the financial statements and the effects thereof on the statements be fully described.

The Principle of Conservatism

The principle of conservatism holds that the accountant should be conservative in his or her estimates and opinions and in the selection of procedures, choosing those that neither unduly understate nor overstate the situation.

The Principle of Materiality

A strict adherence to accounting principles is not required for items of little significance. Consequently, the accountant must always weigh the costs of complying with an accounting principle against the extra accuracy gained thereby, and in those situations where the cost is relatively great and the lack of compliance will have no material effect on the financial statements, compliance is not necessary.

There is no clear-cut distinction between material and immaterial items. Each situation must be individually judged, and an item is material or immaterial as it relates to other items. As a guide, the amount of an item is material if its omission, in the light of the surrounding circumstances, makes it probable that the judgment of a reasonable person would have been changed or influenced.

Implementation Constraints

Two of the principles listed, materiality and conservatism, are different from the other principles. In fact, some regard these as constraints which exert a modifying influence on financial accounting and reporting. The two other constraints are cost-benefit and industry peculiarities.

The cost of preparing and reporting accounting information should not exceed the value or usefulness of such information. Accounting focuses on usefulness and substance over form. Thus, pecularities and practices of an industry may warrant selective exceptions to accounting principles and practices. These exceptions are permitted for specific items where there is a clear precedent in the industry based on uniqueness and usefulness.

Departure from the strict application of accounting principles and concepts must be fully disclosed whether it be on the basis of (*a*) materiality, (*b*) conservatism, (*c*) cost-benefit, or (*d*) industry peculiarity.

Unit-of-Measure Assumption

The unit-of-measure assumption specifies that accounting should measure and report the results of the entity's economic activities in terms of a monetary unit such as the Canadian dollar. The assumption recognizes that the monetary unit of measure is an effective means of communicating financial information. Thus, money is the common denominator—the yardstick used in accounting. Using money allows dissimilar things to be aggregated.

Unfortunately, use of a monetary unit for measurement purposes poses a dilemma. Unlike a yardstick which is always the same length, the dollar changes in value. Therefore, during times of inflation or deflation, dollars of different size are entered in the accounts and intermingled as if they possessed equal purchasing power. Because of the practice of ignoring changes in the purchasing power of a dollar, accounting implicitly assumes that the magnitude of change in the value of the monetary unit is not material. This is incorrect. However, this problem and the efforts of the accounting profession to develop alternative valuation systems that report the effects of changes in prices is beyond the scope of this textbook.

Progress Check

G–4 That a business should be consistent from year to year in its accounting practices most directly relates to the AcSB's concept that information reported in financial statements should be: *(a)* relevant; *(b)* material; *(c)* reliable; *(d)* comparable.

G–5 What are the characteristics of accounting information that make it reliable?

G–6 What is the meaning of the phrase *elements of financial statements?*

SUMMARY OF APPENDIX G IN TERMS OF LEARNING OBJECTIVES

LO 1. Some accounting concepts provide general descriptions of current accounting practices. Other concepts prescribe the practices accountants should follow. These prescriptive concepts are most useful in developing accounting procedures for new types of transactions and making improvements in accounting practice.

LO 2. A bottom-up approach to developing concepts examines current practices and then develops concepts to provide general descriptions of those practices. In contrast, a top-down approach begins by stating accounting objectives and from there, develops concepts that prescribe the types of accounting practices accountants should follow.

LO 3. The AcSB's financial statement concepts identify the broad objectives of financial reporting and the qualitative characteristics accounting information should possess. The elements contained in financial reports are defined and the recognition and measurement criteria to be used are identified.

QUESTIONS

1. Why are concepts developed with a bottom-up approach less useful in leading to accounting improvements than those developed with a top-down approach?

2. What is the starting point in a top-down approach to developing accounting concepts?

3. What is the starting point in a bottom-up approach to developing accounting concepts?

4. What are the basic objectives of external financial reporting according to "Financial Statement Concepts"?

5. What is implied by saying that financial information should have the qualitative characteristic of relevance?

6. What are the characteristics of accounting information that make it reliable?

PROBLEM

Problem G–1
Analytical essay
(LO 1, 2, 3)

Write a brief essay that explains why a top-down approach to developing descriptive accounting concepts is not likely to be effective. Also explain why a bottom-up approach is more likely to be effective. Finally, explain why the conceptual framework reflects a top-down approach to developing concepts.

ANSWERS TO PROGRESS CHECKS

G–1 c

G–2 A top-down approach to developing accounting concepts begins by identifying appropriate objectives of accounting reports.

G–3 A bottom-up approach to developing accounting starts by examining existing accounting practices and determining the general features that characterize those procedures.

G–4 d

G–5 To have the qualitative characteristic of being reliable, accounting information should be free from bias and error, should be verifiable, should faithfully represent what is supposed to be described, and should be neutral.

G–6 The elements of financial statements are the objects and events that financial statements should describe, for example, assets, liabilities, revenues, and expenses.

Accounting for Corporate Income Taxes

After studying Appendix H, you should be able to:

1. **Explain why income taxes for accounting purposes may be different from income taxes for tax purposes.**

2. **Prepare an income tax schedule and journal entries for a company where timing differences exist between accounting and taxable income.**

Financial statements for a business should be prepared in accordance with generally accepted accounting principles. Income tax returns, on the other hand, must be prepared in accordance with income tax laws. As a result, a corporation's *income before taxes* measured in accordance with generally accepted accounting principles is almost never the same as *taxable income* calculated on income tax returns.

ACCOUNTING AND TAXABLE INCOME

LO 1
Explain why income taxes for accounting purposes may be different from income taxes for tax purposes.

You have already learned how to determine net income under GAAP for a profit-oriented entity. However, the determination of taxable income for a corporation, while starting with the accounting net income, is done using the Canadian Income Tax Act. Almost always, this results in taxable income being different from the GAAP accounting income.

A major difference between accounting income and taxable income results from what are known as timing differences. These arise because some items are included as revenue or expense in one period under GAAP, whereas they are included in a different period under the income tax rules. For example:

1. The application of accounting principles for installment sales requires that gross profit on these sales is recognized in accounting income before it is recognized in taxable income under the income tax rules.

2. Accounting principles require an estimate of future costs, such as costs of making good on guarantees; they also require a deduction of such costs from revenue in the year the guaranteed goods are sold. However, tax rules do not permit the deduction of such costs until they are actually incurred.

3. Reported net income also differs from taxable income because the taxpayer uses a method or procedure believed to fairly reflect periodic net income for accounting purposes, but is required to use a different method of procedure for tax purposes. For example, the last-in, first-out inventory method of cost allocation may be used for accounting purposes, but is not permitted for tax purposes. Likewise, many companies use straight-line amortization of capital assets for accounting purposes but are required to use a different procedure, called *capital cost allowances,* for tax purposes.

CAPITAL COST ALLOWANCES

Depreciation (amortization) accounting has been greatly influenced by income tax laws. The 1948 Income Tax Act replaced the complex body of rules that had developed for the purpose of limiting the amount of amortization allowed for tax purposes. The act defined and set a limit on amounts which could be deducted, for tax purposes, in respect to the cost of amortizable assets. These amounts are known as *capital cost allowances* (CCA).

The capital cost allowances are identical in nature and purpose with the accountants' concept of amortization and are based on the declining-balance method, discussed in Chapter 11. For tax purposes, the taxpayer may claim the maximum allowed or any part thereof in any year regardless of the amortization method and the amounts used in the accounting records.

Although capital cost allowances are based on the declining-balance method, certain procedures have been set out by the Regulations of the Act. The more important of these are as follows:

1. All amortizable assets are grouped into a comparatively small number of classes and a maximum rate allowed is prescribed for each group. The assets most commonly in use are set out below according to the class to which they belong, with the maximum rate of allowance for each such class (as at the time of writing).

    Class 1 (4%): Buildings or other structures.
    Class 7 (15%): Ships, scows, canoes, and rowboats.
    Class 8 (20%): Machinery, equipment, and furniture.
    Class 10 (30%): Automobiles, trucks, tractors, and computer hardware.

2. The assets of a designated class are considered to form a separate pool of costs. The costs of asset additions are added to their respective pools of unamortized capital cost. When assets are disposed of, the proceeds (up to the original cost) received from disposal are deducted from the proper pool. The balance of each pool of costs is also diminished by the accumulated capital cost allowance claimed. A capital cost allowance is claimed on the balance, referred to as the *unamortized capital cost* (UCC), in the pool at the end of the fiscal year. However, when there are net additions to the pool, only one half of the amount added is used in the calculation of CCA in the year of the net additions. The effect is that the assets are assumed to have been acquired halfway through the fiscal year.

3. "Losses" and "gains" on disposal of individual assets disappear into the pool of unamortized capital costs except when an asset is sold for more than its capital cost. In this case, proceeds of disposal in excess of the capital cost of the asset are normally treated as a capital gain. Where the proceeds of disposal (excluding the capital gain, if any) exceed the unamortized capital cost of the class immediately before the sale, the amount of the excess is treated as a "recapture" of capital cost allowances previously taken. Such a recapture is considered as ordinary income. When all of the assets in a class are disposed of and the proceeds are less than the unamortized capital cost of the class immediately before the sale, the proceeds less the unamortized capital cost may be deducted in determining the year's taxable income.

Companies must, with few exceptions, use capital cost allowances for tax purposes, but commonly use straight-line amortization in their accounting records. A problem arising from this practice is discussed in the next section.

When one accounting procedure is required for tax purposes and a different procedure is used in the accounting records, a problem arises as to how much income tax expense should be deducted each year on the income statement. If the tax actually incurred in such situations is deducted, reported net income often varies from year to year due to the postponement and later payment of taxes. Consequently, in such cases, since shareholders may be misled by these variations, many accountants are of the opinion that income taxes should be allocated in such a way that any distortion resulting from postponing taxes is removed from the income statement.

To appreciate the problem involved here, assume that a corporation has installed a $100,000 machine, the product of which will produce a half-million dollars of revenue in each of the succeeding four years and $80,000 of income before amortization and taxes. Assume further that the company must pay income taxes at a 40% rate (round number assumed for easy calculation) and that it plans to use straight-line amortization in its records but the capital cost allowance for tax purposes. If the machine has a four-year life and a $10,000 salvage value and if the maximum permitted capital cost allowance rate on this particular machine is 50%, annual amortization calculated by each method will be as follows:

Year	Straight-Line	Capital Cost Allowance
1996	$22,500	$25,000
1997	22,500	37,500
1998	22,500	18,750
1999	22,500	8,750*
Totals	$90,000	$90,000

*Use $8,750 in order to match salvage value.
CCA allowed is $9,375.

In the year of acquisition, only one-half of the CCA otherwise allowed may be claimed. In subsequent years, CCA may be claimed up to the maximum amounts allowed.

Since the company uses capital cost allowance for tax purposes, it will be liable for $22,000 of income tax on the first year's income, $17,000 on the second, $24,500 on the third, and $28,500 on the fourth. The calculation of these taxes is shown in Illustration H–1.

Furthermore, if the company were to deduct its actual tax payable each year in arriving at income to be reported to its shareholders, it would report the amounts shown in Illustration H–2.

Observe in Illustrations H–1 and H–2 that total amortization, $90,000, is the same whether calculated by the straight-line or the declining-balance method. Also

TAXES AND THE DISTORTION OF NET INCOME

LO 2

Prepare an income tax schedule and journal entries when timing differences exist.

Illustration H–1
Calculation of Income
Taxes

Annual Income Taxes	1996	1997	1998	1999	Total
Income before amortization and income taxes	$80,000	$80,000	$80,000	$80,000	$320,000
Amortization for tax purposes (declining-balance)/CCA	25,000	37,500	18,750	8,750	90,000
Taxable income	$55,000	$42,500	$61,250	$71,250	$230,000
Annual income taxes (40% of taxable income).	$22,000	$17,000	$24,500	$28,500	$ 92,000

Illustration H–2   Calculation of Remaining Income

Income after Deducting Actual Tax Liabilities	1996	1997	1998	1999	Total
Income before amortization and income taxes.	$80,000	$80,000	$80,000	$80,000	$320,000
Amortization per books (straight-line) . . .	22,500	22,500	22,500	22,500	90,000
Income before taxes	57,500	57,500	57,500	57,500	230,000
Income taxes (actual liability of each year).	22,000	17,000	24,500	28,500	92,000
Remaining income	$35,500	$40,500	$33,000	$29,000	$138,000

note that the total tax paid over the four years, $92,000, is the same in each case. Then note the distortion of the final income figures in Illustration H–2 due to the postponement of taxes.

If this company should report successive annual income figures of $35,500, $40,500, $33,000, and then $29,000, some of its shareholders might be misled as to the company's earnings trend. Consequently, in cases such as this, many accountants think income taxes should be allocated so that the distortion caused by the postponement of taxes is removed from the income statement. These accountants advocate that

> when one accounting procedure is used in the accounting records and a different procedure is used for tax purposes, the tax expense deducted on the income statement should not be the actual tax liability but the amount that would be payable if the procedure used in the records were also used in calculating the tax.

If the foregoing is applied in this case, the corporation will report to its shareholders in each of the four years the amounts of income shown in Illustration H–3.

In examining Illustration H–2, recall that the company's taxes payable are actually $22,000 in the first year, $17,000 in the second, $24,500 in the third, and $28,500 in the fourth, a total of $92,000. Then observe that when this $92,000 liability is allocated evenly over the four years, the distortion of the annual net incomes due to the postponement of taxes is removed from the published income statements.

Illustration H-3 Tax Expense Based on Accounting Income

Net Income That Should Be Reported to Shareholders	1996	1997	1998	1999	Total
Income before amortization and income taxes.	$80,000	$80,000	$80,000	$80,000	$320,000
Amortization per books (straight-line) . . .	22,500	22,500	22,500	22,500	90,000
Income before taxes	57,500	57,500	57,500	57,500	230,000
Income taxes (amounts based on straight-line amortization).	23,000	23,000	23,000	23,000	92,000
Net income.	$34,500	$34,500	$34,500	$34,500	$138,000

When income taxes are allocated as in Illustration H–3, the tax payable for each year and the deferred income tax are recorded with an adjusting entry. The adjusting entries for the four years of Illustration H–2 and the entries in General Journal form for the payment of the taxes (without explanations) are as follows:

ENTRIES FOR THE ALLOCATION OF TAXES

1996	Income Tax Expense	23,000	
	Income Taxes Payable		22,000
	Deferred Income Tax		1,000
	Income Taxes Payable	22,000	
	Cash		22,000
1997	Income Tax Expense	23,000	
	Income Taxes Payable		17,000
	Deferred Income Tax		6,000
	Income Taxes Payable	17,000	
	Cash		17,000
1998	Income Tax Expense	23,000	
	Deferred Income Tax	1,500	
	Income Taxes Payable		24,500
	Income Taxes Payable	24,500	
	Cash		24,500
1999	Income Tax Expense	23,000	
	Deferred Income Tax	5,500	
	Income Taxes Payable		28,500
	Income Taxes Payable	28,500	
	Cash		28,500

Note: To simplify the illustration, it is assumed that the entire year's tax liability is paid at one time. However, corporations are usually required to pay estimated taxes on a monthly basis.

In the entries the $23,000 debited to Income Tax Expense each year is the amount that is deducted on the income statement in reporting annual net income. Also, the amount credited to Income Taxes Payable each year is the actual tax liability of that year.

Observe in the entries that since the actual tax payable in each of the first two years is less than the amount debited to Income Tax Expense, the difference is credited to *Deferred Income Tax*. Then note that in the last two years, because the actual liability each year is greater than the debit to Income Tax Expense, the difference is debited to Deferred Income Tax. Now observe in the following illustration of the company's Deferred Income Tax account that the debits and credits exactly balance each other out over the four-year period:

Deferred Income Tax

Year	Explanation	Debit	Credit	Balance
1996			1,000	1,000
1997			6,000	7,000
1998		1,500		5,500
1999		5,500		–0–

In passing, it should be observed that many accountants believe the interests of government, business, and the public would be better served if there were more uniformity between taxable income and reported net income. However, since the federal income tax is designed to serve other purposes in addition to raising revenue, it is apt to be some time before this is achieved.

Before concluding this appendix on income taxes, we should mention some additional features of the rules that govern accounting for income taxes.

1. In the example above, we assumed an income tax rate of 40% in each year. However, if the income tax rate changes, we use the rate in effect for that year. When the timing difference reverses, the average rate over the accumulation period should be used to avoid throwing the deferred tax amount into a debit balance (this point is covered more thoroughly in later courses).

2. In the example, 1996 income before taxes was *more than* taxable income because of a timing difference that was expected to reverse in 1998 or 1999. As a result, we recognized a deferred tax balance on the December 31, 1996, balance sheet. In other situations, just the opposite kind of timing difference may occur. In other words, a timing difference that will reverse in the future may cause income before taxes to be *less than* taxable income. These latter situations may, under certain conditions, result in the recognition of a deferred tax debit.

3. The Deferred Income Tax account balance may be reported as a long-term liability or as a current liability, depending on how far in the future the amount will reverse.

4. Federal tax laws generally require corporations to estimate their current year's tax liability and make advance payments of the estimated amount before the final tax return is filed. As a result, the end-of-year entries to record income taxes, such as those shown above, often have to be altered to take

into consideration any previously recorded prepayments.

5. The income tax rate varies depending on the type of organization, small or large, and manufacturing or nonmanufacturing.

LO 1 Explain why income taxes for accounting purposes may be different from income taxes for tax purposes. Accounting income and taxable income will differ when revenues and/or expenses may be included in one period for accounting purposes and in a different period for tax purposes.

LO 2 Prepare an income tax schedule and journal entries for a company where timing differences exist between accounting and taxable income. Reconcile accounting and taxable income by adding or subtracting the items which constitute timing differences. Income tax expense is based on accounting income, income tax payable on taxable income, and the debit or credit to deferred taxes on the net timing differences.

SUMMARY OF APPENDIX H IN TERMS OF LEARNING OBJECTIVES

EXERCISES

Indicate which of the following items might cause timing differences for a corporation:

a.   Sales on account.

b.   Capital cost allowances.

c.   Wages paid to employees.

d.   Property taxes.

e.   Installment sales.

f.   Cost of goods sold.

g.   Warranty expenses.

h.   Rents received in advance.

i.   Cash sales.

Exercise H–1
Timing differences
(LO 1)

a.   Explain why accounting income is usually different from taxable income.

b.   What reasons can you give for the two sets of rules?

Exercise H–2
Taxable vs. accounting income
(LO 1)

Vacon Inc. began operations on January 1, 1996. During 1996, Vacon's operations resulted in a current tax payable of $350,000. In addition, Vacon sold land for $210,000 that had cost $70,000. The sale qualified as an installment sale for tax purposes, so the gain was subject to tax as cash was received. The purchaser agreed to pay for the land on June 1, 1997. Present the December 31, 1996, entry to record Vacon Inc.'s income taxes. Assume a tax rate of 45% and that the profit on the land is fully taxable.

Exercise H–3
Recording corporate income tax expense
(LO 2)

Buster Corporation would have had identical accounting and taxable income for the three years 1996–1998 were it not for the fact that for tax purposes an operational asset that cost $24,000 was amortized $3/6$, $2/6$, $1/6$ (assumed for problem purposes to be acceptable), whereas for accounting purposes, the straight-line method was used. The asset has a three-year op-

Exercise H–4
Recording corporate income tax expense
(LO 2)

erational life and no residual value. Income before amortization and income taxes for the years concerned follow:

	1996	1997	1998
Pretax accounting income (before amortization)	$40,000	$45,000	$50,000

Assume an income tax rate of 40% for each year.

Required

1. Calculate the accounting and taxable income for each year.
2. Prepare journal entries to record the income tax expense for each year.

Exercise H–5
Analyze timing differences; entries
(LO 2)

Castor Corporation reports the following information for the year ended December 31, 1996:

Revenue	$525,000
Expenses	390,000
Net income before tax	$135,000

Additional information:

a. Revenues (above) do not include $30,000 of rent which is taxable in 1996 but was earned at the end of 1996.
b. Capital cost allowances for 1996 are $32,000 greater than the amortization expense included above.
c. Expenses (above) include $12,000 of estimated warranty expenses which are not deductible for tax purposes in 1996.
d. Assume an income tax rate of 40%.

Prepare a journal entry to record income taxes for Castor Corporation on December 31, 1996.

Exercise H–6
Timing differences; entries
(LO 2)

Income tax returns on Vastly Corporation reflected the following:

	Year Ended Dec. 31		
	1996	**1997**	**1998**
Royalty income	$180,000		
Investment income	30,000	$20,000	$40,000
Rent income	10,000	10,000	10,000
	$220,000	$30,000	$50,000
Deductible expenses	30,000	20,000	20,000
Taxable income	$190,000	$10,000	$30,000

Assume the average income tax rate for each year was 40%.

The only differences between taxable income on the tax returns and the pretax accounting income relate to royalty income. For accounting purposes, royalty income was recognized ratably (equally) over the three-year period.

Required

Give journal entries such as would appear at the end of each year to reflect income tax and allocation.   (CGA adapted)

Geac

ANNUAL REPORT
1994

FINANCIAL HIGHLIGHTS

5 YEAR FINANCIAL INFORMATION

(millions of dollars, except per share amounts)	1994	1993	Years Ended April 30 1992	1991	1990
Revenues	152.2	105.1	85.3	82.2	73.5
Income from operations before unusual items & taxes	26.9	17.9	12.7	5.0	5.2
Unusual items	-	(10.7)	-	(9.8)	4.7
Income (loss) before income taxes	26.9	7.2	12.7	(4.8)	9.9
Net income (loss)	22.9	4.5	11.1	(5.5)	8.2
Cash	53.3	40.9	32.0	24.4	13.5
Earnings (loss) per share	$ 0.81	$ 0.17	$ 0.50	$ (0.25)	$ 0.38

SALES BY REGION
for the years ended April 30, 1994 (1993)

Canada 13.7% (18.0%)

USA 44.2% (38.4%)

Europe 24.9% (33.8%)

Australasia 17.2% (9.8%)

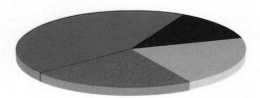

SALES BY DIVISION
for the years ended April 30, 1994 (1993)

Customer Service 35.9% (41.7%)

Library Systems 32.4% (29.0%)

Construction & Property Management 11.5% (7.3%)

Manufacturing & Distribution 10.1% (8.5%)

Financial Systems 6.2% (10.4%)

Hotels and Clubs 3.9% (3.2%)

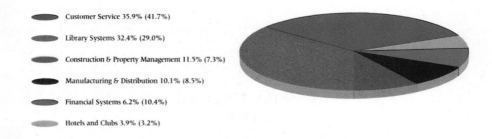

FINANCIAL REVIEW

MANAGEMENT DISCUSSION AND ANALYSIS OF FINANCIAL CONDITION AND RESULTS OF OPERATIONS

Acquisitions

During fiscal 1994, Geac acquired a number of new businesses:

Assets of New Tech Hospitality Systems Pty Ltd., an Australian developer and marketer of hotel and resort software, effective June 30, 1993. Geac initially entered the hotel software market as part of the Jonas and Erickson acquisition in fiscal 1991.

Claymore Systems Group, a Canadian developer of asset valuation software for the real estate industry, effective June 30, 1993. This complements Geac's property management software.

ECI Computer, Inc., a USA based developer of hotel management software with a worldwide customer base, effective August 4, 1993. ECI's advanced Informix based product is targeted at major chains and larger full service hotels.

Datamark International Limited, a New Zealand developer and marketer of manufacturing and distribution software, its Australian subsidiary, Dmark International Pty Limited, both effective September 30, 1993, and the assets of Convergent Solutions Pty Ltd., Datamark's main Australian distributor, effective November 1, 1993. Together with previous strategic acquisitions, these make Geac the largest provider of hardware, software, consulting and support solutions to manufacturers in the fast growing Australasian region.

Assets of Hotel Systems Pty Limited in Australia and Hotel Computer Systems Limited in New Zealand, effective January 31, 1994. Together with New Tech and the Australasian customers of ECI, this makes Geac the largest supplier of hotel and resort management solutions in the region.

These eight acquisitions were made for a total cash consideration of $5.7 million. After their respective dates of acquisition, they contributed about $11 million to fiscal 1994 sales and achieved approximately breakeven operating income. Because of the restructuring and integration of the acquired businesses with Geac's existing business, sales and profitability of the acquired businesses prior to their respective dates of acquisition are not meaningful.

As a result of these acquisitions, Geac included on its balance sheet as other assets $2.2 million of acquired software development and $5.6 million of goodwill. The nature of the assets acquired requires that they be capitalized in accordance with generally accepted accounting principles in Canada.

Results of Operations

Geac reported a net income of $22.9 million for fiscal 1994 compared to a net income of $4.5 million in fiscal 1993. During fiscal 1993, the Company expensed as an unusual item $10.7 million of purchased software research. Income from operations before the unusual item and income taxes increased to $26.9 million (17.9% of sales) from $17.9 million (17.4% of sales) in 1993.

Sales revenue was $150.3 million in fiscal 1994 compared to $102.7 million in fiscal 1993. Service revenue, primarily contracted support of customers' hardware and licensed software, increased to $73.0 million compared to $55.1 million in the prior year. Service revenue represented 49% of sales compared to 54% in fiscal 1993, as new product sales increased more rapidly in a stronger economy. Computer hardware represents about 20% of sales. Higher margin software licences and consulting sold to new and existing customers account for over 30% of sales.

Interest income decreased to $1.8 million from $2.4 million in the prior year due to generally declining average interest rates worldwide.

Provision for income taxes was $4.0 million compared to $2.8 million in fiscal 1993. Geac operates through wholly owned subsidiaries in several countries. The tax consequences of these operations vary significantly based on the results of each legal entity and the tax laws of each country. Future effective tax rates on operating income are likely to be substantially lower than the combined basic Canadian federal and provincial rate of 44% because most countries in which Geac operates have lower effective tax rates and the subsidiaries have a total of $26 million of tax losses and $4 million of favourable timing differences to apply against future income. The utilization of tax losses and timing differences depends on the financial results of individual subsidiaries and, because individual subsidiary future earnings are not certain, some tax losses may expire before they can be used.

Liquidity and Capital Resources

Cash balances of $53.3 million at April 30, 1994 increased by $12.4 million during the year. The Company has no bank borrowings and no long-term debt. Current cash balances and future operating cash flows are more than sufficient to cover foreseeable cash requirements. Commitments at April 30, 1994 consist primarily of lease obligations for office space. No significant fixed asset expenditures are anticipated. In the 1995 fiscal year, cash potentially may be used for the repurchase of the Company's outstanding common shares under a Normal Course Issuer Bid and for the acquisition of new businesses.

Cash is invested in short-term, low risk financial instruments, such as treasury bills and bankers' acceptances. Cash is held in various countries and currencies according to anticipated future needs. Foreign exchange gains included in operations were $0.8 million in fiscal 1994 and $0.1 million in fiscal 1993. Substantially all cash is freely remittable to Canada.

Outlook

Geac's historical and ongoing emphasis is to provide a total solution consisting of hardware, software, service and support to customers in selected vertical markets. Vertical markets are specific groups of current and potential customers where the Company provides complete integrated application software solutions to meet critical system requirements. Vertical markets in which Geac participates include academic and public libraries, leasing and asset finance, consumer banking institutions including credit unions, savings banks and savings and loans, manufacturing and distribution, construction, property management, hotels and clubs.

Geac generally enjoys long-term relationships with its customers, providing hardware and software service, support, maintenance and upgrades as well as consulting in the years following the initial sale. On average, subsequent revenues exceed the initial hardware and software sale. As a result, more than 50% of Geac's annual revenue has been relatively stable. Geac's well established worldwide service network and strong financial position give new and existing customers confidence that Geac support will continue over the life of their systems.

Since 1990, Geac has offered its products on a broad range of industry standard hardware platforms which support a Unix-based Open Systems environment. Geac is now a large worldwide vendor of Unix vertical market application software. Customers benefit from Open Systems solutions because the market for RISC/Unix hardware and peripherals is highly competitive and prices continue to decline rapidly as technology advances. As a result, Geac's revenue from selling equivalent computer processing power has continued to decline. Since the highly competitive hardware market limits hardware revenue and margins, there is a trend towards software and services forming an increasing portion of Geac's sales mix. The primary market trend affecting the Company is the continuing decline in hardware prices. Management continues to focus on operating efficiencies by controlling direct operating expenses and overheads.

MANAGEMENT'S REPORT

The consolidated financial statements and other financial information in this annual report were prepared by management of Geac Computer Corporation Limited, reviewed by the Audit Committee and approved by the Board of Directors.

Management is responsible for the consolidated financial statements and believes that they fairly present the Company's financial condition and results of operations in conformity with generally accepted accounting principles. Management has included in the Company's consolidated financial statements amounts based on estimates and judgements that it believes are reasonable under the circumstances.

To discharge its responsibilities for financial reporting and safeguarding of assets, management believes that it has established appropriate systems of internal accounting control which provide reasonable assurance that the financial records are reliable and form a proper basis for the timely and accurate preparation of financial statements. Consistent with the concept of reasonable assurance, the Company recognizes that the relative cost of maintaining these controls should not exceed their expected benefits. Management further assures the quality of the financial records through careful selection and training of personnel, and through the adoption and communication of financial and other relevant policies.

The shareholders have appointed Deloitte & Touche to audit the consolidated financial statements. Their report outlines the scope of their examination and their opinion.

Stephen J. Sadler
President and
Chief Executive Officer

David G.B. Scott
Vice President,
Finance and Administration

AUDITORS' REPORT

To the Shareholders of Geac Computer Corporation Limited:

We have audited the consolidated balance sheets of Geac Computer Corporation Limited as at April 30, 1994 and 1993 and the consolidated statements of operations, retained earnings and changes in financial position for the years then ended. These financial statements are the responsibility of the Company's management. Our responsibility is to express an opinion on these financial statements based on our audits.

We conducted our audits in accordance with generally accepted auditing standards. Those standards require that we plan and perform an audit to obtain reasonable assurance whether the financial statements are free of material misstatement. An audit includes examining, on a test basis, evidence supporting the amounts and disclosures in the financial statements. An audit also includes assessing the accounting principles used and significant estimates made by management, as well as evaluating the overall financial statement presentation.

In our opinion, these consolidated financial statements present fairly, in all material respects, the financial position of the Company as at April 30, 1994 and 1993 and the results of its operations and the changes in its financial position for the years then ended in accordance with generally accepted accounting principles.

Deloitte & Touche

Chartered Accountants
Markham, Canada
June 17, 1994

CONSOLIDATED BALANCE SHEETS

	April 30	
(thousands of dollars)	**1994**	1993
Assets		
Current assets:		
Cash and short-term investments	**$ 53,327**	$ 40,943
Accounts receivable	**29,389**	21,277
Unbilled receivables	**7,437**	7,591
Inventory (note 2)	**16,269**	16,166
Prepaid expenses	**1,878**	2,534
	108,300	88,511
Fixed assets (note 3)	**16,083**	15,196
Other assets (note 4)	**24,645**	14,165
	$ 149,028	$ 117,872
Liabilities		
Current liabilities:		
Accounts payable and accrued liabilities	**$ 24,327**	$ 21,830
Income taxes payable (note 9)	**1,761**	218
Deferred sales revenue	**25,996**	25,146
	52,084	47,194
Shareholders' Equity		
Share capital (note 5):		
Common shares	**63,611**	61,366
Convertible preference shares	**-**	269
Retained earnings	**32,041**	9,277
Cumulative foreign exchange translation adjustment (note 6)	**1,292**	(234)
	96,944	70,678
	$ 149,028	$ 117,872

Approved by the Board of Directors:

Donald C. Webster
Chairman of the Board

Stephen J. Sadler
President and Chief Executive Officer,
Director

CONSOLIDATED STATEMENTS OF OPERATIONS

(thousands of dollars, except per share amounts)	Years ended April 30 1994	1993
Revenues:		
Sales (note 8)	**$ 150,335**	$ 102,718
Interest income	**1,821**	2,356
	152,156	105,074
Expenses:		
Costs, excluding amounts shown below	**113,137**	77,152
Research and development expenses	**8,469**	8,233
Research and development grants and investment tax credits (note 9)	**(2,093)**	(2,012)
Depreciation and amortization	**5,632**	3,695
Interest expense	**79**	129
	125,224	87,197
Income from operations before unusual item and income taxes	**26,932**	17,877
Unusual item:		
Purchased software research (note 11)	**-**	(10,674)
Income before income taxes	**26,932**	7,203
Provision for income taxes (note 9)	**4,000**	2,750
Net income for the year	**$ 22,932**	$ 4,453
Earnings per share:		
Basic	**$ 0.81**	$ 0.17
Fully diluted	**$ 0.80**	$ 0.17

CONSOLIDATED STATEMENTS OF RETAINED EARNINGS

(thousands of dollars)	Years ended April 30 1994	1993
Retained earnings at the beginning of the year	**$ 9,277**	$ 4,824
Premium on redemption of Series 2 preference shares (note 5)	**(168)**	-
Net income for the year	**22,932**	4,453
Retained earnings at the end of the year	**$ 32,041**	$ 9,277

13

CONSOLIDATED STATEMENTS OF CHANGES
IN FINANCIAL POSITION

(thousands of dollars)	Years ended April 30 1994	1993
Operating activities		
Net income for the year	$ 22,932	$ 4,453
Adjusted for amounts not affecting cash:		
Depreciation of fixed assets	5,352	3,662
Amortization of other assets	2,763	624
Purchased software research (note 11)	-	10,674
	31,047	19,413
Changes in non-cash working capital components	(5,605)	(1,064)
Cash provided by operating activities	25,442	18,349
Investing activities		
Additions to fixed assets, net	(5,435)	(3,341)
Additions to capitalized software development	(5,385)	(1,403)
Acquisitions less cash acquired (note 11)	(5,572)	(21,231)
Foreign exchange translation adjustment	1,526	(267)
Cash used in investing activities	(14,866)	(26,242)
Financing activities		
Issue of common shares	2,245	16,938
Issue of preference shares	-	93
Conversion of preference shares	(74)	(222)
Redemption of Series 2 preference shares	(363)	-
Cash provided by financing activities	1,808	16,809
Cash and short-term investments		
Net cash increase during the year	12,384	8,916
Cash position at the beginning of the year	40,943	32,027
Cash position at the end of the year	$ 53,327	$ 40,943

NOTES TO CONSOLIDATED FINANCIAL STATEMENTS

1. ACCOUNTING POLICIES

Accounting principles
These consolidated financial statements are prepared in conformity with accounting principles generally accepted in Canada.

Basis of consolidation
These consolidated financial statements comprise the financial statements of Geac Computer Corporation Limited and its subsidiary companies.

Inventory
Finished goods inventory is stated at the lower of cost on a first-in first-out basis and net realizable value. Maintenance and service parts are recorded net of a provision for obsolescence which amortizes their cost over an estimated useful life of four to six years.

Fixed assets
Fixed assets are recorded at cost and are depreciated as follows:
- Computers, processing and office equipment - declining balance at rates ranging between 18.5% and 20%.
- Leasehold improvements - straight-line over the lease term.

Goodwill
Goodwill represents the excess of purchase consideration over fair market value of net identifiable assets acquired, and is amortized on a straight-line basis over forty years.

Revenue recognition
The Company's activities are the design, manufacture, sale, service and rental of computer systems and software. System sales revenues are recognized at the time of shipment or upon customer acceptance. The timing of revenue recognition often differs from contract payment schedules, resulting in revenues that have been earned but not billed. These amounts are included in unbilled receivables. Service and rental revenues are recognized rateably over applicable contractual periods or as services are performed. Amounts billed but not yet earned are recorded as deferred revenue.

Research and development costs
Research and development costs relate principally to computer software intended for licensing to end-user customers. All costs up to the date on which the software is considered technically and commercially viable, as well as software maintenance and documentation, are expensed as incurred, net of government grants and other amounts recoverable. Software development, after technical and commercial viability is established, is deferred and amortized on a straight-line basis over its expected useful life, not exceeding four years. The amortization is included in research and development expenses in the statement of operations.

Foreign exchange
All of the Company's foreign subsidiaries are considered self-sustaining. Assets and liabilities of these subsidiaries are translated into Canadian dollars at exchange rates in effect at the balance sheet dates. Income and expense items are translated at average exchange rates for the periods. Accumulated net translation adjustments are included as a separate component of shareholders' equity.

The monetary assets and liabilities of the Corporation which are denominated in foreign currencies are translated at the year-end exchange rates. Revenues and expenses are translated at rates of exchange prevailing on the transaction dates. All exchange gains or losses are recognized currently in earnings.

2. INVENTORY

(thousands of dollars)	April 30 1994	1993
Finished goods	$ 4,914	$ 4,960
Maintenance and service parts	11,355	11,206
	$ 16,269	$ 16,166

15

3. FIXED ASSETS

(thousands of dollars)

	Cost	Accumulated Depreciation	April 30 1994 Net	1993 Net
Computers and processing equipment	$ 39,413	$ 29,184	$ 10,229	$ 9,986
Office equipment	9,104	5,620	3,484	3,499
Leasehold improvements	4,596	2,226	2,370	1,711
	$ 53,113	$ 37,030	$ 16,083	$ 15,196

4. OTHER ASSETS

(thousands of dollars)

	April 30 1994	1993
Acquired capitalized software development (note 11)	$ 7,736	$ 5,510
Capitalized software development	6,788	1,403
Less: Accumulated amortization	(3,074)	(591)
Net capitalized software development	11,450	6,322
Goodwill (note 11)	13,508	7,876
Less: Accumulated amortization	(313)	(33)
Net goodwill	13,195	7,843
	$ 24,645	$ 14,165

5. SHARE CAPITAL

The Company is authorized to issue an unlimited number of common shares and preference shares, issuable in series, each without par value.

As final settlement under the Definitive Proposals accepted by the creditors in 1988, an additional 4,037 Series 2 preference shares were issued during the 1993 fiscal year. Between May 1 and June 15, 1993, 6,108 Series 2 preference shares were converted into 54,972 common shares. The remaining 12,097 Series 2 preference shares were redeemed for $362,910. The premium on this transaction of approximately $168,000 was charged to retained earnings in fiscal 1994.

On May 10, 1994, the Company filed notice of its intention to make a Normal Course Issuer Bid for its common shares through the facilities of The Toronto Stock Exchange. The Company may purchase up to a maximum of 1,436,996 common shares, being 5% of the 28,739,921 common shares outstanding at April 29, 1994. The price at which the Company may purchase such shares will be the market price at the time of any particular transaction. The bid commenced on May 13, 1994 and will terminate on May 12, 1995, unless the maximum number of common shares purchasable thereunder has been acquired before that time. There have been no repurchases as of June 17, 1994.

An analysis of the capital stock account is as follows:

	Number of shares 1994	1993	Thousands of dollars 1994	1993
Common Shares				
Balance at the beginning of the year	27,948,409	22,472,157	$ 61,366	$ 44,428
Issued for cash	741,831	5,311,741	2,171	16,716
Converted from Series 2 preference shares	54,972	164,511	74	222
Balance at the end of the year	28,745,212	27,948,409	$ 63,611	$ 61,366
Series 2 Convertible Preference Shares				
Balance at the beginning of the year	18,205	32,447	$ 269	$ 398
Converted to common shares	(6,108)	(18,279)	(74)	(222)
Issued under Definitive Proposals	-	4,037	-	93
Redeemed for cash	(12,097)	-	(195)	-
Balance at the end of the year	-	18,205	$ -	$ 269

Stock Ownership Plan

An Employee Stock Ownership Plan under which employees may make quarterly purchases of shares in the Company at a 10% discount from the prevailing market price has been in existence since 1984. During 1994, 20,981 shares were issued to employees under this plan (1993 - 25,741) and 120,000 shares were cancelled. The aggregate number of shares still available to be issued under this plan is 115,580 (1993 - 256,561).

Stock Options

Options have been granted to management personnel to purchase common shares at or above the prevailing market price at the time of the grant under the Employee Stock Option Plan. These options are vested or vest at various times over the next 3 years and expire 5 years after vesting.

An analysis of the stock options is as follows:

(thousands of shares)

	1994	1993
Balance at the beginning of the year	1,334	1,821
Options granted	767	171
Options exercised at option prices from $1.10 to $9.25	(720)	(606)
Options cancelled or expired	(68)	(52)
Balance at the end of the year	1,313	1,334

The outstanding options as at April 30, 1994 were granted at prices from $1.10 to $14.50 (1993 - $1.10 to $11.75) per common share.

In addition, other options to senior management personnel to purchase 80,000 common shares at $1.60 per share were outstanding at the beginning of the year and remain outstanding at the end of the year.

6.   CUMULATIVE FOREIGN EXCHANGE TRANSLATION ADJUSTMENT

(thousands of dollars)

	April 30	
	1994	1993
Cumulative unrealized gain (loss) at the beginning of the year	$ (234)	$ 33
Unrealized gain (loss) for the year on translation of net assets	2,190	(495)
Realized (gain) loss on dividends and return of capital paid by foreign operations	(664)	228
	$ 1,292	$ (234)

7.   COMMITMENTS AND CONTINGENCIES

The Company has operating leases on rental equipment for varying terms up to a maximum of four years and has entered into leases for rental of premises for varying terms up to a maximum of thirteen years. Aggregate lease payments in each of the five years ending April 30, 1999 and subsequent are as follows:

(thousands of dollars)

1995	$ 4,965
1996	4,041
1997	3,359
1998	2,440
1999	1,797
2000 and subsequent	5,169
	$ 21,771

As at April 30, 1994, letters of credit are outstanding for approximately $378,000. The Company is potentially liable for approximately $16 million of performance bonds which are routinely issued on its behalf by insurance companies and other third parties in connection with outstanding contracts with various public sector customers. There has never been a claim under any of the Company's performance bonds and any estimated outstanding contract obligations are provided for in the accounts.

There are certain legal actions pending against the Company which management believes are without merit and will not result in any material liability. No benefit has been recorded for certain pending legal actions by the Company against others, the outcome of which cannot be reasonably determined.

8. SEGMENTED INFORMATION

The business of the Company is carried on in one industry segment: the design, manufacture, sale, service and rental of computer systems and software products.

Revenues are derived from system sales and from service and rental agreements, as follows:

(thousands of dollars)	Years ended April 30 1994	1993
System sales	$ 77,291	$ 47,657
Service and rental	73,044	55,061
Total sales revenues	$ 150,335	$ 102,718

The Company operates in four geographic segments as follows:

Year ended April 30, 1994

(thousands of dollars)	Canada	USA	Europe	Australasia	Eliminations	Total
Segment revenue:						
Sales revenues	$ 20,629	$ 66,451	$ 37,425	$ 25,830	$ -	$ 150,335
Transfers between segments	2,065	-	-	-	(2,065)	-
	$ 22,694	$ 66,451	$ 37,425	$ 25,830	$ (2,065)	$ 150,335
Segment operating income	$ 8,483	$ 12,121	$ 6,783	$ 1,982	$ -	$ 29,369
Expenses (income):						
Corporate expenses						4,179
Interest, net						(1,742)
Provision for income taxes						4,000
Net income for the year						$ 22,932
Total identifiable assets	$ 44,056	$ 52,605	$ 36,388	$ 15,979	$ -	$ 149,028

Year ended April 30, 1993

(thousands of dollars)	Canada	USA	Europe	Australasia	Eliminations	Total
Segment revenue:						
Sales revenues	$ 18,485	$ 39,409	$ 34,678	$ 10,146	$ -	$ 102,718
Transfers between segments	4,313	15	-	100	(4,428)	-
	$ 22,798	$ 39,424	$ 34,678	$ 10,246	$ (4,428)	$ 102,718
Segment operating income (loss)	$ 9,519	$ 4,546	$ 5,985	$ (785)	$ -	$ 19,265
Expenses (income):						
Corporate expenses						3,615
Interest, net						(2,227)
Unusual item						10,674
Provision for income taxes						2,750
Net income for the year						$ 4,453
Total identifiable assets	$ 32,721	$ 37,442	$ 39,889	$ 7,820	$ -	$ 117,872

9. INCOME TAXES

Substantially all of the Company's activities are carried out through operating subsidiaries in a number of countries. The income tax effect of operations depends on the tax legislation in each country and the operating results of each subsidiary and the parent Company.

In fiscal 1994, the Company recognized the benefit of $1,800,000 (1993 - $1,800,000) of previously unrealized investment tax credits as their realization became reasonably assured due to the earnings history of the relevant subsidiary. The benefit is included in the statement of operations as a reduction of expense under the caption "Research and development grants and investment tax credits". The Company has remaining unrealized investment tax credits of approximately $4,000,000 (1993 - $5,000,000) which are available to reduce income taxes payable in future years and expire as shown in the table below. The benefit of unrealized investment tax credits will be included in the statement of operations as a reduction in research and development expense when realization is reasonably assured.

The Company has non-capital losses of approximately $26,000,000 (1993 - $30,000,000) which are available for carryforward against taxable income in future years, which expire as shown in the table below and will be recognized when realized by a reduction in the provision for income taxes.

The Company has net favourable timing differences of approximately $4,000,000 (1993 - $4,000,000) which may be applied against taxable income of future years. The timing differences relate primarily to contract revenues, accrued expenses, deferred revenue and depreciation and amortization of assets which are recognized in the financial statements in periods other than those in which they are included in taxable income in accordance with the tax laws of the countries in which the Company and its subsidiaries operate. Timing differences do not expire. When realized, they will be recognized by a reduction in the provision for income taxes.

(thousands of dollars)	Non-capital losses	Investment tax credits
1995		
1996	$ -	$ 300
1997	800	1,000
1998	3,800	600
1999 - 2009	1,000	600
Losses without expiry date	5,000	1,000
	15,400	500
	$ 26,000	$ 4,000

The provision for income taxes reflects an effective tax rate which differs from the corporate tax rate for the following reasons:

(thousands of dollars)	1994	1993
Combined basic Canadian federal and provincial income tax rate	44%	44%
Provision for income taxes based on above rate	$ 11,850	$ 3,170
Increase (decrease) resulting from:		
Permanent differences -		
Purchased software research expensed	-	4,600
Other	1,000	200
Lower rate on earnings of foreign subsidiaries	(80)	(140)
Losses of subsidiaries not tax effected	700	500
Benefit of previously unrecognized losses and timing differences realized in the year	(9,000)	(4,900)
Other	(470)	(680)
Provision for income taxes per statement of operations	$ 4,000	$ 2,750

10. RELATED PARTY TRANSACTIONS

During the year the Company paid $225,000 (1993 - $310,000) for management services including investigation of potential acquisitions to Helix Investments (Canada) Inc. (formerly Helix Investments Limited), a significant shareholder.

11. ACQUISITIONS

Year ended April 30, 1994
During the year ended April 30, 1994, the Company acquired for cash the businesses shown in the table below. New Tech, Convergent, and Hotel Systems were asset purchases. In each of the other acquisitions, the Company acquired all of the issued and outstanding shares of the companies. Acquisitions are accounted for by the purchase method with the results of operations of each business included in the financial statements from the respective dates of acquisition.

The total purchase price was $5,673,000. The acquired businesses included, at fair value, $101,000 of cash, $2,798,000 of other current assets, $2,226,000 of software development which met the Company's criteria for capitalization (note 4), $804,000 of fixed assets, and $5,888,000 of current liabilities.

The difference between the total purchase price and the net fair value of all identifiable assets and liabilities acquired was $5,632,000 and is accounted for as goodwill.

Acquisition	Effective Date
Assets of New Tech Hospitality Systems Pty Ltd.	June 30, 1993
957024 Ontario Inc. (operating as Claymore Systems Group)	June 30, 1993
ECI Computer, Inc.	August 4, 1993
Datamark International Limited	September 30, 1993
Dmark International Pty Limited	September 30, 1993
Assets of Convergent Solutions Pty Ltd.	November 1, 1993
Assets of Hotel Systems Pty Limited	January 31, 1994
Assets of Hotel Computer Systems Limited	January 31, 1994

Year ended April 30, 1993
During the year ended April 30, 1993, the Company acquired for cash the businesses shown in the table below. Albion and McDonnell Douglas Information Systems were asset purchases. In each of the other acquisitions, the Company acquired all of the issued and outstanding shares of the companies. Acquisitions are accounted for by the purchase method with the results of operations of each business included in the financial statements from the respective dates of acquisition.

The total purchase price was $22,421,000. The acquired businesses included, at fair value, $1,190,000 of cash, $25,305,000 of other current assets, $5,510,000 of software development which met the Company's criteria for capitalization (note 4), $5,419,000 of fixed assets and $33,553,000 of current liabilities.

In the CLSI acquisition, $10,674,000 of the purchase price was allocated to purchased software research related to new products which had not achieved technical and commercial viability.

The difference between the total purchase price and the net fair value of all identifiable assets and liabilities acquired, including the purchased software research, was $7,876,000 and is accounted for as goodwill.

Acquisition	Effective Date
Assets of Albion Computing Australia Pty Limited	June 1, 1992
Assets of McDonnell Douglas Information Systems Canada, Inc.	November 30, 1992
CLSI, Inc. and its UK, France, Netherlands and Canadian affiliates	November 30, 1992
Mentat Computer Systems Pty Ltd.	February 26, 1993
Concord Management Systems, Inc.	February 28, 1993
Computer Library Services International Pty Limited and its subsidiary Aldis Pty Limited	March 31, 1993
NBI Canada, Inc., subsequently renamed Geac (Canada) Services Limited	April 30, 1993
MAI United Kingdom Limited	April 30, 1993
Tekserv Computer Services Limited	April 30, 1993

12. COMPARATIVE FIGURES

Certain of the prior year's figures have been reclassified to conform with the current year's presentation.

Comprehensive List of Accounts Used in Exercises and Problems

Current Assets

101	Cash
102	Petty cash
103	Cash equivalents
104	Temporary investments
105	Allowance to reduce temporary investments to market
106	Accounts receivable
107	Allowance for doubtful accounts
108	Legal fees receivable
109	Interest receivable
110	Rent receivable
111	Notes receivable
115	Subscriptions receivable, common shares
116	Subscriptions receivable, preferred shares
119	Merchandise inventory
120	_____ inventory
121	_____ inventory
124	Office supplies
125	Store supplies
126	_____ supplies
128	Prepaid insurance
129	Prepaid interest
130	Prepaid property taxes
131	Prepaid rent
132	Raw materials inventory
133	Goods in process inventory, _____
134	Goods in process inventory, _____
135	Finished goods inventory

Long-Term Investments

141	Investment in _____ shares
142	Investment in _____ bonds
144	Investment in _____
145	Bond sinking fund

Capital Assets

151	Automobiles
152	Accumulated amortization, automobiles
153	Trucks
154	Accumulated amortization, trucks
155	Boats
156	Accumulated amortization, boats
157	Professional library
158	Accumulated amortization, professional library
159	Law library
160	Accumulated amortization, law library
163	Office equipment
164	Accumulated amortization, office equipment
165	Store equipment
166	Accumulated amortization, store equipment
167	_____ equipment
168	Accumulated amortization, _____ equipment
169	Machinery
170	Accumulated amortization, machinery
173	Building _____
174	Accumulated amortization, building _____
175	Building _____
176	Accumulated amortization, building _____
179	Land improvements _____
180	Accumulated amortization, land improvements _____
181	Land improvements _____
182	Accumulated amortization, land improvements _____
183	Land

Natural Resources

185	Mineral deposit
186	Accumulated depletion, mineral deposit

Intangible Assets

191	Patents
192	Leasehold
193	Franchise
194	Copyrights
195	Leasehold improvements
196	Organization costs
197	Deferred income tax debits

Current Liabilities

201	Accounts payable
202	Insurance payable
203	Interest payable
204	Legal fees payable
205	Short-term notes payable
206	Discount on short-term notes payable
207	Office salaries payable
208	Rent payable
209	Salaries payable
210	Wages payable
211	Accrued payroll payable
214	Estimated warranty liability
215	Income taxes payable
216	Common dividend payable
217	Preferred dividend payable
218	UI payable
219	CPP payable
221	Employees' medical insurance payable
222	Employees' retirement program payable
223	Employees' union dues payable
224	PST payable
225	GST payable
226	Estimated vacation pay liability

Unearned Revenues

230	Unearned consulting fees
231	Unearned legal fees
232	Unearned property management fees
233	Unearned _____ fees
234	Unearned _____
235	Unearned janitorial revenue
236	Unearned _____ revenue
238	Unearned rent _____

Long-Term Liabilities

251	Long-term notes payable
252	Discount on notes payable
253	Long-term lease liability
254	Discount on lease liability
255	Bonds payable
256	Discount on bonds payable
257	Premium on bonds payable
258	Deferred income tax credit

Owners' Equity

301	_____, capital
302	_____, withdrawals
303	_____, capital
304	_____, withdrawals
305	_____, capital
306	_____, withdrawals

Corporate Contributed Capital

307	Common shares
309	Common shares subscribed
310	Common stock dividend distributable
313	Contributed capital from the retirement of common shares
315	Preferred shares
317	Preferred shares subscribed

Retained Earnings

318	Retained earnings
319	Cash dividends declared
320	Stock dividends declared

Revenues

401	_____ fees earned
402	_____ fees earned
403	_____ services revenue
404	_____ services revenue
405	Commissions earned
406	Rent earned
407	Dividends earned
408	Earnings from investment in _____
409	Interest earned
410	Sinking fund earnings
413	Sales
414	Sales returns and allowances
415	Sales discounts

Cost of Goods Sold Items

501	Amortization of patents
502	Cost of goods sold
503	Depletion of mine deposit
505	Purchases
506	Purchases returns and allowances
507	Purchases discounts
508	Transportation-in

Manufacturing Accounts

520	Raw materials purchases
521	Freight-in on raw materials
530	Factory payroll
531	Direct labour
540	Factory overhead
541	Indirect materials
542	Indirect labour
543	Factory insurance expired
544	Factory supervision
545	Factory supplies used
546	Factory utilities
547	Miscellaneous production costs
548	Property taxes on factory building
550	Rent on factory building
551	Repairs, factory equipment
552	Small tools written off
560	Amortization of factory equipment
561	Amortization of factory building

Standard Cost Variance Accounts

580	Direct material quantity variance
581	Direct material price variance
582	Direct labour quantity variance
583	Direct labour price variance
584	Factory overhead volume variance
585	Factory overhead controllable variance

Expenses

Amortization (Depreciation and Depletion Expenses)

601	Amortization expense, _____
602	Amortization expense, copyrights
603	Depletion expense, _____
604	Amortization expense, boats
605	Amortization expense, automobiles
606	Amortization expense, building _____
607	Amortization expense, building _____
608	Amortization expense, land improvements _____
609	Amortization expense, land improvements _____
610	Amortization expense, law library
611	Amortization expense, trucks
612	Amortization expense, _____ equipment
613	Amortization expense, _____ equipment
614	Amortization expense, _____
615	Amortization expense, _____

Employee Related Expenses

620	Office salaries expense
621	Sales salaries expense
622	Salaries expense
623	_____ wages expense
624	Employees' benefits expense
625	Payroll taxes expense

Financial Expenses

630	Cash over and short
631	Discounts lost
633	Interest expense

Insurance Expenses

635	Insurance expense, delivery equipment
636	Insurance expense, office equipment
637	Insurance expense, _____

Rental Expenses

640	Rent expense
641	Rent expense, office space
642	Rent expense, selling space
643	Press rental expense
644	Truck rental expense
645	_____ rental expense

Supplies Expense

650	Office supplies expense
651	Store supplies expense
652	_____ supplies expense
653	_____ supplies expense

Miscellaneous Expenses

655	Advertising expense
656	Bad debts expense
657	Blueprinting expense
658	Boat expense
659	Collection expense
661	Concessions expense
662	Credit card expense
663	Delivery expense
664	Dumping expense
667	Equipment expense
668	Food and drinks expense
669	Gas, oil, and repairs expense
671	Gas and oil expense
672	General and administrative expense
673	Janitorial expense
674	Legal fees expense
676	Mileage expense
677	Miscellaneous expenses
678	Mower and tools expense
679	Operating expenses
681	Permits expense
682	Postage expense
683	Property taxes expense
684	Repairs expense, _____
685	Repairs expense, _____
687	Selling expenses
688	Telephone expense
689	Travel and entertainment expense

690	Utilities expense
691	Warranty expense
695	Income taxes expense

Gains and Losses

701	Gain on retirement of bonds
702	Gain on sale of machinery
703	Gain on sale of temporary investments
704	Gain on sale of trucks
705	Gain on _____
801	Loss on disposal of machinery
802	Loss on exchange of equipment
803	Loss on exchange of _____
804	Loss on market decline of temporary investments
805	Loss on retirement of bonds
806	Loss on sale of investments
807	Loss on sale of machinery
808	Loss on sale of _____
809	Loss on _____
810	Loss or gain from liquidation

Clearing Accounts

901	Income summary
902	Manufacturing summary

NOTES

NOTES

NOTES

NOTES

NOTES

NOTES

NOTES

NOTES

NOTE